THE GOLDEN AGE *of* PIRACY

THE GOLDEN AGE *of* PIRACY

The Truth Behind Pirate Myths

BENERSON LITTLE

Skyhorse Publishing

Skyhorse Publishing books may be purchased in bulk at special discounts for sales promotion, corporate gifts, fund-raising, or educational purposes. Special editions can also be created to specifications. For details, contact the Special Sales Department, Skyhorse Publishing, 307 West 36th Street, 11th Floor, New York, NY 10018 or info@skyhorsepublishing.com.

Skyhorse® and Skyhorse Publishing® are registered trademarks of Skyhorse Publishing, Inc.®, a Delaware corporation.

Visit our website at www.skyhorsepublishing.com.

10 9 8 7 6 5 4 3 2 1

Library of Congress Cataloging-in-Publication Data is available on file.

Cover design by Rain Saukas
Cover photo credit iStock

ISBN: 978-1-5107-3875-1
Ebook ISBN: 978-1-5107-1304-8

Printed in the United States of America

For anyone who has ever played at pirates,
searched for buried treasure,
or taken a voyage over the seas
or in their dreams,
but especially for Mary, Courtney, Bree,
and Aidan

Contents

Preface:
Imagining Pirates and Piracy

⸻

I grew up near the sea; first in Key West, Florida, where I was born, then variously along the Gulf Coast of the United States, then the East and West Coasts. As far back as I can remember, I have always been fascinated by the ocean, the great birth mother of humankind. It was not only a pathway to adventure, but it was also, itself, an adventure. It had treasures on its shores and beneath its waves just waiting to be discovered.

When I was ten years old, I read an annotated copy of *Treasure Island*, a gift from an aunt who has since passed away. The story, perfect for a ten-year-old boy, fascinated me, and the annotations helped me understand the background of the story—how a schooner was rigged, how a cannon was loaded, how a flintlock pistol was primed, even if, as I know now, not all the annotations were correct. I already knew something about pirates, or thought I did, mostly from Hollywood swashbucklers filled with tall ships and men with cutlasses who looted towns and buried treasure and, in the end, won the hand of the beautiful lady. But the book made me want to know everything there was to know about pirates.[1]

At the time, my father was away at sea and I lived inland for a year in a small town in Alabama, a state torn by social change and alien to me. Desperately in need of escape, I was determined to find my own buried pirate treasure, and I set about this adventure with a focused passion. On the forty acres—and beyond—in Alabama where my grandparents lived, I went to work looking for evidence of pirates and Indians and pioneers, and of the treasures they must surely have left behind. I slipped quietly through forgotten, overgrown cemeteries surrounded by old timber, inspected rusted whiskey stills, trekked into a swamp where renegade Creek Indians once holed up, clambered through rattlesnake-infested overgrowth looking for a pair of Indian mounds I never found. I discovered arrowheads, old ironwork, and cattle skulls. I once watched in near terror as a silver incandescent ball drifted through the night. I suppose it was ball lightning or marsh gas, perhaps, but I still like to think it was a corpse candle or will o' the wisp, the ghost of some pirate or adventurer bound on an eternal search for his lost treasure.

But never did I find buried pirate treasure. Still, like the treasure of a mere handful of coins that would have made Tom Sawyer happy, my discoveries made me as happy as if I had discovered Captain Flint's own treasure. In fact, one need only read *Tom Sawyer* to understand both the lure of buried treasure and of piracy: Who has not at one time or another wished to run away, set up camp on an island in a river or the sea, and plunder those who pass; who has not wished to discover a hoard of treasure hidden far into the dark passages of a ghostly cave or grotto?

Soon after I first read *Treasure Island*, I discovered an old copy of Alexandre Exquemelin's *The Buccaneers of America* in the school library. I devoured it, although I did not understand many of the terms. Unconsciously, the book set the stage in my mind for an adventure through history, that of discovering the truth about pirates and other sea rovers.

A few years later, I read Rafael Sabatini's *Captain Blood*, then similar novels, and then, often by accidental discovery, the published journals of the pirates themselves. After college, I entered the US Navy and became a Navy SEAL. There, I learned the reality of the sea and men-at-arms and I began to apply what I learned to the stacks of histories and journals of sea rovers. I began to write about pirates and privateers, and always when I wrote I wanted to follow the path to the truth, to the reality of these sea thieves. I discovered that much of what we thought we knew about pirates was wrong. These truths, buried beneath layer upon layer of fascinating, dusty old books and reels and reels of old film, became the treasure I had been seeking since I was young. But they were not what I had expected to find.

Yet, this was not discouraging! The truths, I discovered to my surprise, were even more fascinating than the myths, and seldom did reality detract from the pirate myths we—strangely enough, given that most pirates were cutthroats—hold dear. I discovered that there is room for them both in our learning and mythology. Not only is each fascinating in its own way, but also the path from one to the other—from reality to myth to reality again—is just as fascinating. It is a journey that begins with our history, wends its way through our literature and film, and arrives ultimately at the core of our very culture—our ideals.

Pirates are indeed part of our culture, and understanding how this came to be is a wonderful voyage of discovery, one that reveals both the good and the evil in human behavior. Yet it is also a voyage we need not think too hard about if we do not wish to: the stories themselves carry us away, like dreams that become reality and move too quickly for anything but the thrill itself. Here, within these pages, is what every wishful would-be sea rover, whether relaxing in an armchair or braced on the deck of a schooner in a rolling sea, dreams of: Adventure!

Prologue: The Image of the Pirate

Imagine coming face-to-face with a living, breathing Caribbean pirate from three centuries ago. Do we recognize him as a sea thief? Of course we do. We don't need to see him on the bloody, blackened, splintered deck of a ship, cutlass or rapier in one hand, pistol in the other, with bags of silver and frightened prisoners at his feet, in order to identify him. We already know him well from fiction and film.

We know him by the cunning squint in his steely eyes, by his ambling, rolling seaman's gait, by his cocksure manner. He punctuates his nautical speech with salty language, sprinkled here and there with an "Arr!" and a "Yar!" and occasionally a variety of "Yo-ho-ho!" and "Shiver me timbers!" and "Me hearties!" and "Dead men tell no tales!"[1] His expression might be fierce or jovial as the mood suits him—and according to how drunk he is.

We recognize his cocked hat: a tricorne, we often call it today. It has a feather or two in it and perhaps even a skull and bones on the front. The tops of the tall black boots he wears are folded down beneath his knees.

He has tattoos everywhere—one of them probably a skull and bones—and long, loose hair or even dreadlocks with beads in them here and there. He has a ring in one ear or even both, and rings on his fingers, doubtless stolen from rich Spaniards or English merchants. Perhaps he cut off their fingers to get at the rings more quickly or even slit open their bellies to get the rings after they were swallowed.

He wears breeches and a white shirt with a laced coat on top and over it, a sash, and over all of it, a baldric that holds his sturdy cutlass or rakish rapier when he is not using it. In his sash or belt are two or three pistols. He might have a dagger, too, and a cartridge box, and a squat bottle of rum in one hand while the other plies a willing wench with silver pieces of eight. Often his skin is dirty, his teeth rotting, and over one eye is a patch to cover the empty socket or even, if his eye is still there, to help him see better. He might have a peg leg, and surely on one shoulder is a large, multicolored parrot or small monkey of which he is inordinately fond. Of course, if he is a gentleman pirate, he has probably had a bath and his fashionable attire has a swashbuckling flair.

It is a romantic image, one that has become a warm memory of childhood adventure. The lights always come on when the film ends, we can close the book when we turn out the lamp to sleep, and we always wake from our dreams.

But for the pirate's victim, the image was terrifying. Nowhere do we see the blood on the pirate's hands from the throats he slit to steal the pieces of eight; nowhere do we see the stigma of murder, torture, and rape. Instead, we avoid facing this reality by turning the pirate into a fierce but friendly caricature, and even a hero at times. Some of us even imagine we are pirates—but usually pirates as seen through the eyes of myth, not of cold-blooded reality.

So what, then, does the pirate of the Golden Age, from 1655 to 1725, really look like? Does he resemble what we see on the screen or read in stories? Do we recognize him on a street corner? Of course we do, for the myth is not so far removed from reality in this case, yet the reality is often more interesting than the myth. We do, in fact, know much of what he looks like, but not from the illustrations in Alexandre Exquemelin's late seventeenth-century book, *The Buccaneers of America*, or from Charles Johnson's early eighteenth-century pirate history, for their illustrators almost certainly never saw their subjects and imagined them instead from the text. Rather, we have detailed written descriptions plus artifacts, and, in a great piece of luck, several highly detailed eyewitness illustrations from the 1680s, perhaps the only such illustrations of pirates of the Golden Age.[2]

Our real pirate walks toward us with a seaman's rolling gait. On his head is a hat, a cocked hat perhaps, cocked on one, two, or three sides, or a broad-brimmed hat in the Spanish style, or a knit cap known as a Monmouth hat, similar to a modern navy "watch cap," plain or with a variety of designs woven into it. He might even wear a broad hat whose brim has been cropped short on the sides and left long at the front, akin to a modern baseball cap and worn by the pig- and cattle-hunting *boucaniers*, and by some pirates as well. There may be a feather or even a long plume in his hat, but there is no insignia of skull and bones.[3]

If our pirate is a seaman (not all pirates were professional mariners) and his hair is long, it is usually tied back or even "clubbed" or worn in a tarred "queue," for long, loose hair is dangerous shipboard: it interferes with sight and can get caught in blocks as rigging is hauled through them.[4] Even so, we have eyewitness images of French filibusters with long, loose hair.[5] Perhaps only if he is an African might our pirate have dreadlocks, although if he is a *boucanier*—a hunter of pigs and cattle who often sails with pirates—his hair might be matted with blood and resemble them.[6]

Our pirate might wear a large handkerchief on his head, but probably only for the same reasons non-mariners did: to cover a bald head, to keep sweat from one's eyes, or to cover the head when—if he were a gentlemen, pretended or otherwise—he was not wearing his wig, which in the Caribbean was worn only on formal occasions.[7] If he is a pirate of African descent, he might wear a similar cloth wrap on his head, as many slaves and former slaves do.[8] The modern idea that pirates commonly wore bandanas, handkerchiefs, or scarves on their heads appears to originate from illustrators in the nineteenth century. In all of the eyewitness accounts of pirates, only Anne Bonny and Mary Read, dressed in "Men's Cloaths," are described as wearing handkerchiefs on their heads—and they may have done so in order to help disguise their sex.[9]

Our pirate might wear an eye patch, but only if he has lost an eye in battle or to disease. In fact, black patches were commonly used by persons from all walks of life to cover up not only blind eyes but also any disfiguring scar or blemish on the face.[10] We can disregard the recently argued nonsense that pirates wore eye patches to aid their eyesight at sea. Not only is there no historical evidence to associate pirates with eye patches but it is the result of asking the wrong question, *If pirates wore eye patches, why did they wear them?* rather than *Is there any evidence at all that pirates wore eye patches?*

The myth that lots of pirates wore eye patches has its origin in both literature and our subconscious, with roots as far back as Polyphemus the Cyclops in *The Odyssey*. Its modern origin begins with buccaneer articles that included payment for a lost eye, with real-life one-eyed swashbucklers—such as the old musketeer Heredia in Bernal Díaz del Castillo's eyewitness account of Spanish conquest—and with nineteenth-century novelists, including Sir Walter Scott, who described in detail the eye-patched soldier of fortune Captain Colepepper, and Charles Dickens, who described a pirate with "the one eye and the patch across the nose." In these examples of fact and fiction, there is one common thread: the patches imply eyes lost in battle.[11]

And why are people inclined to believe the myth? Because an eye patch gives a pirate a frightening, fearsome aspect; because readers and filmgoers have seen fictional pirates wear eye patches; and because the myth has been enhanced recently with the suggestion that eye patches might aid eyesight in some circumstances. This last argument has inspired the ridiculous notion that pirates might have worn eye patches intentionally in order to help improve their vision for fighting below deck or improve their night vision or help them use telescopes or navigational instruments. There is zero evidence for this, and, in fact, an eye patch would severely restrict a pirate's vision and destroy his depth perception, as it would anyone's, making it difficult for him to move safely around a ship at sea, much less fight. In reality, the eye patch was never specifically associated with pirates except in fiction and film.[12]

Eye patches notwithstanding, our pirate squints from the sun and between his teeth is a short white clay pipe or, if he's broke, a cheaper one of red clay.[13] He smokes when he can, but never during battle for fear of igniting cartridges or, worse, an incidental powder train to the powder room that might blow up the ship. He smokes cigars when he discovers them among the cargo of his Spanish prey, and he chews tobacco when he cannot smoke it.

He does indeed drink rum, although some writers have suggested the association of rum with pirates is primarily due to literature—"Yo-ho-ho and a bottle of rum!" for example. But rum is cheap, is found everywhere in the Caribbean, and everyone drinks it, but most especially the poor and working classes. Our pirate therefore drinks plenty of it, sometimes straight, sometimes mixed with water, and sometimes in punch. In fact, our pirate drinks anything alcoholic he can get his hands on: "For the pirates being all in a drunken Fit, which held as long as the Liquor lasted." In this case, the liquor was brandy and wine.[14]

Our pirate swears and curses much, even more than common seamen do: "Moreover, the execrable Oaths and Blasphemies I heard among the Ship's Company, shock'd me to such a degree, that in Hell itself I thought there could not be worse; for tho' many Seafaring Men are given to swearing and taking God's Name in vain, yet I could not have imagined, human Nature could ever so far degenerate, as to talk in the manner those abandoned Wretches did."[16]

What our pirate does not say is "Arr!" unless he is from the West Country of England—a Cornishman, in other words—to indicate "yes" or as part of a word, as in "When *arr* we going to attack, Captain?" The idea that pirates talk like this started with Robert Newton, who played Long John Silver in *Treasure Island* in 1950, and continued with Newton's performances in *Blackbeard the Pirate* and in film and television sequels to *Treasure Island*.[16] Our pirate says "yare" occasionally, but only to mean that something is done well or is otherwise fine, as in "the sloop is *yare* at the helm" or a ship is "*yare*-handed."[17] He says "Yo, ho!" or "Yo, hope!" but only when he is heaving on the capstan or hauling on the rigging.

Although he might note that a round shot "shivered"—smashed into splinters—a timber, he does not yet say, "Shiver me timbers!"[18]

But if he is a captain, he surely shouts "My hearts!" when encouraging his men to fight harder, but perhaps not yet "My hearties!" or "Me hearties!" In literature, the former dates to the mid-eighteenth century, the latter to the late eighteenth, although the expression may have been pronounced like these even earlier. By the late nineteenth century, "My hearts!" in its various forms was common in popular literature, including when Tom Sawyer plays pirate.[19]

Our pirate might wear an earring but most sea rovers probably do not. There is no real evidence that pirates and other mariners of European descent of this era wore earrings as part of maritime dress—although some probably did before and certainly did after this time—except for a line in a late seventeenth-century play that speaks of the jewel in a man's ear and also of his gunpowder spot (tattoo), which, depending on how you read it, refers to either a fop or a mariner, probably the former. Some gentlemen as late as the first quarter of the eighteenth century did in fact wear a single earring and some, as discussed below, also had "gunpowder spots," thus the line probably refers to a gentleman.[20]

So, while we may doubt that earrings were commonly worn by seafarers and pirates, we can deduce that at least some pirates who pretended to gentlemanly or foppish airs probably did wear them. More importantly, though, all too often our idea of pirates is that all were of European origin, and we forget that many were of African or Native American origin and were more apt to wear earrings than their European counterparts.[21]

Our pirate might have jewelry around his neck, a coin perhaps, convenient for buying that last dram of rum after all the booty is gone. If he has done well by his plunder and not spent it all on rum, women, and dice, as pirates generally did, he might wear a "necklace of pearls of extraordinary size and inestimable price, with rubies of surpassing beauty" as Captain Nicolas Van Horn did, or a gold chain with a "gold toothpicker hanging at it" as Captain John James did (and many of his crew also wore gold chains), or a "gold chain round his neck, with a diamond cross hanging to it" as Captain Bartholomew Roberts reportedly did.[22] Pirates often wore or carried gentlemanly accessories as well: Captain John Philips wore a "silver hilted sword, silver shoe and knee-buckles, a curious tobacco-box, and two gold rings."[23]

He might have rings on his fingers but probably often not, at least not if he is a common pirate. Rings can cut or break fingers of seamen handling the rigging and hauling great guns, as mariners referred to cannon, in and out of gun ports. (But, for what it's worth, a pirate might indeed threaten to cut a prisoner's finger off if he did not give up his ring.)[24] None of our pirate's jewelry has a skull and bones on it except occasionally as a common *memento mori* that anyone might wear—a reminder that death comes to all.

If he is white, our pirate's skin is bronzed by the sun. He might have a tattoo, or several, but he does not call them tattoos and might not have one at all.[25] If he does, it is probably on his hand or arm and he calls it a "gunpowder spot," for his skin is "pricked" with a needle and crushed gunpowder, or sometimes antimony, is rubbed in for ink. Popular gunpowder spots for Christian pilgrims in non-Christian lands were the cross (especially the Jerusalem Cross), spear, and Jesus and Mary, both for faith and to ensure Christian burial should the traveler chance to die there.[26]

William Dampier, the famous buccaneer, explorer, naval officer, and privateer, wrote of the gunpowder spots "men" sometimes have, the Jerusalem Cross in particular, but we do not know if he were referring to any men or only seamen.[27] In fact, there are records of seamen, soldiers, and civilians, including ladies and gentlemen, with tattoos. William Wycherley wrote a provocative poem about the gunpowder spot pricked on a lady's hand: "Thy Gun-Powder, on thy Hand, shot // Me dead, half-dead with Love before . . ." In the case of gentlemen and ladies, the gunpowder spots were permanent beauty marks, usually on the hand— and this evidence of youth was often later surgically removed.[28]

In fact, buccaneer-surgeon Lionel Wafer attempted at the request of a fellow buccaneer named Bullman to "get out of his Cheek one of these imprinted Pictures, which was made by the *Negroes*." He failed, even after "much scarifying and fetching off a great part of the Skin."[29] Certainly some other sailors and pirates were well-inked: one "saylor" in 1720 Virginia had "on one hand *S. P.* in blew Letters and on the other hand blew Spots, and upon one arm our Savior upon the Cross, and on the other Adam and Eve, all Suppos'd to be done in Gun powder." [30] Pirates who have lived among Native Americans or are Native Americans or Africans or hail from certain lands in the Mediterranean or in the East beyond are often inked as well. But the tattoo as a definite part of maritime culture probably did not exist until seamen began visiting Polynesia in the late eighteenth century.[31]

Occasionally, we might see a monkey or parrot on a pirate shoulder, for exotic pets were popular among travelers, including mariners: an illustration by a late eighteenth ship's surgeon shows a parrot or parakeet in a cage hanging at the break of the quarterdeck of an East Indiaman, for example.[32] One pirate crew even brought away one or two parrots for every man, and a young Barbary macaque was aboard the French privateer *Dauphine* in 1704, almost certainly as someone's pet.[33] Even so, many pirates who had parrots or monkeys probably intended to sell them sooner or later, assuming they had a place to do so, for these exotic pets were as valuable then as they are today.

Our pirate's shirt is plain or checked, often of coarse linen. If he is an early eighteenth-century pirate, he often prefers white shirts as gentlemen wear, to distinguish himself from common merchant seamen, who often wear checked shirts. He probably has a kerchief around his neck, or even a cravat with lace at the ends, and often wears a waistcoat over his shirt and under his coat. In the seventeenth century he wears wide seaman's breeches, open or closed at the knee, or sometimes common narrower breeches secured at the knee, and in the eighteenth, similar breeches or long seaman's trousers. He wears a short tarred seaman's jacket of heavy linen, known as osnabrigs, or a medium-length coat, or even a long coat, sometimes an expensive one, sometimes not. French filibusters often wore blue coats of sackcloth—cheap, in other words.[34]

Only rarely does he wear a gentleman's coat of rich fabric with silver or gold lace.[35] If he happens to be a gentleman, or pretends to be one, he probably dresses as the middle and upper classes do in the Caribbean: in "Thread Stockings, Linnen Drawers and Vest, a Handkerchief tied round their Head, and a Hat above." Only on formal occasions might a gentleman, or a pirate pretending to be one, wear a coat, much less a wig, in the tropical heat and humidity.[36]

In battle, at sea or ashore, he usually carries a musket, cartridge box, sword, a pistol or two, and often a grenade or firepot, and sometimes a boarding ax.[37] Among the buccaneers and filibusters of the late seventeenth century, the musket, not the cutlass or pistol, was the primary weapon, especially the exceptionally long-barreled *fusil boucanier*.[38] Our pirate's sword, usually a cutlass, might hang from a baldric worn across his body, but probably only through the 1670s and rarely afterward except to support the occasional broadsword.[39] Otherwise, he wears his sword in a scabbard hanging from his belt or even slips it through a mere "frog" or loop on his belt. Here and there we might see a pirate with a broadsword, backsword, or smallsword, but only a Spanish or Portuguese pirate or perhaps an Italian might wear a long rapier, and in most cases it is cup-hilted.

He might wear a sash at his waist over his coat, especially if he is French or Spanish (although we know of English pirates who did so, too), and if he wears a baldric, probably over it as well, for this keeps his sword from bouncing about.[40] If he is wearing one, his belt, with or without a baldric, generally goes over his sash.

For convenience in describing the arms on his belt or sash, we will assume our pirate is right handed. At the left front he wears a cartridge box holding twenty to thirty cartridges, the latter being common among buccaneers. The pirates who sacked Veracruz in 1683 carried two cartridge boxes, the second probably worn at the back.[41] Our pirate's brace of pistols is tucked behind at the right front and right side, with the locks toward his body, belt hooks in front, butts to the left. He wears them this way both to protect hammers and primings and for ease of access because he shoots left-handed, with his cutlass in his right. However, if the pistols are very large—as many were, typically eighteen to twenty-two inches long—our pirate might wear them on the outside, via their belt hooks, so that he may have more freedom of movement. Some pirates carried as many as six pistols, but one or two was the norm.[42]

In the early eighteenth century our pirate might wear a brace of pistols slung from silk around his neck as a fad among pirates, mostly to show them off, but this is not a good way to wear pistols unless they are also tucked or hooked into a belt, at least not if you have any running, leaping, climbing, or close fighting to do.[43] Our pirate wears his sword, pistols, and cartridge box when a fight might be imminent, aboard his ship at anchor, especially if there are prisoners or slaves aboard, and when ashore in his own ports—rare and short-lived though they were—or in distant places where there is no law or where he is the law. At Madagascar in 1720, for example, pirates strutted about with a brace of pistols at the waist and a naked sword in hand. As one might expect, this often led to "quarreling and fighting."[44]

Even so, only a few blustering pirates of the early eighteenth century bore arms all the time; they get in the way, for example, of ship handling. Notably, even if pirates could go ashore anywhere they liked, most port cities only permitted gentlemen and those with military duties to bear arms in public except during militia drills and in time of emergency.

And on his feet? He might have a peg leg if he has lost a leg, but peg legs make seafaring, not to mention warfare at sea, difficult and were not as common among pirates as the myth would have us believe. In the 1620s and 1630s, Dutch privateer captain Cornelis Jol was known as "Pie de Palo" or "Wooden Leg." He had moderate success cruising against the Spanish in the Caribbean. In 1678 buccaneer surgeon and writer Alexandre Exquemelin described buccaneer articles that provided disability compensation for the loss of a leg, and in 1724 "Captain" Charles Johnson—a pseudonym—described a whiskered, peg-legged pirate, his belt stuck with several pistols. This possibly fictional pirate is probably the ultimate origin of Long John Silver, not to mention every other Hollywood peg-legged pirate ever filmed. Of course, we cannot forget Captain Ahab. Though not a pirate, his ivory peg leg has influenced our notions of what old seafarers look like.[45]

Our pirate might otherwise be barefoot or, more typically, shod with shoes of cow leather or cheaper pigskin, often with heel plates— "Sparrables of Iron"—to prevent their wearing out so quickly. He never wears these shoes into the powder room, unless he is a fool, for a spark there might blow up his ship.[46]

What he never wears unless he is riding a horse—and a ship is not usually a place for doing so—are high-topped riding boots, known then as jackboots and today often as pirate, musketeer, or bucket boots, which seem a part of every pirate costume in film, television, stage, and illustration, not to mention on Halloween. These boots were made for riding, and only riding. No one wore them for any other reason, and only a foolish sailor would wear them aboard ship. Even ashore, they were the "intolerable cloggs of a nimble footed Seaman."[47]

In fact, they were so stiff that walking in them was uncomfortable and running in them so slow that a dismounted cavalryman in retreat would typically "slip his legs out of his jack boots, and save himself in his stocking feet," as a French officer of the guards once did, fleeing from English sailors who had shot his horse dead.[48] Illustrators and filmmakers have adapted jackboots and earlier similar boots worn by English cavaliers and musketeers (and probably also mistook the heavy, fashionable over-socks, worn through the mid-seventeenth century by French and Spanish foot soldiers, for boots), to pirates for the simple reason that they look the part of a swashbuckler—dashing, dominant, and sexy, in other words.[49] For this same reason do Hollywood directors and costume designers often put women pirates in tall boots.

Yet some seamen—but not pirates—did wear boots. Fishermen often wore fishermen's boots, known as cokers; whalers wore cokers fitted with irons similar to crampons to keep them from slipping off whales as they dispatched the carcass; and sailors in arctic or other cold waters wore boots to keep their feet and lower legs warm.[50] But these were not the boots we see pirates wear on film and in popular illustrations.

In sum, our pirate, head to toe, smells of sweat, tar, rum, and gunpowder, and sometimes of blood as well. He might be tall or short, religious or irreligious, short-tempered or tolerant. He might be black, white, or brown. He is certainly a rebel, even if only by being a thief upon the sea, or for that matter, simply by being a seafarer. In his eyes, he is a "true Buccaneer," an "experienced Soldier and Privateer," a "Gentleman of Fortune," even a "true Cock of the Game and old Sportsman." He might even be a she, although so rarely as to be an extraordinary exception. In fact, he might be any of us, if only in our dreams.[51]

The following twelve chapters, beginning with pirate violence and continuing with pirate society, narrate, describe, and correct many of the myths that have grown up around the Golden Age pirates who cruised the Spanish Main and beyond from 1655 to 1725. This was the era first of the buccaneer and filibuster who sailed against the Spanish from 1655 to 1688 as privateers and quasi-pirates, and by the 1680s often as outright pirates. From 1688 to 1713 many sea rovers served as honest privateers during King William's War and Queen Anne's War, while others turned to piracy, often in the Red Sea. Finally, during the dozen or so years following, many sea rovers turned to true piracy, attacking flags of all nations, and with no pretense of serving under any flag but the black one.

Here we will see these pirates engaged not only in the kernel of truth that is the origin of each myth—when indeed there is a piratical origin—but also in the fascinating reality beyond.

PART I

"For Some Body Must Be Beaten"— Pirate Violence

———⟡———

CHAPTER 1

Death's Head and Marrow Bones

"There are no Men of War belonging to this River; nay, there's no Vessel but mine, no variety of Ensigns or Colours. Deaths Head and Marrow Bones, is the only Flag in a Sable Field."[1]

—*A Pacquet from Parnassus,* 1715

The pirates—and they were pirates, even if they pretended otherwise—knew they could not wait forever. It was nearly too late, almost three hours past midnight. In a couple hours more, the sun would begin to rise and with it the local population. Worse, the sun would be in the filibusters' eyes, making it more difficult to make their way ahead even as it became easier for them to be seen from shore. And if they were spotted this soon, they would have no chance to plunder the countryside of desperately needed provisions or to capture prisoners to guide their way and serve as hostages.

Indecisively they had waited in their several canoes, and much too long, these men who usually knew when it was wise to hesitate and when it was wise to seize the moment. They were seventy in all, nearly all of European extraction, mostly French, but for the half-dozen Africans. Far behind them lay their ship, a small Dutch-built pink or small flute known by the Spanish as an *urqueta*, named *La Chavale (La Cavalle,* the *Mare),* formerly known as the *Saint-Nicolas* of Vlissingen, with just enough men aboard to manage the sails. Immediately ahead lay waves breaking all across the river bar. It was a dangerous crossing even in the best of circumstances, and these men in their small, low-sided dugout canoes had to do so in the darkness of the early morn of December 4, 1688.[2]

They had been long from home, rapaciously cruising a part of the Spanish Main only rarely touched by the pirates of the Caribbean. Strictly speaking, these indomitable intruders were filibusters—the French equivalent of the English buccaneers, men who sailed under their own rules and drifted among legitimate privateering, outright piracy, and the murky area in between. From the Caribbean these sea thieves had sailed in July 1686, in their small vessel of one hundred tons and six guns, having first barely escaped capture at Samana Bay, Hispaniola, in late June by the HMS *Falcon* and HMS *Drake*, a pair of English men-of-war that pounded their thirty-six gun intended consort, the *Golden Fleece*. Commanded by Joseph Banister, an indebted sea captain who turned bold pirate (he made a daring escape under the guns of Port Royal by night in January 1685, receiving only three shots in his hull), their consort was so badly damaged that her captain burned her, then, along with a few of his crew, set sail with these Frenchmen.[3]

Soon they captured a small Spanish bark. Banister and his men parted company aboard the prize and cruised to the Mosquito Coast, only to be soon captured and delivered to Port Royal in a striking manner by the captain and crew of the HMS *Drake*. As the governor of Jamaica put it, "Captain Spragge returned to Port Royal, having succeeded in the task that I assigned to him, with Captain Banister and three of his consorts hanging at his yard-arm, a spectacle of great satisfaction to all good people and of terror to the favourers of pirates, the manner of his punishment being that which will most discourage others, which was the reason why I empowered Captain Spragge to inflict it."[4]

From Hispaniola the French pirates sailed to New York and then toward Brazil and Africa, where just south of the equator they barely escaped alive from a fight with an English East Indiaman of fifty to sixty guns that battered them mercilessly, leaving many pirates dead and most of them wounded. On the coast of Africa, the pirates repaired their ship and tended their wounded. Soon after, they sailed first to the coast of Brazil, then south to the Strait of Magellan and into the South Sea.

Who commanded them has been the subject of some speculation, and, as we will discover, his identity might possibly give us some insight into pirate flags. To the Spaniards in the South Sea, he was generally known as a Dutchman or Fleming, possibly a Frenchman, named Francisco Franco.[5] This is surely the Hispanicization of the Dutch Frans Franco or the French Francis François. However, there are no other records of a filibuster by this name.

It might therefore be tempting to hope it was the veteran filibuster Pierre Lagarde, who had spent three years as the quartermaster of the famous Sieur de Grammont aboard the *Hardy*, formerly the *Saint Nicolas*, the ship of the famous Nicolas Van Horn, who fought a duel with the even more famous Laurens de Graff. After all, Lagarde and Banister, whose ship was destroyed at Samana, had been together at Île-à-Vache not two months before these French pirates arrived at Samana. Lagarde, commanding his "*fregattela*"—little frigate—named *La Subtile*, was also at Île-à-Vache a few months before that, hoping to sail to the South Sea and join Frenchmen already there. Unfortunately, Lagarde was giving a deposition in Martinique in January 1687 at the same time the French pirates were en route from Newfoundland to Brazil.[6]

To discover who Franco might really have been, we begin by taking a close look at the highly detailed journal of the voyage. From the handwriting it is clear that François Massertie, a Frenchman, was the author, although he identifies himself as such only very late in the voyage. Could he have been the captain? Francisco Franco could be a double wordplay on François. However, if Massertie were the captain, he only commanded after the original captain and a few of the crew departed on their own in a captured barque. This man, who doubtless commanded at Acaponeta, was very likely deposed by vote of the crew, and, rather than serve in a common capacity, chose to set sail on his own, along with eight of his most loyal followers—quite a bold act for nine men to set out sea roving in a small vessel in a Spanish ocean.[7]

So who else might have taken the nom de guerre of Francisco Franco? François Le Sage (or Lesage) is a likely candidate. He was yet another famous Dutch filibuster. Two years earlier he tried to sail into the South Sea, as the Pacific was then commonly known, but was turned back by weather and raided slave ships on the Guinea Coast of Africa instead. However, the ruthless Le Sage was apparently not in command of the South Sea voyage, for he is believed to have been in the service of the Compagnie de l'Orient at the time.[8] Nonetheless, part of his crew may have desired to attempt the South Sea again.

And there is indeed a connection to Le Sage: several French scholars believe the captain was the famous Michel Andresson, a Dutch or French filibuster commonly known as "Captain Michel," sailing under the false name of Guillaume Mimbrat after being accused of piracy. Governor Pierre-Paul Tarin de Cussy of Saint-Domingue had confiscated his ship, *La Mutine*, formerly the *La Paz* captured off Cartagena in 1683, and Andresson, along with many of his former crew, joined Le Sage on his attempt to sail into the South Sea. After capturing several Dutch prizes on the African coast, Andresson and his followers returned to the Caribbean aboard one of them. Buccaneers often used false names, and perhaps Andresson pretended to be Francisco Franco before he was turned out of office and set sail with eight followers, eventually crossing the Pacific and sailing into the South China Sea as far as Siam (Thailand).[9]

Andresson is an ideal candidate. A bold and experienced captain, he participated in the sack of Veracruz in 1683, was with Laurens de Graff when French filibusters under his command captured three Spanish ships sent to capture them off Cartagena in the same year, and a year later plundered two rich Dutch ships off Havana, Cuba. Such a captain would have been quite familiar with the conventions and tactics of buccaneers and filibusters, *including their use of flags at sea and ashore*.[10]

Under the command of Franco, whoever he was—but we will assume quite reasonably that he was the famous Michel Andresson—these dangerous men licked their wounds, then sailed around Cape Horn and into the South Sea. North they now cruised, sometimes plundering, sometimes escaping by the skin of their teeth from the valiant crews of Spanish men-of-war, as far as La Paz in the Gulf of California, where they made a winter base and translated its name as Port de Paix (Port of Peace), perhaps also after the French port of the same name on the northern shore of Hispaniola across from the island of Tortuga.

And now they lay before the breakers on the shallow bar before the Acaponeta River, almost two hundred miles south of the Gulf of California on the Mexican coast. Some of the filibusters were probably seasick and dry heaving over the gunwales of the canoes, for nothing compares to a small boat or canoe in a swell to cause this illness—and even seamen of this era were known to get seasick at times, especially in small boats adrift in a short, choppy sea.[11] Given the breakers and the coming dawn, Captain Franco could not wait forever. Or as Massertie put it, "Where there is the necessity, there is never too much risk!"[12]

Franco gave the order, and with the word of command passed from canoe to canoe, the filibusters put their backs into their oars or paddles—canoes used by pirates and other Anglo-Europeans were usually rowed, not paddled, unless they were very small—and stroked toward the bar, aiming for areas where the white foam of breaking waves did not show. Of course, it is often impossible to know on a dark night when a wave might break upon you, until it actually does. The filibusters' arms would have been lashed inside the canoes, and their cartridge boxes well waxed to help waterproof them.[13]

But the pirate gods, whoever they were—Castor and Pollux, the Gemini Twins, some said, because they had been pirates, although others said they were the gods of pirate hunters because they had hunted pirates—were on their side.[14] This attack would not fail as it had a year before. One canoe touched the bar, but was spared capsizing. No men were lost. Once safely past the bar, the filibusters rowed into the lagoon at the mouth of the river and made camp on a small island. The next night they rowed quietly up the river until they found the main road to Acaponeta. Quietly they went ashore, then marched, all seventy of them, for another hour, then slept until an hour before dawn.

Their arms at the ready, they marched forward, knowing well that soon the alarm would be given. At a small house in the darkness they kidnapped a man and forced him to be their guide. A troop of Spanish cavalry rode quickly by, just missing them. It made so much noise that the filibusters could not have missed hearing them coming. Onward they marched and seized a small town with no resistance. The pirates took the mayor, the wife of the chief captain, and all of the priests captive.

The next morning they marched to Acaponeta, which lay on the road from Mexico City in the south to New Mexico in the north. The countryside was alarmed: this would be no picnic. In a ragged line the filibusters surged up the road, their prisoners and stores at the center. The path led across a hot, dusty, arid region whose dull flatness was relieved by adobe houses; by palm, guava, and banana trees; and by fields of grasses, low bushes, and cassava plants. Gnats and mosquitoes swarmed around the filibusters as they strode, long-barreled buccaneer muskets in hand.

By midday, three or four hundred armed Spaniards, all mounted, lay nervously in wait behind a nearby hill, perhaps more nervously than the filibusters as they had lain in wait before the breakers at the mouth of the river. A year ago they had repulsed thirty filibusters as they tried to come ashore. But today there were seventy and they were already ashore. It would not be easy to force them back, and Franco knew what he was doing. But the Spanish had tricks up their sleeves as well. Their plan was simple: hundreds of Native Americans lay in wait along the road, and when they ambushed the pirates, the cavalry would charge while the pirates were distracted. The pirates would be cut to pieces.

But the filibusters were not fools. They knew the Native Americans were there, and it was time to send them a message. The pirates furled the white banner of France they marched under, and in its place they raised high a "red flag with a death's head at the center and two crossed bones below the head, in white, in the middle of the red."[15]

The flag meant they would give no quarter.

At Franco's order, the pirates fired musket volleys into the grasses where the Native Americans, who had been given a cow to slaughter and *eau de vie* to drink as encouragement to fight, lay hiding. The hot lead balls, whizzing by ears, cutting leaves, and killing and wounding warriors, scattered the Spanish allies. Hearing the fusillade, the mounted Spanish soldiery dashed to the road in a cloud of dust, expecting that the filibusters had been attacked by surprise—but when they realized their error they reined up and retreated, keeping their distance.

The rest of the attack was anticlimactic. The Spanish cavalry, most of it probably composed of poorly trained and armed militia and volunteers, chose discretion over battlefield valor. Captain Franco led his men into Acaponeta unmolested and held it to ransom, using hostages, including the governor, as a means of additional persuasion. The Spaniards promised them one hundred thousand pieces of eight, eight hundred carts of wheat, two hundred mule loads of corn, and eight hundred salted cattle. This was an enormous ransom for so small a place! Too enormous, in fact—the filibusters should have been suspicious. The Spaniards, no fools either, delayed as long as they could, providing five cows and two loads of wheat per day, giving time for a small man-of-war to be dispatched from Acapulco to catch the pirates off guard.

Soon enough the filibusters aboard *La Chevale* sighted an unknown sail. The filibusters lowered their flag to half-mast and fired a cannon, the signal for those ashore to return to the ship. Quickly Franco and his men returned to their small pink. The unknown sail quickly turned into a Spaniard mounting twenty-two guns and bearing 143 men; the filibusters bore less than half of each. Franco knew that his ship and men might not be able to survive a long battering by the Spaniard's guns. He chose to board instead, a tactic favored by French filibusters.

After an afternoon and night of playing cat and mouse, on New Year's Day 1689, the helmsman steered *La Chevale* close, but just as the filibusters fired their first broadside—jokingly they referred to it as "throwing a biscuit" at the Spaniards, perhaps because the pirate ship's guns were so small—the wind died. For four hours, the ships drifted alongside each other, each trying to smother the other with iron, fire, and lead. Perhaps the filibusters hoisted their red flag with skull and bones aloft, hoping to inspire dread or even terror in the Spanish crew.[16]

But the Spanish crew did not seem afraid, even though their guns did little damage. The filibusters might well have captured the man-of-war had they been able to come alongside. Instead, they could only follow conventional tactics: batter the Spaniard's hull with their cannon and fire muskets and swivel cannon at the enemy's gun ports to keep them closed, at any head that appeared, and at the sails and rigging. They were too close to aim their cannon into the rigging.[17]

Eventually, the swell of the sea pushed the ships apart, and when the wind came up, each ship bore away to nurse its wounds and wounded, although the Spanish claimed they pursued the pirates for two more days, and the French claimed the Spanish ship fled. The filibusters' losses were two men killed and eighteen wounded, almost a third of their force. They gave up the attack and planned new adventures. These pirates continued their bloody trade in the South Sea until 1693. The South Sea Spaniards were never able to dislodge them.

The red banner the filibuster crew flew at Acaponeta, and which they may well have flown in their fight with the Spanish man-of-war, is the first known instance of Golden Age pirates of European origin flying the famous skull and crossbones. Importantly, this death's head and crossbones were depicted on a red field, not a black one. And, unlike the famous black flag of pirates, this red flag was intended as a warning of "no quarter," not as the first warning to surrender, as pirates commonly used the skull and bones. French pirates were particularly fond of the red flag of no quarter, and used it often.[18]

Can we assume that the use of a skull and crossed bones on the red flag of no quarter was commonplace at this time? Did other buccaneers and filibusters use it as well? Unfortunately, to date we have no way of knowing. Buccaneer flags are seldom described in journals, except when they are unusual. The fact that Massertie described the flag in detail suggests that the skull and crossed bones were not typical of the red banner of no quarter—or at least not to him. But perhaps this was not the first time that the veteran Captain Michel Andresson, if indeed he were pretending to be Franco, had flown the flag.

Notably, the flag used at Acaponeta was not called the Jolly Roger, nor even the "*joli rouge*" ("pretty red"), which many books, repeating a long-standing myth, incorrectly suggest may be the origin of the term Jolly Roger.

The Myth of *Le Joli Rouge*

In fact, *le joli rouge* does not appear at all among the journals of French pirates, privateers, and men-of-war, or any other sea rovers or mariners of any nationality, as a term for a flag or anything else. If you want to find the term in the age of sail, you need to look in books about painting and flowers, not in those about cannon and cutlass.

The origin of the mythical *joli rouge* almost certainly lies in the French revolution of 1848, with roots in the original French revolution. An unknown writer argued in 1921 that the term was a misattribution based on the *bonnet rouge* or red Phrygian 'liberty cap' and the associated terror and violence of the French revolutionaries who began to wear it circa 1789, but he did not provide his evidence.[19]

Even so, if this is the case, then *joli rouge* cannot be the origin of Jolly Roger because the events upon which it is based came later than the original accounts that used the name. But how is *joli rouge* derived from the cap of the French revolutionaries? The author did not explain, but using his clues we can trace a very strong argument. First we need to look beyond the original French revolution, to that of 1848. By now the French *tricolor* of blue, white, and red was no longer the flag of revolution, but of established government—of convention, not rebellion. A new flag was needed. The new French revolutionaries appropriated the color of the *bonnet rouge* to their new banner.

Often associated with this adoption of the red flag, which signified both death and life, were the death's head and crossbones. One such flag was red with a death's head capped by a Phrygian bonnet with fleur de lys on it, over crossed bones, with a hatchet and torch, and the motto (translated) of "Long Live Blanqui [a noted revolutionary] or Die."[20] And it was indeed a "*joli*" flag. In fact, the only reference the author has found to any flag as a *joli rouge* is an incidental description by Nineteenth-century historian and political writer Hippolyte Castille, of the 1848 revolutionary banner as the pretty red flag—"*le joli drapeau rouge*"—floating on the morning breeze from the Seine.[21]

From here it was but a simple misstep backward from the pretty red revolutionary flag, often enough with skull and bones, to the pirate's fantasy *joli rouge* and his real Jolly Roger. Or perhaps it is the other way around: the black pirate banner with skull and bones, together with the red banner of no quarter, inspires the revolutionary banner, which inspires the myth of *le joli rouge*.

But as already noted, the pirate flag flown at Acaponeta was neither a Jolly Roger nor a *joli rouge*, nor was it a banner of nineteenth-century socialist revolution. Rather, it was a unique early instance of the piratical skull and crossbones, and not quite what we have come to expect.[22]

The Colors of Fear and Death

So is this red flag the origin of the black flag with skull and crossbones that has come to be known as the Jolly Roger? It might be, but it is more likely not, or at least not its sole origin. Rather, it is probably part of a common theme that runs through time across both land and sea. Until the early eighteenth century, a black flag flown at sea aboard European ships typically meant mourning: a captain or admiral had died, or perhaps a prince or king. To indicate a willingness to fight, especially to neither give nor receive quarter, a red flag, often known as the "bloody flag," "bloody banner," "flag of no quarter," "*pavillon de combat*," "*pavillon sans quartier*," and "*bloed-vlag*," was flown at sea, and occasionally ashore.

A nineteenth-century historian traces this red banner's origin at sea to the red *baucents*—medieval pavilions or banners—flown in the thirteenth century AD, and probably earlier, by French ships of war. A document dating to 1292 notes that these red banners sent a message of "certain and mortal strife." Ashore, the red banner has a more ancient recorded lineage: Lodowick Lloyd "Esquier" in 1602 traces the red flag to Hannibal of Carthage, and before him to Alexander the Great. Tamerlane employed it, too. Without doubt, the red banner, given its obvious connotation of spilled blood, and therefore of threat and violence, has originated independently many times throughout history:

"While the Red Flags breathe on their Top-masts high Terror and War . . . ," wrote poet Andrew Marvel in 1667.[23]

Early on, anyone at sea might fly the red banner: naval men-of-war, privateers, pirates, even merchantmen (a merchantman was any ship carrying merchant cargo). Later, beginning in the late seventeenth and early eighteenth centuries, the red flag was largely abandoned by many navies, and retained only by privateers and pirates as a threat that no quarter would be given, or at least that quarter *might* not be given. But beginning in the early eighteenth century, a new wave of pirates who originated in the Americas began to fly a black flag.

But why not black before this, and red only as a banner of no quarter? Foremost, until the early eighteenth century, most pirates and quasi-pirates—buccaneers and filibusters, for example—flew the naval ensigns of their home countries. English buccaneers flew the Cross of St. George or the English naval ensign with a red field and a Cross of St. George in the canton. French filibusters usually flew the "*pavillon blanc,*" or white banner of France. Spanish pirates flew a white ensign with a red Cross of Burgundy, except for Spanish pirates from "Biscay," who often flew the reverse, a red ensign with a white Cross of Burgundy. Dutch sea rovers often flew the tricolor of the Netherlands or the "States General" flag with a lion holding a cutting sword and a sheaf of arrows on a red field.[24]

Only rarely did Golden Age pirates prior to 1716 fly their own distinct colors. Each company of buccaneers that crossed the Isthmus of Darien in 1680 had its own distinct banner, for example, but none was black and none bore a skull and crossbones—and none was flown at sea, as far as we know. Instead, at sea they flew the ensigns of England and France. When three "pirate kings" at Madagascar went to war around 1720, each flew his national colors: English, Danish, or Scottish, rather than the black flag of piracy.[25]

Why did most pirates fly the colors of their home countries? Because it was a pretense of legitimacy: they did not want to be hanged. Local governments often quietly supported their piracy, or at least looked the other way because it was profitable to do so. Pirates pretended that their crimes were in fact legitimate, even when they knew they were not. Further, most pirates of this era remained loyal in many respects to their home nations, even when they were part of a multinational, multicultural band of brethren pirates.

But much of this changed with the coming of the cutthroats who came to be defined by their rejection of nation-states and by their unity under their own colors. After Queen Anne's War ended in 1713, privateers were no longer necessary and diminished trade meant fewer seafaring jobs. A brief attempt to turn former privateers into pirate hunters hunting Spanish pirates failed when the hunters set their sights on honest Spanish shipping, attempting to continue a sea-roving tradition begun in 1655. But no longer would blind eyes be turned to pirates who attacked the Spanish. In retaliation, pirates now set their sights on the shipping of all nations. The final period of the Great Age of Piracy had begun.

And this is when we see the black flag become synonymous with piracy, although it had been flown by pirates of European origin before this time, at least once. In 1700, at Brava Island in the Cape Verdes, the HMS *Poole* chased and briefly trapped French pirates commanded by Emanuel Wynne. The pirates, the *Poole*'s captain noted in his log, flew a black flag with skull, crossbones, and hourglass. But there are no other accounts of European or American pirates flying such a flag around this time, and Wynne cannot be considered as one of the great band of pirates who came into being after Queen Anne's War ended in 1713.[26]

Curiously, a poem published in 1702 described Charon, the ferryman of the River Styx, as flying a "sable" flag with "Death's Head and Marrow Bones." Charon ferried souls—who had to pay him a tiny silver coin called an obol—to Hades.[27] The meaning of the skull and crossbones on a black flag was clearly obvious. This was without doubt the perfect symbolism for a pirate willing to stand against all nations. Even so, not all pirates chose black. At least two, one of them French and the other almost certainly so, chose white flags with black skull and bones or black skeletons. Very likely, the white flag with black bones was a symbol both of piracy and of French nationality—and a reminder to us that even pirates who claimed no flag or nationality but that of piracy still held significant attachment to their national origins.[28] Even some notorious early eighteenth-century English pirates who flew the black flag were not known to "drink any other Health than King George's." And when they heard that King George I had died, these same pirates lowered their black flag to half-mast.[29]

Yet might we not wonder why the great majority of pirates, beholden now to none but themselves, chose black instead of the traditional bloody red? Foremost and obviously, in many cultures black represents death—the eternal sleep, the impenetrable blackness, the void of nonexistence. Further, grieving is a somber time, typically one of darkness, not of light. Black clothing, draperies, flags, even sword hilts and sword knots were all used in the West to indicate grief. It therefore seems obvious that Western pirates would likewise choose black. Still, why choose black rather than red as their forebears, even recent ones, had? Red, as noted, is the color of blood: of anger, violence, rage, warfare—of death as it happens. Red can be viewed as an opposite of white, for the white flag of surrender is a request that no blood, or no more blood, be spilled.

There are two compelling reasons. The first is identity. Unlike most pirates of the past, the sea thieves who now flew the black flag considered themselves as apart from any nation, at least nominally or rhetorically. The red flag had been used by all sorts of nationalities at sea and by all sorts of vessels at sea, ranging from man-of-war to common pirate. The black flag, however, as a banner of identity would, at sea, be unique to pirates alone. As a French eyewitness to a pirate attack put it, these new pirates wanted "by these sorts of liveries to distinguish themselves from others [other sea rovers, that is] who sail the sea."[30]

The second reason relates to the first, as well as to the symbolism of the color itself. Black flags were not flown just at times of mourning. Importantly, the black flag is the true antithesis of the white flag: it indicates the opposite of surrender and has been used in centuries past both to threaten death to the besieged, and especially by the besieged to indicate defiance, that they would neither give nor take quarter. The symbolism was well known in the seventeenth century: "the black Flag of defiance, death and destruction."[31] In 1714 at the siege of Barcelona, for example, the besieged Catalonians planted a black flag with a death's head in a breach in a wall of Montjuïc Castle to send a message that they expected no quarter and would fight to the death.[32]

This defiant siege mentality is important to understanding another of the reasons pirates may have chosen black: theirs was also a defiant siege mentality—they saw themselves as physically and psychologically besieged, for in their eyes they stood defiantly against the world. They needed no flash of inspiration to realize this, for it was written into the maritime law of the time. *Pirata est hostis humani generis*: A pirate is an enemy of all mankind.[33]

Death's Head and Marrow Bones

Inseparably associated with the black flag of piracy are the symbols or devices arrayed upon its sable field. The meanings are usually obvious. The skull or "death's head" and crossed bones below or behind were the most common "mortuary" and *memento mori* (reminder of death) symbol at the time, and for centuries before. It was used on tombstones, in paintings, on mortuary rings and watches, and in various architectures.

Strictly speaking, a "death's head" was only a skull, but the term appears to have also been used at times to indicate a skull with crossbones. Sometimes the crossbones were called "marrow bones"—the femur or thighbones. To be on one's marrow bones was to be on one's knees. A "death" or "anatomy," also often used as a mortuary symbol, was usually a full skeleton, although at times the term "death" indicated only a skull. Typically, these symbols were used to remind people that the clock was ticking, that death would come inevitably sooner or later. Often, an hourglass, sometimes with wings to remind one that "time is flying," was associated with the skull and crossbones or anatomy.

The skull and bones was also used at times, for obvious reasons, to strike fear into one's enemies. The combination was used in antiquity by the Thracians, then by the Romans and Turks, and in the Middle Ages by many peoples.[34] As far as we know, it was used ashore far more often than at sea. The use by Catalans defending Barcelona in 1714 has already been noted, for example, and a seventeenth-century Swedish cavalry regiment had long used the skull and crossbones as a device on their hats. In fact, the best-known skull and crossbones ever recovered from a shipwreck of the Golden Age—a gold button or pin—belonged to a cavalry officer who died when the Swedish man-of-war *Kronan* blew up and sank during battle in 1676.[35] Clearly, the use of the skull and crossbones was well known for many centuries as both a mortuary symbol and as one of terror.

To discover why, soon after 1700, the iconic skull and crossbones became the symbol of piracy, we must take a look at how the early eighteenth-century American pirates designed and used their flags.

Bartholomew Roberts's Legacy

As Bartholomew Roberts lay spilling his blood onto the powder-blackened deck of his *Royal Fortune*, his best days were long behind him. Not only would he soon bleed to death from the grapeshot wound in his neck, but also almost his entire crew would soon surrender meekly after their mainmast was shot "by the board." No grand exit for them—they had not even inflicted a single casualty on the victorious pirate hunters—nor any pride at their exit from him, had he lived. A few of his crew tried to kill themselves by blowing up some powder, but they failed miserably, succeeding only in charring their flesh. Many of the survivors would hang, their lifeless bodies tarred in chains and gently swinging with the breezes for a long time afterward as a warning to other seamen who might choose to sail under the black flag.[36]

Roberts, of whom we will say much more later, had neither the time nor the inclination to ponder his legacy as he lay dying. For one thing, one of his crew was reportedly busy upbraiding him for cowardice, at least until he realized Roberts's throat had turned thickly scarlet. It was quite the legacy indeed that Roberts left—a swath of plundering terror from the Caribbean to North America to Brazil to Africa: a great number of vessels captured, exceeding that of any other pirate of the early eighteenth century, and hundreds of slaves captured aboard slave ships and many of them ransomed back to their owners. So successful was he that his name—"the pirate Roberts" as he was usually known—became the byword for piracy for a few years. Even today, some consider him the greatest pirate ever, but this is another chapter.

However, his real legacy may be the name he gave to his black flags. Like many men, Roberts had turned pirate in the years immediately following the end of Queen Anne's War in 1713. Many seamen had been privateers, and with peace came the eventual disbandment of these lawful plunderers: the brief attempt to turn them into pirate hunters failed miserably. In general, many seamen were put out of work after the war. Piracy was an alternative for the daring, the disenfranchised, and the foolish.

Around 1716, these pirates began flying the black flag, often with a death's head, with or without crossbones but probably more often with, and often with an hourglass, which was also a maritime symbol. Half-hourglasses were used to keep time aboard ships. Other symbols included a powder horn or pistol, daggers or swords, an arm or a full figure holding a sword, and a heart pierced by a dart. In spite of written descriptions, it is impossible to know exactly what these symbols looked like on pirate flags and how they were often arrayed. Seventeenth- and eighteenth-century gravestones show a remarkable variety of arrangements of these symbols, for example.

Pirates were not the only ones to use some of these non-mortuary symbols. A blowing horn (a cow's horn used for sounding calls) resembling a powder horn was used in the late seventeenth century on the flag of Hoorn in the Netherlands, for example, and in 1693 the black general of the Akwamus, who had captured Fort Christiansborg (now Osu Castle) from the Danes at Accra on the Guinea Coast of Africa, flew a white flag "with a black man painted in the middle brandishing a scymiter."[37]

The black flag anointed with these various devices became a symbol of unity and identity, for reasons already discussed. And these pirates revered their black flag as much as patriots of any kingdom or republic did theirs: the crew of Captain Spriggs hoisted their black flag, gave three huzzahs, and "fir'd all the Guns in the Ship, with repeated Shouts," when one of their prisoners finally, but voluntarily, agreed to join their crew. Very likely this was a common ceremony.[38]

No matter its devices, the black flag, flown variously as an ensign at the stern, at the main-masthead, and as a jack at the bow, was used not only to unify the crew but most especially to inspire fear among the prey, and it was arguably the most effective weapon in the pirate arsenal at this time—flying the flag was a tactic of threatened violence, of inducing fear and thus surrender by its threat. Pirate prey were primarily merchant-men, most of them poorly armed and with small crews. These men were easily frightened, or at least easily intimidated. But the crews aboard many larger ships came to be easily intimidated as well, once they learned what the black flag meant. The color was far more important than the images upon it, for the images might not be easily identified except up fairly close, even with a telescope.

In theory, pirates usually flew the black flag first, then, if the prey did not surrender, the red to indicate that no quarter would be given. The articles of the French pirate Jean Thomas Dulaien of the late 1720s pro-vided that no quarter was to be given *only* if the enemy fired three or more cannon shot after the red flag was raised.[39] In other words, black meant "Surrender now or we'll give no quarter!" Strictly speaking, red meant "Too late, we'll give you no quarter, don't expect us to leave any survivors, we'll probably murder you all!" If the pirates captured their prey, they might do as they pleased to their victims: they might murder them all, or some of them, or none.

In practice, however, the use of the black and red flags varied among pirates, or at least their interpretation did among pirate prey. Some thought the black flag was a new version of the red flag of no quarter, used instead of the red.[40] Others considered it a warning to be heeded lest the red flag suddenly fly to the masthead. In fact, pirate prisoner Captain Richard Hawkins wrote that "When they [Spriggs and his crew] fight under *Jolly Roger* they give Quarter, which they do not when they fight under the Red or Bloody flag."[41] In one battle, a small group of pirates alternated between white and black colors, then flew the bloody red, then finally hoisted black again, as if unsure which to use.[42] Most early eighteenth-century pirates appear to have used both red and black, more often flying the black first, then the red as a final threat.

Bartholomew Roberts and crew flew several black pirate flags over his career. His first had a death's head and cutlass on it.[43] Further, aboard a sloop captured at St. Kitts by these pirates, one of the crew scrawled in chalk, "For our word's sake we let thee go, But to Creoles we are a foe," alongside a drawing of a "Death's head and arm with a Cutlace."[44] This is certainly evidence of the black flag and it symbols being more than merely an instrument of terror. Clearly it is also a symbol of identity, in this case left as a calling card to remind merchant seamen precisely who was there.

Amusingly, at the same time aboard a different captured sloop, another pirate scrawled, "In thee I find content of mind." The verse has perhaps confused some pirate historians, but it is nothing more than a common seventeenth- and eighteenth-century wedding motto often inscribed on wedding rings. It just goes to show that pirates had a sense of humor. (So did people getting married back then: "Let me in thee most happy bee" and "Lye still Joan, and don't wince" are also wedding ring mottos from those years.) And pirate humor may have had a role in the creation of the Jolly Roger, as we shall soon see.[45]

Another of Roberts's flags reportedly depicted a pirate with the skull of a Barbadian and a Martinican underfoot, for according to Charles Johnson, Roberts detested the Barbadians and Martinicans who had fitted out armed vessels against him, in one case forcing him to flee with his tail between his legs.[46] Most famous, though, were his flags depicting full skeletons—"deaths" or "anatomies," as they were often known—although Roberts was not the first to fly such a flag.

In August 1717 an English pirate ship of fourteen guns and at least one hundred forty men flew a flag described as "black, with a skeleton in the middle, holding in one hand a dart and in the other an hourglass." Three months later an unidentified pirate in a ship of eighteen to twenty guns flew a black flag with a full skeleton depicted on it. In March of 1718, a pirate flew a white flag with a full skeleton, and in October 1718 Richard Worley flew a "black Flagg with a humane Skelleton on it which so much terrified" a merchant crew that they refused to fight.[47]

Roberts's most famous flag, flown in 1722 aboard the *Royal Fortune* at Whydah on the West African coast, was described by Charles Johnson as having "a Death [skeleton] in it, with an hour-glass in one hand and cross-bones in the other, a dart by it, and underneath a heart dropping three drops of blood." This was almost certainly the flag known in Johnson's famous book, *A General History of the Robberies and Murders of the Most Notorious Pirates*, first published in 1724 and then in an expanded edition in 1726, as Jolly Roger.[48]

The Fake Flags

Unfortunately, once the combination of truth and myth of the symbol of pirate skull and crossbones took hold over the centuries, nearly every pirate was credited with flying it and, even more inaccurately, of sporting the skull and bones as a symbol on their clothing.[49] Henry Every, a Red Sea pirate during the 1690s, is often depicted as flying a black flag with a skull wearing a scarf and an earring, with crossbones below, but he never actually flew any black flag or skull and bones. His pirate flag is a twentieth-century fantasy.

One of his contemporary Red Sea pirates, Thomas Tew, is usually depicted as flying a black flag with an arm grasping a sword. As described shortly, this was a common device, but there is no evidence Tew ever flew a flag with this device. Captain William Kidd, who also sailed at this time and was technically a pirate-hunting privateer even when he was flirting with piracy in the Red Sea and environs, flew either English colors or a "red broad pennant."[50] Stories, however, often depict him as sailing "under the black flag."

Many other pirate flags depicted today, such as those purportedly of Stede Bonnet, Calico Jack Rackam, and Blackbeard, are modern inventions without historical basis. The pirate flag we know incorrectly as Calico Jack's, with crossed cutlasses under a skull, may well have been inspired by the flag used in the 1935 film version of *Captain Blood*, that of a pair of cutlass-holding arms crossed beneath a skull. And this film flag may have been inspired by the early flag of Bartholomew Roberts, that of a death's head and an arm holding a cutlass, or by the Dutch red battle ensign with an arm holding a cutlass, or by the seventeenth-century flag of Algiers (a notorious haven of Barbary corsairs), or even by a Barbary corsair flag of no quarter. We simply do not know what the pirate flags of these three pirate captains really looked like—Rackam's only recorded flag is a white pendant—except that Blackbeard's was a black flag with a "death's head," and not the commonly attributed black flag with horned skeleton.[51] Similarly, the purported pirate flags of Christopher Moody and John Quelch are misattributions: Moody's is actually the Barbary corsair flag of no quarter described later in this chapter and Quelch never flew a pirate flag.[52]

In fact, even the accuracy of modern depictions of authentic pirate flags is limited, for there are no existing pirate flags from the Golden Age, nor any illustrations of them, with one possible exception, that of the flag of the aforementioned French pirate Dulaien. In 1729 a wood printing block was made, reportedly from an existing illustration, and from it several prints were produced. A wood printing block claimed to be the original was acquired in the late nineteenth century, and its image was published in 1881. The flag was black, with a skull and crossbones below on the hoist and a naked man holding a cutlass in one hand over the skull and bones and an hourglass in the other, on the fly. The symbols on this flag are identical to those flown by Captain Kennedy aboard the *John and Martha* in 1716.[53]

Previously, in 1842, a different illustration of the flag had been published, based on a drawing in a manuscript in the French archives. The two images are identical in their use of symbols but are otherwise two entirely different interpretations. It is possible that the archives illustration was the inspiration for the woodcut, for the woodcut image is the mirror of the archives image. In any case, neither exactly matches a vague written description of the flag, perhaps made from memory and which therefore could be its description: black, with "white markings, such as figures of men, cutlass, remnants of our bones, and hourglasses." The point of all this should be obvious. Without an original Golden Age pirate flag in our hands, we can never know precisely what any of these flags looked like.[54]

The origin of our modern popular but fanciful renditions is a series of several books whose illustrations were passed from one to the next, with few or no changes. The earliest publication of this series discovered to date—and probably the origin—is Basil Lubbock's *The Blackwall Frigates*, published in 1922. The book includes a plate of eight pirate flags, three of which are misattributions, although otherwise mostly accurate, and one is a fanciful flag taken from an illustration in Charles Johnson's pirate chronicle.[55]

Most of these flags, with names now added, were reproduced in Charles Grey's 1933 book, *Pirates of the Eastern Seas*. Patrick Pringle's *Jolly Roger: The Story of the Great Age of Piracy*, published two decades later, includes nine pirate flags, all reproduced exactly from Grey's book. In 1959, Hans Leip's *Bordbuch des Satans* (*Log of the Satans*) includes some very similar flags clearly inspired by Lubbock, Grey, and Pringle, although two have been miscaptioned. Leip also adds three new flags, all imaginary: those of Calico Jack Rackam, Stede Bonnet, and Henry Every.[56]

Most of Leip's pirate flags were reproduced exactly in 1961 in *Pirates of the Spanish Main*, part of the American Heritage Junior Library, with credit to Leip's book. *Pirates of the Spanish Main* became a classic source of historical pirate lore—and mythical pirate flags—to literally thousands of young readers who imagined themselves pirates, not to mention to publishers of subsequent books on piracy. Similarly identified flags, some accurate, some, like those in the other books, not, were published in 1978 in *The Pirates*, a title in the popular Time-Life series "The Seafarers." It is no surprise that inaccurate images of pirate flags would appear in pirate books: for many publishers, the main purpose of images in a book is to get readers to buy it. The image of the "Jolly Roger," whether accurate or not, is the perfect lure.[57]

The Real Origin of the Jolly Roger

In late 1721, the year before Roberts left his blood on his decks, his body in the sea, and his soul, if he had one, in hell, Ned Low turned pirate. Doubtless mentally ill, he was a cruel villain of a man who ruthlessly, needlessly, joyfully tortured common seamen, often to death. Perhaps because of his gruesome ways—other pirates may have been entranced by his cowardly cruelty, wondering what he would do next—he managed to build a flotilla of pirate vessels around him. All were no doubt familiar with Bartholomew Roberts and his Jolly Roger.[58]

According to Charles Johnson, Low's chief lieutenant, Francis Spriggs, flew the same black ensign Low did.[59] Spriggs's was described by an eyewitness as black, "in the Middle of which is a large white Skeleton, with a Dart in one Hand, striking a bleeding Heart, and in the other an Hourglass." This is for all practical purposes the same flag identified by French merchantmen in August 1717, demonstrating clearly that the flag had been around for at least several years.[60]

For a fact—we have Captain Hawkins's eyewitness account just quoted—Spriggs's crew called this flag "Jolly Roger."[61] Very likely, Ned Low also called his identical flag Jolly Roger. Although these flags were identical, there was nothing new about the symbols used on them: they were common mortuary symbols, even the bleeding heart.[62]

Charles Harris, another of Low's lieutenants, flew an identical flag, except for its color: "under their own deep Blew Flagg which was hoisted up on their Gallows [as the pirates were hanged], and had pourtraied on the middle of it, an Anatomy with an Hour-Glass in one hand, and a dart in the Heart with 3 drops of blood proceeding from it, in the other."[63] Perhaps Harris wanted to be different or perhaps he did not have any black fabric or perhaps this account is incorrect, for another notes that the flag was black.[64] A newspaper reported that Harris's crew called their flag "Old Roger"—perhaps because the flag had faded from black to blue—or because the newspaper reported the name incorrectly, mistaking Jolly Roger for Old Roger. An early twentieth-century author suggested that Old Roger might be the merchant seaman's term and Jolly Roger the pirate's term, although this could not be the case if the newspaper report is correct.[65]

We also know, according to a witness, that the crew of Captain Anstis called its flag Jolly Roger, although we have no description of the flag itself. It should be noted that this is the only known instance in which a merchant seaman of this era *may have* identified a pirate flag as a Jolly Roger upon sighting it: usually it is a pirate naming it and a witness reporting it. It is therefore possible that the name was well known among seamen by 1725, but it might also mean nothing more than that the seaman Charles Maning learned its name after he was captured or possibly that the 1724 edition of Charles Johnson's pirate chronicle had made the name well known everywhere.[66]

This adds up to three known crews who called their flag Jolly Roger—those of Roberts, Spriggs, and Anstis—and perhaps at least seven in all who did, if we consider that Captain Harris's Old Roger was probably a Jolly Roger and that Ned Low and John Philips also flew flags identical to those, described in detail, belonging to Roberts, Spriggs, and Harris and therefore may have named theirs Jolly Roger, too. The seventh may have been that of Howell Davis, Roberts's predecessor: more on this in a moment.[67]

One important fact to remember is that, with the possible but unlikely exception of Anstis's flag, none of these "Rogers" was a skull and crossbones, unlike many pirate flags. All had a full skeleton as the main image. Perhaps there was some intended or incidental association with the woman- and child-devouring hobgoblin "Raw-Head and Bloody-Bones," a specter used to frighten small children: "[A]nd now Death, Pox on him for a Raw-head and Bloody-bones, has toss'd me out of the Frying-pan into the Fire."[68]

But where does the name Jolly Roger come from? Not from most records of the time, in which pirate flags were usually referred to as "black flags" or, occasionally, "black colors." In fact, the term Jolly Roger appears as few as four, arguably five, times in writing at the time.[69]

So again, where does the name come from? Most likely, it has several origins—but not "*joli rouge*," as we have already discussed, nor "Ali Raja," nor any other popular, highly speculative but completely lacking-in-evidence theories. Before we review the evidence for the origin of Jolly Roger, we need to remember that names and symbols often have multiple, at times coincidental, even synergistic origins. We need especially to remember that meanings often change over time and that origins are often forgotten, sometimes in only a few years, and new meanings ascribed. This chapter has already demonstrated this in the case of the myth of *joli rouge*. We can even take a look at the image of Jolly Roger today to see how much it has changed in three centuries, for it no longer carries the same sense of dread as once it did—no longer does it convey the immediate sense of the physical and psychological terror of torture, rape, and murder.

Looking first at the origin and meaning of "roger," we find, as many have before, that Old Roger was a term for the devil.[70] This makes piratical sense: a skeleton intended to strike fear into merchant seamen's hearts might well be named after the devil. But "roger" had a few other meanings. By most accounts, it derives from rogue: Roger is a rogue, after all, and so is the devil, thus this name for the devil.

Looking more broadly, we find a popular song of the time, "Jolly Roger Twangdillo," composed around 1707, which reminds us of other meanings of "roger." In the lyrics, Jolly Roger is a rich farmer whose money attracts many women suitors. The farmer was named Roger for a reason: not only was he a rogue, but "roger" was also a word for a man's penis, and was also beginning to be used as a verb that meant to have sex—specifically, for a man to use his penis, to "roger," that is. Jolly Roger the farmer was happy for a reason. Add to this the obvious addition of "Jolly" to "Roger" because skulls have a single expression: a grin. Roger is obviously jolly, perhaps doubly so.[71]

Some historians argue that at least part of the origin of Jolly Roger may lie in the following somewhat ambiguous line about pirates in *The Weekly Packet*, in December 1719: "and then they would go into Providence, to their old Friend Johnny Rogers; and lay down their Standard, which they hoisted at Main-topmast-head, with a Gun and Sword, which they call'd Johnny Rogers." Johnny Rogers was a nickname for Woodes Rogers, the pirate-hunting governor of New Providence, and the line *may* indicate that it was also the name given to Davis's flag. Howell Davis was the predecessor of Bartholomew Roberts, the pirate who made Jolly Roger famous—an obvious connection that strengthens the argument. It could also be, given the errors in newspapers at the time, that the second use of "Johnny Rogers" is a writer, editor, or printer error for "Jolly Roger." "Gun and Sword" might refer to the symbols on the flag but more likely refers to the symbolic act of laying down colors and arms as a sign of submission.[72]

Add to this line of reasoning the fact that "Roger" was also early eighteenth-century cant for a thief-taker—for a law enforcement officer, that is.[73] Flying the image of a dead, now skeletal thief-taker, especially if he were the pirate-hunting devil, Woodes Rogers, might indeed be a pirate's inside joke: to wit, a thief-taker was a "dick"—and hopefully soon a dead one.

It is incontestable that men of violence, no matter whether their causes are lawful or unlawful, use a disproportionate amount of the language and symbolism of physical domination, often sexual. Pirates of the Golden Age were no exception. When we consider their gallows humor, their sexist, male-dominated society of violence, their mentality of the besieged, their pervasive mentality of domination, it is easy to see that Jolly Roger may have had several origins and interpretations. One of the most significant interpretations, and perhaps one of its origins, too, may have been an inside joke about turning society on its head and predicting exactly what would happen to a merchant crew if they did not surrender immediately: they'd "be screwed."[74]

Yet it seems that four written uses of Jolly Roger, or five if we count "Johnny Roger," should not have exploded into the name—and arguably an incorrect one at that—for the classic skull and bones pirate flag. Yet they did, and it was all largely due to three writers. Charles Johnson's book on pirates was, and remains, immensely popular and widely read, including by popular writers Sir Walter Scott, author of *The Pirate*, and Robert Louis Stevenson, author of *Treasure Island*. Both Scott in 1822 and Stevenson in 1883 used the name to refer to the black pirate flag in general, although it was already part of sea language and street slang and was used by at least one other novelist after Scott but prior to Stevenson. However, none of these authors describes his or her Jolly Roger flag in detail.[75]

Why, then, is the name today associated with the skull and bones and not with a full skeleton? Foremost, because many readers of all eras do not look too closely at what they read: a pirate flag is obviously a black flag with skull and bones; some pirates called their flag Jolly Roger; therefore all pirate flags are Jolly Rogers, or so they assume. The skull and bones is a much simpler symbol, after all. In fact, Francis Grose's dictionary of the *Vulgar Tongue* in 1788 defines Jolly Roger as *any* pirate flag, and Smyth's *Sailor's Word-Book* of 1867 defines it as a white skull on a black flag. But ultimately it was Stevenson who introduced the term to the world at large, where it was taken culturally to heart. The rest is history.[76]

This still leaves us with a lingering question: Where, then, did the "skull and bones" itself originate as a pirate flag? Was it just an accident that one or more pirates had the idea to use these symbols of death? At some point, this was indeed the case; we just do not know when it first happened. We do have some clues, though, but as we consider them we should recall one of the most common logical fallacies: *post hoc, ergo propter hoc* (after this, therefore because of this). We need to remember, again, that the same or similar ideas are often developed independently over time, or even in parallel, and are not necessarily inspired by previous occurrence.

We must therefore consider the possibility that the early eighteenth-century "Golden Age" pirates may well have gotten the idea of flying the skull and bones from the Barbary corsairs of North Africa, for they had apparently been using the skull and crossbones at times on some of their red "no quarter" flags (a bit of a misnomer, since Barbary corsairs invariably took prisoners to keep or sell as slaves), possibly since at least the early seventeenth century. A 1719 illustration of a Barbary corsair flag of no quarter has a red field, with a winged hourglass, an arm holding a cutting sword, and a skull and crossbones—very similar, in fact, to the first known black flag of Bartholomew Roberts. Its written description is of a richly appointed flag, as Barbary corsair flags often were.[77]

The earliest specific reference to pirate flags I have found dates to 1679 in John Crowne's *The Ambitious Statesman, or The Loyal Favourite*, in which a character says, "Oonst. Now, I find his tricks; he secretly //
Puts pirates' colours out at both our sterns, // That we might fight each

other in mistake; // Then he shou'd share the ruins of us both!" The reference could be either to the false colors commonly used, and at times even fought under, by both European pirates and Barbary corsairs, or to the legitimate state or "no quarter" flags of Barbary corsairs, whose depredations were notorious at this time. There was no specific identifiable "pirate flag" of European pirates at this time.[78]

All this said, the ultimate origin of the skull and bones as a symbol of maritime terror may still lie in the West, for Muslim corsairs may have been using Western Judeo-Christian symbols to strike fear into Western seafarers and coastal inhabitants. They may even have been imitating the use of skull and bones by Western raiders of earlier eras.

In fact, of the three purportedly authentic pirate flags still in existence, none are from the Golden Age. However, two of them are believed to be from North Africa. One, purchased by a Finnish mariner, is believed to date to the eighteenth or early nineteenth century. The other was reportedly captured from North African corsairs circa 1790 by British naval officer Richard Curry. However, given Curry's record of service, he almost certainly captured it later, circa 1801 to 1802, during operations along the Egyptian coast or on the Nile.[79] Both flags are simple skull and crossbones, but the Curry flag is red—a flag of no quarter, virtually identical to that flown by Captain Franco and his South Sea pirates in 1688. Barbary and Levantine corsairs commonly flew the red flag of no quarter in battle as necessary and may have reserved the death's head for this flag.[80]

Barbary corsairs inspired terror throughout the Mediterranean and beyond, and merchantmen often surrendered immediately as soon as they knew who was attacking. The early eighteenth-century pirates were trying to inspire just as much fear—and often did. Their black flag was no mere threat of violence but a promise of very real violence, of torture and murder if captain and crew did not surrender. Unheeded, it was often followed by the red banner that conveyed a message of "death guaranteed."

Above all, we must not forget the real purpose of these flags, that of terrifying merchant captains and crews, of inspiring them to surrender *without a fight*. Fear was an easy tactic and often a profitable one. Fighting put pirate lives and pirate vessels at risk, and pirates were all about profit with as few hard knocks as possible. In fact, pirates captured most vessels without a fight, relying solely on the terror they inspired. And there were ways other than the death's head and marrow bones on a black field, or of a bloody red banner, to inflict the violence of intimidation and fear.

CHAPTER 2

"False Optics" and Blackbeard the Pirate

———— ∞∞∞ ————

"We had not been ashore many hours before a rumour spread the town that Pirates were landed, which alarumed them to their arms, so they set a watch and guards about our house all night, which in the morning early drew off, being ashamed to be seen by three men, for we were no more."[1]

—Jeremy Roche, *His Second Journal*, 1677

On May 22, 1718, the *Crowley*, a merchantman bound for London, weighed her anchors and set sail in the Cooper River under the guidance of a pilot. Not half a mile to the north of her river anchorage lay Charlestown, the great capital of South Carolina, through which flowed exports of rice, pitch, tar, turpentine, and, especially, deer and cattle hides. Under light sail the *Crowley* slipped down the river, her hold filled with rice and other goods, toward the sea and away from the small but usually bustling city, one whose spirit and profit had been battered down by recent war with the Yamasee and allied tribes, not to mention just before that by Queen Anne's War, fought against the French and, in particular to the Carolinians, against the Spanish.[2]

But the war was over now, or mostly so, and the residents of Charlestown, as well as of the farms and plantations inland, thanked Providence for the fairly small loss of life among the white settlers. Providence, however, had done them no favors when it came to their economy. The Indian war was caused by the encroachment of white settlers and traders onto Native American lands, not just for homesteads but also for trade and Native American slavery. The usual English, French, and Spanish political machinations and their manipulations of Native American tribes did not help. The war had severely interrupted the critical flow of deer hides from Native American tribes, and of the rice, cattle, and naval stores produced by white settlers and their many African and Native American slaves. Charlestown was ready to move forward.[3]

The merchantman had sailed south first, down the river, but only briefly, then east, past Marsh Island, separated from Hog Island only by a narrow creek to the north and Boone's Island to the south. The passage required both the timing of the tide as well as a pilot to avoid the sandbars in the river, and indeed, ahead of the *Crowley* was a small pilot craft which would later return the pilot to Charlestown.

The *Crowley* followed the pilot boat through one of the channels in the large bar of sand and silt at the river mouth, then put her pilot over the side into the craft that would carry him downriver. The *Crowley* intended to make her course north, leaving "Sillivant's Island"—Sullivan's Island, that is—and the entrance to the Ashley and the Cooper Rivers behind her.[4] To larboard, her crew aloft might have noticed the sand dunes that ran for two or three miles along the coast, but their attention in fact was most likely on the sea—and on the ship rapidly approaching.

It was a fairly small ship, at least as compared to large merchantmen. It was a common sort and size used for trade to the Americas and was likely seeking a pilot to carry it across the bar. And indeed, the pilot boat had not long ago come alongside the ship. Even at this relatively close range, neither the captain of the *Crowley* on deck with his telescope nor his lookout aloft could be sure what she was, but both surely supposed she was an inbound merchantman. As the two ships came closer, it became apparent that the unknown ship had clean lines, might be Dutch built, and was of roughly two hundred to three hundred tons burthen.[5]

The ship turned her course toward the *Crowley*, whose captain now surely began to have misgivings. Maybe the vessel only wanted to "speak" to him regarding a pilot, but it was obvious that she already had one, and through his telescope Captain Robert Clark probably thought he could discern the ship's armament: a single row of gun ports indicating as many as twenty guns, as cannon were known to seamen, and perhaps a few more on the quarterdeck.[6]

The guns were mostly six-pounders. Small yoke-mounted cannon, doubtless a miscellaneous collection of muzzle-loading "swivels" and breech-loading patereros, were in place in their stations at the rail between each great gun. Twenty great guns at least, and perhaps as many swivels—the armament of a sixth-rate man-of-war, the smallest of rated warships. Not a great ship by any means, but certainly sufficient to frighten all but the largest merchantmen. This was no true forty-gun ship, as some have suggested it was, for such ships typically ranged from four hundred to six hundred tons. The *Queen Anne's Revenge* was nowhere near this size.[7]

Unfortunately, it was by now too late for the *Crowley* to come about and flee if her captain were so inclined, much less fight if he thought he must. And it might take an hour to get his merchant ship ready for action. Captain Clark's heart surely dropped into his stomach as the approaching frigate came within a quarter mile. Even without his telescope, he could see that her decks and the lower parts of her shrouds were covered with men, most of them armed and waving cutlasses. Their shouts soon carried easily over the water, not clear enough that their words could be made out yet, but still clear enough to recognize that these armed men were not sending friendly greetings.

Then up flew the black flag! Captain Clark, his crew, and his passengers knew this meant surrender immediately or be damned. Whether Captain Clark could see what the device on the black flag was—a death's head, with or without crossed bones—did not matter. None flew the black flag but pirates.[8]

Even if Captain Clark could have run away, he now knew it would ultimately have been pointless. The pirate ship clearly "had the legs of him." Fighting would have been pointless as well, for the crew of the *Crowley* was vastly outnumbered and aboard were several prominent Charlestown citizens, including children. They had no time to prepare their closed quarters and attempt to retreat safely within them as they fled under sail into the security of the Cooper River at Charlestown. Some captains condemned merchant commanders who surrendered too easily; one referred to them as "Cowardly Villains, that Surrender up their Ship at the Whistling of a Shot."[9] Perhaps if Captain Clark had had more time, he might have put up a fight.

Instead, he ordered his crew to strike their colors, if he had even been flying them at all (ships flew their flags only on certain occasions), and lower their topsails in submission. He needed no prodding to do what came next: he "lay by" in the lee of the pirate ship and waited to be boarded.

As Captain Clark waited anxiously to meet his pirate captors, he surely surveyed the pirate ship before him with his telescope. One pirate on the quarterdeck may have stood out from the rest. He was a tall, lean man, with a great black beard, long and wide, probably twisted or braided into "tails" and tied with ribbons, much as seamen twisted their hair into queues.[10] Over his shoulders he may have worn a sling "with three brace of pistols, hanging in holsters, like bandoliers."[11] Perhaps the bearded man also had slow matches, used to fire cannon and light grenades, tucked under his hat, giving him a demonic appearance.[12] He was the notorious Edward Teach, or Thatch, better known as Blackbeard, and his reputation preceded him, striking fear into common merchant seamen everywhere.

Blackbeard is commonly regarded as the fiercest pirate ever, and therefore is considered by many as the fiercest fighter of them all. Indeed, pirates of the Golden Age in general have a reputation for fearsome fighting ability, and much of it was well deserved. But not all pirates were as fierce as many believe. In fact, for many, their reputations for fierceness and fighting ability far exceeded the reality. And so it was with

Blackbeard, a man whose image was mightier than his reality, although it, like the black flag and red banner of no quarter, served him well, as such images did many pirates.

Blackbeard's dark, hairy visage, matches included, were part of the fearsome image that struck terror into readers of Charles Johnson's book on pirates, and perhaps to merchant seamen, fishermen, and seaside inhabitants as well. But in fact, we have only Johnson's word for the matches.[13] The man behind the pseudonym of Charles Johnson was an avid researcher and extraordinarily fond of detail. But he also had a novelist's eye and a penchant for exaggeration, and altered or even invented facts when it suited his narrative. He invented an entire chapter in his pirate book, for example, which we will take a look at later. In fact, the lines he quotes from Blackbeard's purported logbook—"Such a day, rum all out . . ." and so forth, all very nautically swashbuckling and romantic—are probably Johnson's, not Blackbeard's, but we will never know for certain.[14] As for the matches, no account by any man who actually saw this pirate mentions them.

Still, pirates, privateers, merchant seamen, and naval seamen tasked with throwing grenades in battle sometimes carried the burning slow match, needed to light the grenade fuses, in their hats, but it was more usual to tie it around a wrist or pin it to their clothing or hat with a match case, although one image of Jean Bart, the famous French privateer in the service of France, shows him with a length of lighted match held in his teeth.[15] Very likely Charles Johnson saw this popular print. Slow match was designed to burn very hot because it was used to ignite gunpowder, which is not as sensitive to heat and flame as is commonly believed. Slow match could thus easily ignite hair, and a pirate's greasy, tarry flaming beard would have been a hellish spectacle—and one probably never repeated. It is probably safe to say that Captain Clark saw no matches burning from under the pirate captain's hat.

Even so, Captain Clark knew immediately who this man was. And the ship that lay before them, its great guns and swivels aimed at the *Crowley*, was the infamous *Queen Anne's Revenge*. Nearby were three sloops. One was the *Revenge*, originally outfitted by dilettante pirate

Stede Bonnet, who, now stripped of his command and largely impotent for the moment as a pirate, paced the deck of Blackbeard's ship. It was a pirate fleet, or at least a pirate flotilla.

By now the fear of crew and passengers was obvious. Wealthy Samuel Wragg, a member of the Council of the Province of Carolina, surely consoled his wife and four-year-old son, William. The unknown inspires fear more than anything else, and no one aboard the *Crowley* knew what was going to happen. Most probably feared the worst: beatings, torture, rape, murder, or even that they would all be blown up or burned to death on their ship.

Members of Blackbeard's crew boarded the *Crowley*, roughly and rudely shoving anyone aside who dared stand in their way, as pirates invariably did. From stem to stern and truck to keel, they searched the ship, doubtless striking even more fear into the prisoners via the typical fearful pirate manner of waving cutlasses, swearing, and threatening to "clap a pistol" to the heads of the innocent. The pirates ferried the Carolina passengers and Captain Clark to the *Queen Anne's Revenge*. Here the prisoners stood before the great pirate, his dark visage hidden behind his beard, intimidating each and every one. Here would burning matches illuminating his face and beard have been most effective!

According to Johnson, writing in the style of a novel, Blackbeard carefully examined the prisoners as to their goods aboard, the lading of the vessels they owned, the condition of other vessels in Charlestown harbor, and "when they thought they would sail and whither bound."[16] Then he ordered them imprisoned in the hold of the *Crowley* along with its crew.

Soon, though, Blackbeard recalled the principal captured citizens to his great cabin and demanded of them a chest of medicines. It was a curious request. Not that medicines were unnecessary—they were indeed vital—but, given that Blackbeard was effectively blockading Charlestown, capturing every vessel that happened by and putting grave fear into resident and mariner alike, one would at least expect a demand for ransom or tribute in the form of coin and cargo or even a threat to sack the town itself. But he made no such demands.

Blackbeard sent a prisoner named Marks ashore with Captain Richards of the pirate sloop *Revenge*, along with two or three other pirates, to procure the medicines, which the governor at first refused. The Carolina prisoners, Samuel Wragg in particular, were held hostage, and Blackbeard threatened to "imediately put to death all the persons that were in their possession and burn their ships etc. and threatn'd to come over the barr for to burn the ships that lay before the Towne and to beat it about our ears" if the medicines were not delivered.[17] The medicines, finally agreed to, were not delivered on time, and Blackbeard was furious, but in fact all was well. Routine delays hindered Mr. Marks and the pirates in their mission. Meanwhile, the pirate emissaries strode through the town truculently, scaring women and children and perhaps many merchants and tradesmen as well. But there were others who would not have been so easily frightened and they bring us back to the question of why Blackbeard did not demand a greater ransom or even attack the town.

Why indeed would the pirates, whose fleet now numbered eight vessels, including those captured, set sail after such a paltry demand? The medicines—perhaps to cure syphilis, some historians have suggested—were worth three or four hundred pounds, a considerable sum but nothing on the order of what might have been extracted even from a city with a diminished economy. The fact is, Blackbeard was in a precarious position. He dared not attack the town. Not only would there be severe retribution—an English force would surely be dispatched against him sooner or later if he succeeded—but also he was highly unlikely to succeed in an attack on Charlestown. His men were not soldier-seamen like the buccaneers of the late seventeenth century. They were not veterans of land warfare. In fact, many probably had limited experience in serious battle at sea or ashore.

Even those who had once been privateers may have had little fighting experience, and probably none at all ashore, for privateers, like pirates, preyed on weaker merchantmen and tended to run from hard fights. To attack Charlestown would first require running the gauntlet of Fort Johnson. Only in Hollywood films and Disney rides do pirates successfully cannonade strong forts. Second, pirates usually attacked towns from the land, but to attack Charlestown by land would require a long slog through rough country, including river and stream crossings. Such attacks were typically made by surprise, with pirates marching by night and hiding by day, and then, whenever possible, attacking at night.

But Blackbeard and his pirates would not have this element of surprise and thus would be vulnerable to counterattack. Third, notwithstanding local political and economic strife, Charlestown could summon veterans, including doughty scouts, rangers, and privateersmen, of Indian wars, of raids upon the Spanish, of defense against attack by the French and Spanish. Many of these men were experienced in brutal close combats with intrepid Native American warriors, and many were also veterans of the fights against the Spanish in North America during Queen Anne's War, and had even expelled an attempted French raid. They would not shrink from a fight with pirates. Last, an attack on the town would leave Blackbeard's ships undermanned and vulnerable even to a well-armed passing merchantman.

There were other risks as well. The residents of Charlestown might soon have outfitted a ship with volunteers and sent it against the pirates. Colonies often did this, but not always successfully. There were plenty of stout seamen and volunteers, many of whom were combat veterans, in Charlestown and in the countryside who could have manned such a ship or a pair of well-armed sloops. And soon enough they did, for not long after Blackbeard eventually departed, two sloops were fitted out under the command of Colonel William Rhett. Although Rhett did not find Blackbeard, he and his crew did capture Stede Bonnet, now in command again, and his *Royal James*, although his consort Richard Worley escaped.[18]

Not long after, learning that the infamous pirate Christopher Moody was headed their way, the governor and people of Charlestown outfitted a four-vessel squadron, including the former pirate sloop *Royal James*, mounting sixty-eight guns between them and manned by three hundred fighting volunteers. They found and engaged their pirate, but he turned out to be the briefly notorious Richard Worley commanding the *New*

York's Revenge, a sloop of six guns and forty men, flying a black flag with the likeness of a human skeleton on it—not the skull and bones often depicted today as his flag. It was no contest, yet the pirates fought for several hours. The pirate sloop was battered from all sides and Worley was killed in action during close combat. The pirate's consort, the *New York Revenge's Revenge*, until recently the merchantman *Eagle Galley*, was chased and captured intact, her hold filled with indentured servants, both men and women.[19]

Let none say that South Carolinians could not defend themselves against mere pirates, for South Carolinians had already defended against Native American attacks, sacked St. Augustine, and fought off a combined attack by the French and Spanish. Pirates were but a small threat by comparison.

Part of the problem is that some historians quote the trial of Stede Bonnet and similar documents wherein it is noted that Charlestown had been "reduc'd very low by the Calamities of the Indian War and heavy Taxes," and therefore assume that the colonial city could not defend itself. The issue is compounded by statements to the effect that "the Town is at present in a very indifferent condition of making much resistance if them [the pirates] or any other enemye should attempt it." In fact, the first statement refers only to Charlestown's ability to raise money for armed sloops and other defenses, and not to its ability to raise capable armed men to defend against or attack pirates, privateers, Native Americans, and French and Spanish soldiery. The second is an excuse for the embarrassment of being blockaded by a pirate, for it is followed by a plea for help: "we were very desirious to get them off our coast by fair means which we could not doe otherwise for want of such helps as other Governments are supply'd with from the Crown."[20]

Blackbeard had more than just Charlestown defenses to worry about. He also had to prepare for the possibility of an English man-of-war catching him off guard. An English navy sixth rate, fully armed and manned—not one too long on station or in port, whose stores were almost depleted, whose powder was low, and half of whose crew was unfit for duty, but one well manned and properly fitted for cruising—could almost certainly have taken the pirate, but the fight might have been a bloody one, at least at first. But even an English sixth rate in poor condition could fight most pirates at least to a draw. Still, better to have a fifth rate to fight these pirates, or even a fourth. These ships had more guns, and larger ones at that, and bigger crews, and could take on pirates who sailed well-armed frigates.

But there was a problem. Too few such men-of-war were to be had among the English colonies and there was none at Charlestown. Blackbeard knew this, but it was better not to risk the possibility of one being summoned from another of the colonies and better as well not to risk the possibility of attack or pursuit from Charlestown itself. The man was no fool: he knew that the hostages he held were his main weapon. In the end, he sailed away with both his chest of medicines and the plunder from the vessels he had captured. He had blockaded the port for no more than ten days. Had he not by accident of timing captured the *Crowley* and her important South Carolina passengers, he probably would not even have been able to extort the medicines.

If Blackbeard were truly the fierce pirate that myth has made him out to be, if he were truly the fierce fighter many believe he was, and with a crew as large as he had, he could have made Charlestown pay through the nose purely out of fear of his martial prowess and pirate brutality. He might have even sacked the city. Yet he did neither.

The Pirate as Fierce Warrior

The blockade of Charlestown, while intriguing, even bold, seems hardly the stuff of great pirate legend. Yet it was, in fact, Blackbeard's most notorious act of piracy, and it was greatly aided by the "false optics" of fear—"[F]or their eyes so mistered [misted] in looking at us as we came in from the sea that they fancied we rowed with at least 20 oars aside and had a multitude of men, such is the nature of Fear to multiply or magnifie objects through her false Optics," wrote mariner Jeremy Roche after his small boat, manned with a crew of three and carrying six swivel guns tucked away in her lockers, landed at Lyde, England, and were mistaken as pirates, frightening the entire town by their sudden, unusual presence.[21]

During Blackbeard's entire career, he captured no large, rich ships after a fight, he sacked no towns or cities, he defeated no men-of-war sent to capture him, although legend mistakenly claims he fought the HMS *Scarborough* to a standstill. In fact, he never fired a shot at her. His richest prizes were a French "Guinea-man" with a cargo of more than 400 slaves; *La Concorde*, which he refitted as his *Queen Anne's Revenge*; and the *Crowley*, which he plundered of 1,500 pounds sterling, roughly $350,000 today, a paltry sum when shared among one hundred fifty and possibly more than three hundred men. Neither ship put up a fight. He captured prizes of less value as well, such as the *Protestant Caesar* loaded with fifty tons of logwood, but again without a fight, although the prize had, not long before, fought one of his sloops to a draw and escaped. But confronted by the *Queen Anne's Revenge* and three sloops manned by pirates, the crew refused to fight. Spaniards they would have fought, they said, but not pirates, although Spanish pirates and *guardas costas*, often one and the same, were as violent and cruel as Blackbeard or any of his ilk.[22]

It was all about image as much as deeds and it was this combination that gave pirates their renown: black and bloody flags, a fearsome visage or famous name, a reputation for violence and cruelty. Even so, Blackbeard did have one singular act judged by many as even greater than his greatest act of piracy, one that sealed his reputation and lofted him into legend. It was also his last.

In 1718 Governor Alexander Spotswood of Virginia procured the support of two English men-of-war and sent two hired sloops, commanded by Lieutenant Robert Maynard and manned with English naval seamen, to destroy the pirate Blackbeard. The famous sea rover was holed up in his sloop at Ocracoke Inlet, North Carolina, and had made Bath-Town his base after accepting the king's amnesty. Many of his fans and supporters today claim he was no longer engaged in piracy, and some did then as well, but many others at the time did not believe this. Some at the time tried to excuse his alleged plundering of sloops in the river by claiming it was, strictly speaking, not piracy because it did not occur at sea. But this is quibbling. For merchants, ship owners, and crews, an attack on a vessel anywhere was piracy. Blackbeard was also accused of extorting goods from locals, and further, he had plundered a French merchantman but reportedly pretended it "was a Wrack, w'ch they had found at Sea without either Men or Papers." What happened to the French crew is not noted. Governor Spotswood was not going to permit a "Gang of Pirates" to operate with impunity in nearby North Carolina, legalities of jurisdiction be damned.[23]

As the pirate hunting sloops came near Blackbeard's sloop at anchor in Ocracoke, the naval and pirate commanders exchanged greetings and refused to accept any quarter. The engagement began, desultorily at first, then more violently. A pair of broadsides fired from four three-pounders wracked the hired sloops, which had no great guns mounted nor significant cover, killing and wounding many men. Maynard's consort fell away astern, its crew too much killed and wounded to continue.[24]

Immediately after, Blackbeard cut his cables and the battle became a running fight. Maynard did his best to keep away from Blackbeard's broadside and Blackbeard did his best to escape with the tide. The attack might best be described as an early eighteenth-century "naval special operation," the sort conducted today by Navy SEALs and similar units, in which navy seamen, aboard sloops with no cannon and no cover, made a direct assault on a pirate sloop armed with cannon and whose crew had plenty of protection behind their bulwarks.

Soon, Blackbeard's sloop ran aground. Maynard seized the opportunity and ran his sloop alongside the pirate. As the pirate hunting sloop came board-and-board (touching Blackbeard's sloop), Blackbeard and his small crew flung case bottles filled with gunpowder, scrap metal, slugs, and small shot onto its deck, where they exploded in balls of burning, scorching flame and great volumes of smoke, into the latter of which the famous pirate and his men quickly leaped, expecting to rain terror via pistol shot and cutlass edge on any survivors.[25]

But only Maynard, a seaman named Demelt, and perhaps one other were on deck when the grenades exploded. As Blackbeard and his pirate crew boarded, Maynard's men suddenly surged from below deck, pistols and cutlasses in hand. It was, according to Maynard, thirteen English naval men against eleven pirates. Surely such nearly even odds would weigh heavily in favor of the pirates, popularly known today as among the fiercest of warriors, and led by the fiercest of pirate captains!

But they did not. The English seamen attacked swiftly and fiercely, cutlass and pistol in hand. These men were not pirates who fought only when they had no choice, but men bred and trained to fight at sea—to close with an enemy and destroy him. At close range, they fired pistols, surely even pressing some into pirate ribs as they squeezed triggers and swung cutlasses down upon heads, necks, and limbs, cracking skulls, shearing off cheeks and ears, and cutting through arms like heavy cleavers through thick beef brisket. Maynard closed on Blackbeard, as did Demelt and a Scotsman and probably other naval men as well.

To his credit, Blackbeard fought back stoutly. The two commanders faced each other immediately and each fired a pistol at the other; Maynard's found its mark. Without hesitation the men closed quickly and attacked with their swords. Maynard thrust his sword at Blackbeard's belly. The stomach and gut were popular targets of thrusts, for there were no ribs or cartilage to catch a blade.[26] Unfortunately, according to a newspaper account, Maynard's blade bent at the hilt when it struck Blackbeard's cartridge box. Most likely, Maynard thrust his sword powerfully at Blackbeard, but the blade missed and stuck in Blackbeard's cartridge box instead, which would probably have been made of leather and lined with thin wood, or even held a solid block of wood with holes drilled in it for cartridges.[27] The blade could have been trapped there briefly, allowing Blackbeard to strike at Maynard as he twisted his arm upward in an attempt to free the blade and protect himself with a hanging parry from a counterstroke. Blackbeard's powerful stroke broke the hilt of Maynard's sword, cut his fingers, and probably bent his blade at the hilt as well.[28]

Demelt attacked Blackbeard at almost the same time, slashing the pirate's face. He was followed immediately by a Scotsman, who swung his Highland broadsword at Blackbeard's neck, cutting partway through it. Highlanders were well known for their prowess with the broadsword and they were adept at removing head or limb from body.

And that day was no exception. Blackbeard was still standing, but not for long. Most of his men already lay dead on the deck of the small hired sloop. The Highlander swung again, this time striking Blackbeard's head from his body. "No man is Hercules against the multitude," at least not when engaged in open battle with swords, not even Blackbeard.[29] According to Johnson, the pirate reportedly died with five "shot" in him and twenty sword cuts to his face, neck, and body. Maynard's men were "miserably cut and mangled"—but all those who had fought hand to hand against Blackbeard and his men were still alive.[30] Not one of Blackbeard's men who boarded the English hired naval sloop survived the combat.

So what should we make of the vaunted fighting ability of the early eighteenth-century pirates and especially of the fierce fighter Blackbeard? Sure, Blackbeard's men fought bravely in the end, refusing to ask for quarter, but their skill and vigor were nothing compared to those of the English naval seamen who attacked them—seamen who were trained to close with the enemy and fight him until he was dead or he surrendered. The pirates of Blackbeard's age were not the buccaneers and filibusters of the previous century, who fought Spaniards in open land battle, sacked cities, and engaged powerful Spanish men-of-war deliberately. Buccaneers and filibusters had part-origins in the French hunters called *boucaniers,* who fought the Spaniards guerrilla-style on Saint-Domingue (modern-day Haiti), and in the English soldiers who, battered badly at first, learned their trade combating Spanish guerrilla tactics on Jamaica.[31]

But the pirates of the early eighteenth century were men who rarely ever had to fire more than a single shot in order to plunder their prey. At nearly even odds—and one account says the boarding pirates outnumbered their enemy—the defending naval seamen wiped out the pirate boarding party to a man, without a single loss of their own.

A Fearsome Visage

Looked at objectively, Blackbeard was a capable seaman of unknown antecedents and age (although one scholar has recently argued with some merit that he was born in Jamaica of a well-off family, was formally educated, and had served aboard the HMS *Windsor*) who turned pirate and created a fearsome image that made his job of robbing rich merchants of their investments and working-class crews of the fruits of their labor much, much easier.[32] But in spite of his image, he was ultimately successful for the same reason most pirates of the period from 1716 to 1724 were: most of the time there was no one to stop him. But there should have been.

So here we have it—a great fearsome image! Blackbeard was a pirate whose appearance, coupled with his reputation, is said to have struck terror into anyone who saw him. Doubtless it did strike fear into many hearts, but so can any common seaman-turned-pirate (or, for that matter, any common thug) who puts a pistol to your head. Still, a fearsome visage may have enough effect that a pistol to the head is unnecessary.

But herein lies the problem. For any merchantman with a small crew and light armament, and indeed even for some with larger crews and better armament, the sight of the black flag at a mile or more distant, coupled with a well-armed vessel easily gaining in pursuit, with what was obviously a large number of men on deck brandishing cutlasses and other weapons, was more than enough to compel most to surrender. Blackbeard's fierce visage, much less his bandoliers filled with pistols, could not be recognized until within 200 to 250 yards and would have been difficult to pick out from among a large crew. Even a telescope would not have increased this range enough to make much of a difference. Most fearful merchantmen would already have struck their colors, or at least would have been already resigned to doing so, by the time Blackbeard was close enough to be recognized.

So why the image? Why Blackbeard's or any pirate's? First, Blackbeard may have believed that seamen would spread word of it around. Even so, there was no way to know that a black flag with a death's head belonged to Blackbeard and not to some other pirate. The flag of a devil's skeleton stabbing a heart with a spear, often attributed to Blackbeard, is a horned version of the flag that came to be known as the Jolly Roger, and there is no evidence Blackbeard ever flew such a flag. The only one we know Blackbeard flew was a black flag with, according to the *Boston News-Letter* and the London *Weekly-Journal, or, Saturday's-Post*, a death's head, which may or may not have had crossed bones beneath or behind: "a large Ship and a Sloop with Black Flags and Deaths Heads in them and three more Sloops with Bloody Flags," stated the captain of the *Protestant Caesar*.[33] In fact, the devices on flags were often difficult to recognize at long range. The color—black—was the most important aspect. Even if Blackbeard flew his own recognizable flag, it might still have been difficult to make out the details and know it was his until the merchant vessel had already surrendered.[34]

More likely, Blackbeard's violent image—*if indeed he had such an image during his lifetime*—was intended as much for his crew as for his prey, or even more so. Pirates of this era were democratic, of which more will be said later. They voted their captains into office and they could vote them out of office. And pirate captains had limited authority, except in battle. Yet Blackbeard and a handful of other pirate captains of his time may have wielded more authority than their articles likely permitted. Some may have done so via fear created by a combination of image and occasional brutality, others simply via good leadership. In Blackbeard's case, we lack the evidence to determine his true leadership style.

According to Charles Johnson, Blackbeard was cruel, even going so far as to light brimstone (sulfur) and other combustibles below deck, saying, "Let us make a Hell of our own, and try how long we can bear it." Similarly, Johnson writes that Blackbeard once randomly shot his gunner Israel Hands through the knee for the sport of it. Very likely, these examples of brutality are invented. Blackbeard's comment about creating a hell of their own is very similar to that attributed to "The Grand Pyrate, Captain George Cusack" in 1668: "I will make you officers in Hell under me[!]" he said as he flung a Bible overboard. Johnson, or even Blackbeard himself, may have been inspired by Cusack, whose story was told by author and political pamphleteer Roger L'Estrange.[35]

In fact, such abuse typically led to a mutiny against a pirate captain. After all, some researchers claim pirates were merely common seamen who rebelled against excessive behavior in their merchant captains in the first place. If so, would not pirates rebel against similar pirate captains? Ned Low, for example, murdered one of his men in his sleep after a disagreement, for which his crew marooned him at sea.[36] Perhaps Blackbeard's crew feared him tremendously, yet there is great strength in numbers. His crew could have deposed him at any time. Why they did not, given his purported abusive behavior, is unknown. Perhaps his fearsome image did the trick, working as well or better on his crew than on his prey. Even if this is the case, Charles Johnson probably made up the fiercest aspects of Blackbeard's character. Most likely, Blackbeard was neither as evil nor as colorful as Johnson made him out to be.

In sum, Blackbeard was not, among other praise heaped upon him, "the nastiest pirate ever," as a Hollywood producer has proclaimed he was.[37] There were many far more brutal men who lived far nastier lives as pirates far longer than Blackbeard did. But hyperbole helps sell books and movies. Nor was Blackbeard probably the "boldest and most notorious of the sea rovers who infested the coastal waters of the English southern colonies in the New World in the early 1700s," as historian Robert E. Lee has written.[38] And if he was, he committed few piracies there overall, even fewer while he lived at Ocracoke, and some fans of his claim he committed none at all while at Ocracoke. He might well have settled there in order to reintegrate himself into colonial life—but even this would not prove he was not still a pirate, for pirates had long been favored in the Carolinas for the goods and money they brought.

Blackbeard was not even a "knight of the black flag," as historian Lee has also stated, unless knights were brutal brigands who stole by force of arms from others.[39] But here Lee may unintentionally have a point, for a fair number of knights were little more than brigands, especially from the point of view of the serfs who served them and the poor whom some knights robbed and occasionally murdered.

As far as we know, Blackbeard may never even have fought a real pitched battle as a pirate or an accused pirate but for one—and he lost it, his last and the only fight that mattered, when Lieutenant Robert Maynard and two small Virginia sloops filled with volunteer British seamen attacked and defeated him at Ocracoke Inlet.

The reality is that little is actually known about Blackbeard and other pirates, leading some scholars and other writers to make all sorts of speculative claims, even bordering on conspiracy theory. Some researchers, often adhering to Marxist ideology, argue that pirates were not just the victims of bad press, but were victims, period, persecuted for atrocities invented by a British government threatened by piratical independence—and especially by the piratical threat to commerce and the slave trade.[40] This was not how pirates were viewed by their victims, however, and ignores the fact that much of the reason for early eighteenth-century piracy had to do with privateers refusing to give up their traditional trade. And if Charles Johnson, whoever he was, truly intended to vilify pirates for the sake of government propaganda, the plan backfired, for Blackbeard soon became a folk hero. Much more likely, Johnson made Blackbeard larger than life for the same reason writers and editors have often enhanced biographies and "true life" stories: to increase book sales.

The study of piracy has long had a problem separating fact from fiction. We know so little, yet much of what we know is confounded by popular myth and purposeful ideological speculation, dating from the days of the pirates themselves to the present. Part of the problem lies in the romantic nature of piracy itself: many people want to see themselves as pirates, at least after a fashion—but not as those who torture, rape, or murder. Most do not even wish to be seen as lawless men or women who steal, via the threat of violence or its actual infliction, not only from the rich but from the poor as well, most of them innocent. Nor do most promoters of most ideologies wish their icons to be identified as cutthroats—it's usually, but not always, bad for business.

Therefore, for the sake of self-image or institutional image, the image of the pirate is often sanitized, both in scholarship and popular imagery, and the sea thief becomes not a criminal but a victim exercising righteous violence. In the case of Blackbeard, much of the scholarship devoted to him is intended to improve his image. Some scholars even argue that he was not really a violent man at all—but it's hard not to be violent in a violent trade, and we should not forget that even the threat of force is a form of violence. How much difference is there between the thief who murders indiscriminately and the thief who murders only if his victim resists? Only that one is more "trigger happy" than the other. Otherwise, each is willing to commit murder—and will.[41]

As one would expect of a pirate elevated to folk hero status, a fair number of his fans believe that Blackbeard was treacherously undone. People do not like to believe that their heroes are mortal, and when they are proved so, it must have been by deceit, subterfuge, and treachery. Not in fair fight are they defeated, but by a turncoat, or by a king's agent disguised as a pirate, the latter of which is yet another myth. It first originated popularly in James Fenimore Cooper's *The Red Rover* and later in Hollywood several times, including in the present day in NBC's *Crossbones*.

Some Blackbeard fans even believe the pirate was "murdered" by Maynard and his men, for the pirate hunters lacked legitimate authority to pursue the pirate, or at least so goes the argument. But the fact is, Blackbeard was defeated face-to-face in a fight as fair as any. As for what he was doing in Ocracoke after having accepted amnesty, he was not there to engage in open, honest trade, but rather, at the very least, to dispose of goods he had pirated from a French merchantman. He may have believed that at Ocracoke and Bath-Town he had a protected base of operations, but he failed to recognize that piracy was thriving for only two reasons: a lack of naval strength and the mobility and dispersion of pirates across the waters. The combination made it difficult to track pirates down. Settling at Ocracoke was Blackbeard's undoing.

If Blackbeard was not the greatest of pirates, was he at least a great one? Of course he was. He did well by piracy during his short tenure. He captured more vessels than most pirates of his era did, was possibly less cruel than many of his contemporaries, almost certainly less so than the worst of pirates, and once for more than a week managed to blockade one of the most prominent cities in the North American colonies.

Above all, though, Blackbeard's greatest triumph was his image, and indeed it was a fierce one—but only enough to frighten some merchant seamen, lubberly shore-based merchants, and armchair adventurers. Not by a long shot was it powerful enough to intimidate, much less terrorize, the English naval seamen who killed him in action. Like the black flag, the image of the pirate as fierce warrior and hell fiend, whether substance or mere superficiality, was but one more tactic based on fear, one whose purpose was ultimately surrender without a fight. The fact is, many storytellers, including Hollywood filmmakers, and even some historians, have long accustomed us to see such men, whose image was created by fear or to inspire fear, or both, and which was magnified by the "false optics" of fear and imagination, as folk heroes—in other words, to translate their violent image and deeds into a heroism undeserved.

CHAPTER 3

Pirate Ships and Pirate Prey

———⊗⊗⊗———

"Notwithstanding, while the smoke of the powder continued very thick, as amidst a dark fog or mist, they sent four canoes very well manned, and boarded the ship with great agility, whereby they compelled the Spaniards to surrender."[1]
—Alexandre Exquemelin, *The Buccaneers of America,* 1684

Black and bloody flags, cutlasses waved in the air, and fearsome, angry faces, no matter how often they were successful, were still insufficient at times to compel surrender at sea and, in particular, ashore. In such cases the practical execution of arms was required, and, given that pirates were, by definition at the time, thieves on or from the sea, armed vessels were indispensable to the piratical goal of profit by force of arms. The common image of the "pirate ship" and its prey is of the pirate in his pirate galleon attacking Spanish treasure galleons, but this Howard Pyle and Hollywood picture is far too simplistic and, frankly, more myth than substance. We can begin to correct this misunderstanding by looking at typical sort of pirate attack from the late seventeenth century and going from there.

The attack lasted but half an hour and ended when Captain Richard Sawkins ran forward, braving a hail of harquebus shot, lances, and arrows, and by "main strength" pulled up two or three poles of the short stockade fort—more of a palisade, really—behind which the Spaniards fought.[2] Flinging the last pole down, he charged at the head of the buccaneers into Santa Maria, pistol and cutlass in hand.[3]

Immediately, the defending Spaniards and their Native American allies called for quarter. As many as seventy of the two hundred defenders lay dead, most of them cut down by the accurate musketry of the buccaneers. For his part, Sawkins had taken an arrow to the head but soon recovered, as did the only other injured buccaneer. He had been shot in the hand.

But the slaughter was not over. The buccaneers' Native American allies, venting a long hatred of the Spaniards, whose garrison at Santa Maria had murdered and abused many of them, dragged many inhabitants from the town and butchered them with lances. Hearing the cries of the murdered, the buccaneers, guilty themselves of murder at times, stopped their allies from dragging anyone else from the town. Their Indian allies had reportedly killed as many Spaniards afterward as the buccaneers had done during the fight. The ground inside and out was stained the dark purple of an abattoir.

It was April 25, 1680. Since April 11, the buccaneers had marched and canoed across the Isthmus of Darien, now known as the Isthmus of Panama, struggling through marsh and over mountain, imitating Henry Morgan and his buccaneers of eleven years past, and with the same ultimate purpose: to sack the great city of Panama.

As soon as Santa Maria, known formally as Real de Santa Maria, was secure, the buccaneers came together for a council. They first elected John Coxon as their general—that is, the commander who would lead them into battle against Panama. Then came the great question: Who would attack Panama? Santa Maria had little plunder and was a great disappointment, but, as one buccaneer put it, "Disappointment is an incentive to revenge, and good resolution the commander of success."[4] The buccaneers' "hungry appetite for gold and riches" was stronger than ever and Panama was one of the richest cities on the Spanish Main.[5] Of the 327 men, only a dozen declined, although Coxon himself was none too keen.

New Panama was stronger than the Old Panama sacked by Henry Morgan and burned to the ground, and the buccaneer force was far smaller than Morgan's when he captured the rich prize. Worse, the governor of Santa Maria had escaped down the river with several chests of gold dust. Soon enough, Panama, roughly one hundred fifty miles away by river and sea, would be warned of the coming of the buccaneers.

Before setting out in their canoes, the buccaneers burned Santa Maria, largely to pacify their Native American allies. It was no great place— except to those who lived there. A garrison town that collected gold dust panned in the river by forced Native American labor and sent it Panama, it was little more than small, simple thatched houses made of cane, a church, and a rude "stockado fort."[6] The surviving Spaniards pleaded to go with the buccaneers, so that the Native Americans might not murder them. But the buccaneers had no room and refused them a place in their canoes. Yet follow them the inhabitants did, on small rafts known as "barklogs" and in old canoes. They had to, if they wanted to live.

For a day and a half the buccaneers, soaked by rain showers, broiled by the sun, and besieged by swarms of mosquitoes and gnats, rowed down the Santa Maria River (modern-day Río Tuira) in thirty-five canoes large and small, along with two piraguas (large one- or two-masted canoes) until they reached the open sea. Of course, this is not at all what we expect of pirates, at least not according to the myth. They should be sailing instead in galleons with grand, high sterns and galleries, two or more decks of brass cannon, and masts with large, billowing sails painted with designs—not struggling through rivers in tiny dugout canoes with barely enough room for men and muskets. The fact is, pirates used the vessels most suitable—and available—to their missions of plunder. And true galleons were not only useless on rivers and in shallow waters, but, as we shall see, they were also vessels pirates of this age would seldom encounter.

Fighting a strong tidal current, the buccaneers reached a small key and rested, such as they could. Already soaked from the sea washing over the low sides of their canoes, they endured a severe downpour during the night. Cold, wet, and hungry, not to mention as vulnerable as sitting ducks amid the Pacific part of the Spanish Main, they waited for what the day would bring.

For four days more, the buccaneers and two of their Native American companions—"Captain Andreas" and his son, "King Golden-Cap," who legitimized the invasion by acting as the authority under which the pirates raided—made their way from island to island, from Tuesday to Friday, toward Panama and its riches.[7] En route, they captured a handful of Spanish barks. One of these they made their "admiral" or command ship, putting 137 men from the smallest and most easily swamped or capsized canoes aboard under the command of "that sea artist and valiant commander" Bartholomew Sharp, as buccaneer Basil Ringrose described him.[8] Nearly two hundred buccaneers remained in canoes that variously carried from six to fifteen men.

"Death unto Each Other"

On Friday morning, St. George's Day, the buccaneers came in sight of Panama. It was a new city, built some miles from Old Panama, which was burned by Henry Morgan and his buccaneers in 1671. It was a pleasant sight to the buccaneers, made so not only by their anticipation but also by its simple Spanish beauty. Captain Coxon dispatched the bark commanded by Bartholomew Sharp to seek water, of which the buccaneers were in desperate need. All of the buccaneers were exhausted from rowing and paddling.

Most of the city's shipping lay at anchor at Perico Island, roughly six miles from Panama. Here, cargoes were loaded from and unloaded into warehouses. Quickly the buccaneers put their backs into their oars and paddles, hoping to capture the five large ships and three large barks they espied at anchor. Attacking Panama directly at the moment was out of the question, given the missing 137 men in Sharp's bark.

Suddenly the three barks made sail and set a course directly for the buccaneers. By now the pirate canoes and piraguas were spread out. Far out in front of the oared fleet were five canoes carrying thirty-six men. The remaining one hundred forty or so trailed far behind, especially those in the piraguas, which were heavier and slower. Rapidly the three barks sailed toward the buccaneers. It was immediately obvious what they were: *armadillos*, or "little men-of-war," outfitted in Panama.[9] The buccaneers feared that the barks, which probably ranged from fifty to one hundred tons and whose upper decks lay six to ten feet above the canoes, would simply run them over.

Quickly the pirates pulled even harder at their oars and paddles, changing course and making as much speed as they could, trying to slip around the barks and into the eye of the wind. And they did! Now the barks could not run them over and the canoes could maneuver at will, for the barks could not sail directly into the wind.

As the buccaneers slipped into the wind's eye, the piraguas had time to catch up. But even now they numbered only sixty-eight men, with almost a hundred and thirty more en route behind them. Their odds were long, if counted by the numbers, for arrayed before them were three well-manned barks. The admiral was manned with eighty-six "Biscayners" or Basques, all volunteers, some of the best mariners and fighting men of Spain, and was commanded by Don Jacinto de Barahona.[10] The vice admiral or second-in-command bark bore seventy-seven Africans under the command of the Andalusian officer Don Francisco de Peralta. The rear admiral or third-in-command bark was manned with sixty-five *mestizos* (men of mixed Spanish and Native American blood) under the command of Don Diego de Carabajal.

It was two hundred twenty-eight against sixty-eight, or more than three against one. The Spaniards knew what happened when Henry Morgan took the city in 1670: he looted and burned it, and, many said, his men committed atrocities upon the men and women there. They did not intend to let this happen again; they would stop the buccaneers in their tracks. Worst of all for the buccaneers, though, they had to fight from low-sided canoes. The enemy had the high ground, which is as dangerous at sea as it is ashore.

The buccaneers swore that "rather than drown in the sea, or beg quarter of the Spaniard," they would "run the 'extreamest' hazard of fire and sword."[11] Carabajal's bark worked its way between the buccaneers and fired musket volleys port and starboard, wounding five buccaneers. But as soon as the smoke cleared, the buccaneers opened fire, taking aimed shots and killing several enemies with their first volley. It is no easy thing to load and fire a musket, especially a long-barreled "buccaneer gun," accurately from any canoe. Even lying back to load, as much under cover as they could be, the buccaneers were still exposed. As some pirates fired, others reloaded. They kept up a furious fire, with never a lull, forcing Spanish heads down as each buccaneer breathed a sigh of relief each time he heard the *crack-thump* of a musket ball striking a canoe gunwale instead of him.[12]

Now sailed the Spanish admiral Barahona among the buccaneers. Carabajal slipped away as the pirates turned their scourging fire onto the incoming Biscayners. The helmsman fell dead; the bark turned into the wind, its sails aback. The buccaneers rowed swiftly under the stern of the bark and opened fire, a fusillade so furious that it cut the bark's mainsheet and main brace, leaving the vessel unable to be maneuvered, and killed any man who tried to take the helm or knot the parted rigging.

Meanwhile, Captain Sawkins, who so far had commanded the attack on the admiral, abandoned his canoe—it was shot to pieces—and boarded a piragua. Immediately, he made for the vice admiral, Peralta. Here the fight was even more furious. Sawkins, ever a valiant man, laid the piragua alongside the bark. Buccaneers and Spanish Africans fired their muskets furiously at each other at close range; they both gave and received "death unto each other" as fast as they could load.[13] Neither side would yield. Both the bilges of the dugout canoes and the deck of the bark ran red.

Suddenly Carabajal's bark came about and charged to the admiral's aid. Two canoes under the command of Captain Springer rowed into its path and opened fire, exchanging a fierce hail of fire and lead until most of the *mestizo* crew were killed or wounded. It was, a witness reported, a "bloody massacre."[14] Carabajal had no choice but to retreat. By now the buccaneers had shifted well under the stern of the admiral's bark, still under a hail of fire and grenade. Here they drove wedges into the rudder so that it could not be worked. Barahona, valiantly leading his Biscayners, fell dead, and with him his pilot.

Captains Coxon and Peter Harris surged at the head of their men up the bark's side. But there was still fight in the Spaniards. Harris was shot through both legs, yet with Coxon's help made it to the deck. Now it was cutlass and pistol at close, tight quarters. Cutlasses lay into flesh like cleavers into meat; pistols left bloody holes in men and powder burns on their clothing. The bark surrendered almost immediately.[15]

Carabajal, badly battered and with few men still able to fight, had fled the scene. Barahona was dead, his bark captured. But Peralta and his Africans refused to surrender. Stoutly they fought, firing and reloading as fast as they could. Try as they might, the buccaneers could not board. Thrice Peralta and his crew had beaten Sawkins and the piragua from alongside. Two more buccaneer canoes came to Sawkins's aid, yet still Peralta and his men would not surrender.

Suddenly there was an explosion astern, burning many of Peralta's men and hurling some into the sea. A buccaneer grenade had ignited a jar of powder. Peralta, burned severely in his hands, leapt overboard anyway and swam several of his African fighters back to the bark, rescuing them. And still they fought! Yet soon after, another jar of powder exploded, and it fired several more on the forecastle. A thick cloud of smoke drifted over the deck and above the surrounding waters. On the air was the smell of burned powder and burned flesh. Down the bark's sides flowed small rivers of human blood. Aboard the bark itself, "scarce one place in the ship was found that was free from blood."[16] Peralta's valiant crew were to a man now "killed, desperately wounded, or horribly burnt."[17] Only twenty-five still lived, and of these only eight could still bear arms.

The fight was over. It had lasted three hours, from half an hour after sunrise until late morning. Among the buccaneers, eleven were dead and thirty-four wounded. Spanish valor had been extraordinary and was held in the highest regard by the buccaneer victors. But the buccaneer victory was nothing short of incredible. Outnumbered more than three to one and fighting from open canoes against an enemy in higher-sided barks with much better protection, the buccaneers had prevailed. These men were not merely pirates but sea warriors as well.

The Spanish viceroy, however, placed much of the blame for the defeat on "accidents of water and wind," and in some ways this is true, although the term "accidents" is a stretch.[18] The buccaneers not only used their outstanding musketry to their best advantage, but they also outmaneuvered the Spanish barks, although it is quite possible that the wind was on their side when they did. It was a classic buccaneer engagement, of canoe or small craft against an armed Spanish bark—quite possibly the most common type of pirate engagement on the late seventeenth-century Spanish Main. Yet nowhere was a galleon to be seen—at least not yet.

Now the buccaneers set their eyes on the greatest ship at anchor at Perico. Yet when they reached her, they found hardly a man aboard. Those who were left had drilled a hole in her hull and tried to set her afire, but the buccaneers quickly stopped the leak and put out the flames. The great vessel was the *Santísima Trinidad*, or, as the pirates translated it, *Blessed Trinity*, a four-hundred-ton treasure ship, one that many today would call a galleon.[19] According to a buccaneer believed to be Edward Povey, the ship was the same one that escaped in 1671 at the sack of Panama with much of the city's wealth and wealthiest.[20] The buccaneer captain sent to capture her, Robert Searles, who had led the sack of St. Augustine in 1668, was drunk and engaged in "lascivious exercises"—without doubt a euphemism for rape—with several women and let her get away.[21]

This time, her cargo was more mundane: wine, sugar, sweetmeats (fruit pieces preserved with sugar), hides, soap, and flour, along with, at least according to the Spanish viceroy, gunpowder and slow match intended for the garrisons of Peru. But also aboard were 60,000 pieces of eight intended for these garrisons. Given the size of the buccaneer army, this was not a great sum of silver. Still, each buccaneer's share came to 247 of the crude coins. It was a good start, especially after the disappointment of Santa Maria. The buccaneers set sail aboard the *Trinity*—after all, she was the best sailor in the South Sea—and eventually, after much plundering of Peru and Chile, sailed her around Cape Horn and to the Caribbean.

The *Santísima Trinidad* is often referred to as a galleon, a type of ship typically described as a large, well-armed Spanish treasure ship with a high stern and a hold filled with the riches of the New World: gold, silver, pearls, and emeralds, plus the more mundane, including logwood and other dye woods, hides, and medicines. The reefs and shallows of Florida and the Bahamas are littered with wrecks of these great ships. But to these buccaneers, this prize was not a galleon. Although it is possible the *Trinity* may have been one of the last true galleons, she was probably one in name only, and only because she had at least once been a Spanish treasure ship, to which the term was often still applied, no matter what sort or size she actually was. A 1683 encyclopedia of geography describes the term galleon as no longer in use except by the Italians, and especially by the Spanish, who reserved it for their ships trading from Spain to the New World "without regard to size or type of construction."[22]

In reality, although Exquemelin calls her a galleon, the *Trinity* was more likely a large common merchantman, for Don Melchor de Liñán y Cisneros, the viceroy of Peru, referred to her simply as a *navío*—a ship, as opposed to a *fragata* or *galeón*.[23] She might also have been a large frigate, which was a seventeenth-century term for a type of swift hull belonging to a ship, often a man-of-war, of no more than two decks running the full length from bow to stern. The buccaneers who captured the *Trinity* referred to her only as a "ship," "great ship," or "larger ship," and kept her only because she was the best sailor in the South Sea, not to mention a "good, strong and tight" vessel.[24] But even as a great "treasure galleon," she may have been the only one ever sailed by pirates of the Golden Age, from 1655 to 1725. And she did not have even a single cannon aboard.

Almost certainly, pirates never or almost never captured or sailed real galleons during the Golden Age, for the true galleon no longer existed as a type of ship construction after the 1640s, and those remaining were mostly gone by 1660, except for a few still built and used solely in the treasure fleets into the early eighteenth century.[25]

If any Golden Age pirates did sail true galleons, it was only briefly during the first few years of the era. The name galleon, however, remained in use in reference to Spanish treasure ships, even among the Spanish, in spite of the fact that by the first decade of the eighteenth century a galleon was a rare sight, although the term was also still used occasionally by the Spanish to indicate a stout Spanish man-of-war.[26] Privateer Woodes Rogers noted only one ship built "Galeon-fashion, very high with Galleries," among all the Spanish ships he encountered in the South Sea in 1709, other than the two Manila galleons themselves, and it was a common unarmed merchantman, not a treasure ship.[27]

Yet even true Spanish treasure ships, whatever their build, were seldom under attack except in the South Sea. Those that belonged to the great treasure fleets known as the *Flota* and the *Galeones* were far too well protected, and pirates of the Golden Age never captured a single one except for a few of the Honduras *urcas* or their *pataches* (scouting consorts), or perhaps an occasional registry ship or other small treasure ship sailing independently of the treasure fleets. Pirates often lay in wait for the few ships of the *Flota* and *Galeones* that sailed alone, such as the Honduras *urcas* and the *patache de Margarita*, but only occasionally did they capture them. As for the great treasure ships of the great Atlantic treasure fleets, they were far too well protected, as were the Manila galleons, not that pirates did not have their collective eye on them: "At this council it was determined to go to the isle of Savona, there to wait for the *flota* which was then expected from Spain, and take any of the Spanish vessels that might chance to straggle from the rest," writes Exquemelin of Henry Morgan and his small fleet of buccaneers.[28] But there were plenty of other types of vessel to sail—and to attack.

Rakish Sloops and Ships with Teeth

Pirates often sailed vessels other than ships. For example, the dugout canoe was one of the most common of pirate vessels. In the late seventeenth century, buccaneers and filibusters used them for raids up rivers on the Spanish Main, towed them astern or carried them aboard their larger vessels, and often began their piratical careers aboard them, working their way up from canoe to small merchant bark to *barcalonga*, tarteen, or sloop, and finally—sometimes—to frigate, small or large, the smaller vessel capturing the larger.[29] And sometimes they fought barks and small ships with canoes, as the buccaneers at Perico did. Sometimes they even fought great ships, such as the four- or five-hundred-ton "hulk" of the Honduras *urca*, a large-bellied flat-bottomed cargo carrier.[30] Famous cutthroat pirate François l'Ollonois captured a hulk this way.[31]

In the late seventeenth century, the *barque longue*, or in Spanish, *barcalonga*, the common bark, and the sloop were the most common vessels among the pirates of the Caribbean. A *barque longue* was a long, narrow, open-decked vessel with shallow draft. It carried one or two masts and one or two sails, although some carried topsails as well. The sails of Spanish *barcalongas*, and perhaps those of some of the French *barque longues*, were lugsails that could be easily changed from side to side for tacking. The best pirate craft were those that could escape to windward (toward the wind). Pirate craft in the Caribbean also needed to be able to sail against the prevailing trade winds, and the lugsail made this easier.[32]

However, the sloop deserves the most fame as a pirate vessel, especially the sort called "Bermuda," named for its place of construction, although in fact it had originated in Jamaica. Sloop builders shifted to Bermuda after the timber ran out in Jamaica. These sloops were swift vessels, built of cedar, with hulls well tallowed and chalked for speed, fore and aft rigged with an enormous mainsail, and in the eighteenth century, with a tall single mast raked strikingly aft and a long bowsprit thrust piercingly forward like a Spanish rapier. You could not miss recognizing one, even at a distance. As Jamaica sloops they were popular in the second half of the seventeenth century, and as Bermuda sloops grew even more so in the eighteenth. There are only a few significant pirates who never sailed a Jamaica or Bermuda sloop at one time or another.[33]

By chance, we have an outstandingly detailed description of a pirate sloop, whose short story is in itself a fascinating one. In early 1718, Captain

Charles Pinkethman set sail from Jamaica aboard the sloop *Nathaniel & Charles*, intending to make his fortune upon the Spanish treasure wrecks in the Bahamas. Unfortunately, his dreams of salvaged silver were short-lived. He died en route, leaving the sloop's master, suitably named Tempest, to take his place. At Walker's Cay, in the Abaco Islands of the Bahamas, they put their African or Native American divers to work, but to little profit. Weighing their anchor, they sailed with another sloop to Bimini and worked a wreck there, but it, too, held little profit.[34]

A mutinous sort named Greenway commanded the consort sloop. Failing at treasure hunting, he had sniffed the air and caught the whiff of piracy. Bad fortune had discouraged Tempest's crew, leaving them vulnerable to the temptation of piracy, now beginning to flourish in the Caribbean and Americas. Greenway lured them with golden dreams, assuring them that piracy was far more profitable than hunting for treasure on sunken wrecks.

Under the influence of Greenway, Tempest's crew mutinied, "took possession of this sloop and all the arms, and threatened to shoot Captain Tempest and all that would not go with them under Greenway's command."[35] Yet in spite of the threats, Tempest and more than a dozen steadfast seamen refused to join the pirates. Relenting eventually, the pirates transferred some of them to another sloop and let them go. But they didn't release all the seamen. The new pirates forced several to remain behind.

West now the sloop sailed, to Florida to fish for silver—a curious way to begin a pirate cruise that was instigated by failing at fishing for silver—but Spaniards on the shore welcomed them with volleys of lead. Sailing north, Greenway brought his sloop into an inlet south of Charlestown, South Carolina, and fitted her with a new mast. At sea again, they captured and released a small sloop, ran from a twenty-four-gun French merchantman, and sighted the Spanish treasure fleet but ran when they realized a Spanish man-of-war was lying in wait for them. So much for "plucking a crow" with Spanish galleons! Near Bermuda, they captured two sloops, kept one, and forced a few men to join the pirate crew.

Pirates of the early eighteenth century often forced freemen, seamen, and fishermen to join their crews, unlike the late seventeenth-century buccaneers and filibusters, who forced only slaves and the occasional Spanish pilot. Thirteen of these forced men wanted to be rid of their captors. All they needed was an opportunity; a chance to maroon themselves ashore would be ideal. But they got better than they could wish for.

On July 17, 1718, the pirates sighted and gave chase to a ship. Ranging up close, the pirates hoisted their black flag, fired a cannon and, for emphasis, a volley of muskets at the ship. Immediately, the merchantman lowered her topsails, lay by in the trough of the sea, and waited to be boarded. Captain Greenway, greedy as ever, clambered into the sloop's boat, along with his gunner, doctor, and a few other officers, leaving the pirate crew and forced men behind.

Suddenly, the wind filled the ship's sails, which were balanced against each other as she lay by, and pushed the ship down upon the sloop, smashing into her quarter. But rather than worry about the accident, the pirate crew leaped aboard the ship, rabidly looking for plunder. It was every man for himself. They ran about the ship, pillaging as they could and paying no attention to the sloop they had just left nor to their captain. After all, pirate captains had absolute authority only in battle. Just a few pirates were left aboard the sloop.

The forced men seized the moment. Richard Appleton, one of the few to be armed, took the helm and ordered John Robeson below to secure the stores. He shouted to the black men aboard—slaves probably, but possibly freemen, perhaps even divers—to hoist the sails. Immediately, a pirate realized what was happening. He seized a musket, aimed it at Appleton, and "snapped it," as pulling the trigger was known due to the sound of the flint striking steel.[36] But it misfired, and again so.

Swiftly, he reversed it in his hands and swung the butt at Appleton, cracking it over his head. Appleton went down. But the black men aboard had no more reason to want to be with the pirates than the forced white men did. One of them shot the pirate in the belly with a pistol, and another shot him in the leg. Quickly they trussed up the pirate and seven of his fellows, all of whom were mostly drunk, put them all in a canoe, and set them adrift. To Philadelphia the pirate prisoners—the "forced men" from Tempest's crew—and their black comrades sailed and gave themselves up, where all—at least the white seamen—were "well used and civilly entreated for the service they had done."[37]

Thankfully, the council at Philadelphia kept a detailed inventory of the sloop, probably the most detailed we have of a pirate craft of the Golden Age. She had a full set of sails, including a jib, a flying jib, and a spritsail, plus three anchors, and tools, lumber, tar, and other sundries for making repairs. For navigation, she had three compasses; for maneuvering in calm or light airs, a set of oars or sweeps; for feeding her pirate crew, thirteen half barrels of beef and pork; for cooking, a kettle and two iron pots; for treating her sick and wounded, a doctor's chest; for tricking the prey, a pair of false colors and pennants, and a jack; and for intimidating the prey, a black pirate flag and a red "no quarter" flag.[38]

More important to her purpose, she mounted ten cannon of small caliber, along with two small "swivel guns" that loaded from the muzzle, and nine patereros (a form of small swivel cannon) that loaded from the breech. But six of the patereros were old and may have been unserviceable. She also had ten "organ" barrels belonging to a small bit of rail-mounted artillery known as an organ: a sheaf of musket barrels made to fire together, more accurate than a common swivel.[39]

The sloop also carried two hundred round shot for her cannon, which is really not all that many, four kegs of scrap metal for loading in canvas bags and firing in a murderous hail at men, and thirty-two barrels of gunpowder. She carried fifty-three grenades, vital for boarding a ship under fire, and thirty muskets, just as vital for attacking a ship. Muskets were used to suppress enemy fire and often made the difference even when ships were fighting with their great guns broadside to broadside. In fact, the musket was the principal weapon of the pirate.[40]

Sloops like this were the most common seagoing pirate vessels of the Golden Age, and the ones we should most associate with pirates. Certainly the most common was not the galleon, which by the eighteenth century no longer really existed except in name; only a handful of real galleons, known by the design of their hulls, still sailed. Even so, many pirates did sail ships and other three-mast vessels. Most were small frigates, usually of only one or two hundred tons and of ten to twenty guns of two- to six-pound caliber, often with as many swivel cannon mounted on the rails. But some pirates captured large merchantmen or slave ships, converted them to pirate ships, and sailed the seas with ships of forty or even fifty guns. These ships were often slow compared to their prey, or at least no swifter, and slow compared to pirate hunters. Further, they were expensive to maintain and required a lot of maintenance— and pirates were generally a lazy lot.[41] Most of the time, pirates preferred lighter, swifter vessels—fast enough to overtake prey and run from a pirate hunter and armed well enough to make a stout fight if it came to that. Often large pirate ships were accompanied by light, swift craft, as we have already seen in the case of Blackbeard's pirate flotilla.

The Most Famous Attack on a Galleon

If pirates did not sail galleons or really even attack them during the Golden Age, why, then, do we think they did? Foremost, because during the late sixteenth and early seventeenth centuries, pirates *did* attack galleons and sometimes sailed them as well. It is an easy matter to confuse the symbols and images of one era with another; Hollywood does it all the time. Also, Spanish treasure ships continued to be referred to as galleons for a long time afterward, even if they were not actually galleons. In the popular mind, *any* Spanish ship with treasure aboard was a treasure galleon.

Looking closer, we can probably lay a substantial part of the responsibility on two men: a writer who also happened to be a buccaneer surgeon, and an illustrator who also happened to be a writer. Buccaneer surgeon Alexandre Exquemelin's magnificent history of the buccaneers, *The Buccaneers of America*, recounts among many of its largely factual stories that of Pierre le Grand, who sailed from Tortuga, just off the coast of Saint-Domingue (modern-day Haiti), the island refuge of hunters known as *boucaniers*, as well as of other deserters, shipwrecked seamen, and various fortune hunters. Prior to its becoming a buccaneer haven, the island subsisted on a small trade in tobacco, *boucan* (smoked pork strips), and hides.[42]

Le Grand and his small crew of twenty-eight filibusters, most of them probably Frenchmen, had put to sea in search of "purchase," as prey was known to pirates. Their craft was small—a boat, Exquemelin says, but likely a canoe, piragua, or *barcalonga*, although eighteenth-century historian Pierre-François-Xavier de Charlevoix writes that it mounted four great guns, which would make it a decked vessel, a bark perhaps.[43] Their provisions nearly gone, the pirates feared they might perish if they did not soon go ashore.

Suddenly, they sighted a great ship of the Spanish *Flota*, or so the story goes. By its colors they knew it to be the vice admiral, or second-in-command, a rich ship. The *Flota*, like the *Galeones*, was a large Spanish fleet that traded from Spain to the Spanish Main and back, and throughout the seventeenth century some of its ships were true galleons, although others were a variety of common round merchant hulls known generically as *naos*, and *urcas*, the Spanish name for the Dutch fluyt design, a flat-bottomed three-mast vessel with a pinked stern and sharp tumblehome. Exquemelin's English editions indeed refer to the *Flota* ship as a galleon, although the Dutch and Spanish editions merely call it a ship.

The pirates set sail in pursuit and swore an oath to behave courageously. The vice admiral himself, doubtless a proud, even arrogant man, ignored them, however, conceiving them to be much too small to do him and his ship harm. To him, the small craft was a "pitiful thing."[44] Night came. Under its shroud, the pirates slipped close by the ship. They not only appreciated the Spaniard's scorn but also used it to their advantage. Unseen, they came alongside and drilled holes in the hull of their vessel so that they would have no retreat. They must do or die.

Quickly they clambered aboard via the main shrouds, for this was by far the best place to board a large ship. Pistol and cutlass in hand, they cut down anyone in their path. The cutlass is an effective tool for dispatching the unwary. It can split a skull, and if it fails to do this, its sheer weight will crack a skull and render the owner unconscious. The pirates ran to the great cabin and put a pistol to the captain's breast, shocking him speechless. Whether he dropped his hand of cards or held them petrified was not recorded. The pirates forced him to give up the ship. Others seized the gunroom and arms and quickly gained control of the decks, doubtless by stationing armed men at the ladders.

"Jesus bless us!" a Spaniard cried when he realized what was happening. "Are these devils, or what are they!"[45]

Pierre le Grand and his crew sailed the great ship to France and, it is implied, lived happily ever after, or at least as happy as pirates might if they did not too quickly squander their booty. According to Exquemelin, this great deed inspired other *boucaniers* and fortune hunters on Tortuga to turn pirate, or, more correctly, filibuster or *flibustier*, a word derived from "freebooter," which is in turn derived from the Dutch word *vrijbutier*.[46] In fact, the *boucaniers* and fortune hunters of Tortuga and Hispaniola needed no inspiration other than the obvious: there were Spanish ships in the Caribbean rich for the taking.

Unfortunately, we do not know exactly when this happened, or even whether it's true, although the tactics and Spanish hubris ring true enough, or even whether Pierre le Grand actually existed. The filibuster historian Jean-Baptiste Lepers, who wrote in the early eighteenth century, gives his name as "Picore," and historian Pierre-François-Xavier de Charlevoix, writing not long after, suggests the attack took place between 1661 and 1665.[47] There was in fact a Pierre le Grand mentioned as having sacked Sancti Spíritus in Cuba in 1665.[48] Doubtless, any successful pirate or fortune hunter named Pierre probably soon became known as Pierre le Grand—the capture of even a fairly rich ship would surely inspire the appellation. Almost certainly, the truth of the tale has been grossly exaggerated, for there is no record of pirates capturing the vice admiral of a *Flota*.[49]

There is a similar tale of another pirate, Michel le Basque, whose real name may well have been Michel d'Artigue, who is said to have captured the "*Margarita*," perhaps the *patache de Margarita*, perhaps simply the *Santa Margarita*, part of the Spanish treasure fleet, right from under the cannon in the forts at Portobello. If the story—it is no more than a couple of brief descriptions several decades later—is to be believed, the booty amounted to one million pieces of eight, an incredible sum whose loss would have made news even across the sea in Europe. In fact, several scholars note that Michel le Basque did capture a ship off Portobello in 1668 while commanding l'Ollonois's *Dauphin*, but not a treasure ship filled with a million Spanish dollars. Without doubt, the truth was greatly exaggerated in similar fashion to that of Pierre le Grand.[50]

Exquemelin's account of le Grand's capture of the treasure galleon influenced generations of writers and illustrators, one of whom was Howard Pyle. In "With the Buccaneers," which was reprinted in *Howard Pyle's Book of Pirates*, as were many of his stories, he invents a tale of Captain Henry Morgan capturing a Spanish galleon by stealth in Portobello harbor. In fact, the tale is nothing more than that of Pierre le Grand with a change in actors and location, perhaps inspired as well by the tale of Michel le Basque. Doubtless this story also helped inspire the myth of pirates and Spanish galleons, but it was Pyle's ability as a painter that really did the trick. There are few who are unfamiliar with his famous painting, *An Attack on a Galleon*, from his story, "The Fate of a Treasure-Town." Indeed, the illustration is a fixture in nearly all illustrated books on piracy. Without doubt, Pyle based his powerful painting on the exploit of Pierre le Grand, although Pyle's attackers have two boats, not one. The painting has influenced generations of novelists, illustrators, screenwriters, and set directors who in turn depicted pirate ships as pirate galleons and Spanish treasure frigates as treasure galleons.[51]

Is it, then, in any way fair to say that Golden Age pirates regularly attacked and captured galleons? Of course it is: Howard Pyle's magnificent paintbrush has proved they did. Even though we know the pirate's treasure galleon may be one in name only, our hearts and souls refuse the truth. It will do us no harm if, in this one instance, we do not let reality betray our own romantic, swashbuckling illusions.

CHAPTER 4

Not by Walking the Plank

———— ⊗⊗⊗ ————

"[W]hen having made fast a Block to the Yard-Arm, and re[e]ved a Rope in it; they [the Spanish pirates] took the Mate and twisted a piece of Sea-net about his Head till his Eyes were ready to start out, and then Hanged him up by the two Thumbs, that they might make him confess what Money there was a Board, but when they saw they could make him confess nothing by that Punishment, they made fast the Rope about his Neck, and their Men asked the Commander, whether they should hoist him up or not?"[1]
—Anon., *Sad and Dreadful News from New England*, 1684

Pirate violence was not limited to threatening images and reputations and to the violence of attacking armed ships and shores. Indeed, the violence against victims in the aftermath of a pirate attack, most of them innocent and all of them unable to defend themselves, was often as brutal and surely caused far greater psychological damage than did the assault against armed defenders. In a fashion that fed upon itself, pirate cruelty against prisoners helped magnify their image as fiends from hell, although this was almost certainly not the primary purpose of such cruelty. From courage in battle to cowardice against prisoners was but a small step for many pirates, and for that matter, many others as well, then and now. Misconceptions and even myths have grown from tales of pirate cruelty, not the least of which is that surrounding the forcing of prisoners to "walk the plank" to their deaths.

"I am no common man," the prisoner remonstrated, his back straight and his head held high to indicate his social status among the rabble that had captured him. "You would do well to understand this. Harm me at your peril!"[2]

"What are you, then?" asked one of his captors, laughing. "A rich Syracusan merchant making his living in trade of goods as opposed to honest force of arms? Or a Rhodian noble, one of the pirate-hunting butchers? Perhaps you are an Aegyptian prince who has spent too much time with his slave women and has taken a sea voyage to escape them— or to escape his wife's ire at being neglected for the sake of young nubile women?"

Several other Cilicians—for these men who had captured him were Cilician pirates, members of a sea-thieving navy a thousand-sail strong from the Cilician coast (modern-day Turkey)—laughed along with him.

"Well?" continued the interrogator. "What are you? Who are you to strut about upon our deck as if we ought to recognize you and bow and scrape before you?" After each question and answer, he paused to translate from the Roman language, Latin, into his crew's tongue, Cilician. He wanted them to miss nothing of the exchange.

The prisoner cleared his throat and tilted his head even higher. "*Ego sum Romanus—I* am a Roman!" he said, pointedly referencing the fact that *he* himself was indeed a citizen of the great city and empire. "You must put me ashore immediately, and then perhaps there will be no consequences for you!"

"A Roman? A Roman!" his captors muttered, looking back and forth among themselves in surprise.

"Indeed, that changes things," the prisoner's interrogator said, rubbing his beard. He was the captain of the pirate vessel, a *hemiolia*, a swift craft that could chase under both sail and oar. It even had a gilded mast, a sail of woven purple fabric, and oars plated with silver, as some pirate craft did.

The Cilicians had turned to piracy a century or so earlier, around the middle of the second century BCE, first as privateers and mercenaries serving Mithridates IV in his wars against Rome. Later, as Rome was busy fighting its civil wars, the Cilicians expanded into outright piracy, unable to resist the temptation of the great lucrative trade in slaves, trade goods such as olive oil and wine, and ransom. Well organized, they sacked more than four hundred villages, towns, and cities, and extracted tribute from many others. Often they raided miles inland. They violated the temples of the Roman gods. Their mariners were of the finest, their pilots the most experienced, and, not surprisingly, their bacchanals ashore rivaled those of the wealthy Romans.[3]

"Yet you are not clothed as a Roman," the captain continued, tilting his head slightly to the side as he addressed his prisoner. "Here, someone bring this man Roman shoes. And a toga as well! Hurry now, help him dress himself. By the gods, sir, it is a good thing you told us that you are a Roman! What a mistake we might have made! All of you, everyone, bow to this man. We humbly beseech you, Roman sir, to forgive us."

The pirates slapped their thighs and dropped to their knees, their heads bowed to the deck. Several, though, failed to conceal smiles; one pirate choked briefly as he tried to keep a laugh from bursting forth. The prisoner, his mind overwhelmed with fear and bourgeois hubris, failed to notice any of this.

"You had best put me ashore immediately!" the prisoner ordered. "Rome protects her citizens!"

"Indeed, Roman sir, we shall, just as soon as you have finished dressing. I suggest you dress as a Roman at all times from now on. That way, if we capture you again, we will know you for what you are."

The prisoner finished dressing, then cleared his throat. His attitude was not nearly as tremulous now. Rather, a haughty arrogance had overtaken it. Doubt and fear still showed, but only through the cracks. "I shall follow your advice from now on," he replied. "How soon before you can put me ashore? The sooner the better for you, you know."

"Sooner than you might think, Roman sir," the Cilician captain said and bowed with a grin. "A ladder!" he ordered.

Quickly one of his men secured the ladder to the gunwale. The foot of the ladder dragged in the Mediterranean. The sea was a brilliant blue under the clear bright sky.

"As I promised," the pirate captain said, gesturing to the ladder. "Over the side with you, Roman sir."

At first, the prisoner thought this was a joke. Soon, though, as the wolfishly grinning crew advanced on him, some gripping their weapons, he quickly realized it was anything but.

"It's only a few miles to shore. Even a fat merchant—you are a merchant, aren't you?—can walk that far before noon. Get going."

The prisoner did not move. "You can't do this to me! I'm a Roman! The gods know this, I'm a Roman!"

"It matters nothing to us what you be. You wanted to go ashore, so you're going ashore."

"But I am not a Roman! I'm not!"

"Too late for remonstrance now. And like I said, Roman or not, you'll take the ladder and walk home." The pirate's grin was replaced with the twisted rictus of a murderer.

Still refusing to go overboard of his own volition, the prisoner was grabbed by several pirates. The man struggled violently, showing surprising strength in his final moments. The pirates threw him, still struggling violently, overboard. Overwhelmed by numbers, even a stout man would have been forced into the sea. If nothing else, an ax or a sword to the head would have ended the argument.

The *hemiolia* rowed slowly away, its crew catcalling the man overboard as he tried in vain, pleading for mercy, to catch the parting vessel. "*Ave atque vale!*" the captain shouted, giving the traditional Roman salutation and valediction: "Hail and farewell!"

The death of the man in the sea was certain. He lacked the strength to swim even a mile, much less several. Even if he could keep himself on the surface, eventually fatigue and hypothermia—no matter how warm the water—would set in, and he would no longer be able to bear himself above the briny deep. Soon enough this man would weary and slip beneath the surface of the water, where his body would briefly, violently grasp in gasping spasms at life. His mind filled with nothing but panic, he would soon pass out from holding his breath, or attempt one last gasping breath, which would both choke him and quickly render him unconscious, to die soon after, perhaps already at the bottom of the sea.

The year could have been almost any during the first two-thirds of the first century BCE. The words spoken are fictional, but words like them were surely spoken many times. The tale itself comes to us from Plutarch, who described the infamous Cilician pirates in detail. Even the young Julius Caesar was once captured by them, but he was well aware of how to deal with them, having briefly served in an expedition against them. Entertaining them with jovial threats of how he would put them to death when he was free, Caesar arranged for the state to ransom him, then quickly put together a private naval force that attacked the pirates at night and captured them. When the local governor decided to sell the pirates as slaves to benefit his own purse, Caesar preempted him. He ordered every pirate crucified, but, to show his mercy, let their throats be slit so they would not suffer on the cross.[4]

So powerful were the Cilician pirates that they eventually threatened Rome's grain supply. Rome was happy to buy slaves from the Cilician pirates but could not permit pirates to threaten a critical resource. In response, the Roman senate authorized the greatest pirate-hunting expedition in history. In three months, without the loss of a single ship, a combined force of warships and legionnaires commanded by Pompey the Great swept the pirates from the sea and destroyed the mighty pirate empire. But unlike Caesar, Pompey did not crucify his prisoners. Instead, he resettled most and made them into farmers. Some took service under the Romans at sea. Pompey understood that piracy was the Cilician livelihood. He gave them an alternative.[5]

As for putting prisoners over the side, Plutarch's story of the Cilician pirates is probably nothing more, at best, than the ultimate source of the inspiration for the myth of seventeenth- and eighteenth-century pirates forcing prisoners to walk the plank. Throughout the ages, pirates have often forced prisoners overboard. In antiquity, pirates—the term is used loosely here for any sea rover—kept most prisoners as slaves, ransoming only the wealthy. Even so, they killed useless prisoners and threw their bodies overboard, or even threw prisoners overboard alive. In the Middle Ages, prisoners who were not wealthy enough to be ransomed—most of them, in other words—were usually thrown overboard alive and left to flail briefly in terror at the mercy of the sea. The salt waters are seldom merciful to anyone thrown naked into their grasp. In *The Canterbury Tales*, Geoffrey Chaucer repeated what was probably a dark joke at the time: the sailor—whether pirate or patriot, or even both—sent his prisoners home by the sea.[6]

Even so, there was no plank. Although there is more to the story of walking the plank to be told before this chapter is through, the reality was that pirates had many far more common means of abusing and killing prisoners.

Of Pirates and Prisoners

In 1668, seventeen hundred years after the fall of the Cilician pirate empire, a small pirate fleet of seven hundred men in six vessels, one of them an *urca*, or round-bellied, flat-bottomed trading ship, captured recently from the Spanish at Maracaibo, Venezuela, cast their anchors at Matamano, a turtle-fishing village on the south side of Cuba. Commanding the expedition was Jean David Nau, better known as l'Ollonois or l'Ollonais from his birthplace at the small seaport of Sables d'Olonne, France.[7]

L'Ollonois may have been the most brutal of his era, but other pirates were nearly as cruel, perhaps just less often or on a smaller scale. Many of l'Ollonois's men had been with him at Maracaibo, but all had quickly squandered their booty, as filibusters and buccaneers were wont to do. "All the flood-tide brings in, the ebb-tide carries away," wrote Exquemelin, buccaneer surgeon and author.[8] Others aboard, though, were tobacco farmers undertaking their first sea-roving expedition. Wide-eyed at the success of the raid on Maracaibo, they "threw away their hoes" and took up the musket and cutlass.[9]

At Matamano the pirates stole canoes—the sole means of support for the turtle fishermen, or *variadors* as they were known in Spanish—along with some of the fishermen themselves, and set a course for Cape Gracias a Dios, some 520 miles south. L'Ollonois intended a raid into Lake Nicaragua, and he required canoes to ascend upriver. But the wind did not cooperate, and the pirates soon found themselves becalmed and carried by the current into the Gulf of Honduras. L'Ollonois, who commanded the *urca*, could not beat back to windward. The prevailing wind and current pushed his great ship west, and he lost sight of his smaller vessels.

Needing provisions for the great raid ahead—l'Ollonois's were almost spent—the filibusters raided all along the coast of the Gulf of Honduras. Village after village they raided, most of them inhabited by Native Americans, who remained, after all, the largest population on the Spanish Main. Corn, pigs, chickens, and turkeys fell into pirate hands, so many that many small villages were left to starve. Not even monkeys were safe from the pirates' appetite.

L'Ollonois soon set a course for Puerto Caballos, known today as Puerto Cortés, on the west coast of the Bay of Honduras. Here the pirates captured a twenty-four-gun Spanish merchant ship. Perhaps they simply anchored and pointed their cannon at the Spaniard, or slipped alongside during the night and boarded her quickly and violently. Ashore, the filibusters pillaged whatever foodstuffs they could find. The warehouses, filled mostly with hides, they burned, having no need for them. They were after greater plunder.

L'Ollonois needed information, and he wanted it quickly. He knew that some men might lie to save their families, and he knew that some men might lie to protect state secrets, even under great torture. But few enough men will lie to protect their own wealth, or what little they may have, much less that of others. Immediately, he ordered his men to take prisoners, and he examined them personally "on the rack."[10]

The expression is not to be taken literally. It was simply a term for torture, and it originated with the real rack often used in a variety of inquisitions. Unlike many abusive sea rovers, l'Ollonois did not ask questions first and afterward torture prisoners if he did not believe them. He put them directly to the pain. Whenever a prisoner did not answer him immediately, he hacked him to pieces with his cutlass, then licked the blood from the blade, making it clear that he wished this dead man were the last dead Spaniard in the world. And for the poor prisoner who agreed to lead him to a town or to money and then got lost? He was "inflicted with a thousand torments—and then put to death at the end of it all."[11]

The torments used by pirates were actually common ones that, particularly among those that often led to death, were far worse than forcing someone to walk the plank. Many writers have assumed the pirates invented these torments, but all had long been in use. When a buccaneer tortured a prisoner by tying a line around his head, then tightening it with a stick as one would a tourniquet, he was simply making use of a forehead tourniquet, a device long used in formal inquisitions—and they would often use sharp beads strung on a line to make the pain worse. For buccaneers—they called it "woolding" (wolding)—it may have been inspired by the seaman's term for a line wrapped around a mast or spar and tightened or for a cable wrapped around a hull and tightened.[12] Certainly the name was taken from the practice. Rafael Sabatini, by the way, got the origin of this torture right in his famous novel *Captain Blood*; he knew well the Inquisitorial origin of this "rosary of pain that has wrought the conversion of many a stubborn heretic."[13]

Any man who claimed he had nothing to offer up to the pirates—no gold, no silver, no more grain or livestock—was often tortured anyway. "If he won't confess, string him up!" was the cry.[14] If the prisoner continued to tell the truth but was not believed, he might be killed. If he lied and could produce nothing, he surely was killed. To "string a prisoner up" was to strappado him: that is, to tie his hands behind his back and hoist him up by his wrists. Here, his arms nearly tearing from their sockets, he could be beaten with the back of a cutlass blade or cut with the edge of a knife or cutlass.[15] Or—and often all were done to him—he could be hoisted higher and then dropped, causing great pain and tearing apart the muscles and tendons of his shoulders. Pirates might hang stones from his neck and feet until he screamed in pain or burn palm leaves under his face, suffocating him.

Another prisoner—or any prisoner, indeed—might find slow match placed between his fingers and toes. Slow match, used to fire cannon and matchlock muskets, burns very hot and very slowly. It could burn flesh to the bone.

Still another might be tied spread-eagled to a table or cart wheel or even staked to the ground. Sometimes pirates would stake a man above the ground, face down, via his thumbs and big toes, then beat the cords holding him up, causing his muscles and tendons to tear. If this failed, they might set a fire beneath him or place heavy stones on his back—or do both, and many other tortures as well. Some prisoners were stabbed several times while tied up, then left to die. Others were strung up by their testicles until the weight of the body tore them loose.[16] Some were crucified. Some were tied up, then their feet were coated with lard and placed in the fire.

Perhaps the only torture common to the period that does not appear to have been used regularly—at least of those that did not require much in the way of special equipment—was the water torture, although a 1681 illustration does show it being used by buccaneers.[17] Disney also depicts a form of it in the *Pirates of the Caribbean* attraction at some of its theme parks: buccaneers sacking a Spanish town (or at least this was the presentation until the *Pirates of the Caribbean* films came out) drop the tied-up *alcalde* (mayor) into a well repeatedly. "Speak up, you bilge rat! Where be the treasure?" demands the pirate captain. "Don't tell him, Carlos! Don't be chicken!" shouts the *alcalde's* wife. "I weel not talk!" sputters her husband in a stereotyped Hollywood Hispanic accent after spitting out a stream of water.[18] But in reality *alcaldes* and everyone else almost always did talk, even if it were often only to tell lies in the hope of appeasing their torturers and stopping the pain.[19]

When l'Ollonois and his pirates had the information they needed— or were simply sated, or the town had been plundered of everything valuable—they moved on. Instead of bodies drowned as a result of walking the plank, the aftermath was littered with the dead, the dying, and the permanently disfigured and disabled.

From Puerto Caballos on the coast of Honduras, l'Ollonois led his men inland toward a town called San Pedro. But the Spaniards were ready for him. From barricade to barricade and ambush to ambush, he led his men on the road to the town. He had prisoners brought before him and demanded of them which other route he could take. When they told him there was no other, he used his cutlass to split the chest of one of the prisoners open, tore out his heart, chewed on it, then threw it in the face of another prisoner, telling him to find another way or have his heart ripped out, too. And when there was no other way, he cried, "God's death! The Spanish buggers will pay me for this!"[20]

L'Ollonois continued his assaults on both towns and prisoners until one day he met his end at the hands of Native Americans who, too, had suffered at his hands. Suffice it to say that he learned firsthand what torture felt like. The ashes of his dismembered body were scattered to the wind.

Violence and other forms of cruelty were often the resort of men in search of wealth by force of arms and they had other means than those just described. Walking the plank was simply unnecessary. For example, if a pirate needed to get rid of a crew, he might simply "cast them overboard" as did Irish pirate Francis Bodkin in 1670. He and his crew of Irish and English plundered a vessel returning from Virginia with tobacco, but pretended to authorities that it was a derelict found with no crew aboard. The pirates were acquitted of murder for obvious lack of evidence but were found guilty of another piracy.[21]

Or, if a pirate objected to a Spanish priest or friar aboard a bark just captured in the South Sea, he might shoot him, then heave him aboard while he was still alive.[22] The priest would bleed to death or drown in the sea. Perhaps a shark was trailing the ship—they often did—and it would make a meal of the innocent victim, possibly even accelerating the process of death in an even more painful, anguishing way. Not for nothing did French filibusters refer to sharks as *requins*—reportedly from requiems, masses for the dead.[23] However, pirates do not seem to have ever in fact deliberately fed their prisoners to sharks, although sharks did kill some crew, and probably slaves, who jumped overboard from the ship *Porcupine* when Bartholomew Roberts burned it.[24]

If Spaniards did not pay their city's ransom on time, filibusters might do as those with whom Raveneau de Lussan sailed the South Sea did in the late seventeenth century: decapitate a few hostages and send their heads to the dilatory Spanish officials.[25] Never mind the terror in the eyes and minds of the men as they waited to die. If buccaneers had a problem storming a castle, they might put Spanish prisoners in front of the attackers. Even so, buccaneers could not assume that the defenders would not fire. Often they would. They did so at Portobello in 1668 and at Arica in 1681, although in the latter case the prisoners, at a signal from the fort, escaped into a sally port.[26] If captured Spaniards refused to show a buccaneer crew the road to the hog yards they wanted to plunder for provisions, the buccaneers might tie them to wooden stakes and roast them "alive between two fires" as Rock the Brazilian did.[27]

A psychotic pirate or a sociopathic sea thief, one of which Ned Low surely was, might cut the ears and lips from prisoners whom he did not like, then broil the excised flesh and force the hapless prisoners to eat it. He might hang prisoners because he did not like their race or religion. For fun, he might haul them aloft, let them choke until they were almost dead, let them down for a moment, and then repeat the process until they were dead. And his crew? He might shoot one of them in his sleep because he disagreed with the pirate captain. Even so, the disturbed pirate captain might find himself marooned in a boat and then hanged if he was captured by English, French, Spanish, Dutch, or Portuguese authorities.[28]

And what of women and children? The Dutch edition of Exquemelin's *The Buccaneers of America*, published in 1678, provides many gruesome details of abuse, including rape and mothers being refused food for their infants. Some historians might argue that Exquemelin sensationalized the violence, in which case we can look elsewhere, for there are, sadly, many other examples. At the sack of Portobello by Henry Morgan in 1668, "a woman there was by some set bare upon a baking stone and roasted, because she did not confess of money which she had only in their conceit." John Style also wrote that he heard buccaneers boast of this, although one sick buccaneer, probably dying, did confess with "sorrow" to the torture and murder.[29]

At Veracruz in 1683, filibusters under the command of Laurens de Graff, Nicolas Van Horn, and the Sieur de Grammont, stripped women and children, along with men, shut them up in a church, and left them to suffer for days from thirst and hunger. Fray Juan de Avila recounted the screams in the church at night as pirates came and took whichever women prisoners they wanted, and raped them "without anyone stopping them." And if a husband had the temerity to protest, the pirates beat or even murdered him.[30]

Henry Every's crew raped the many women aboard the "Great Mogul" Aurangzeb's ship the "*Gunsway*" in 1695. According to an East India Company report, an old woman "they abused very much, and forced severall other Women, which Caused one person of Quality, his Wife and Nurse, to kill themselves to prevent the Husbands seing them (and their being) ravished."[31] An account by Mughal historian Khafi Khan, who had access to eyewitnesses, or at least to persons who had such access, provides similar corroboration: "When they had laden their ship, they brought the royal ship to shore near one of their settlements, and busied themselves for a week searching for plunder, stripping the men, and dishonouring [raping] the women, both old and young. They then left the ship, carrying off the men. Several honourable women, when they found an opportunity, threw them selves into the sea, to preserve their chastity, and some others killed themselves with knives and daggers."[32]

In 1698, Dirk Chivers, commanding the pirate ship *Soldado* in whose company were the *Mocha* Frigate and the "very leaky" *Pellican*, captured a rich pilgrim ship in the Red Sea. "The Women Passengers, about Sixty, were kept aboard, and inhumanly abused [raped]; to avoid which Indignity Five stabbed themselves."[33] In 1720, after Bartholomew Roberts plundered ships and fishing vessels at Trepassey harbor, he captured the brigantine *Essex*: the pirates "did him [the *Essex*] considerable damage, and abused [raped] several Women that was Passengers on Board."[34]

Even so, pirate prisoner William Snelgrave noted that the pirates who captured him had a rule that "should they take a Prize at Sea, that has any Women on board, no one dares, on pain of death, to force them against their Inclinations."[35] The rule, along with a "no women aboard in harbor" rule, was designed not to protect women, but to prevent disruptions among the crew over women: "This being a good political Rule to prevent disturbances amongst them, it is strictly observed."[36] However, considering the aggressive, alcohol-fueled sexism and cruelty of many pirates, it is likely that such rules about women prisoners often had little effect.

Probably not all pirates were so cruel, but invariably the pirate's priority was to satisfy his lusts—foremost for Spanish silver, but also for rum and women—first. A prisoner's needs always came second, if at all.

Pirate Cruelty in the Old and New Worlds

Occasionally, scholars question whether buccaneers, filibusters, and pirates in general were as brutal as they are described in some accounts. Would all pirates have thought nothing of making prisoners walk the plank, if in fact any ever did this, or of committing the tortures just described? Were their acts of torture sensationalized? Sensationalism sells, after all, then and now. Surely not all pirates were as cruel, or at least as often, or so the revisionist argument goes.

Some scholars also note that Spanish accounts often do not mention torture and rape by buccaneers or filibusters, although Fray de Avila clearly does. Unfortunately, ugly as it may seem, torture was relatively commonplace in the New World in the late seventeenth century, and it was only recently frowned upon in the Old—and there are plenty of eyewitness accounts to prove it. All European nations had a history of torture as a means of extracting criminal and religious confessions, as well as of learning the enemy's secrets. In the New World, slaves were tortured for infractions and put to death via horrible means—starving to death in cages, for example, or being crushed in the rollers of the cane press in a sugar mill.[37] Native American tribes were likewise often cruelly treated and sometimes even largely exterminated, and Europeans, both mariners and local inhabitants, were brutalized by sea rovers in the quest for wealth. To doubt that many a man will torture another in order to grow rich or win a battle—or sometimes, just because he can—is to ignore both history and, unfortunately, human nature.

However, in all of these journals, associated stories written at the time, and legal depositions of the pirates of the Golden Age, from 1655 to 1725, never is there even a hint that a plank "was run out over the gunwale, and lashed down," as Rafael Sabatini described was done to put Colonel Bishop, a greedy, cruel, pompous ass of a man, overboard in his famous 1922 novel *Captain Blood: His Odyssey*.[38] Never is there a suggestion that anyone was "made to walk the plank for their impudence," as in Sir Walter Scott's *The Pirate* exactly a century earlier.[39]

"A Plank Is Made Fast on the Gangway . . ."

But this does not mean that no one ever really walked the plank. In 1817 much of South America was aflame in social and political rebellion. General Simón Bolívar was leading an army and navy against Spain, trying to wrest loose a four-century hold on New Granada. Not only did many New Granadans flock to his banner, but soldiers of fortune and adventurous men of conscience from other nations did so as well. Blacks from Santo Domingo and escaped slaves from the various Spanish colonies joined the rebel ranks. Privateers, including Jean Lafitte (sometimes spelled Laffite) of New Orleans, put to sea under Colombian commissions in order to enrich themselves while also aiding the cause. Doubtless, though, profit was their foremost motive. Anyone's commission would have served.

In 1817 James Hackett, in company with other volunteers, sailed from Great Britain aboard the *Britannia* to join the ranks of the Independents of what is today Colombia and Venezuela fighting against the Royalists of Spain. Their surprise was palpable upon arrival. The Independent army was ill-equipped by modern standards, the climate was overbearing to those unaccustomed to it, and the customs of warfare were alien. One observer described the crews of Independent gunboats as "manned entirely by wild and savage-looking Indians" of both sexes, naked, painted with red ochre, and decorated with coconut fiber.[40] But this had little bearing on barbarity. The finely dressed—by European standards, that is—officers of Spanish men-of-war and privateers had already proved their barbarity at sea many times over.[41]

In that same year, 1817, a small merchant vessel proceeded to the Spanish Main. The captain could have been from any of many American nations or places. His crew was doubtless a mixture of races, nationalities, and languages. On "the Main," they traded with the Independents, provisions for mules. They put to sea and set a course for Trinidad, but before they arrived they were captured by a Spanish cruiser. The captain and crews of Royalist cruisers, like those of the Independents, often behaved no better than pirates.

The Spanish captain inspected the vessel's papers. The vessel, probably a schooner, rolled back and forth as it rose each time from the trough of the sea and over a rising swell. The mules brayed; the motion disturbed them. Under sail, the rolling and pitching was tolerable, but not now as the schooner lay by in the lee of the Spanish cruiser. From the schooner's papers the captain learned all he needed to know about the cargo. Mules from the Independents. The schooner was aiding the rebels. It mattered not whether this were for nothing more than mere profit, that the aid was not politically motivated. There was but one thing to do. No trial was necessary. Captain and crew must die, every single one of them.

James Hackett described the common process of murdering prisoners at sea: "It is a melancholy truth, that the sanguinary and ferocious character of the warfare, which has reflected lasting disgrace on the contending parties on the Continent of South America, also governs the proceedings of the hostile navies; the indiscriminate destruction of prisoners is most generally accomplished by compelling the ill-fated captives to pass through the ceremony, which is technically called *Walking the Plank*. For this purpose, a plank is made fast on the gang-way of the ship, with one end projecting some feet beyond the side; the wretched victims are then forced, in succession, to proceed along the fatal board, and precipitate themselves from its extremity into the ocean; whilst those who instinctively clinging to life hesitate prompt obedience to the brutal mandate, are soon compelled at the point of a spear to resign themselves to a watery grave, to avoid the aggravated cruelties of their inhuman conquerors."[42]

Hackett's book was published in 1818. Four years later, Sir Walter Scott published his book *The Pirate* in three small volumes. So famous was he that the book did not even give his name, merely that it was written by the author of *Waverly, Kenilworth*, and so forth. He mentions walking the plank only twice, and never as part of the plot, but only as a descriptive term in the dialogue. Probably he read Hackett's book and the barbarity of walking the plank was perhaps common knowledge by then. It needed no description. After this year there was an explosion in literary plank walking. Nearly every pirate story used the image, and when motion pictures came along so did they.

Still, the term was around before Hackett wrote his book. It was described in the 1788 edition of *The Classical Dictionary of the Vulgar Tongue* as "a mode of destroying devoted persons or officers in a mutiny on ship-board, by blindfolding them, and obliging them to walk on a plank laid over the ship's side; by this means, as the mutineers suppose, avoiding the penalty of murder."[43] Alas, there is no mention of pirates. Purportedly, the mutiny actually took place, but if it did, the details are still buried in old dusty records.

Three years later, in 1791, the term reared its ugly but soon-to-be-romantic head in the evidence given in support of a British bill to abolish the slave trade. Two Guinea-men (slave ships trading from the Guinea Coast of Africa to the Americas) smuggling slaves to Cuba in 1779 found themselves in distress, having consumed most of their water and provisions. They needed to go ashore for succor, and the Isle of Pines was nearby. And yet they did not. The captains had a purpose, but just as they were likely to implement it a British man-of-war, the HMS *Hunter*, arrived on the scene and gave aid to both the crew and its slave cargo. The aid was far more precious than the slaves knew.[44]

The British captain asked why the ships were in shoal water, and why, given its nearness, they had not released their slaves on the Isle of Pines. Because, they replied without hesitation, they would have lost their insurance on the slaves. Had the *Hunter* not shown up, the slavers' crews would have forced most of the slaves to "walk the plank"—to "jump overboard" and drown. Insurance would cover dead slaves.

But in fact, the phrase was probably not used by the men who were accused of preparing to make slaves practice it in 1779. Apparently, the captains did not know the meaning of the phrase, which was later inserted in the evidence. They did know, however, to force men over the side to die.

Whatever its origin, the idea of "walking the plank" is an ancient one. Storytellers have given us the mythical details, well established by 1830 in reference not to mutineers but to pirates: a plank lashed over the gunwale or out the gangway, the prisoner's hands tied behind his back, his eyes blindfolded. The crew forces him at cutlass point to make his way cautiously, fearfully out the plank, wondering each moment when he will fall into the sea and drown. Howard Pyle has romantically depicted this murder-in-progress.[45]

There was also a somewhat amusing use of the term, depending, of course, on one's point of view regarding sailors and rum. Aboard some nineteenth-century merchant ships, whenever a sailor appeared to be drunk, an officer would make him "walk the plank" to determine his fitness for duty. Ordered to the quarterdeck, he was made to try to walk a straight line along a plank. One such sailor reportedly gave the following reply to a question about his sobriety: "No, sir, I'm sober, only had *three* half-pints of rum between *two* of us all day, besides a few handfuls of beer." "Why, Tom, when do you call yourself *tipsy*?" "When I cannot walk straight upon a plank," said Tom. "Then of course when you *cannot* walk straight upon a plank you *must be drunk*." "No master, never drunk when I can hold on a rope." "Then when, in God's name, do you account yourself drunk?" "When I lay on my back and catch at the sky, swearing it is the main-top [the large platform on the mainmast] painted blue."[46]

Humorous drunken seamen notwithstanding, it is still hard even today to reconcile the reality of walking the plank with the steadfast image storytellers have implanted. The myth of pirates of the Golden Age forcing prisoners to walk the plank has become both accepted fact and escapist fantasy. Who among us has never jumped off a diving board when a child, pretending he or she was walking the plank at point of sword? Perhaps Captain Hook in *Peter Pan* sums it up best:

> "Yo ho, yo ho, the frisky plank
> You walks along it so,
> Till it goes down and you goes down
> To Davy Jones below!"[47]

But Peter can fly, Wendy and her brothers deserve a happy ending and so must not die, and the only danger the plank offers Hook himself is that of the crocodile waiting for him below—and Hook deserves his fate. For most people, this fantasy-myth is as close to the reality of pirate brutality as they ever want to come.

CHAPTER 5

"False Optics" and the Great Pirate Roberts

—∞∞∞—

"The Weymouth and Swallow Men of War carried the Pirates to Cape Coast, where they were tried and condemn'd, several of whom were hanging in Chains when I was there; others who upon Trial appear'd less criminal had the Favour of the Court to indent with the Company's Agents for Ten Years Servitude; one of whom I saw at Commenda, and was told he behaved very quietly and well."[1]
—William Smith, *A New Voyage to Guinea*, 1745

The pirate sloop sailed boldly into the harbor at Trepassey in Newfoundland on June 21, 1720, "her black colors flying, drums beating and trumpets sounding."[2] Surely all trembled at her sight, including the twenty-two larger vessels in the harbor, most of them sloops, all of them there to trade in cod caught by fishermen who tried to keep warm by drinking black strap, a concoction of spruce beer, made by boiling spruce or fir twigs, molasses, and yeast, fermented with rum and more molasses.[3]

The captain of the pirate sloop, perhaps dressed, as Charles Johnson described, in crimson damask waistcoat and breeches, with a red feather in his hat, gold chain and diamond cross around his neck, and two brace of pistols hanging from a silken sling slung over his shoulders pirate fashion, knew there were no great riches to be had here.[4] But there were provisions, sloops, and even a ship or two that could be fashioned for piratical purpose.

In the harbor, the crews of the larger vessels, which included a Bristol galley and the merchantman *Bideford Merchant*, all fled ashore at the sight of the eighty-ton pirate sloop, which was armed with only ten or twelve small cannon and no more than a hundred sixty men, and perhaps as few as sixty.

At least one man, though, considered fighting the pirates. The captain of the *Bideford Merchant* ordered his crew to make his ship ready for engaging, but cold feet—or a cowardly crew—took root, and both captain and crew abandoned the ship as it was, colors flying, guns loaded, all entirely prepared for battle except for the men required to do the actual fighting.[5] Perhaps the literal meaning of the harbor's name struck at them unconsciously. In French, a *trépassé* is a dead man.

There was little reason for the pirate captain's easy victory, and little excuse for those who ran away, surrendering the important fishery to the cutthroat pirate. As Governor Alexander Spotswood of Virginia would later put it, "Considering the boldness of this fellow, who last year with no more than a sloop of 10 guns and 60 men, ventured into Trepassey in Newfoundland where there were a great number of merchant ships, upwards of 1,200 men and 40 ps. of cannon, and yet for want of courage in this headless multitude, plundered and burnt divers ships there, and made such as he pleased prisoners . . ."[6]

The pirate's name was Bartholomew Roberts, although he was often known as John Roberts in documents of the day.[7] He had little experience as a pirate captain, yet he would become in a short time one of the most notorious of his era. Quickly he came to embody both myth and reality of pirate violence: of dread-inspiring Jolly Roger, grand piratical image, ship-to-ship battle, and cruelty both to cruel shipmaster and innocent seaman. Today he is considered by many to be, quite literally, "the greatest pirate of them all."[8] This honor—such as pirate honors are—is based largely on the four to five hundred vessels he captured during his short reign. Although we will examine this claim to fame shortly, even it cannot compare to some of the great pirates of antiquity, many of whose names are now lost to history, but whose numbers were counted by the tens of thousands, whose fleets were counted by the many hundreds, and whose depredations were stemmed only by the powerful naval fleets of grand states and great empires.[9]

Further, although Roberts was certainly the greatest pirate of this brief reign, there were pirates of the "modern age"—of the past four centuries—who were greater. Some buccaneers and filibusters of the late seventeenth century cruised longer and more successfully than he did. What they lacked in numbers of vessels captured at sea they made up for in towns and cities sacked, and in the occasional extraordinarily rich ship—and such ships usually put up a bloody fight. These earlier pirates sacked cities and fought aggressive Spanish men-of-war and great Spanish *urcas* (large, round-bellied cargo ships) ferrying rich payrolls or holds filled with dyes, dyewoods, chocolate, gemstones, and silver, among other New World riches. But not Roberts, not really. Indeed, only a few pirates of the early eighteenth century ever attacked powerful ships ready and willing to put up a stout fight. None ever sacked any significant town or city.

Further, we cannot forget Eastern pirates such as Kanhoji Angria of India, who was Roberts's contemporary, and Cheng I Sao of China, who came afterward and commanded a fleet of five hundred pirate junks.[10] Both of these pirates left far greater destruction in their wakes. Roberts was a great pirate, but was he the greatest pirate ever? To his fans, of course, he was. But in reality, he reigned as the "greatest pirate" only among the Western pirates of the early eighteenth century. Nonetheless, as one of the last great pirates of the Golden Age, and one who embodied the full range of myth and reality, a close look at Roberts is extraordinarily useful in understanding pirate violence, not to mention the many myths that grew up around men such as he.

Roberts put his crew to work immediately in Trepassey Harbor, plundering the sloops and ships. He ordered his men to cut down the masts of the *Bideford Merchant* and cut the ship's shrouds and anchor cables to pieces. He ordered the same of other vessels as well. His men fired the *Bideford Merchant*'s loaded guns, an exultation of the pirate over his prey, and a warning to all that they must not resist. The galley— a frigate-built ship that carried oars to use in calms or light winds—he converted to use as a pirate ship.

Accounts differ as to the destruction Roberts and his men wrought. According to Charles Johnson's famous early eighteenth-century book, *A General History of the Robberies and Murders of the Most Notorious Pirates*, Roberts's men burned the sloops and fishing shallops in the harbor, and they would have surged ashore, cutlass and pistol in hand, to destroy the cod-drying racks and warehouses filled with barrels of salt cod. But according to a newspaper report at the time, Roberts, other than the sloops and ships he clearly captured, only "made himself Master of the said Harbour, and the Ships there, being 22 Sail, and 250 Shallops," and threatened to burn everything as well as hang one of the ship or sloop captains for not being there to welcome him. The most damage his pirates did ashore was to get drunk with some of the fishermen. Roberts himself never went ashore.[11]

Trepassey Bay is more than fourteen miles wide at its mouth, and Trepassey Harbor within the bay is more than five miles deep: if the fishing boats were spread throughout even part of the bay or harbor, it would have been difficult if not impossible for the pirates to collect, plunder, and burn them all in the short time they were there, even if there were as many as one hundred sixty pirates, as one account has it, in a ten- or twelve-gun sloop. A more accurate number of the pirates who sailed into Trepassey is probably between sixty and one hundred. For a fact, though, according to the *Weekly Journal*, a contemporary newspaper, Roberts eventually "destroyed about 30 sail, French and English, on the [Grand] Banks."[12]

But this was not Roberts's greatest act of piracy, although it counts among his greatest. Greater, at least in terms of booty, was the capture of a rich Portuguese ship, which he soon lost when one of his officers mutinied and sailed away with it. Greater, again in terms of booty, were the dozen slave ships he captured at Whydah on the West African coast in 1722, most of which he held for ransom, including their cargoes of slaves. But it is this uncontested raid on Trepassey Harbor that put Roberts over the top when it comes to the claim of greatest pirate ever.

Barbarously Successful—But Not the Greatest

Here, in the cod-fishing harbor of Trepassey, is both the reason and the defect in the claim that Roberts was the "greatest pirate of them all."[13] The unofficial title is based on the four to five hundred vessels he captured during his short career from 1719 to 1722, not even three entire years. However, 250 of that number are the fishing shallops he trapped in Trepassey. But if we are going to credit Roberts with these 250 fishing boats, we might as well credit every town-capturing pirate, buccaneer, and privateer with the small craft they trapped in harbor, no matter how small the value, no matter whether they were plundered or not.

Harbors were always filled with canoes, piraguas, and boats used for fishing, ferrying goods, and local travel. If we add these, in leaps and bounds the number of vessels "captured" by town-raiding sea rovers would surge, surely leaving many to compete with Roberts's own famous but misleading number of four to five hundred.

It is far more accurate to estimate that the pirate Roberts captured or destroyed 200 to 250 vessels—still an extraordinary number—and add a footnote that he *may have* captured 250 small fishing boats in harbor, in the sense that they were there and he was in control, and he may have, but probably had not, wantonly destroyed as many as 150 of them as he did other vessels.

This wanton destruction leads us to two other myths regarding the "great pirate" Bartholomew Roberts. And he was indeed a great pirate! But both myth and scholarly but wishful thinking have blown the reality of his nature and piracies all out of proportion. First, pirates like Roberts are regarded by many of their fans and some scholars as abused seamen who rebelled and sought revenge on the merchants and shipmasters who had exploited them. However, more often than not, when pirates like Roberts pretended to be "dispensing justice" by abusing captains, the violence was arbitrary, having little if anything to do with a captain's behavior toward his crew, and more to do with whether the captain—or whoever was on the receiving end—had for any reason angered the pirates.[14]

In a typical example, Roberts is considered as a "dispenser of justice" against cruel captains and others because he "mercilessly" beat a surgeon, Thomas Tarlton, for refusing to aid a seaman marooned on the coast of Africa. Tarlton had even denied the seaman "a small supply of biscuit and salt meat." But Tarlton had refused to help the seaman, George Wilson, because he had seen him among the pirates of Roberts's crew and was certain he was a pirate himself. After Roberts and others beat Tarlton nearly to death, two pirates, Moody and Harper, went looking for him, intending to clap a pistol to his head and kill him, but several captured Liverpool seamen hid him under a staysail until the pirates' fury abated.[15]

Still, there may be some truth in the idea of pirates "dispensing justice" against cruel merchant captains, and of making a better life for themselves than they had had under these captains. But this neither explains nor excuses the excessive abuse pirates like Roberts inflicted upon the common seamen and fishermen they captured, of which there are numerous convincing accounts. One sums it up well: "Captain Roberts called the *Onslow* People aft, and asked who was willing to go [pirating], and who not? for he would force no body; therefore supposes they were at their choice; and afterwards told them, he saw they were willing, but wanted some force."[16] And thus the violence and abuse to convince the unwilling that they were in fact willing. Of the 165 of Roberts's men tried for their lives, 74 were acquitted. Most, if not all, were men who had served unwillingly in the pirate crews.[17]

How was the violence inflicted by pirates on their prisoners—violence inflicted either to convince prisoners to join their captors, or simply out of sheer cruelty—any different from the abuse some of them received at the hands of some merchant captains? It was worse. And if Roberts did in fact burn many or even all of the vessels in Trepassey Harbor and destroy the fisheries there, he was putting hundreds of common working men out of work and putting their well-being, even their lives and those of their families, in jeopardy. Anytime he destroyed a ship or robbed common seamen, he was harming the livelihoods of working men.

It is hard to excuse a pirate who claimed to be rebelling against the "disagreeable superiority of some masters he was acquainted with" when he in fact barbarously abused prisoners for refusing to join the pirates, or even for no reason at all except spite or pique. At times, Roberts even beat seamen and fishermen for *not* fighting back.[18] On at least one occasion, his crew was reported to have raped captured women passengers, although, again, it is popularly believed that Roberts respected women prisoners.[19] And in spite of a popular belief that he murdered no prisoners, at least two were shot for attempting to escape while he commanded. Some might argue that, strictly speaking, these two murdered men were not prisoners, but pirate crew, but most likely they were forced men, or men who had joined only after threats and abuse.[20] Even if they were not forced or intimidated into joining, the fact that Roberts and the men serving under him would put two of their shipmates to death after a "trial" for "desertion" is telling. The late seventeenth-century buccaneers permitted any member of a crew to leave at any time—but not so these "egalitarian" pirates of the early eighteenth century.[21]

In early 1721, Roberts sailed into Martinique and captured fourteen French sloops. He showed no sympathy toward their crews, for he "barbarously abused some they almost whip't to death others had their ears cut off others they fixed to the yard arms and fired at them as a mark and all their actions look'd like practicing of cruelty, and at last they sunk and burnt thirteen of the fourteen sail and let the other return with the poor tormented men to Martinique to tell the storie."[22] At roughly the same time, he whipped the chief mate of the *Lloyd Galley* "within an inch of his life, by reason he had conceal'd two gold rings in his pocket." So much for revenge against cruel captains only![23] The account of the trial of many of Roberts's crew is filled with similar abuse toward common seamen, much of it intended to intimidate them into joining the pirates.[24]

Close on the heels of the myth of Roberts as a violent rebel against merchants and merchant captains is the myth of Roberts as an antislavery pirate, or at least as a pirate who "despised the brutal ways of slave-trading captains."[25] To refer to him thus is misleading: Roberts was anti-captain in general, including anti–slave captain, as well as anti–common seaman and anti-slave. He especially hated any captain or crewman who dared fight when Roberts expected cowed surrender. There is no evidence that he despised slave-ship captains more than any other.

This myth of scholarly origin implies that Roberts despised the slave trade as well, but this is far from the truth. Like many pirates, Roberts took slaves into his crew, some perhaps as freemen, others as slaves: we will deal with the status of the large number of black men at times among his crew soon enough.[26] None of this stopped Roberts from trading in slaves, however, especially by holding slave ships and their slave cargoes for ransom. In no way could Roberts, or any pirate, be considered anti-slavery.[27]

At times, he treated these enslaved men, women, and children worse than he did merchant captains, their crews, and the common fishermen he captured and abused. In 1722, while on the coast of Africa, Roberts sailed boldly into Whydah Harbor, a noted and notorious "factory" for slave trading. Pronounced "hwhi-duh" (modern-day Ouidah, Benin), the port was noted at times for delivering as many as one thousand slaves per month to European traders. Roberts captured a dozen slave ships here, and he ransomed all but one.

The recalcitrant captain of this ship refused to pay sufficient ransom to Roberts. Ever the practical cutthroat, Roberts had to send a message: he would burn the ship. He set his men about unshackling the slaves below, but when he realized the process was taking too much of his time, he simply followed his cutthroat nature and ordered the slave ship *Porcupine* burned with a "considerable number of Negroes aboard." However, the burning of the ship may have had little to do with the time taken to unshackle slaves, for the pirates took the time to tar the ship's decks so that it would better take fire.[28]

Author Charles Johnson reported that roughly eighty burned to death, most still shackled in the fetid slave hold of the ship. Not only did Royal Navy Captain Chaloner Ogle corroborate this, noting in his report that Roberts had burned a cargo of slaves to death, but so did one of the *Porcupine*'s crew, Richard Wood, who joined the pirates but was later acquitted of piracy: "he was glad to get on board the Pyrate to save himself, many of the Negro Slaves being burnt or drowned, unable to help themselves being fetter'd."[29] Roberts was as likely to enter former slaves into his crew, in whatever capacity, as he was to treat them as mere cargo that could be destroyed as mindlessly as he might burn a fishing shallop that made up a common worker's livelihood.

Often, one hears of Bartholomew Roberts described as a fearsome pirate, as a real tough man in a fight. Surely, the reasoning goes, he must have been, for he captured so many ships. And we expect pirates to be tough, to be men of physical, personal violence. But successful pirate leadership did not always go hand in hand with hand-to-hand fighting ability. According to Charles Johnson, Captain Roberts, furious once with an insult given him by one of his drunken crew, ran the man through with a sword, killing him.[30]

And there might have been an end to it, except that one of the now dead man's friends, named Jones, suggested loudly to Roberts that the pirate captain be treated the same way. Roberts, recognizing a threat when he heard one, shoved his sword through Jones as well. But Jones was of far tougher stuff than either his dead shipmate or Roberts. Unarmed, his wound notwithstanding, and with Roberts still armed with a sword, Jones grabbed Roberts, threw him over a cannon, and beat the hell out of him.[31] Roberts was a successful pirate, but in the "badass" category he could not compare to the pirate Jones, who, unarmed and with a sword wound in his torso, gave his armed pirate captain a thorough thrashing.

As a side note, Roberts is often referred to today by the nickname or nom de guerre "Black Bart," a sinister sort of name suggesting violence, but there is no evidence that this name was ever used for him while he lived. Perhaps it derives in part from "Blackbeard"—whose name was reminiscent of Barbarossa or "Red Beard," the name of two great Barbary corsairs—and in part from the nineteenth-century Old West stagecoach robber Black Bart. Its ultimate origin is apparently a poem by Welshman

I. D. Hooson.[32] After all, Blackbeard had a wickedly descriptive name, so why not Bartholomew Roberts? And Roberts was described as a "Tall black Man," which at the time usually meant a white man of dark or olive complexion, or with black hair.[33] The old buccaneers and filibusters often had descriptive names, and so why not their heirs? Even "Ned Low," a contemporary of Roberts, has a ring to it, for example, and he was indeed a man of low parts and character. Roberts perhaps had no need of such figurative appellations: "the Great Pirate Roberts" and "the famous Captain Roberts," as he was at least once each described at the time, was more than sufficient.[34]

But most pirates were known by their deeds, not by a frightening name or fearsome visage. If a man becomes notorious enough, even a very common name and common face will serve to inspire fear. He need not be of stern mien or become known as "the Dread Pirate Roberts" of *The Princess Bride* fame to inspire fear. His deeds, or even mere reputation, will serve well enough. And so it was with Bartholomew Roberts and many others.

Roberts was not even the last of the great pirates of the Golden Age, as many books and "common knowledge" note. This honor belongs to Ned Low and Francis Spriggs, whose deaths, along with that of Roberts about two years before, were noted by governors, merchants, and merchant captains of the era as ending the reign of piracy that lasted from roughly 1716 to 1724.

Swinging Sun-Dried in a Sea Breeze

After Trepassey, Bartholomew Roberts led a long, successful cruise as a pirate captain, reportedly claiming as his motto, "A merry life and a short one."[35] He kept on the move, plundering another two hundred or more ships and sloops, always staying a step ahead of pirate-hunting men-of-war. The fact is, there were not very many men-of-war in pursuit, and often none at all. And on those rare occasions when he did engage them, he was happy to escape alive, and he was invariably furious as well.

Unfortunately for Roberts, the Royal Navy was bound to catch up to him sooner or later. His luck held for a long time, at least relative to the short reigns of pirates of the early eighteenth century, but luck never lasts forever. Fortune, invariably depicted as a woman in this era, always found, sooner or later, someone new to favor, leaving her to quickly forget the old.

In February 1722, we find Roberts at sea off the Guinea Coast of Africa, aboard his *Royal Fortune* in swift pursuit of a large ship flying French colors. Already Roberts recognized her for what she really was: the HMS *Swallow*, a fourth-rate pirate hunter bristling with two complete decks of great guns—eighteen-pounders on the lower deck, nine-pounders above, and smaller guns on the forecastle and quarterdeck. Already the *Swallow*, commanded by Chaloner Ogle, had captured Roberts's consort, the *Ranger*, luring her into range by sailing slovenly, with "bad Steerage" and "Tacks on Board, tho' before the Wind, and the Main-Yard braced."[36] Any capable seaman should have recognized that something was out of order. A broadside "alow and aloft" within musket shot made it clear who hunted whom. Now it was the *Royal Fortune*'s turn.[37]

According to Charles Johnson, Roberts intended to run alongside the *Swallow* at musket-shot range or closer—within 250 yards—and fire a broadside after receiving the *Swallow*'s. It was a grand gesture of bravado. A wiser captain would fire first, hoping to damage the *Swallow* enough to escape. But Roberts reportedly had other plans. If he could not escape after the broadside, he swore he would run his ship aground or board the *Swallow* and blow both ships to hell.

Roberts ranged his *Royal Fortune* alongside at pistol shot, a distance generally considered at sea to be yardarm to yardarm, his gun ports open.[38] Immediately, the *Swallow* struck her false French colors, hoisted her British naval ensign, and fired a thunderous broadside, shooting the pirate's mizzen topmast by the board and shattering some of his rigging. Almost certainly, no matter what Roberts is reported to have wished about receiving the first broadside, the highly trained British gun crews simply fired first—and brutally effectively.

Roberts ordered a broadside from the *Royal Fortune* forthwith. A cloud of gray-white smoke temporarily obscured the *Swallow*, but it was apparent that no real damage was done. Roberts ordered a swift retreat. After all, their great boasts notwithstanding, pirates were after money, not hard knocks, much less swinging lifeless in a sea breeze as a warning to seamen and a precarious perch for sea birds. The *Royal Fortune* bore away under as much sail as she could bear, the *Swallow* in swift pursuit.

For two and a half hours the ships fought a running fight at half–gunshot range, roughly 150 yards, the *Swallow* ranging on the *Royal Fortune*'s quarter as she could, firing chase guns and some of her bow guns into the pirate ship's hull and rigging. About two hours after the fight began, the *Swallow*, thanks to a favorable wind, came alongside and engaged again with full broadsides. Soon, the pirate's main-topmast was shot by the board. With its main-topmast gone, the pirate ship was effectively dead in the water, leaving her crew little choice but to surrender. Half an hour later they did. Roberts, however, did not witness his crew give up. He was already dead, having bled out his dark life after a grape-shot hit him in the throat. His body was now far behind, food for fishes, for his crew had thrown him overboard, per his wishes.

Of course, his crew did not blow up their ship and themselves all to hell, as many often promised they would do. Pirates almost never fought to the death or killed themselves rather than be captured, or even tried to. This is yet another pirate myth. A few pirates did fight to the death, notably Blackbeard and his part of his small crew. A few of Roberts's men did fire powder in the forecastle when capture was imminent: it scorched several terribly.[39] All but one lived to stand trial, as did those captured members of Blackbeard's crew who were said to have been ready to blow themselves up rather than be taken and hanged. Any of these pirates might have put pistols to their heads, yet they did not. Only two or three Golden Age pirates we know of ever did: Captain George Lowther and one of Charles Harris's crew each killed himself with a pistol, and one of Captain Phillips's crew apparently committed suicide by placing himself in front of the muzzle of a cannon, the bore unswabbed and vent unstopped, while he was ramming home a cartridge to fire a second signal.[40] The cartridge exploded and "blew him into pieces." [41] The rest of captured or about-to-be-captured pirates usually went meekly to trial—and the gallows.

Cutthroats as Folk Heroes

The early myths, strongly associated with violence and the cruelty of pirates such as Bartholomew Roberts and Edward "Blackbeard" Teach, helped turn them into folk heroes, which in turn exaggerated early myths, created new ones, and propagated all. Many of these pirates had indeed panache, flair, and style. In particular, they were larger than life, or at least so it seemed, and we like to believe they would have been easily picked out of a crowd. We see them as violent rebels, standing up to convention and armed authority, and herein lies their greatest appeal. They were everything that many people wish they were, or at least wish they were just a little bit, but almost never are.

Similar are the tales of Captain William Kidd, who failed as both pirate hunter and pirate, and was hanged—twice, actually, the rope breaking the first time—and of Henry Every, who captured one great ship, then escaped to England. Both men sailed during the late seventeenth century, and both had popular songs and even plays written about them. Folklore has elevated all of these men to heroic—even epic—status, and in so doing has exaggerated their deeds, sanitized many of their cruelties, and given them a far greater reputation than they deserve.

Indeed, it has turned Bartholomew Roberts, Blackbeard, William Kidd, and Henry Every into men persecuted by the powers that be. In these myths, Blackbeard was an innocent man "murdered" by the Royal Navy and the government of Virginia; Roberts hated slave-ship captains and was chased down and killed by the Royal Navy because he was interfering with the slave trade; Kidd was not a pirate nor even a would-be pirate, but a victim and scapegoat of government machinations; and Every was a true pirate king who got away with his great robbery, and in the popular mind retired wealthy—something most of us can only dream of.

The facts, however, speak otherwise. Roberts, who became a pirate simply for the thrill of it, hated all merchant captains and was anything but antislavery, having captured slaves for profit and having even burned part of a cargo of slaves to death. Blackbeard had, by many credible accounts, engaged in piracy after he had accepted amnesty. Kidd, although he was in fact made a political scapegoat, did attempt and even commit piracy. And Every was a pirate who had the good fortune to capture an extraordinarily rich ship whose women passengers his crew raped repeatedly, after which he fled across the sea to die in obscurity and, reportedly, poverty, a hunted, haunted man. Facts must often be revised or forgotten to elevate criminals into folk heroes, especially in the case of those men and women who singed the beard of the powers that be, only to wither or die at their hand in the end.

However we may judge these men, and occasionally women as well—as folk heroes who should be revered, or as cutthroat pirate scum who deserved to hang by the neck a hundred times—we should look beyond their fame or infamy and recognize one inalterable fact: these pirates left a legacy based on actual deeds, however misguided or misbegotten, however vainglorious or violent. Today, far too many people far too often revere celebrities of great fame but little if any substance. We can pass no such judgment on Blackbeard, Bartholomew Roberts, and other famous pirates, for while they have left us with grand, exaggerated images of themselves and their violence, these images are based in part on actual exploits, deeds, and crimes of great significance. They deserve their great place in the grand mythology of the sea.

CHAPTER 6

Epic Combat at Sea

—∞∞∞—

"[A]nd about eight or nine in the morning she came under our stern, ranging up our starboard quarter. Then our capt. ask'd, Where he was bound? He answer'd, Aboard us, the drummer beating a point of war. The captain told him, Win her, and have her. He thereupon boarded us for four or five hours, cutting our poop and ensign-staff, and his shot cut many of our shrouds. Our ship being very much pester'd, we play'd but three or four of our guns; yet we beat his gunnel in, and made him put off, and lie upon the careen."[1]
—Robert Everard, *A Relation of Three Years Sufferings*, 1693

None of the previous chapters' various descriptions, demythologizing, and demystifying of pirate violence should lead the reader to the conclusion that sea battles between pirates and prey or pirates and pirate hunters were never epic violent combats. In fact, one such sea battle has already been described, that of the buccaneers in canoes who fought Spanish pirate hunters in barks near Panama. Still, however brutal and courageous on both sides, this famous little battle, most of which was fought with musket, grenade, and firepot, is not quite what storytellers have led us to believe about pirates and sea battles. Is there, then, any truth to the Hollywood depiction of sea battles associated with

pirates? Of great ship-to-ship actions? Not of running fights but of brutal tactical engagements under sail, each ship and crew trying to batter
the other into submission or retreat? And if so, what brought these grand
engagements about? To examine these questions we turn first to April
1675.

The buccaneer captain aboard the tiny brigantine surely kept a close
eye on both his helmsman at the tiller and the prey in the offing. At first,
the small frigate commanding the buccaneer's rapt attention had kept to
her westerly course along the southern coast of Hispaniola, doubtless
observing in turn the tiny, faraway brigantine, revealed at first only by a
gray speck that was in reality a set of small sails rising slowly over the
horizon. The captain's Spanish counterpart wondered who was aboard
this tiny vessel, for any sail in the Caribbean could be an enemy, ranging
from a man-of-war to a pirate. Time would soon tell.[2]

The brigantine—so far unconfirmed by the Spanish captain as
belonging to a buccaneer or filibuster, common terms for the notorious
breed of Spanish-hunting Caribbean sea rovers—soon changed course,
intending to cut the Spaniard off. Only a cruiser—a pirate, privateer, or
man-of-war—would do this. The chase was on!

After England made peace with Spain in 1674 and "privateers," as the
buccaneer pirates of Jamaica were known, were outlawed, a man named
Bennett joined the crew of a Jamaica merchant brigantine trading to
Surinam—or so captain and crew probably claimed they were doing—but
soon turned pirate instead. At Petit Goave, the haven of French filibusters,
command was shifted to a man named Harris, who had the misfortune to
drown while trying to climb aboard the brigantine in heavy weather in
order to avoid capture by authorities at Petit Goave who sought him for
piracy. Jones, the original captain, had been captured ashore, imprisoned
on order of the governor, and died within twenty-four hours.

Bennett was elected to take Harris's place. He directed the brigantine
to Tortuga, received a French commission from the governor, and set out
to capture Spanish vessels. The English considered him a pirate commanding a brigantine he had "run away with"—stolen, thereby incur-
ring the governor's wrath—from Jamaica.

Bennett's brigantine might not have been much larger than the fifteen-ton *Virgin Queen* he had commanded as part of Henry Morgan's expedition against Panama a few years past.[3] If so, her deck was probably no more than thirty-five feet long and no more than eight or ten abeam, with a draft of but four or five. Bennett's crew was forty-five men, his armament just four small guns (cannon), and he was an Englishman unlawfully bearing a French privateering commission against Spain.[4]

Running from the brigantine was a small hired frigate, a *fragatella*, of fifty tons burthen—that is, a very small ship, three-masted, as ships by definition were, with swift, clean lines—bearing as much sail as she could. Still, at fifty tons she may have been two and a half times the size of the brigantine: her deck may have been sixty feet long, her beam twelve or thirteen, her draft six or seven. She was, unlike the brigantine, fairly well armed, perhaps with a handful of cannon of small caliber, probably three-pounders, and surely as many as a dozen swivel guns, which were small cannon mounted on a vessel's rails. The Spaniard was manned with sixty men, many of them soldiers, and for good reason, for aboard was the payroll, or *situado,* intended for the garrisons on Santo Domingo, the Spanish half of the island of Hispaniola, known today as Santo Domingo. And it was because of this rich cargo that the Spanish captain would fight only if he had no other choice. Only one thought was on his mind: escape. Then he'd sail as swiftly as possible to safety under the guns of the forts at Santo Domingo.

For the buccaneers, the small frigate would make an incredible prize, as close to being a real treasure ship with a reasonable prospect of capture as any of them might ever see. The payroll amounted to 46,471 pieces of eight, and there was probably some private silver aboard as well: enough to make forty-five men wealthy, even after deducting shares owed for disability compensation; carpenter's work; the surgeon's chest; provisioning the brigantine with food, supplies, and gunpowder; and the French king's 10 percent.

Put another way, there were enough silver coins aboard to fill fifteen and a half of the king's *cajónes de plata,* or treasure chests. Except for the captain, whose shares ranged from two to, rarely, as many as six depending on the articles he and the crew signed, plus a few more if he owned the buccaneer vessel, each man would receive one equal share, which might be as many as seven hundred pieces of eight in the case of this frigate—as much as the average seaman might make in seven or eight years.[5]

The details of the chase may have been lost to history. But however it transpired that the frigate's master, Bernardo Ferrer Espejo, recognized an enemy, he knew that duty required foremost that he protect his cargo. In other words, it was his duty to flee.

Chases were often all-day affairs. The Spanish captain would have longed for nightfall, for this was his best chance of escape. He would have given orders to the crew that there would be no lights after dusk, and when the night grew very dark—it would help if there were no moon, for moonlight glinted off sails, revealing the vessel—he would alter course, try not to run aground on the many coral reefs in the Caribbean, and eventually return to his original course to Santo Domingo. But Bennett was no fool, either. Even if the Spaniard managed to prolong the chase until darkness and slip away among the dark, tortuous waters of the Caribbean, Bennett knew the frigate would eventually have to turn back on course for the Spanish capital. If the frigate escaped, Bennett and his buccaneers need only sail toward Santo Domingo and lie in wait.[6]

And if the Spanish in Santo Domingo sent a sloop or small frigate after him? Bennett was prepared for a fight. When it came to pieces of eight and valuable cargoes of dyes and dyewoods, chocolate, tobacco, and other New World commodities, buccaneers and filibusters were unwilling to run unless defeat was likely. The two or three handfuls of buccaneers aboard the brigantine were not going to let anyone get in the way of nearly fifty thousand pieces of eight.

Of course, instead of running, the Spanish captain may have tried to bluff by sailing straight at the brigantine, cannon and muskets loaded, men ready to fight but many probably hoping they would not have to. The brigantine, after all, was so small that it could not be manned with more men than the frigate. Surely the brigantine's captain and crew, if they were indeed buccaneers or filibusters, would choose to seek weaker prey when they saw the frigate fearlessly approaching.

Either scenario could have happened, or even several others. But whichever actually did, the brigantine had probably lain in wait off Santo Domingo, just over the horizon, often with only its lower sails set. It may have lurked here for weeks if it had intelligence of the *situado* ship. The most common route for Spanish vessels from Havana to Santo Domingo was north along the east Florida coast, then northeast once the reefs and islands of the Bahamas were safely past, then east into the Atlantic, and finally south to the Mona Passage between Hispaniola and Puerto Rico. It was a long route, yet was considered safer (especially March through June) than beating to windward south of Cuba and Hispaniola.[7]

Bennett's brigantine may even have scouted near the coastline at times, its sails furled with light, easily broken line so that they could be quickly set, making it difficult for the frigate or any other vessel to spot it against the backdrop of the great island of Hispaniola. One thing it did not do was cruise on the open sea for prey. Only by accident could a pirate find another vessel there.

The buccaneer crew may even have come across the frigate opportunistically, but it is more likely that they had been expecting the frigate for weeks, having learned of its general timing by their usual intelligence methods. They bartered and bribed for information while trading with Spaniards; they brutally interrogated Spaniards captured during attacks at sea and ashore, torturing them and threatening them with death if they refused to talk or were not believed; and they sometimes received information from Jewish merchants who helped manage much of the trade in the region.[8]

On deck, the buccaneer captain had waited patiently for the cry of "A sail! A sail!" Each time he heard this cry, he shouted aloft, "How stands she?" and then barked orders for the chase. And then he had waited patiently in anticipation, perhaps irritated at the amount of time it would take to discover what kind of vessel he chased, perhaps irritated at the way the helmsman steered or the way his crew set and trimmed the sails. He and his crew itched for Spanish silver, and this chase, if successful, would go a long way toward scratching that itch.

Blades and Wit Sparking

The anticipation notwithstanding, we all know how the chase will end according to the myth, at least if the pirate catches up with its prey. There will be a fight. Broadsides will blaze, buccaneers will swing from the rigging and swarm onto the enemy's decks, and, after the attackers hack and slash with cutlasses for a few minutes, the Spaniard will strike its colors.

Captain Bennett conning the brigantine—giving orders to the helmsman—was a veteran seaman and sea warrior, intrepid and aggressive and no fool. During the expedition against Panama in 1670, he had commanded the *Virgin Queen*, a tiny, fifteen-ton vessel armed with no cannon but manned with thirty courageous, violent men fully ready to sack one of the greatest cities on the Spanish Main.[9] Bennett was a strong leader and expert tactician, and the small complement of men in the tiny buccaneer brigantine was happy to follow him in his attacks against much larger, much better-manned vessels—provided, of course, that the payoff was worth the risk.

Slowly or quickly, inexorably or with enough speed that both crews stumbled over themselves in order to make their vessels ready for engaging in time, the Spanish frigate and buccaneer brigantine came within a hundred yards, well within range of the long-barreled muskets known as *fusils boucanier*, or "buccaneer guns," and well within point-blank range of the Spanish cannon.

There are few people who have lived in modern society for the past hundred years who are not familiar with the striking image of what surely must happen next. The rakish pirate vessel blazes away, broadside to broadside, against the vile Spanish frigate whose fearful crew puts up a valiant defense in spite of the odds against them. The black flag with skull and bones flies erect and snapping in the strong breeze as the two vessels under full sail spit flame and iron at each other at close range. Round shot (cannonballs) shatter masts, yards, and rigging and send them crashing down to crack the skulls of men below. The crews wave cutlasses defiantly at each other, each swearing to slaughter the other, but the outcome, as we all well know and expect, is inevitable.

The pirate brigantine edges in toward the prey, grappling hooks arc through the air, and soon the pirates board. Some leap from ship to ship while others swing spectacularly through the air from ropes all too conveniently placed. On the deck of the innocent merchantman or venal Spaniard—or so Hollywood would have us believe—the crews engage in a melee of clashing cutlasses and the occasional crack of pistol. The fight is soon over, often after the ships' captains engage each other with rapiers, blades and wit sparking and riposting, until the pirate commander swiftly slips his steel point to his enemy's throat and orders him to surrender.

So powerfully has this image been imprinted on us that we believe in it religiously: the pirate prey always fights back, the battles are always epic, and every fight ends with steel upon steel on open decks. And indeed, it seems a glorious image, providing, of course, that we ignore the blood washing across the decks and out the scuppers into the sea.

But the battle we expect did not happen. The *Buen Jesús de las Almas* simply struck her colors, probably the red cross of Burgundy on a white background, or perhaps a Spanish royal ensign. There may have been a brief running fight, buccaneers firing nonstop at the decks and gun ports of the fleeing frigate, forcing its crew to keep under cover, unable to return fire. Indeed, only during such running fights would we see vessels under full sail. In any other fight, they sailed only under topsails, perhaps the fore course, and perhaps a fore and aft sail as necessary—fighting sails, those that could be manned with a small number of men. There was no black flag to cast fear, either; as we have already seen, it would not be used by Caribbean pirates until the next century.

The fact is, most pirates of all ages captured their prey by intimidating them into surrender. The great sea battles of Golden Age pirates (1655 to 1725) we are accustomed to seeing on the big screen were actually few and far between, and most were fought in the late seventeenth century between buccaneers or filibusters and Spanish merchantmen and men-of-war. Pirates used speed, ambush, or ruse to get close, and once they were in range, the mere threat of force was usually sufficient to induce surrender. In the early eighteenth century, pirates used the various black flags with depictions of skull and crossed bones or full skeletons to great effect. The end result was that most pirate prey surrendered without a fight. And if the prey were too "stout," often—but not always!—pirates sailed away, seeking easier prey or a better plan.

The myth of *every* pirate attack at sea being a battle of Hollywood proportion is just that, a myth, like the myth of pirate ships bombarding Spanish forts into submission, followed by pirate crews surging ashore to loot the town. In fact, the guns of pirate ships were too small and too few to damage a fort of any significance. Most Spanish forts could easily have sunk any pirate ship foolish enough to engage them. A good-sized ship was required to successfully attack even a small battery or very small fort. Henry Morgan was ecstatic at the assignment of the fifth-rate HMS *Oxford* to him in 1669, "for he had not a single vessel in his fleet fit to prevail against a fort if the need arose."[10] Unfortunately, the ship exploded, killing most of the men aboard, Henry Morgan and a handful of others excepted, before it had a chance to engage anything. In any case it could only have prevailed against a very small fort.

In 1686, the English fifth-rate HMS *Falcon* of thirty-six guns and the sixth-rate HMS *Drake* of sixteen guns expended nearly all of their powder in a two-day cannonade to destroy the pirate Banister's ship and his makeshift battery ashore at the Bay of Samana. Both English men-of-war received damage, lost twenty-three men between them, and, due to a combination of shallow water and enemy fire, could not approach Banister's careened ship (although they had shot her to pieces) to burn her—all against what was nothing more than great guns mounted behind a rude earthwork, and pirates armed with muskets.[11]

Also in 1686, the thirty-six gun HMS *Dartmouth* barely escaped from under the guns of the Castillo San Felipe del Morro, the great fortification at San Juan, Puerto Rico, after seeking a Spanish pirate but being rebuffed by the governor and ordered instead to proceed into Spanish custody: "The forts at once opened fire, which I returned until we were out of range. There were one hundred and fifty guns bearing on the ship, several batteries to pass, the shore lined with small shot, and the channel so narrow that we were forced to go within pistol shot. Two of my men were killed and two more wounded; the ship had several shots right through her, fifty shot through her foresail, and most of her running rigging shot away." This was the damage from doing nothing more than running away and living to fight another day. Had she stayed to fight, the HMS *Dartmouth* would have been sunk.[12]

Even so, ships did sometimes successfully cannonade Spanish Caribbean forts. Of the first plundering attack on a Spanish town following the capture of Port Royal in 1655, one eyewitness wrote that "Wee lately with 120 men and 12 frigotts tooke the towne of St. Martha on the Terra firma, where were 2 castles containing 32 piece of ordnance, out of which wee beat the enemie by our ordnance . . ."[13] The term "castles" can be a bit misleading, however. Here it has been used as a euphemism for fortifications of any size, and perhaps as a bit of exaggeration on the part of the writer as well. The defenses at Santa Marta were in fact fairly rudimentary. The San Vincente "castle," for example, consisted only of a very small, low rectangular fort or "*plataforma*" surrounded by a triangular wooden palisade with a few additional gunports.[14]

Our idea of pirate ships routinely defeating forts is probably due to Rafael Sabatini's *Captain Blood*, and he probably got the idea from the French expedition against Cartagena in 1697, but the vessels that bombarded the Spanish forts were great ships of the line, and bomb vessels as well. Sabatini may also have been influenced by Clement Downing's history of the Indian wars, in which East India Company men-of-war attack Indian forts, but these forts were usually poorly defended. The myth was expanded to an audience of many millions, first by the 1935 film version of *Captain Blood*, then by Disney's Pirates of the Caribbean attraction, whose duel between ship and fort owes much to the film.[15]

Instead, pirates typically landed ashore in secret, marched by night to the town, and stormed the walls of forts and castles. Here, ashore, not at sea, ship against ship or ship against fort, did they fight most of their great battles—and these land battles were fought only by the buccaneers of the second half of the seventeenth century, not by the pirates of the early eighteenth.

As for Captain Bennett, his victory was of the common sort against an uncommon prize. Indeed, so easy was Bennett's victory that Spanish authorities accused the frigate's master, Ferrer Espejo, of complicity and arrested him. As for Bennett, he was suddenly rich, or at least very well-off, at least for the time being. The capture of the *situado* frigate had come as most prizes did, with a lot of work but without a real fight. Yet this prize should never have been taken so easily.

Siege Warfare at Sea

Obviously, though, not all chases at sea ended without a fight, or without much of one. There were indeed bloody battles great and small between pirates and pirate hunters, between pirates and courageous merchant captains and crews, and between pirates and treasure-bearing Spanish men-of-war. They were in the minority, but they were real, at times epic, and they are the true source of the myth of every pirate attack being a classic Hollywood-style sea battle. However, even they were not usually fought as we see on the big screen.

Continuing our tale of Captain Bennett, soon after he captured the *Buen Jesús de las Almas*, he happened upon a shipwrecked Henry Morgan—now Sir Henry Morgan—on Île-à-Vache.

Sir Henry advised him not to return to Jamaica yet, but to take his prize instead to Petit Goave. A year or so later we find Bennett, buoyed by his success against such great odds, where he is in the company of Bernard Le Moigne, a French filibuster captain, and his crew of the powerful *Toison d'Or (Golden Fleece)*. With Le Moigne's ship is a consort vessel, the *Toison* (Fleece), possibly commanded by Bennett, but just as likely Bennett was serving in a lesser capacity aboard one of the ships.[16] Their goal: to capture the rich Honduras *urca* known as the "*gran*" (great) *San Pablo*—built in Ostend, 477 tons—and her *patache*, or scouting consort, the *Nuestra Señora de Agua Santa y San Francisco Sales*.[17]

Not long past, Bennett had been a pariah in the eyes of the Jamaican government, but as soon as Sir Henry Morgan had established his presence in Port Royal, Jamaica, as lieutenant governor, he had assured

Bennett, as well as other English and French buccaneers, of their welcome in Jamaica—and doubtless of the welcome of the *urca*'s silver and goods as well. Bennett even lawfully sold the brigantine in Port Royal.[18]

The filibuster vessels, under French colors and commission, first set sail to Trujillo in the Gulf of Honduras, seeking the Honduras prize. Here they found and captured the *Concordia* instead, a twenty-two-gun frigate intended as reinforcement for their ultimate prey, a great *urca* often of seven or eight hundred tons, filled with New World riches: indigo and achiote dyes, chocolate and medicines, and, of course, silver, much of it in the form of pieces of eight. The Dutch, who invented the ship, referred to such great round-bellied flat-bottomed cargo carriers as fluyts; the English referred to the Honduras *urca* as the "hulk," probably because it was large and hulk sounds a lot like *urca*. And the "hulk," with her high sides and steep tumblehome that would have made her difficult to board, was a floating fortification.[19]

Bennett, as we have already established, was no fool, but there is often but a hairbreadth difference between a fool and a hero. The French sea rovers were well-manned. Not for Captain Bennett a mere forty-five men this time! Bennett was in command of either the *Toison*, if her captain had taken command of the prize, or the more powerful *Concordia* itself. Here were three vessels arrayed against the *urca* and its *patache*, with sixty-two great guns and surely more than four hundred men. There was no way they could lose.

Pirates had two means of attacking a ship at sea: pummel it from long range with great guns and muskets, then, when the prey's sails and rigging were shattered, when many of its crew were dead or bleeding their lives away or were filled with splinters and lead, too injured to fight back, board and finish the job. But pirates did not swing from ship to ship; the myth originated with Hollywood, perhaps inspired by a line in James Fenimore Cooper's *The Red Rover: A Tale*, in which a pirate captain swings from the poop deck to quell a mutiny below.[20] Or perhaps it was just a Hollywood director who had the original idea.

In reality, pirates leaped from their forecastle to the other ship, often from the fore chains to the enemy's main chains, with a brave soul or two leaping from the cathead, and then into the waist between forecastle and quarterdeck, first tossing grenades and firepots aboard to maim or kill as many defenders as possible. If the Spanish crewmen were still on deck, the filibusters engaged them hand to hand in a bloody melee, pistols cracking and filling the air with smoke and cutlasses swinging and cleaving ears from heads and sometimes heads from torsos.

The other way to capture a ship that fought back was to close swiftly, as with any other prey, keeping low to the deck to stay under cover, firing muskets to suppress the enemy, then board and attack the enemy who had retreated to "closed quarters," a form of siege warfare at sea. The pirates would hack holes in the decks with boarding axes and iron crows and toss firepots and grenades into the holes to burn and choke the crew within, forcing them either to surrender or to die one at a time as they tried to sally forth from the hell created when gunpowder ignited in the confined space 'tween decks.

Often, pirates would try not to attack the Honduras *urca* itself, but would attack the storehouses up the Rio Dulce instead. Unfortunately, the storehouses up the river at Lake Izabal were already empty, their goods now aboard the *urca* at Puerto Cavallos for safety, rather than at the usual port, Trujillo. Aware that pirates were looking for the ship, the authorities removed her cargo and built a fortified platform with twelve cannon from the *urca* to defend the port and town. Eventually, or so it was believed, the pirates would leave.

But the sea rover captains were patient, and instead of seeking other prey, they holed up at Roatán Island nearby. It was three months after the capture of the *Concordia* that the great Honduras *urca* and its patache finally sailed. We have only two sparse accounts of Bennett and his consorts' fight against the hulk, but we have enough similar accounts—and we know how the battle ended—to describe with great certainty what probably happened. The best way to capture the hulk was to take it at anchor by surprise after Native Americans, *mestizos* (people of mixed Spanish and Native American blood), and African slaves loaded the rich cargo aboard. Every pirate knew this. Timing was everything, for if the local Spaniards got word that pirates were in the area, they might unload the hulk and send the cargo ashore, as they had already done once, or set sail immediately if the *urca* was already loaded. And set sail is what the hulk and her consort did.

Bennett and his consorts set out in pursuit. Finally, in the Gulf of Mexico, they espied their prey. Sighting the pirates—or rather, the buccaneers and filibusters who were today legitimate privateers flying the white ensign of France, although to the Spanish they were but thieving pirate dogs, and many of them Protestants at that—the Spanish crew "made ready for engaging" the enemy.

Surely the pirates fired many broadsides at the great ship, but the small artillery of most pirates and privateers could not do much damage to such thick, tall sides.

"Let them blaze away with their little guns!" Captain Mateo Perez de Garay might have shouted. "They must board us to capture us, and this they will never do!"

The Spanish gunners wrought havoc on the three well-armed attacking ships and their large crews anyway.[21] Quite likely the three vessels attempted to close on the hulk and prepare for boarding, for this was the most common filibuster tactic at sea. But filibuster musketry could do little to clear the high decks—ranging from twelve to twenty-five feet or more above the water—of men. Coming alongside under a withering fire from Spanish musketeers and great guns—if indeed they managed to come alongside at all!—Bennett and his buccaneers and filibusters were surely met with a hail of "fireworks."

Spanish defenders would have hurled iron grenades, burning torches, firepots, fat incendiary fuses called *saucissons* (sausages), and perhaps even powder kegs wrapped with slow match, which would ignite the many pounds of powder inside when the cask hit the deck and burst down upon pirate heads.

The bombs and incendiaries would burn many buccaneers to the bone and send shards of iron fragmentation into the flesh of others. The burns would have been the worst injuries, immediately incapacitating many men, leaving them screaming in pain, although those with the worst burns might have felt relatively little pain at all, their nerves having been severely torched.

Bennett, so successful against the *situado* frigate, whose crew outnumbered his three to one but fought little, if at all, would not fare so well today. Reckless valor cannot always carry the day, nor even can careful planning. With the loss of many pirates—or more correctly, privateers, more or less, at least for the moment—the attackers broke off the engagement.

Fray Francisco Ximénez, the late seventeenth-century Guatemalan historian and chronicler, wrote of the "Gran San Pablo . . . which encountered the enemy, who had three men-of-war. From all of them she defended herself, and maltreated them much, in spite of carrying much merchandise from the realm of Guatemala."[22] But the *Gran San Pablo* was not yet done with enemies. Off the coast of Spain, she was attacked by a fleet of Barbary corsairs—and she beat them off, too. Her crew believed that Santa Rosa (de Lima) kept them safe, for aboard were one thousand pieces of eight to buy stained glass for her namesake church. Doubtless the courage, leadership, seamanship, and martial skill of her captain played a great role as well.[23]

An English report from 1677 summed up the battle just as succinctly: "[T]wo French vessels lately well beaten by a Spanish hulk in the Gulf of Mexico with the loss of eighty men, Captain Bennett killed in the engagement."[24]

Myth and Reality Almost as One

But it is not Captain Bennett, nor the tactics he and the French filibusters used, although together they are indeed a fine example of the fierce Hollywood-style battles between pirates and their prey, that concern us now. Rather, the story carries us to another man, Dutchman Laurens-Cornille Baldran, who would later style himself "Sieur de Graff."[25]

Laurens de Graff, as he came to be known and whose connection to Captain Bennett we will explain shortly, would one day become in reality everything we have come to expect of a Hollywood pirate captain, outclassing by far his heirs such as Blackbeard and Bartholomew Roberts. De Graff was a true swashbuckler, with an appearance to match: tall, blond, handsome, with a mustache in the Spanish style, one with long, pointed handlebar ends. When he went ashore after he became famous, he was accompanied by musicians playing violins and trumpets, and by a crowd of admirers. Doubtless de Graff dressed in rakish finery, perhaps even in the Spanish style. From a sword belt hung a serviceable sword that he knew how to wield well. De Graff spoke Dutch, Spanish, and French fluently. According to buccaneer-surgeon Alexandre Exquemelin, he believed anything was possible, and once he set his mind on something, many believed it was as good as done.[26]

The French referred to him as Capitaine Laurent, the English as Captain Laurence. But the Spanish called him Lorencillo, which means "Little Lorenzo," Lorenzo being the Spanish version of his name. It was an affectionate nickname, an endearment, and did not necessarily refer to actual physical stature, although some Spanish detractors have described de Graff as short, thus the diminutive name. Most likely, the nickname dated to his days as a gunner in the service of Spain and had nothing to do with stature, or only in its opposite sense. It may have been intended in the same way as the nickname "Little John" was for Robin Hood's giant companion.

De Graff had, by most accounts at the time, served as a gunner in Spain's Armada de Barlovento.[27] Strictly speaking, he would have required a special license or a blind eye turned by Spanish officials in order both to sail to the New World and to remain there, but good gunners were always in demand and this would not have been a problem to arrange. Spanish gunners aboard the treasure fleets, armadas, and registry ships (ships licensed to sail independently of the treasure fleets) were swashbuckling men of special stature. So valuable were they to the protection of Spanish treasure that they could not be arrested for debt, they could bear swords and firearms, they could be tried for crimes only by the General of Artillery or his lieutenant, they could wear what clothing they pleased, ignoring Spanish sumptuary laws that restricted certain clothing and jewelry to certain classes, and they received numerous other protections and special privileges as well.[28] De Graff was a swashbuckling seafarer long before he became a pirate.

According to the popular history, in Veracruz de Graff joined the pirate-hunting Armada de Barlovento and served it for three years. Then, one day, buccaneers or filibusters captured his ship and carried it to Saint-Domingue, doubtless to Petit Goave, or so the story goes. But the fact is, Caribbean pirates and privateers captured no ships of the Armada de Barlovento in 1675 or 1676, the approximate time French records state that he became a filibuster or pirate. Indeed, buccaneers and filibusters always steered clear of the pirate-hunting fleet.

So is it a mere myth that de Graff's ship was captured by filibusters? The story has a romantic notion to it, making us want to believe it. It seems to be right out of the plot of a Hollywood swashbuckler, the idea of a seaman in the service of Spain being captured by pirates and then turning pirate. Is it indeed possible? It must be, for we have seen the movie already, or imagine we have.

Recalling the *Buen Jesús de las Almas*, we noted that it was a *situado* ship. The *situado*, or payrolls and other subsidies, were doled out sparingly and often years late from Spanish coffers. The treasure was ferried by the Armada de Barlovento from Veracruz to Havana, where it was separated into smaller quantities according to destination, and then loaded aboard smaller men-of-war, which then ferried each *situado*.[29]

We mentioned earlier that the pirates Bennett sailed with captured a well-armed ship named *Concordia*, and it, along with the *Buen Jesús de las Almas*, are in fact the only likely candidates for a ship associated with the Armada de Barlovento or Spanish escorts and pirate hunters to have been captured by buccaneers or filibusters around this time. Given the circumstances, it is very likely that Laurens de Graff was a gunner aboard one of these ships, and in fact one historian has uncovered sufficient evidence to place de Graff aboard the *Concordia* when she was captured on October 6, 1676. Seizing the moment, de Graff volunteered to serve with his captors—and might very well have fought in the attack against the *Gran San Pablo*. If so, he would have first established his credentials as a gunner and a leader here.[30]

De Graff was already an extraordinarily talented fighting seaman with long experience, probably aboard Dutch ships and almost certainly aboard a Spanish registry ship trading from the Canary Islands to Havana, where upon one voyage the ship and its cargo were impounded, and some officers arrested, in the Spanish city on charges of smuggling— a common practice, smuggling—and de Graff was left to seek other employment.[31] Spanish gunners were highly qualified and had to pass a rigorous certification. At sea, they serviced and manned the great guns and also took their turns at the helm, thus they also knew much of seamanship. Dutch gunners, whose profession de Graff surely followed before he set sail with the Spanish, were also highly qualified and much in demand, just like English gunners, perhaps even more so than their Spanish counterparts. Add all of this together, not forgetting that de Graff doubtless knew the Caribbean well and had learned how the Armada de Barlovento and other Spanish pirate hunters operated and fought, and we have a man who could one day be a great pirate hunter— or a great pirate.

De Graff set out quickly to become the latter, although he would have referred to himself only as a filibuster, never as a pirate. His successes came rapidly. By late 1678 or early 1679 he commanded a *barque longue* and soon after captured a small ship. With it in 1681 he captured a small Dutch merchantman from Amsterdam, *De Tijger* (the *Tiger*), of twelve guns. He mounted it with sixteen more, and retained the ship's fierce name, altering it only to make it French, *Le Tigre*. With a ship of twenty-eight guns, a *barque longue*, and a crew of two hundred or more between them, de Graff was a force to be reckoned with. He was now the most powerful pirate in the Caribbean.[32]

Indeed, so quickly had his reputation grown that Sir Henry Morgan, who knew a thing or two about great pirates, dispatched the HMS *Norwich*, a small fifth-rate of 250 tons and roughly twenty-eight guns, accompanied by a sloop captured from the pirate Everson and now manned with pirate hunters, to capture the "great and mischievous pirate" whom he referred to as "Laurence." To the frigate's crew he added forty veteran soldiers "that the frigate might be the better able to deal with him [de Graff] and to free him [the frigate] from danger of being worsted or taken." But the HMS *Norwich* never encountered *Le Tigre*.[33]

In 1682, putting his firsthand knowledge of Spanish tactics to use, de Graff ambushed a ship of the great pirate-hunting flotilla. Called *Francesa*, her real name was the *Santíssimo Sacramento*. She was a French prize frigate of 240 tons now in the service of Spain. Aboard were the *situados* bound for Santo Domingo, Puerto Rico, and, according to one document, Santiago de Cuba—120,000 pieces of eight!

De Graff lay in wait in the Mona Passage near Puerto Rico. Sighting the Spanish man-of-war, he immediately gave chase in his *Tigre*—and the Spanish man-of-war, in spite of being manned with 250 men and armed with twenty-six great guns and ten swivel guns, ran. Again, a *situado* frigate's duty was to protect its cargo at all cost. *Tigre* chased *Francesa* through the Mona Passage toward Santo Domingo. De Graff's feline vessel was clean and swift, but so was *Francesa*.

East of Hispaniola, *Tigre* caught up with the *Francesa* and engaged her. De Graff was a magnificent gunner, and he had trained his crew of one hundred or a few more well. He did not close with the Spaniard and attempt to board, for this might be suicide given the size of the Spanish crew. Instead, he wielded his ship like a sword, maneuvering and striking to best advantage, crossing his enemy's bow and stern whenever he could, raking the *Francesa* fore and aft. His great guns cut rigging, tore sails, and splintered yards. Never did he let the Spaniard get close enough to board, for this was the enemy's strength. He "maintained a stout fight at a distance," guns blazing away, battering the Spaniard.[34]

The Spaniard fought back just as stoutly, but much less effectively. At first, the ship was hindered by its cluttered decks, which had to be cleared to work the guns. After a couple of hours, de Graff had lost eight or nine men killed and sixteen or seventeen wounded. But aboard *La Francesa*, fifty or more lay dead or in need of the surgeon's knife. The ship itself was well battered and likely to become a floating hulk soon. If *La Francesa* could not maneuver, then the fight was over. As was written in 1684 of a fight between buccaneers commanded by Bartholomew Português and a twenty-gun Spanish ship, "For some body must be beaten, and it seems the Pyrate would not, therefore the others must," so it went in the case of de Graff versus the Spanish captain, Manuel Delgado.[35] Wounded in the upper thigh and with his belly "somewhat torn by a great shot from one of Laurence's quarter-deck guns," Delgado surrendered to spare his men the inevitable slaughter.[36] De Graff graciously put the captain ashore, along with a surgeon and a servant to attend him.

The Dutch filibuster's feat was incredible: he had captured a Spanish man-of-war, not merely an armed Spanish escort or hired ship outfitted to chase pirates, but one of the Armada de Barlovento itself, the great Spanish pirate-hunting fleet. He was one of only two Caribbean rovers who ever did, the other being Henry Morgan, who did so at Maracaibo. More important, he was the only one of his era ever to capture a ship of the Armada de Barlovento after a true ship-to-ship engagement, and he was one of the few who probably could have. Most pirates never had to engage in pitched Hollywood-style battles when they captured their prey, although the myth would have us believe they always did. Yet a few pirates truly did fight and win on this epic scale, and de Graff was one of them.

When the plunder was shared, each man's share came to seven hundred pieces of eight. De Graff mounted *La Francesa* with thirty guns and made her name French, *La Françoise*. The Spanish viceroy was livid, and so were his superiors in Spain. But de Graff would yet anger and humiliate them even more.

In May of 1683 he was one of the leaders of the brutal sack of the port city of Veracruz, Mexico, and in December of the same year he again put his skill to effective use in another great sea battle. This time, sailing in the company of Captains Andresson, aka Michel (who may have later commanded at Acaponeta, described earlier), and Jan Willems, aka Yanky, not to mention several others, de Graff sailed to the coast of Cartagena to cruise upon the Spanish. This impudent threat was too much for the Spanish authorities to bear. Don Juan Pando de Estrada, "Governor and Captain General of the City of Cartagena de Indias," had fitted out two powerful new slave frigates newly arrived. The frigates belonged to the *asiento de negros* (slave monopoly) granted to Juan Barroso de Pozo and Nicolas Porcia, and had just carried both Porcia and the new governor himself to the great city: the *San Francisco Javier y San Lucas Evangelista* of 263 or 273 tons and thirty-four or more guns, and the *San Joseph* (named as the *Nuestra Señora de la Paz* in some records) of 208 tons and thirty or more guns. Both were Dutch-built, as were all of the nine *asiento* ships except for one built in Genoa, Italy. Accompanying the two armed slave ships was a barque or galliot of six guns and twelve patereros (swivel guns). The governor sent them as *armadillas*, or locally armed ships, commanded by the famous Andrés de Pez, to engage the arrogant filibusters and bring them in dead or alive. One account suggests there were as many as eight hundred men sent against the pirates. In fact, the Spanish were woefully undermanned for the pirates they were about to engage: their combined crews numbered only three hundred fifty fighting men.[37]

Facing the Spaniards were de Graff's *Françoise*—the former *Francesa*—of thirty guns and two hundred fighting men; Michel Andresson's *Tigre* (formerly de Graff's ship) of twenty-six and one hundred eighty, respectively; and Jan Willem, aka Yanky's, *Padre Ramos* of twenty-four guns and one hundred fifty men. Among de Graff's squadron at this time were also five smaller pirate vessels whose crews likely numbered at least two hundred in all, with at least twenty-two additional great guns among them, and whose captains were likewise capable, some of them famous, filibusters: François le Sage commanding a small prize, Pierre Bart, aka Bréha, and his *barque longue Diligent* of eight guns, Jean Blot and his *Cagone* or *Guagone* of eight guns, François Grogniet, aka Chasse-Marée, and his *Saint Joseph* of six guns and seventy men, and an unidentified English captain, quite possibly George Spurre, and his small sloop.

De Graff and his squadron took the weather gage and attacked swiftly, closing on the Spaniards, who had not suspected such a large force. The *San Francisco* ran aground; de Graff's filibusters boarded and captured her. The *San Joseph* fought back fiercely for four hours until, having been boarded and a bloody battle waged at closed quarters, she struck. Captain Yanky captured the galliot. De Graff, ever the showman, put the prisoners aboard the galliot and sent them ashore with a letter to the new governor of Cartagena, thanking him for sending such good ships as Christmas presents.

As is ever the case, records are inconsistent: a French account claims the battle lasted but an hour and a half, other accounts four or five hours. The same French account notes that the filibusters killed or wounded the greater part of the Spanish defenders, but had only thirty-four casualties among their own, divided equally between killed and wounded. Spanish records claim ninety Spaniards killed and twenty filibusters. An English account claims the Spanish lost eighty men aboard the *San Joseph*. In any case, victory was clearly on the side of the filibusters. The capture of the two great ships, intended to transport slaves to Spanish colonies, was a financial blow not only to the slave-trade *asiento*, but also to the Dutch and English who helped provide the slaves. As Sir Thomas Lynch, governor of Jamaica, put it, "The Governor took the *Lapaz* [*San Joseph*] and *St. Francisco*, two great ships intended to fetch negroes, and sent them out, where they were lost. This made Porcio rave indeed, because the great stress of the Assiento's business depended on these ships."[38]

Slaves were required for plantations under the colonial system, and trade with the colonies was vital to Europe. Nothing, including pirates, must hinder the colonial economies. De Graff had to be stopped, as did his brethren. As a result of de Graff's success, rapidly approaching from the figurative horizon—and soon to be the real horizon—was one of the greatest sea battles ever fought between pirate and pirate hunter.

The Rare, Real, Truly Epic Fight at Sea

De Graff's victories thrust his star even higher into the heavens. In 1685 he commanded *Le Neptune*, as he now called the *San Francisco*, now mounted with forty-eight or fifty guns and carrying a crew of three hundred, at the equally brutal sack of Campeche, Mexico. He was one of the few buccaneers, filibusters, or outright pirates of the age of sail ever to command a great, heavily armed ship. Still, the *Neptune* was but of medium tonnage, as compared to most men-of-war.[39]

After the sack—rape is surely a better word—of Campeche, the raiders scattered at the sight of the Armada de Barlovento, although the pirate-hunting armada picked off a few of them. Three days later, off the north Yucatán coast of Mexico, de Graff's lookout sighted two ships. The larger was the *Nuestra Señora de Jonjón*, an *urca* or frigate of roughly 335 tons and twenty to thirty guns.

Hers was a swashbuckling history: captured by pirates, she was recaptured in 1680 at Laguna de Términos, Mexico, by infamous Spanish sea rovers Pedro de Castro and Juan Corso. De Castro renamed her *León Coronado* and turned her against pirates and smugglers, and surely honest English ships, too, whose cargoes were sold at cut-rate prices and the profit distributed among captain, crew, and local *armadores* and officials who had invested in the *guarda costa* (coast guard vessel) and issued her commission. Because her draft was too deep to make a good *guarda costa*, *León Coronado* was taken into the Armada de Barlovento in 1682 and became a pirate hunter of the Spanish navy under her original name, *Nuestra Señora del Jonjón*.[40] Built in Campeche, she was named for a local patron saint, the Virgin of Jonjon of the convent in Pachihomhom at Cabo Catoche. (The ruins of the church can be seen today, and are known as the Boca Iglesia at Yalahau.)[41]

The smaller vessel was the eight-gun *Jesús, María y José*, a *patache* or small escort ship of unknown rig, formerly known as the *Sevillana*. Both were part of the pirate-hunting Armada de Barlovento. The *Jesús, María y José* immediately set all sail and a course away from the pirates, desperate to inform the famous, now elderly Admiral Andrés de Ochoa y Zárate that the greatest of pirates was nearby. The *Jonjón* wisely kept her distance. Soon enough, the captain of the *patache* informed the admiral of the opportunity to destroy the man who so successfully scourged the Spanish Main.

Within a day the main force of the Armada de Barlovento came in sight of de Graff, and a powerful squadron it was. The Spanish *Capitana* or flagship was the Dutch-built *Santo Cristo de Burgos*, of 650 tons and fifty-six guns, her stern with an image of Christ crucified, wearing a skirt that fell to beneath the knees. Aboard her was the Armada's commander-in-chief, Andrés de Ochoa, ill to the point of physical incapacitation but refusing to leave his quarterdeck. The *Almirante* or vice-admiral was the

Dutch-built *Nuestra Señora de la Conceptión*, of fifty-two guns, probably 550 tons, and commanded by Antonio de Astina.[42]

We know much of what the ships looked like, thanks to a drawing of the port of Portobello in 1682, which includes the two ships at anchor.[43] They are typically Dutch, although both appear, unusually, to have the semi-open stern gallery seen on some Spanish ships at this time.[44] Dutch ships, at least those sailed by the Dutch themselves, did not have these galleries. The *Burgos* also has a high poop, and possibly an awning over it. Gunports run the full length of her gundeck and upper deck, and there are gunports on the forecastle and quarterdeck as well. The ship is adorned with three very large flags: an ensign at the stern, a flag at the main-masthead, and a jack at the bowsprit. The *Conceptión* is a bit smaller, but similar. The ships are exactly what we have come to expect great Spanish ships to look like. Surely de Graff's ship looked similar. Here is the exception that proves the rule, here is the reality of the myth of the pirate "galleon" engaging great Spanish "galleons" in epic combat! Yet all three ships were Dutch built.

Further, both of the large pirate hunters were more lightly armed than we might expect—in fact, over-gunning is an historical error often made in novels and films, especially those depicting ships of the seventeenth and early eighteenth centuries. Based on the armament of similar ships of the Armada de Barlovento circa 1700, the *Burgos* was probably armed with twelve-pounders on the gundeck, perhaps a few sixteen- or eighteen-pounders (culverins) as well, with demi-culverins shooting eight-pound shot on the deck above, and four-pounders on the "*castillos*," that is, on the forecastle and quarterdeck, and possibly the poop.[45]

The *Conceptión* was likely armed with twelve-pounders, or even ten-pounders if twelves were unavailable, on the gundeck, sakers of five- or six-pound shot on the upper, with smaller guns on the quarterdeck and, possibly, the poop.[46] Accompanying these two great ships was the recently captured pirate ship *Reglita*, itself originally a Spanish prize, of twenty-two guns, probably of six- or four-pound shot, commanded by *présador* or prize-master Pedro de Iriarte.

And it was by these three ships that de Graff found himself trapped to leeward in his *Neptune* of as many as fifty guns, though we must doubt that these were all great guns, given the tonnage of his ship.[47] His ship probably had ports for no more than thirty-five to forty great guns of no more than eight- and four-pound shot; the rest were almost certainly various swivel cannon. Put plainly, he was heavily outgunned!

Unable to gain the weather gage so necessary to give him a fighting chance against two large men-of-war—or to escape them—de Graff ordered the *Neptune* to lie by and prepare for battle. In the language of the day, he had "catch'd a Tartar." The Armada was not idle either. During the night, the two powerful Spanish men-of-war brought filibuster prisoners aboard to help man the guns against their filibuster brethren—or die.

The battle began early the next morning. De Graff could surely have fought off, perhaps even captured, one of these great men-of-war, but two at once? Still, de Graff knew his business and just how serious the situation was. Before battle began he spoke boldly to his crew, as recounted by buccaneer-surgeon Alexandre Exquemelin:

"You are too experienced to not understand the peril we are running, and too brave to fear it," he said. "It is necessary here to be cautious of all yet to risk all, to defend and attack at the same time. Valor, deception, fear, and even despair must all be put to use on this occasion; where, if we fall into the hands of our enemies, nothing awaits us but all sorts of infamies, from the most cruel of torments to, finally, the end of life. We must therefore escape their barbarity; and to escape, we must fight."[48]

The great ships of the Armada sailed bravely down upon the waiting *Neptune* and her cornered pirate crew. Coming into range, the *Burgos* fired a warning shot from a bow chaser. The *Neptune* made no response. Onward sailed the *Burgos*, the *Concepción* not far behind. And here the Armada made its first tactical mistake, sailing on each side of the *Neptune*. In this position, the Spaniards could not fire on the enemy without also firing into each other. Only in Hollywood can two ships sail closely one on each side of another ship and destroy it, as in *Pirates of the Caribbean: At World's End*. In reality, it could be suicide or nearly so.[49] Of course, Rafael Sabatini, doubtless inspired by Exquemelin's description of the battle, got the tactic right in *Captain Blood*, with his hero emulating de Graff by sailing between the Spanish men-of-war *Milagrosa* and *Hidalga*.[50]

De Graff shouted orders to fire starboard and larboard. First one side, then the other of the *Neptune* blazed iron into the pair of pirate hunters. Immediately de Graff topped the broadsides off with an enormous discharge of musketry. Buccaneer surgeon Alexandre Exquemelin claimed that the musketry alone killed or wounded fifty Spaniards, and this might be true: filibusters and buccaneers were known for their ability with their long-barreled muskets. The *Burgos*, ready to fight, let loose its own powerful broadside in return.

Spanish records, however, give a slightly different account of this first *phrase d'armes*, perhaps truthfully, perhaps to cover up a grave error. Admiral Andrés de Ochoa y Zárate, the records suggest, believed de Graff would speak to him, surely to discuss terms, and so approached the pirate. After all, de Graff was outnumbered, outgunned, and outmanned. But when the admiral's ship came into close range, de Graff let his great guns do the talking.

For the next twelve hours de Graff maneuvered his ship defensively such that his enemy could seldom or never bring two broadsides to bear on him at once. Never did de Graff gain the weather gage, yet in spite of this the Armada ships never boarded him. In fact, they feared to do so. De Graff had a large crew that was clearly proving its prowess in open-sea battle. If the Spaniards were to board, they first had to outmaneuver de Graff, and both ships must board his ship, one first, then the other alongside the first. Once one had boarded, the other must cease firing, but the pirate had no such restriction. Perhaps most threatening, they knew too well de Graff's prowess as a gunner. He might slaughter far too many of their men as they came near to board, for boarders, if there are many of them, must be massed on deck just before they board, and thus are vulnerable.

And de Graff made sure the Armada captains and crews understood how dangerous it would be to try to board. At one point, de Graff ordered his helmsmen to close with the *Burgos* and his gun crews to aim a broadside at close range at the mainmast. In this age broadsides were not fired as in Hollywood films, all guns firing at once or almost so, with each gun captain simultaneously touching his match to his gun. Rather, these great guns were often fired by a few gunners, gunner's mates, or officers who went from one gun to the next and then the next, or they were aimed and fired *individually* by each gun's captain, all in order to ensure good aim.

In either case, a real broadside in this era was a ragged, slow-motion series of ear-cracking explosions of fire and smoke that ripped from iron into wood and flesh. Buccaneer-surgeon Alexandre Exquemelin claims that de Graff himself aimed the gun that dismasted the *Burgos*. And it's likely de Graff did aim several or more of his guns in this broadside, but the mainmast of the *Burgos*, although damaged, did not fall. Even so, the broadside was so effective that the Spaniards abandoned any thought of boarding the *Neptune*.

Surely emulating *Le Tigre* in its fight against *La Francesa*, the larger, less maneuverable *Neptune* twisted and turned as the fight continued, engaging first one ship, then the other, but taking no unnecessary risks. De Graff wanted to batter his enemies down, one, then the other, however long it took. The *Concepción*, valiantly bearing the brunt of the fight, fired at least sixty full broadsides at the *Neptune*, and *Burgos* at least fourteen. The Spanish officers would later claim their powder was bad, and maybe it was. Yet it was powerful enough to kill five Spanish gunners when their great gun exploded.

But de Graff's powder was not bad, and moreover, his crew knew how to load, aim, and fire accurately. Smoke covered the water between the ships as they blazed away. Men bled and died on each side, including de Graff himself, wounded in the leg. He was carried below, and his crew lost heart. But as soon as de Graff heard his guns slacking, he rose, climbed back to his quarterdeck, and, sword in one hand, pistol in the other, rallied his filibuster crew.

The battle continued until nightfall, when all three ships stood off from each other to tend to their wounded, knot their shattered rigging, repair the leaks in their hulls, and pump the water from their holds. The *Neptune* was in terrible condition. Although only nine of her crew had been killed and but ten or twelve wounded, the *Neptune* herself had taken a beating, for the Spanish broadsides had not been ineffective. Her foretopmast was shattered. Far worse, she had been hulled at the water-line by so many round shot that she was listing severely due to the water that continued to flood her hold in spite of the plugs pounded into the hull by the ship's carpenter and mates. Through the night de Graff's crew worked to lighten *Neptune*, to right her and prepare her for battle on the morn.

At dawn the next morning the *Neptune* had finally gained the weather gage—and the *Burgos* and *Concepción* were in no mood to engage her again. Their crews were battered and almost beaten, with dozens killed and wounded. They had expended most of their powder and shot, and the upper works of the *Burgos* were shattered. During the night the elderly admiral had been given his last rites in expectation of his death: he would live but two more days. With a single exception, the Armada officers believed that calling off the fight was the best course. Only Pedro de Iriarte wanted to chase the pirate and renew the fight, more for the sense of honor and reputation than for tactical wisdom. Surely every one of them felt shamed by their failure to capture, at odds of two to one of ships and guns in their favor, this notorious pirate who had once been one of them.

One historian suggests that the exploding great gun—a cannon, that is—that killed five crewmen aboard one of the ships caused the Spanish failure. But a single gun exploding and killing a few crewmen aboard one of two large ships would not cause defeat. Either of the two ships alone should have been able to fight de Graff to a standstill. Two together should have defeated him. Perhaps the exploding gun was the last straw, so to speak, after a long and brutal fight.[51]

His ship battered and in need of much repair, de Graff sailed away, perhaps the only pirate to have ever captured a ship of the Armada de Barlovento in single combat, and certainly the only one ever to have engaged and defeated the pirate-hunting Armada with a single ship.

De Graff and others like him prove that there really were pirate bat-tles and pirate heroes—if one can rightly call any pirate a hero—in the epic Hollywood mold. But they were the exception. Most ships were captured without a fight, for pirates generally preferred to capture ships without a fight if they could. The myth that every ship was captured after a valiant fight was promoted by great swashbuckler novelists like Rafael Sabatini and by the great swashbuckling films of Hollywood. Great sea fights are far more exciting to read about or watch than simple surrender is. These creators of swashbuckling fare have been a double-edged sword. They have kept the memory alive, albeit an altered memory, of epic pirates and pirate sea battles, but they have turned them into myth as well.

And it is this myth of "glorious" pirate violence, of ships with billowing sails blazing away at each other, filling the air with billowing gunpowder clouds and the din of battle, that in part sustains the popular image and causes us to turn a blind eye toward pirate misdeeds: of theft, torture, and rape, of violence inflicted on the innocent. For the pirate, violence was usually a means to an end, occasionally an end in itself. Still, there was much more to pirates and piracy than violence. There was also pirate society and a social order, with customs, traditions, rules, and behaviors that sustained both the violence and the organization necessary to inflict it on the scale piracy required. This pirate society, which ultimately enabled pirate plunder, has been mythologized as much as pirate violence itself.

PART II

"The Custom of the Coast" —Pirate Society

CHAPTER 7

Thief or Rebel?

———— ⚬⚬⚬ ————

"But these Privateers [pirates or buccaneers] (for so they were as we afterwards understood) hated them the more for their Treachery, and loved us the better, confessing that they were Rebels too, adding, That if the Duke of Monmouth had had One Thousand of them, they would soon have put to flight the King's Army."[1]
—Dr. Henry Pitman, *A Relation of the Great Sufferings*, 1689

For Golden Age pirates, piracy was not a culture most were born into, unlike some other piratical cultures before and after, but one they joined voluntarily or were forced into. As such, motivation is vital to understanding the myth and reality of piracy. Today, pirates are often popularly, and at times even by scholars, viewed as rebels, as men who became pirates in order to seek revenge upon the agents of the social or political injustice who harmed them in the first place. And if pirates are not always seen as rebels in pursuit of revenge, they are still often seen as rebels who turned to piracy due to some great social or political injustice. But just how true is this idea of the pirate as thieving rebel against injustice, an idea which has become a staple in fiction, film, and popular culture?

It was a rough time for Governor Richard Cony of the Somers Isles, as Bermuda was often still known. His subjects had turned against him. They had accused him of swearing and cursing, of killing a widow's hog, of forcing tavern owners to pay unlawful fees, of requiring unlawful oaths of his subjects. Indeed, many Bermudans were furious that Governor Cony demanded that they produce their cargoes, pay customs duties, and not sail from port until the customs house had cleared their vessels. He even refused to sell or give away the common lands—the king's lands, that is—of St. George's Island without the king's consent, much less without rent, as the sheriff, Richard Stafford, had recently tried to do.[2]

In particular, the Bermudans considered these restrictions to be nothing less than tyranny. They shouted that they were a "free-born people" and "esteem[ed] all government, not of their own making, to be slavery."[3] It was the beginning of an American Revolution in miniature.

Part of the problem, of course, was that King James II had revoked the colony's private charter in 1684 and put Bermuda under the direct control of the English government, not that the Bermudans had liked the Somers Isles Company much better. It was a time of rebellion in England, too: James II, many believed, was a secret Papist. His dead brother's bastard son, James, Duke of Monmouth, had just turned against him and tried to raise the West Country of England against him in hopes of marching on London and seizing the throne. When news reached the island that Monmouth had been crowned, the crowd turned ugly and tried to seize arms and control of the colony. But in fact the rebellion in England had failed. Monmouth's only reward was the dull ax of a sloppy headsman who mangled the beheading, not to mention Monmouth's foolish neck. When news came of the rebellion's failure, one Bermudan captain flew his ship's ensign bottom side up, an act of near treason.

The Bermudans, many of whom remained inspired by the Monmouth rebellion, wanted no part of this new governor who served James II. They shouted that he and the king were trying to enslave them. They demanded their rights, including that no man be deprived of his property "without legal trial."[4] They pointed to a book, *The Liberty of the Subjects of England*, which explained their rights but which James II considered seditious.[5] They were furious that when the king dissolved the Somers Isles Company, he had not "left them to their own election of governor and government."[6]

The disgruntled inhabitants were now close to open rebellion, and even demanded access to the government's arms and powder. Poor Governor Cony had few enough allies even though he was in fact only doing his job, however badly or well, no different from what any other colonial governor did. Unfortunately for Cony, the Bermudans, who were accustomed to doing as they pleased, had practically besieged him in his own house.

To cap it all, on a late November day in 1685 a small frigate of ten guns, eight *patereros* (breech-loading swivel cannon), and one hundred men sailed into St. George's harbor and dropped anchor. The arrival of any vessel was news. Bermudans quickly learned that the frigate, named *Josiah*, was commanded by Bartholomew Sharp—"Bat" Sharp to those who knew him well—a notorious buccaneer who had started his career under Henry Morgan, led a pillaging expedition in the South Sea, been acquitted of piracy in London, stolen a small vessel and sneaked back to the Caribbean, and participated in the brutal sack of Campeche, Mexico, under the command of the infamous filibusters Laurens de Graff and the Sieur de Grammont.[7] In fact, Sharp still had plunder from Campeche in his hold.

We know what will happen next, for Hollywood has shown us often enough. The pirates, who are only pirates because of their ill treatment at the hands of an unjust government, will join forces with the rebels and overthrow the English governor. And when the tyrant in England is finally overthrown, the pirates will return to being peaceable citizens. The rights of the common man prevail over those of despotic government! Each man will have a vote in the affairs of his government, just as pirates do in theirs! Pirates, after all, were rebels who stood against the tyranny of governments, or at least this is what we have been told in many tales and even by some scholars.

Rebel Pirates—But Not Revolutionaries

The last thing Governor Cony needed was a hundred veteran pirates, all of whom bore arms, coming ashore and joining the rebels. In fact, some pirates strongly supported the failed Monmouth rebels. Yet there was something curious about Sharp's small frigate. It flew the colors (the flags and pennant) of an English man-of-war. Of course, pirates of this age usually sailed under their national colors, so this might not mean anything. Yet when Bartholomew Sharp came ashore, he was accompanied not by his quartermaster, who aboard pirate ships, and even aboard most legitimate Caribbean privateers, was second-in-command. Rather, he was accompanied by his lieutenant, Paul Abney, and his ship's master, Thomas Walley. A "lieutenant" was not an officer found aboard pirate ships, but only aboard men-of-war and non-buccaneer privateers.

More curiously, Captain Sharp had an impressive piece of paper in his pocket. It turned out that in early 1684, Sharp had conned William Stapleton, governor of the Leeward Islands, into granting him a commission to "take and apprehend savage Indians and pirates."[8] Sharp was no pirate after all! He was now a king's man, a pirate hunter—set a thief to catch a thief!—and an Indian fighter. But appearances are often deceiving.

The fact that Sharp bore a commission from the governor actually meant very little. Stapleton's authority to issue the commission was debatable. As far as Sharp was concerned, the piece of paper was not only a means of avoiding being hanged, but also a mere pretense for piracy or other skullduggery, not to mention the cover of legitimacy under which he intended to sell his slave cargo, the product of large-scale piracy at Campeche. Even his small frigate was stolen, although to be fair, Sharp had stolen it from a pirate named Thomas Henley, who had stolen it from a Spaniard and sold it to a merchant in Boston who was investing in treasure hunting and piracy.

The infamous pirate captain immediately went ashore and sized up the situation. He was in desperate need of stores, and although he surely had plunder from Campeche with which to buy provisions, he claimed to be destitute except for the few Indian slaves he had aboard. He needed a place to unload the thirty members of his human cargo. Given that they were pirate plunder from Campeche, the slaves were hard to sell except by "stealth," as smuggling was known, and Bartholomew Sharp the pirate was not exactly welcome everywhere, his commission notwithstanding.

Sharp, ever a bold fellow, did what any king's privateer would do: he made straight for the governor's house. There, he explained that he needed provisions paid for at least in part by the sale of his Native American cargo. In turn, the governor explained the local situation. Surely Sharp grinned. He knew an opportunity when he saw one. He assured the governor he was no pirate. Campeche? The French had forced him to go along. And his previous piracies? They were not piracy at all—had he not in fact been acquitted of charges of piracy in 1682?[9] Those acts, in Sharp's eyes at least, were mere privateering, and had been in England's best interest. And anyway, he had been acquitted in London of all charges by a jury that hated Spaniards. The governor and pirate came to terms. Sharp and his men set about their work. The first thing they had to do was sell their slaves.

Selling the slaves was easy, for there was a ready market. The locals here had no qualms about trading with a pirate. After all, not too long ago they had purchased £3,000 to £4,000 worth of goods from the pirate Henley, whose ship Sharp had stolen. Immediately, the rebelliously inclined tried to draw Sharp to their side. Surely they did so respectfully. It was one thing to push a prisoner-pirate around, but quite another to pressure one who had a hundred men and a small frigate at his disposal.

Right here, according to the myth, is where Sharp should secretly side with the rebels. Or if he does not, here is where the plot will begin to thicken, leading Sharp to eventually change his mind, realize the error of his ways, and support the rebels, just as in the film *The Crimson Pirate*, starring Burt Lancaster, or *Swashbuckler*, starring Robert Shaw.

But Sharp was not a Hollywood pirate, and Bermuda in turmoil was not a Hollywood soundstage. At first, the rebels tried to bribe Captain Sharp to side with them, or at least take no role in Bermudan politics.

He refused to do either. Instead, he immediately threw his support behind the governor and against the people, or at least against the rebels, for not all Bermudans were in rebellion. Quickly the rebels—who had been happy to buy slaves from him—turned against him, using words and indirect action as their primary weapons. They were rebels, after all, but not fools. They shouted that Governor Cony was consorting with a known pirate. They refused to sell provisions to Sharp and his buccaneers. They prepared arms and made plans to take control of the government.

The leaders of what Cony considered to be a rabble included William Peniston, a fisherman by trade but now both a tobacco trader and a preacher of the fire-and-brimstone sort, as well as, at least formerly, a con artist and Fifth Monarchist who believed he would be one of Jesus Christ's saints when the Fifth Monarch—Jesus Christ—returned. Led by Fifth Monarchist Thomas Venner, he was among those who had tried to capture London in 1661 and hold it for Christ's coming. As one might expect, fifty men were not enough to capture London, much less hold it, even on Christ's behalf.

Venner and ten others were hanged, drawn, and quartered, but Peniston escaped with nothing more than the stigma of a branded criminal—not to mention the actual brand on his shoulder. At Peniston's side in Bermuda was "old William Righton," a loudmouth former tailor and preacher who now pretended to be a lawyer and also traded in tobacco. He even owned a small vessel to carry his tobacco.[10]

These descriptions are not necessarily meant to paint these men in a bad light. We have to remember that the Americas then were a place where men and women found new beginnings, where social status meant less, where even a branded criminal might retire as a wealthy merchant on a landed estate—something much more difficult in England, for example. In many ways, Peniston and Righton probably regarded themselves as new men in the New World, as business entrepreneurs who also happened to be seeking religious freedom, even if a bit extreme, not to mention a bit hypocritical. Above all, they did not like their government interfering with their profits.

Governor Cony first tasked Sharp and his crew with dealing with William Righton. The merchant trader had not only refused to pay customs duties on his shiploads of tobacco, but he had also broken out of jail, doubtless with the complicity of the sheriff, and sailed his cargo to Pennsylvania, and no one would arrest him. Now, though, he had returned to his house, some twenty miles away. His ship lay at anchor nearby. Sharp's men quickly descended on the house and the vessel, but they found the house abandoned and the vessel without its rudder. Depending on whom you believe, the pirates either behaved riotously at Righton's house, shouting "bloody oaths" at the Bermudans and calling them rebels who wanted to murder the governor, or behaved with the utmost restraint and decorum.[11] Either way, the rebels exploded in even louder, angrier charges.

And they did more. They took up arms, and two of them, William Keele and George Bascom, led parties of men and captured two of the island's forts. Quickly the mini-rebellion had escalated. By now even Sharp had his hands full. He could not risk a bloody confrontation. He had to temper his buccaneer inclination toward brutality, for these were Englishmen here in Bermuda. Intimidation—the threat of force backed by the judicious use of force as necessary—had to be his weapon. Here he could neither rack prisoners nor burn homes. He had to make it clear to the rebels that he would follow the governor's orders and that he had enough men to do so, but without acting like a buccaneer, although the fact that he was indeed a pirate surely gave the rebels pause.

Sharp prepared to march on the forts, but his men were spread wide and thin. They had to protect their frigate, the governor, and themselves—and recapture the forts. Probably Sharp considered the consequences of an attack on the forts with the small body of men available. Blood would be spilled. Sharp would be blamed because he was a pirate, his commission notwithstanding. What, then, he wondered, should he do?

Suddenly, by good fortune, a second small frigate, the *Prosperous*, came to anchor in St. George's harbor. Governor, rebel, and pirate each cast his eye on it, wondering who it might be and how the arrival might shift the balance of power. The captain who strode ashore was Edward Conaway, treasure hunter, fortune hunter, would-be privateer—and pirate. Perhaps Conaway would side with the rebels and against Sharp, and also prove another myth—that of pirates fighting each other over treasure or treasure maps, or simply because they did not like each other—to be true. Pirate and rebel would fight against pirate and government.

But Conaway and his thirty privateer-pirates were unaware of such tales. Pirates, in fact, did not go around helping overthrow local governors, tyrannical or otherwise, except when they were Spanish, and then only to steal from them and their subjects. And only rarely did pirate crews ever get in fights with each other. Instead, Conaway and his crew immediately allied themselves with Sharp and his buccaneers and charged the forts, forcing the rebels to flee without firing a shot. In the words of Governor Cony, they "outdured" the insolence of the rebels.[12]

Sharp himself arrested the deputy sheriff, Richard Stafford, and threw him in irons aboard the *Josiah*. Here the sheriff's friends could not help him. In no time at all, the large band of seagoing rogues restored order in Bermuda. In the king's name, the pirates held the forts, incarcerated the deputy sheriff, and enforced the governor's orders. The rebels fled to the countryside, fearing the pirates would follow. Still, their words rang with defiance and rebellion, even if they were from a safe place: if "Captains Sharp and Con[a]way opposed the country, the country would oppose them, and would be in readiness in an hour's time; that unless they came civilly they must expect blows; and that it would be a long time before they took Bascom and Keele again."[13]

But Sharp and Conaway had no reason to chase after them. The governor was safe and owed the buccaneers a great debt. Sharp even wrote a letter to the English secretary of state, advising him of the situation. It seems a curious matter, that of a pirate supporting the very government that pirates in stories and myths are supposed to oppose. But the fact is, pirates invariably acted foremost for profit. And supporting Governor Cony was in Sharp's best interest. In particular, it helped make up for his recent piracies. Had Sharp sided with the rebels, he might have been charged with both piracy and treason. A hanged man cannot grow rich.

The rebels, of course, remained outraged. One of them, Peniston, briefly had his revenge, or thought he did. He filed a writ detailing seven charges against Captain Sharp "as to his suspicious departure from Jamaica, and acts of piracy at Campeachy and elsewhere" and served it upon the pirate. Sharp merely grinned and either "wiped his breech" with the paper, or rolled it up and used it to light his pipe—probably both—as Peniston turned purple with rage.[14]

Unfortunately, Captain George St. Lo, a strict naval officer who had no love for pirates or former pirates, arrived and, after a brief investigation, arrested Sharp, along with five of the rebel ringleaders, and took him to Nevis for trial on charges of piracy for stealing Henley's *Resolution* at Jamaica in October 1684 and participating in the sack of Campeche in October 1685. But Sharp had the last laugh, as usual: The jury would not accept the word of a "Spaniard nor of a Christian Indian"—nor, apparently, even of an English naval officer like Captain St. Lo—and "God-damned all Indians and Spaniards for a crew of dogs, who should not take away an Englishman's life."[15] Sharp was acquitted and his ship restored to him. St. Lo, however, was in hot water.

Bartholomew Sharp continued his life of skullduggery until his death in 1702 in the St. Thomas jail. Imprisoned for attempting to escape the debts he had accrued as a failed planter, his case was not helped by the fact that he was unable to keep a civil tongue in his head. He probably died of the same malady that had paralyzed his hands: a fitting end for a pirate, some surely said, although doubtless others thought the old adventurer who had scourged the Spanish and helped break the rebellion at Bermuda deserved better.[16]

Equality, Democracy, and Profit

Where, then, did we get the idea that pirates were rebels who wanted to see the overthrow of governments, and at times even helped do so? Hollywood has been a great source of this myth, often portraying pirates as rebels siding with the downtrodden, the objects of tyranny, and the underdog. Given the choice between a good narrative and the truth, Hollywood invariably chooses the former. Ultimately, the myth derives from the language of some of the pirates of the early eighteenth century. In his early eighteenth-century pirate history, Charles Johnson made it seem by their language that pirates really were rebels. Unfortunately, Johnson most likely made up much of the highly detailed pirate dialogue in the book, as probably did the unknown editor of *The Four Years Voyages of Capt. George Roberts*, which also has much pirate talk of rebellion.

But even if we ignore these two books, there are still plenty of examples provided by real witnesses, usually pirate-prisoners. Captain Howell Davis, who captured more than one hundred vessels and whom the infamous Bartholomew Roberts would succeed as captain, said that "their reasons for going a-pirating were to revenge themselves on base merchants, and cruel commanders of ships."[17] Captain Thomas Cocklyn, an associate, drank to the health of "King James the Third"—to the pretender to the throne, that is, and by doing so committed an act of both rebellion and treason.[18] Pirate John Phillips, captured from a fishing boat at Newfoundland, perhaps at Trepassy Bay, by Bartholomew Roberts, abused prisoner John Wingfield, "calling him a Supercargo Son of a B—h, that he starved the Men, and that it was such Dogs as he that put Men a Pyrating."[19]

But the fact is, in spite of their rebellious talk, pirates of all ages were and are motivated foremost by plunder, whether by need or greed, or both, as Thucydides noted twenty-five hundred years ago.[20] Certainly a sense of adventure permeates piracy, and without it perhaps many men would not have turned to sea thieving, but pirates were foremost seeking wealth by force of arms on the sea. Even so, it is common to believe today, in part due to scholarly works, that pirates were motivated entirely by economic wrongs and had no choice but to turn to piracy to feed themselves, or that pirates were motivated by political injustice and took to the sea to revenge themselves. Economic injustice in particular is often attributed to the early eighteenth-century pirates of the Golden Age, to Howell Davis, Bartholomew Roberts, and their ilk, for example. From these examples are all pirates often assumed to be so motivated.

And need has in fact often played a significant role in piracy. At the end of Queen Anne's War in 1712–1713, there was a rise in Spanish piracy in the Caribbean, probably due to the lack of employment of Spanish privateers now that peace had been made. This so restricted English trade that the anonymous "Gentleman" who wrote a tract entitled *The Importance of Jamaica to Great-Britain* in 1741 believed it "occasion'd the rise of pirates; for after the peace the sailors went cheerfully into the merchants service, and were well contented with their employments, till they had been not only cruelly and inhumanely treated, but losing their wages, whereby their families were expos'd to want and other hardships, they thought it hard to be so used and insulted by the Spaniards, and not to have a power to stand in their own defence."[21] At first they attacked only Spanish vessels, and Spanish *guardas costas* were indeed a menace, often confiscating any English ship if it had any cargo—"fruits of the Indies"—aboard that might be construed as coming from the Spanish New World colonies.[22] But when the English government revoked their commissions, they began to attack ships of all flags. Thus goes the argument of economics and revenge.

But hand in hand with need as a cause of piracy go greed and opportunism. The aforementioned anonymous gentleman fails to mention that at the end of the war the English government at Jamaica commissioned "14 sloops mann'd with about 3,000 men to clear those seas [of Spanish pirates], but the remedy was worse than the disease," much like the disease of Spanish privateers who quickly turned pirate.[23] The "privateers" attacked honest Spanish shipping, dove unlawfully for silver on Spanish wrecks, and robbed Spanish salvors of treasure they had recovered.[24] Very quickly they went from hunting Spanish pirates to hunting any Spanish vessels. In similar fashion, some modern Somali pirates claim to have turned to sea thieving for reasons of economic vengeance—yet they did not attack the intruding "pirate" fishing vessels that were depriving them of their livelihood; they attacked honest commercial shipping instead.[25] Former privateers not wanting to give up their traditional trade—one that had been strongly favored in the Caribbean since 1655, and in place for decades prior—probably accounted as much for the rise in piracy as did economic hardship, although it may be argued that the loss of one's trade, however necessary to political, economic, or social advancement, is a significant hardship.

Later, after the great rise of piracy, many of the pirates who believed or pretended, as Captain Davis did, that they were revenging themselves on cruel merchants and captains, not to mention a society that left many of them unemployed, leaped at the possibility of returning to privateering and "enriching themselves in a legal way, by going a privateering, which many of them had privately done."[26] The word enriching is key; for all of the Golden Age, pirates went to sea primarily to plunder. Most of the talk of rebellion occurred in the early eighteenth century by pirates who knew they could not in any way claim to be legitimate. Some might pretend "to be *Robbin Hoods Men*"—but they did not give to the poor, except that the poor were themselves.[27] For any pirate, rebellion consisted of nothing more than going to sea to steal. This was the extent of their rebellion; there was no revolution, and much of the rebellion consisted of violence against all races and classes. And when their stint at piracy was over, most pirates slipped quietly back into society—assuming, of course, that they had managed to avoid the noose.

Still, did Golden Age pirates at least believe in equality, which at the time was considered a form of rebellion? Of course they did—but only among themselves.[28] They permitted every free adult male a vote in the affairs of the crew and cruise, although among some large crews, pirates voted for representatives who then voted in council. Only captains might have two votes. Arguably, pirate crews were the first true democracies in the New World, and they came into being at least a century and a half before the American Revolution. However, there is no evidence that pirate democracy influenced, much less inspired, the democracy that developed out of the American Revolution, although some pirate historians make this argument.

Pirates believed in equality in other ways as well. They divided their plunder almost equally. Most pirates received a single equal share. The captain usually received two. The quartermaster, master, surgeon, and specialist officers such as the gunner might receive one and a half, though not always.[29] Boys often received a half share, except among the early eighteenth-century pirates, who allowed them no share, even boys as old as seventeen, at least according to the practice of Bartholomew Roberts and his crew.[30] Pirates divided their spoils as soon after they stole them as they could, each man doing what he pleased with his. Some gambled with theirs, usually ashore (this helped prevent conflict aboard ship), and became richer or poorer. Some invested theirs, especially among the late seventeenth-century buccaneers and filibusters. Bartholomew Sharp owned land in Jamaica, for example, and Laurens de Graff owned a large sugar plantation on Saint-Domingue, with more than one hundred slaves.[31] But most pirates squandered their shares of plunder on rum, prostitutes, and related extravagant, debauched celebration.

Among the buccaneers and filibusters of the seventeenth century, the pirate vessel's owner received shares, negotiated between captain and crew, for its maintenance. Often, captains owned their ships. Captains were sometimes rewarded with a prize ship, especially if it was better than the one he was sailing. Sometimes they bought them with money from previous cruises. Of course, if pirates did not agree to the shares a captain wanted for his ship, they would not sail with him. A large group of filibusters once refused to sail with the great Dutch filibuster Laurens de Graff for this reason. Instead, they crossed into the South Sea.[32]

Captains liked the shares they received for their ships—two and half to a dozen for a small ship or frigate, thirty or more for a large ship like Nicholas Van Horn's *Saint Nicholas* or Laurens de Graff's *Neptune*.[33] Why? Because if the cruise were a successful one, only a small part of the shares would be necessary to maintain the ship. The rest would go into the owner's hat, so to speak. Captains and other owners could get rich this way, and many did. Only the early eighteenth-century Golden Age pirates do not appear to have followed this practice.

One important aspect of pirate shares was that disability compensation and the cost of the surgeon's chest were always paid for first, before the remaining plunder was divided among the pirate crew. And if there were not enough pieces of eight to compensate the wounded for their injuries, pirates usually continued their cruise until they had stolen enough for that compensation.

Pirates believed in equality in more ways than just votes, shares, and disability compensation. They were usually an international lot. Although most Golden Age pirates came from England, Scotland, Wales, Ireland, France, and the Netherlands, others came from Spain, Portugal, Denmark, the German states, the Italian states, and other European nations and places. Among them were "Levanters" from the Eastern Mediterranean lands and islands such as Greece. There were also Native Americans in their crews, and Africans, not to mention mulattos, *mestizos*, and other people of mixed race. There were occasionally even a few Asians among Caribbean pirate crews. They or their ancestors had made it to the New World from China, Japan, and the Philippines via the Manila galleon that annually crossed the Pacific.[34]

The 198 pirates aboard *La Trompeuse* in 1684 included "French, Scotch, Dutch, English [twelve], Spaniards, Portugals, Negroes, Indians, Mullattos, Swedes, Irish, Jersey men, and New Englanders."[35] However, among the early eighteenth-century pirates, white Britons predominated, although there were plenty of French and Spaniards among their separate crews. We will discuss the status of Africans among these later crews shortly. Except in the case of those Africans and Native Americans who were kept as slaves rather than as free members of the pirate crew, all pirate crewmembers were treated equally in voting, shares, and other compensation.

Indeed, pirates were in many ways far more democratic and egalitarian than their contemporaries. However, what pirates did not do was try to overthrow governments or come to the aid of rebels trying to overthrow governments, except on the rare occasion when it was in their best interest to do so. And those rare occasions were limited to assisting native peoples whose help the pirates needed.

Rebel Surgeon and Pirate Captain

Rebel pirate rhetoric, real and imagined, is not the sole origin of the myth of the rebel pirate, and it may indeed not even be the greatest influence on the myth in popular culture. Instead, the mishap of an English surgeon in 1685 is arguably as much or more to blame.

His name was Henry Pitman. In early July 1685, the West Country of England was in an uproar. The Duke of Monmouth, Protestant champion and bastard son of Charles II, had landed, hoping to raise a following large enough to overthrow the Catholic King James II. Men, most of whom had little experience with arms, were flocking to his banner with whatever weapons they had or could improvise. The atmosphere of hope and fear, of treason and rebellion, of arms and armed men, was intoxicating. Dr. Pitman, a sea surgeon, had only recently returned from a trading voyage to Italy and had gone to visit family in Sandford, Somersetshire, England.[36]

Of course, the excitement of history in the making was too much to ignore. Incited by both his own curiosity and that of some of his acquaintances, Pitman and a few friends rode to Taunton to view the duke's forces. Satisfied they had seen history, however it might turn out, they headed for home, but they quickly realized that they might be taken for rebels by the Lord of Oxford's troop of horse. Foolishly, but fearing they had no choice, they returned to the rebel lines to await a "more safe and convenient opportunity."[37] Pitman actually had little choice, for he had lost his horse, probably to the rebel army.

Pitman quickly came to regret fortune's hand. A night sneak attack by the rebels failed. The royal army routed the novice warriors, slaughtering many. The number of wounded was just as appalling. Already Dr. Pitman's humanity had been appealed to by the rebels and local citizens, who, "miserably lamenting the want [lack] of chirurgeons," desired him to assist with the wounded. Pitman's "pity and compassion" on his "brethren in Christianity" gave him no other choice. By the time the forces met at Sedgemoor, he had long been busy dressing the wounds of both rebel soldiers and the king's soldiers. And now he had his hands both full and bloody.[38]

As the king's forces swept through the rabble that once had been a rebel army, arresting everyone in sight and hanging many, Pitman fled, knowing a noose might await him. The countryside was under martial law and the rights of Englishmen had been abandoned or ignored. Captured on the road, he was thrown into jail and eventually brought to court. Pitman and the accused rebels quickly learned that men who pleaded "not guilty" were summarily hanged. Immediately, the accused rebels, except for three or four men of vast courage and conviction, pleaded guilty. Again, Pitman and his brethren were told this was their only salvation. But it was all a lie. The rule was "Confess, and be hanged!"[39] Judge Jeffries, following the desires of his king, was a butcher who sentenced accused rebels to death so quickly that they might just as well have dispensed with the trials, except that they provided a pretense of justice.

Pitman was sentenced to be hanged, drawn, and quartered. Two hundred thirty-eight of the rebels were drawn in carts or on sledges to the gallows, where a rope tightened around their necks when they were pushed off a ladder, leaving no support beneath their feet. They strangled, or nearly so, on the gallows, then were brought down, many still alive, only to be castrated, their bellies cut open and their bowels pulled out, and then beheaded and cut into four quarters, which went on display at "every spot where two roads met, on every market-place, on the green of every large village which had furnished Monmouth with soldiers."[40] Heads and limbs were stuck on poles, and entire bodies were encaged in iron frames in a gruesome display.

But Dr. Pitman was lucky. He and the remainder had their sentences commuted to "transportation." The "rebels convict" were sold as chattel and sent to Barbados as indentured servants. Here they lived on salt beef, salt fish, and corn cakes and were worked hard by their masters. Pitman, fed up with his treatment, swore he would not work as a surgeon anymore, but would rather work "in the field with the Negroes." His owner exploded in rage, lashing his head, arms, and back with a cane until it splintered into sharp blades that stripped even more flesh from his bones, then put him in the stocks for twelve hours until his owner's wife, moved by "pity or shame," ordered his release.[41]

Pitman had had enough. Gathering a few like-minded men together, they prevailed upon a debtor named John Nuthall to buy a boat from a slave ship in the harbor. Unfortunately, no sale could be final until notice was given to the government, and the magistrate quickly became suspicious of the purchase of a boat by a debtor. Pitman ordered Nuthall to sink the boat, so that the magistrate would stop inquiring, thinking it was lost. They would recover it later.

Pitman and his confederates now prepared for their voyage, hiding the necessary stores in a warehouse under the supervision of rebel convict John Whicker. They waited until May 9, 1687, the night of a celebration in honor of the governor of Nevis. All the town was "revelling, drinking, and feasting to excess."[42] In secret, they put to sea, setting a westerly course, their only real option, given the prevailing wind direction. But the boat was terribly leaky, and they spent much of their time bailing water out of it. They smeared tallow from their candles onto rags and stuffed them into the leaky seams, but to little avail. Soon, all were seasick and had no strength to bail. There was no chance they would make it as far as their destination, the Dutch colony on the island of Curaçao. Indeed, they were in danger of drowning at sea, a predicament in some ways far worse than their servitude at Barbados. Still, they were free, and masters of their destiny!

Real Pirate Rebellion

The "rebels convict" made landfall at "Saltatudos" or "Salt Tortuga" near the Isla de Margarita, off the coast of modern-day Venezuela. They were marooned, to use the term of the day, but at least they would not sink at sea and drown. Very quickly, though, they discovered that they were not alone. There were other men on the island, Englishmen who introduced themselves as in distress.

In fact, they were buccaneers, formerly part of the crew of Captain Jan Willems, better known as Yanky, and his forty-eight-gun *Dauphine*. In late summer or fall of 1686 they had set off along the Florida coast seeking canoes for a raid on St. Augustine, sponsored in part by the government of

Carolina, which in this case had no scruples about recruiting pirates as allies, especially in revenge for a recent Spanish pirate attack led by Alejandro Tomás de León in response to Carolinian encroachments on Spanish territory, and in particular to Carolinian-inspired Native American attacks on "Spanish Indians." Not only were Charlestown merchant traders encroaching on Florida in their thirst for deer skins and Native American slaves, but so were the Scottish colonists of nearby Port Royal, Carolina. The Spanish rovers and their Native American allies destroyed the Scottish colony and burned numerous Carolinian plantations.[43]

But the buccaneers now on Salt Tortuga missed all of this. On the gulf coast of Florida they were attacked by Native Americans, missed their rendezvous with Captain Yanky, and were thus forced to set out on their own, eventually landing at Salt Tortuga some two thousand miles distant by sea. Clearly, given the great distance between Florida and Venezuela, there was more to their adventure than they admitted or Dr. Pitman remembered. Most likely, they set out on their own piratical cruise along the Spanish Main, but found little prey or plunder, and ended up on Salt Tortuga "hoping to meet here with some Vessel loading of Salt, in which they might get passage for some English Port . . ."[44] As for the reprisal attack on St. Augustine, it never took place, for it was forbidden when the new governor, James Colleton, arrived. Captain Yanky and his bold crew, along with their consort, Captain Jacob Everson and his crew, went on their way.

Hoping to ingratiate himself with the buccaneers, John Nuthall told them that, unlike himself and one other, the rest of his companions were Monmouth rebels. But Nuthall's words did not have the desired effect: the pirates were in fact pleased that these lost men were rebels, and despised Nuthall for his petty treachery. These marooned buccaneers even claimed to be rebels, too, and they swore that if Monmouth had had "1,000 of them, they would soon have put to flight the King's army," which might well have been true.[45] Quickly, the buccaneers tried to recruit the escaped rebels. They wanted to head to sea in their canoe, and they needed the rebels convict's boat for materials. And besides, as they suggested to the marooned men, it was better to be armed and at sea than unarmed and stranded ashore, prey to every Spaniard who happened by. But Dr. Pitman and his confederates declined, which prompted the buccaneers to burn their boat as inducement, after first stealing its sails. From its ashes, they recovered its nails and used them to nail planks to the gunwales of their canoe to make it more seaworthy.

Soon, the buccaneers left on their own accord, leaving the rebels convict to scour the island for turtles and turtle eggs and other such fodder they could eat. The buccaneers had shown them where to find water, but still the marooned rebels suffered. They hiked miles from the well to the beaches where they found turtles and back again, over and over. Their shoes and clothing wore out, and they despaired of rescue, which might not be for months, when the salt sloops finally arrived to "rake" salt from the shallow ponds on the island.

After three months, they suddenly sighted a large ship with a sloop as a companion. A boat came ashore, and one of its crew invited Dr. Pitman aboard. It turned out that the buccaneers who had burned their boat were not such foul men after all, for they had told the ship of the marooned men and their plight. The ship's crew helped Dr. Pitman up the side and welcomed him with trumpets. The captain invited him into the great cabin and fed him well with "wine and choice provisions."[46] They gave him shoes and stockings and linen to make new clothes. Rescue was at hand!

But only for Dr. Pitman. The ship was a pirate vessel, and not even her captain—whom Pitman was careful not to name—could prevail upon her crew to accept the rebels convict aboard, except for Pitman. The captain had but two votes in such matters; he was overruled by his crew, who would not let him take aboard stranded men whose politics they probably agreed with. So much for being a brotherhood of rebels. Even so, the pirates left food and supplies for the marooned escapees. Dr. Pitman eventually found his way home, thanks to the pirates who rescued him.

And what has this small odyssey to do with the myth of the rebel pirate? Anyone who has read Rafael Sabatini's *Captain Blood: His Odyssey* has already guessed. Dr. Pitman's true tale was the basis for Sabatini's famous swashbuckler. Twice the novel has been made into a major motion picture, the second time in 1935 starring Errol Flynn and Olivia de Havilland. It tells the story of a doctor unjustly convicted in the aftermath of the Monmouth Rebellion and transported to Barbados, where he escapes and, along with other rebels convict, turns pirate, inspired by their terrible treatment at the hands of King James II and his minions. The novel and its film versions have done as much to inspire our belief in the rebel pirate—in the man (or woman) who turns pirate for political reasons and acts on his or her social conscience.

Captain Blood, of course, was a gentleman pirate, unlike the majority of pirates who came from the poor, working, and middle classes. In fact, all of Sabatini's heroes were gentlemen, either by birth or by character. Thus, when King James II was deposed, Blood became a pirate no more. But he and his fictional crew were the only such pirates to do so. Although some men did turn pirate in response to ill treatment at the hands of their government or of cruel merchants and captains or of Spanish pirates, this was the extent of their rebellion.

But to fans of Rafael Sabatini's novel, none of this matters. We accept both truths—that of the reality of pirate rebellion and also that of pirate rebellion in fiction, in which the pirate rebel struggles with his conscience and in the end does the right thing. If nothing else, the false image of the pirate rebelling against government and trying to overthrow it has served to inspire real acts of conscience against injustice and even tyranny, proving that myth and legend still have a great place even in our modern world.

CHAPTER 8

Dueling and Democracy

———⊂∞⊃———

"The chief pirate was a heretic who had a Spanish companion and partner by the name of Nesilio [Lorencillo]. The two quarreled over the division of the loot between them, so Nesilio killed the heretical chief and took over the leadership of the pirates."[1]

—Elias al-Mûsili, *An Arab's Journey to Colonial Spanish America*, 1683

The myths surrounding Golden Age pirates notwithstanding, one incontrovertible cultural fact is that these pirates functioned as extraordinary micro-democracies. In fact, one can argue that pirate democracy was a grand form of rebellion, one that stood defiantly against the reigning social order—against the rule of kings and nobility. Even so, the reality of pirate democracy has not escaped its distortion by pirate mythology.

The three men involved in the disagreement were Dutch, as were most members of the crews. Two of the three were captains of buccaneer vessels, and the third was the friend of one and the quartermaster of the other. The three were mostly quiet now, as was the expectant crew ranged 'round the deck of one of the small vessels. Many of them stood on the gunwales or in the shrouds. On deeds, not words, was their focus today.[2]

At center were the two Dutch captains. Each had a cutlass in hand. Each intended to wound or even kill the other in a mythic duel pitting two famous pirates of the Caribbean against each other. The outcome would effectively determine command of the expedition between the two captains.

The loudest of these two armed men was "Garret Garretson alias Rocky."[3] Many buccaneers used *noms de guerre*, and Garretson was more commonly known as Rock the Brazilian, Roche Brasiliano, or just plain Rock or Rocky. Born in Groningen, the Netherlands, he had lived for many years in New Holland, as the Dutch portion of Brazil was known. In 1654 the Portuguese captured Recife, the capital of New Holland, and effectively turned New Holland back to Portuguese rule. Within a few years, Garretson had ventured to Port Royal, Jamaica, and there did what many wandering spirits did. He joined the buccaneers.

His timing was perfect. Captured by the English in 1655, Port Royal had almost immediately become a haven for sea rovers. The English-speaking among these quasi-pirates (for often enough their scourging of the Spanish Main was lawful) referred to themselves as buccaneers. Rock the Brazilian went to sea with them first as a common buccaneer, but via his fierce nature, he quickly made a name for himself and drew many supporters to his side. He was a loud, aggressive, threatening man, the sort whom lesser spirits often see as a leader. And sometimes such men do make good leaders.

Before long, Rock and his faction parted company with their original captain. As already noted, buccaneers were permitted to leave a voyage at any time if they chose to do so, as long as they paid for the victuals they had eaten during the voyage.[4] "Mutinies"—for so they called these democratic ruptures—were common among these adventurous, independent men, all of whom considered themselves not only equals but also leaders. But even leaders must have a leader, and soon Rocky commanded the "mutineers." We do not know the year, but it was probably no later than 1663.

The new captain and crew had but a small vessel. Soon they sighted a sail on the horizon and gave chase. It turned out to be a ship from

Spain, perhaps a "registry" ship, as those with licenses to sail independently of the treasure fleets were called. The details of the battle are
absent, but the Spaniard, reasonably well armed, surely put up a fight.
Spaniards usually did if they were armed. We can assume Captain Rock
fought at the head of his crew, leading from the front as buccaneer captains were expected to do. No buccaneer captain could command for
long if he did not.

We must pity the Spaniards who stood up to him as he and his men
boarded, cutlass and pistol in hand amid the grenades and firepots they
flung on the Spanish deck, for Captain Rock was known as a violent
man among men of violence. He once roasted a Spaniard between two
fires, as one would a butchered hog, when the man refused to point the
way to the hog yards Rock and his men intended to raid for provisions.
When drunk in Port Royal, he was reputed to "roam the town like a
madman" and chop an arm or a leg from the first person he came across.[5]

Of course, this chopping and cleaving of limbs in his home port was
probably an exaggeration. Surely he did not get away with this more
than once. But that would have been enough to secure his reputation.
Even Dr. Hans Sloane, the famous physician, botanist, and zoologist
who had examined the dying, probably cirrhotic ex-buccaneer Sir Henry
Morgan in 1688, attested to the fame earned by Captain Rock's violent
nature. He wrote that "Rockey a Privateer" (in Port Royal, *privateer* was
a polite word for a buccaneer) had a reputation for killing sharks with
daggers—while swimming in the sea with them. (Of course, some Carib
Indians and Native American divers were known to do the same thing.)
"Rockey" certainly had courage to go along with his brutality, a combination not nearly as common as most people would like to believe.[6]

In early 1668, Rock was made captain of an eighty-ton, twelve-gun
Spanish prize sold in Port Royal at the behest of infamously murderous
filibuster and pirate Jean David Nau, better known in the Caribbean as
François l'Ollonois. Rock's quartermaster was Jelles de Lecat, or "Yellows,"
as he was named among the buccaneers. One of the buccaneers among
the crew was reportedly Jan Erasmus Reyning, a man of noble mien, one
who did not tolerate cruelty and who was also a purported investor in the

voyage. Captain Rock and his crew cruised between Cartagena and the Mosquito Coast, pausing to help Henry Morgan sack Portobello in July 1668.

In the same year, according to Reyning's seventeenth-century biographer, Dr. David van der Sterre, the buccaneers lay at anchor taking on provisions. Espying a Spanish brigantine under oars in the calm airs, Captain Rock ordered his crew aboard and just in time got his own men to their oars to intercept the attacker. Rocky himself led the way, deftly bringing his vessel alongside to board. The buccaneers threw grappling hooks onto the rails and into the rigging of the Spanish brigantine, then drew the vessels together, board-and-board, and under fire lashed each to the other.

For an hour, buccaneer and Spaniard blazed away at each other with small cannon, swivel guns, muskets, and grenades. With cutlass and pistol, the buccaneers cut down any Spaniard in the open, but doubtless many of the Spanish crew retreated within to the "closed quarters," where they fired muskets through loopholes at the buccaneer boarders and tossed grenades among them. Otherwise, the boarding fight would never have lasted an hour. As the fight raged, both vessels, their crews locked in mortal combat, drifted in a cloud of smoke punctuated by bright flashes of gunpowder. Even the two brigantines, lashed together as they were, seemed to intend death to the other.[7]

With boarding axes and iron crows, the buccaneers surely made breaches in deck and bulkhead planks, then hurled grenades and firepots into the holes to flush the defenders out by searing them to the bone with exploding gunpowder and choking them with the resulting smoke. Only a few Spaniards survived the fight, one of them reportedly a boy who escaped death by hanging outboard from the brigantine's rail astern. Captain Rock and his men returned to Port Royal. There they outfitted the Spanish prize as a buccaneer vessel with the Brazilian as captain. Buccaneer captains were often rewarded with prize ships, especially if they were better than their existing vessels.

Rocky was by now a notable buccaneer captain—a man esteemed by many, yet who "made all Jamaica tremble."[8] He set sail again, this time in consort with his former vessel. Commanding it now, according to van der Sterre, was Jan Erasmus Reyning, a famous Dutch sea rover whose authenticated life reads like a novel. Born in 1640 in Vlissingen to a transplanted Danish seaman and a Dutch mother, Reyning went to sea at the age of ten and soon saw action aboard a privateer, probably by the age of twelve or thirteen. In 1667, he sailed to the New World, first to Cayenne, South America, then to Tortuga, the famous haunt of the French buccaneers, known in their language as *flibustiers* (filibusters). He toiled briefly as a tobacco farmer, then as the servant of a *boucanier*, or hunter, before signing with Dutch privateer Captain Casten. In 1668, he signed aboard Captain Rock's vessel in Port Royal. Soon a third vessel was added, that of Joseph Bradley, probably his *May-Flower* of seventy tons and fourteen guns.

The buccaneers set a course for Blewfields on the coast of Nicaragua. Here they cruised for Spanish vessels and cut and stole logwood, a valuable dyewood. Jelles de Lecat had remained Rocky's quartermaster, but reportedly quarreled with him often. Captain Rock, never a man to let anyone challenge his authority, in a fit of anger struck Yellows across the shoulders with the back of a "*sabel*," defined as a "short broad Sword" or a "short and crooked sword"—a cutlass, that is.[9] Such blows could break bones. When Reyning heard about this, he was furious and challenged Rocky to a duel that in essence amounted to a duel over de facto command of the expedition. A victory would either break up the consortship or leave Reyning with enough regard that he might now be seen as the "admiral," at least of the two Dutch buccaneer vessels.

What happened next is based on van der Sterre's account. The men eyed each other warily and began circling, which, in the fencing language of the day, was called "traversing." For a right-hander moving to the right, perhaps the most effective way to traverse was to move the front foot first, then the rear, while keeping the adversary's sword to the left if possible; moving to the left, one moved the rear foot first, then the front, while keeping the adversary's sword to the right. This way, his legs did not cross, which could put the swordsman off balance if he were suddenly attacked in this position. Others, however, believed that one should always move the back foot first, whether to the right or the left, at least if retreating. Traversing was very useful in gaining an advantage in attacking with cutting weapons, though somewhat less so with thrusting weapons such as rapiers, except to gain better ground or to put one's opponent on worse ground.[10]

So here they were, the brutal veteran buccaneer confronting the well-blooded privateer new to buccaneering, cutlasses in hand. As the story goes, the men attacked simultaneously, a mistake we might well expect of aggressive, strong-willed men who had many times wielded cutlasses in battle. In a duel, one may often—and should!—take time to get a feel for the adversary, if the adversary permits, of course. But in battle, one must be able to attack and defend *immediately*. There was seldom time for patient, calculated swordplay.

In this first pass, Rocky wounded Reyning slightly in the belly. But Reyning fought back and cut Rocky on the chin, perhaps with an "outside"—a back cut to Rocky's right side—that only just clipped him. In return, Rocky cut Reyning in the knee, but was himself cut on his undefended forehead. This may well have been a classic exchange: Rocky feinted a cut to the head, then cut swiftly to the leg as Reyning raised his cutlass to parry, then slashed down at Rocky, striking his forehead. *Snickersnee!* went these blades back and forth—cut and thrust! It is an appropriate term, *snickersnee*, for the fight at hand. From the Dutch, it originally meant to "stab (or "stick") and cut"—to cut and thrust, in other words, although now it refers to a long fighting knife.[11] It's also the phrase Lewis Carroll turned into *snicker-snack*, the sound made by the vorpal sword in "Jabberwocky."

According to the account, Rocky now lost control of the duel. Where at first control of the fight went back and forth, as it will between swordsmen of similar ability, now it belonged to Reyning. Again he attacked, wounding Rocky first in the arm, then on the forehead, this time perhaps from a "hanging guard"—the hand as high as the head, the point lower, aimed toward the adversary. If it was timed right, all he had to do was twist his arm sharply, flipping the blade over, and aim for the head.

Facial wounds bleed profusely, and Captain Rock might not have been able to see. Rocky surrendered—at least as the story goes.

Later, Rocky reportedly sought to obtain a Spanish rapier—"een spaense Degen"—with which to challenge Reyning, and Reyning in turn was willing to challenge him with pistols, but a second duel never took place.[12] The two captains and crews parted company instead. Both continued as buccaneers, even fighting under Henry Morgan at Panama in 1671. Rocky continued plundering Spaniards until at least 1673—and was also shipwrecked one more time. At some point after this year, he probably retired to the island of Jamaica, for he still was recalled fondly, if fearfully, some fifteen years later. Reyning's fame continued to grow: he went on to serve the Spanish as a *guarda costa*, then the Netherlands as both a privateer and a naval officer.

When Cut and Thrust Were Real

So here we have it: a duel between pirate captains, almost as we might imagine it. But there is a problem with the story of this formal combat between these two dominant, domineering buccaneers. There are no other historical accounts of dueling for command among buccaneers and filibusters in the late seventeenth century, nor among the pirates of the early eighteenth century. Even the duel between Rock the Brazilian and Jan Erasmus Reyning was really a fight to settle pecking order or to defend a friend, as opposed to one that would confer command, although in fact the winner could probably now call the shots had the loser bothered to stick around.

In fact, not only does van der Sterre describe the fight between Rocky and Reyning in detail, he also mentions another, in which an unidentified captain placed two "zabels" on deck as a challenge to a crewman who had upbraided him for cowardice. The men fought, the captain chased the crewman into the sea—and followed him.[13] But even this was not a duel between captains, or even for command per se, if in fact it even happened.

Although duels are occasionally mentioned in accounts of pirates of this era, only rarely are they described. Occasionally, there are circumstances in which we might suspect a duel. Captain Robert Searles, who sacked St. Augustine and sailed with Henry Morgan against Panama, was "afterwards killed in the Western Lagune [at Laguna de Términos, Mexico], by one of his Company as they were cutting logwood together."[14] However, we do not know whether Searles's death resulted from a duel, a brawl, or outright murder, and in any case it was not a fight between captains. Of all the confirmed duels between pirates of the Golden Age, there is only one known duel between pirate captains for any reason. What, then, should we make of van der Sterre's accounts?

First, although duels could have been fought aboard ships, there really was not room for them. Hollywood pirate ships are usually large ships with lots of deck space, but most real pirate vessels were much, much smaller. Add cannon, other fittings, and rigging, and most decks would be too small to provide anywhere near the space normally allotted for an affair of honor. Even a large deck was far too cluttered for duelists to be able to move around much.

The fact that the duelists' wounds were fairly superficial suggests that they fought at longer distance, making tighter, lighter cuts, not the sweeping slashes we think pirates used in fights, but which are usually very dangerous to the one who makes them. If he misses, he will probably get cut unless he has a shield or "targe," or rides past his target on horseback. Broad, sweeping slashes with a cutlass were best used against the unarmed, the retreating, and the unaware, and occasionally against the adversary over whom the attacker momentarily had a clear advantage in fencing "time." But there probably was not enough space for the tight, light-cutting swordplay in which fencers endeavor to keep proper distance. Much less was there a lot of space for any large, sweeping cuts, should either have been so foolishly inclined or so lucky to have a safe opportunity to do so.

The cutlass, although often looked down upon by non-mariners of the day, was in fact the ideal sword for shipboard fighting—and it was aboard ship that most sword-to-sword fighting took place in this era.

The cutlass was short enough to make it less likely to catch on rigging and fittings or injure a crewmate accidentally in the cramped conditions of a fight on deck, and it had great virtue at close quarters or "handy grips." It was well suited to counteractions at this range, and could also be easily drawn back to make a cut or thrust, which longer blades could not. Its pommel and hilt could be used to "pummel" effectively, breaking bones in the face, and its short, heavy blade was capable of making devastating cuts at close range, even with a short cutting stroke, for the cutlass could act much as a cleaver. If Rock and Reyning had fought close, as the confines of a small vessel's deck would have forced them to do, their injuries should have been severe. At the range of a couple of feet, the hand drawn tightly but powerfully downward and backward, a cutlass can cut right through a brisket or haunch of meat a foot thick—not to mention an arm.

The wounds of close-quarters battle are well described in this example from a seventeenth-century surgical text: "Particularly at the Battel of Worchester, a soldier came to us where we were dressing, with his sword in his hand, the Blade broken off near the Hilt, with many wounds on his Head. I seeing the Hairy scalp of one side of his Head hanging down his Neck, went to him, and calling my Friend Will. Clarke to me with a Sponge to cleanse the Wound, we saw six pieces of the Scull sticking on it: some of them were of the first Table, others of both Tables [layers of skull bone]. Besides which there were various Fissures, *Sedes* [impressions in the skull made by the point of a sharp instrument or weapon], and some Fractures, with Depression, made by Sword, Musketstock, &c."[15]

Doubtless a bit of exaggeration follows, but the cleaving and hacking described in one edition of Exquemelin's *The Buccaneers of America* is entirely possible with the cutlass: "Never did the Spaniards feel better carvers of Mans-flesh; they would take off a Mans Arm at the shoulders, as ye cut off the Wing of a Capon; split a Spanish Mazard [head or skull] as exactly as a Butcher cleaves a Calf's Head, and dissect the Thorax with more dexterity than a Hangman when he goes to take out the Heart of a Traitor."[16] An allegorical illustration on a 1685 French chart of Léogane on Saint-Domingue shows a man who has just split another, without doubt a Spaniard, in half horizontally with a cutlass.[17]

The cutlass was an excellent weapon for clearing decks thick with smoke and men: "for some we cut in pieces, and the rest we drove over board," wrote one mariner of a bloody sea fight.[18] But there are few detailed accounts of its use. Exquemelin recounts an adventure of Alexandre, nicknamed Bras de Fer (Iron Arm), when he attacked the armed shore party of a heavily armed Spanish merchantman, sword-in-hand. Bras de Fer attacked the leader—but missed his head, cutting instead through the length of the wide-brimmed Spanish hat. Worse, as he renewed his attack, Bras de Fer tripped over a root, and instantly his adversary was upon him. Only by dint of his powerful wrist, doubtless that of his sword hand, was Bras de Fer able to spring his opponent's sword from his hand and thereby gain time to call for help.[19]

William Smith, a surveyor aboard a slave ship in 1726, describes a close fight against Africans at the water's edge: "[O]ne of them full of Revenge, and regardless of his Life, got out into the Water behind me, resolving to cleave my Skull with a *Turkish* Scimitar, which *Ridley* perceiving, leap'd out of the Canoe, and just came time enough to give him a Back Stroke, which took the Fellow's Wrist as it was coming down upon my Head, and cut his Hand off almost. *Ridley* with the violent Force of the Blow at once snap'd his Cutlass and disarm'd the Negroe, whose Scimitar falling into the Water, *Ridley* laid hold'of, and us'd instead of his Cutlass." So fierce was the fighting that flashes from the sparking blades could be seen in the darkness by the crew aboard a sloop anchored nearby.[20]

As for the quality of swordplay among pirates and other sea rovers, it surely varied, as it did among soldiers ashore. The fact that swordplay was vital during boarding actions suggests that many pirates had at least some skill in it, although it may have been like that of many soldiers ashore who "do not regularly always observe this Method [formal training]; and most part thrust on any way, without troubling themselves much with the Tierce, Cuart, or Feint; but make use of their Swords to attack or to defend themselves, according to the small talent that God Almighty has given them."[21]

Referring to the pirate Henry Every and his crew, Indian historian Khafi Khan wrote in the late seventeenth century that "The Christians are not bold in the use of the sword," but this was clearly not the case with many Western naval and sea rover crews.[22] Perhaps he was referring to the fact that Western seamen in general favored firearms over the sword or was merely taking pride in Eastern swordplay or in Eastern courage sword-in-hand. Of course, some privateer captains did provide instruction and practice in swordplay to their crews.[23] Perhaps some pirate captains did as well, even if only informally. Doubtless any pirate who was a gentleman or so pretended was instructed in the use of the sword, and surely any pirate who wished to be the first to board an enemy ship was as well.

But the sword was not the only dueling weapon among pirates. Not only did the pig- and cattle-hunting *boucaniers* of Hispaniola fight their duels with muskets, but many buccaneers and filibusters did as well, for this was the Caribbean pirate's primary arm—not the cutlass, nor the sword in any form. These musket duelists drew lots to see who would fire first, then stood at a specified distance apart, probably at least fifty yards, for they were excellent shots out to a hundred yards. First one fired, then, if still standing, the other. A surgeon examined any dead body to make sure there had been no back shooting. Such duels could only be fought ashore.[24]

Early eighteenth-century pirates often fought duels with pistols ashore, to be followed by cutlasses if necessary. The articles of Bartholomew Roberts and his crew reportedly provided that "The Quarter-Master of the Ship, when the Parties will not come to any Reconciliation, accompanies them on Shore with what Assistance he thinks proper, and turns the Disputants Back to Back, at so many Paces Distance: At the Word of Command, they turn and fire immediately, (or else the Piece is knocked out of their Hands:) If both miss they come to their Cutlashes, and then he is declared Victor who draws the first Blood."[25] There were other methods of dueling with pistols during this era, and it is likely that pirates may have used them as well.

Even among those pirates who preferred the sword—and surely many did—a duel was always better fought ashore where there was room to move and maneuver. In fact, every other duel noted in pirate journals of the period was fought ashore, and for good reason. Besides safety to bystanders and fairness to the antagonists, fighting ashore gave the angry duelists a chance to cool off, at least in the case of an affront given at sea. It also helped prevent the crew from dividing even further into factions aboard ship. Duels aboard ship, while they might be a diverting entertainment to some, would ultimately have been a distraction that disturbed the good order required for safety at sea. If Rocky and Reyning fought a duel, they would almost certainly have done it ashore.

Second, Rocky's dispute with his quartermaster was none of Reyning's business. The dispute was between Captain Rock and his quartermaster, Yellows, who could have challenged him for the blow. Only in battle did buccaneer captains have absolute authority. The dispute would have been settled between the two, or even by a vote among the rest of the crew, if they believed Captain Rock was out of line. Reyning's intervention was unusual, unless he was already looking to pick a fight.

Third, many details noted by van der Sterre cannot be corroborated elsewhere. In particular, buccaneer surgeon Alexandre Exquemelin is the major source of information on Rock, and although Exquemelin is not always entirely accurate, he is fairly reliable. But he does not mention any duel or other conflict between Rock and Reyning. In fact, he does not mention Reyning in any edition of his books. Van der Sterre was a doctor hired by the Dutch West India Company to take care of slaves on Curaçao.[26] His knowledge of Reyning's escapades came from Reyning and others, but it was hearsay, not firsthand eyewitness knowledge. Exquemelin, however, had participated in some of the events he wrote about, and was therefore not only much closer to his sources, but also had much personal experience of how buccaneering worked.

Last, there are the duelists themselves: How likely is it that a man who could leap into the sea, daggers in hand, and kill sharks would give up so easily in a fight? But perhaps the arm wound incapacitated him, or he bled too much from his head wounds to be able to see.

So again, what should we make of van der Sterre's description? Although it might well depict the dueling practices of Dutch pirates and privateers—and the Dutch were indeed fond of dueling, with both knife and sword, especially the backsword and cutlass—it is just as likely a heavily fictionalized account, with many details invented by the author. In fact, it has too many details of the sort a novelist uses to give the flavor of truth. Typically, these are missing from factual accounts.

So why invent and add them to a factual account? Because conflict is vital for book sales, and duels make for great action—especially those between two famous pirates. Such "part fact, part fiction" accounts were common in the period. The most famous example is *The Memoirs of d'Artagnan*, from which Alexandre Dumas took not only the plot for his famous novel *The Three Musketeers*, but his characters as well. Van der Sterre gave his readers what they expected: a duel, in great detail, between captains on the deck of a ship. All this being said, there remains the remote possibility that the duel happened much as Reyning's biographer described it.

The "Art" of the Duel

Although Reyning's perhaps very fictional biography was popular in the Netherlands at the time, it is not likely the source of the storytelling myth of dueling for command among pirates. Written in Dutch, it was never translated into English and probably had little effect on the creators of swashbuckling fiction and film in English, for these artists, along with a handful of illustrators, remain the greatest influence on pirate myths and modern "pirate culture." In their world, duels were almost always fought on a sandy shore on a small island or key in the Caribbean, with a clear blue sky above and turquoise waters lapping gently on shores sheltered by coconut palms, with the cry of a parrot or the lyrics of a sea shanty floating somewhere in the background. And why not? It's what Caribbean shores are like, and this is where pirates actually fought their duels.

It should come as no surprise that writers of swashbuckling fare old and new, not to mention Hollywood, have often played up conflict between pirate captains, leaving us with the impression that they often fought duels for command or whenever they disagreed with each other. After all, it makes a great plot device when necessary, and entire plots can be built around it.

Indeed, two of the greatest pirate duels in fiction and film—duels that have left us much of our image of what pirate duels were all about—take place between pirate captains. Could they be the origin of the myth? Foremost is the famous duel between Captain Peter Blood and the pirate Levasseur in the 1935 film version of Rafael Sabatini's famous novel, *Captain Blood*. Captain Blood's name—an appropriately sanguinary name that made an excellent eponymous title—was probably inspired at least in part by Colonel Thomas Blood, who stole the Crown Jewels from the Tower of London but was soon captured.[27] Captain Blood's brief nemesis, the villainous, lascivious Captain Levasseur, kidnapper and erstwhile ravisher—rapist, that is—of women, was named after an early governor of the island of Tortuga, the famous buccaneer and fili-buster haunt just off the north coast of the island of Hispaniola.

The two actors fought with stage rapiers—that is, rapier hilts mounted with épée blades used in sport fencing. These blades, light by comparison to real rapier blades, permitted Hollywood-style sword-play—a flashy combination of classical foil and saber, made with wide and comparatively slower movements (otherwise the audience could not follow the blades)—and doubtless spared the actor's arms as well. The large size of the shells at the hilts pronounces them as rapiers, but per-haps the armorer or fight director had them enlarged to meet audience expectations, or so they could be better seen on screen, or both.

Of course, real French, English, and Dutch pirates at this time, if they used thrusting swords at all, would not have used rapiers, but "transitional rapiers" (to use a modern term) or "small-swords," which were light thrusting swords descended from the rapier, and which were confusingly often referred to as rapiers. More confusingly, these épée-bladed stage rapiers were actually more similar to the transitional rapiers and smallswords than to rapiers, and thus more historically correct. Again, though, only Spanish, Portuguese, and some Italian pirates might have used real rapiers.

The duel begins with the now-famous lines, "You do not take her while I live!" to which Peter Blood replies, "Then I'll take her when you're dead."[28] The lines also give away the duel's provocation as well, at least to those who have never seen the film or read the book. It was fought over the perception of a woman's honor, with Peter Blood displaying great chivalry, as one would expect of a romantic hero. The duel proceeds apace. In the Errol Flynn film version, there are close-ups hilt-to-hilt, and long shots of elegant fencing poses as well, along with rougher swordplay. It ends as we would expect, with Captain Blood impaling the rascal pirate. For those with an interest in swordplay or trivia, the leftward lunge off the line (assuming a right-hander)—a sneaky move, but not a dishonorable one—made by Errol Flynn as Captain Blood when he runs Levasseur through, was known as *intagliata* in some of the Italian schools. In the book, however, Levasseur is defeated only by "practiced skill."[29] The details are left to our imagination.

Sabatini also wrote *The Black Swan*, another pirate novel set in the same period, which was later made into a film of the same name starring Tyrone Power and Maureen O'Hara. The entire plot leads to a duel between Captain Charles de Bernis, a former buccaneer, and the villain Captain Tom Leach, an outright pirate, at the climax. Once more, though, it is not a duel over command, but one fought in large part over a woman's honor, although a pirate-hunting plot enters as well. In fact, there are no records of pirates of this era dueling over a woman's honor, or even over her possession, although such duels were otherwise common.

When pirates fought over a woman, it was mostly likely while drunk in a tavern or "stew," as houses of prostitution were known. Again, the duel Sabatini describes is what we have come to expect, and more. It is a brief tour de force, man against man, and may the *more cunning* man win. The villain loses, of course, this time by the hero de Bernis pivoting and "making in his turn a lunging movement outward upon the left knee"—in other words, an *intagliata*, or perhaps what in English was known as "volting" or "avolting," which the fight director appropriated from the novel and gave to the 1935 film version of *Captain Blood*.[30]

Pirate Democracy, Plus an Unquestioned Duel

If not from real pirate duels or from these two famous film duels, where, then, does the myth of pirates dueling for command originate? We can look back even further in cinematic history, to silent film actor Douglas Fairbanks, who single-handedly created the modern movie swashbuckler genre in 1920 with *The Mark of Zorro*. In his 1926 film, *The Black Pirate*, Fairbanks's character challenges a pirate captain and defeats him in a duel with rapiers and daggers by cunningly forcing his adversary to trip backward and impale himself on a dagger placed there for the purpose. At last, a duel for command! Or at least one that will lead to command.

Although we might argue that this film inspired the myth of pirates dueling for command, it actually has a much deeper origin, an innate one deriving from our aggressive, violent, competitive, hierarchical nature. We naturally expect that pirates would fight for command. Something deep within tells us this is how it was, or at least how it should have been. Prior to *The Black Pirate*, the famous illustrator Howard Pyle exploited this well in his painting *Which Shall Be Captain?*

Two pirates, armed with daggers, are locked hand-to-wrist, legs braced and pushing against the adversary, each man trying to wrest his bodkin free and kill the other while the crew watches expectantly. Nearby is an unburied treasure chest and a pair of shovels. We don't even need to read the accompanying story by Don C. Seitz; the picture *is* the story. Of course pirates fought duels for command. One look and we know this must be true, so effective is Pyle at appealing to our inner nature. A few years earlier, he had painted a similar duel for command titled *Why*

Don't You End It? for *To Have and to Hold* by Mary Johnston. Her novel was a significant influence on Rafael Sabatini's writing.[31]

This image has been repeated many times, most lately in *Pirates of the Caribbean: The Black Pearl* in 2003, when Barbossa draws his sword and dares any man of his mutinous crew to challenge him. Perhaps Seitz and other authors got the idea from pirate Bartholomew Roberts, who once challenged any of his crew who did not like the way he treated them, that "They might go ashore and take satisfaction of him, if they thought fit, at sword or pistol, for he neither valued nor feared any of them."[32] But even this is not the same as a duel for command.

Ultimately, the myth originates from our expectation that leaders will fight for command, and that the strongest should lead. This is how it often is in much of the animal kingdom, of which we are in fact merely a somewhat-civilized member. But strength is not as simple as it seems. Although we greatly admire strength in its many physical forms—raw muscular strength, not to mention speed and endurance—we humans are at the top of the food chain not because we are great physical predators. Indeed, we are much weaker physically than any comparable animal of our size.

What we are is smarter by leaps and bounds. We know how to best use our limited strengths and minimize our many weaknesses, and we can also innovate in ways that only a few animals even have a hint of, and which none can match us at by an order of magnitude in the thousands. Charles de Bernis wins his duel not merely by being a strong, skilled fencer, but above all by outsmarting his adversary—within the rules of the duel, of course. Strength and skill were mandatory—but so was cunning.

And so it was with pirate leaders, especially during the Golden Age. They did not fight physically for command. Rather, they were elected democratically, as were quartermasters, by a vote of the entire crew, each man having a single vote, captains excepted with two votes.[33] Even other officers, boatswain and carpenter for example, were usually elected.[34] This is how both Rocky and Reyning earned their commands. The best man—the man whom the majority believed could put pieces of eight in their hats (for this was usually where they received their spoils when the division was made and pirates took their individual shares)—won. Even this democratic victory came with restrictions: pirate captains commanded absolutely only in battle, and could be deposed by vote at any time but during battle. Never could his position be challenged in the form of a duel, with command going or returning to the victor.

A pirate captain therefore had no need to prove his mettle in a duel in which victory might actually prove meaningless. Firearms, the musket especially, and great guns (cannon) were the pirate's real arms, those that made up the greater part of his success. To these we must add the more intangible weapons of courage, flexibility, knowledge, and, most vital of all, leadership. With these did a pirate succeed.

Pirates had no need to prove their courage in a duel. They proved it in battle. For a pirate, a duel settled only personal quarrels and proved only skill in limited single combat—or lack thereof—and perhaps that, for a moment, fortune favored one man over another.

Ships, however, were almost never captured after single combat between the captains of the attacker and the attacked, as Reyning is said to have once done, and which French privateer René Duguay-Trouin once actually did.[35] Ships were captured by pirate crews working together under the command of a captain they had chosen. And certainly, ships were never captured as a result of a swordfight between a pirate captain, who had won his place by dueling for it, and the captain of the ship he intended to capture. In fact, pirate duels in general seem to have been less common than we think. Dueling, after all, could be divisive among crews, and it was vital that pirate crews work together. Only in extreme cases do pirates appear to have challenged each other, at least while they were part of a pirate crew or pirate expedition.

Captain versus Captain

We cannot leave the subject of dueling versus democracy without describing the sole confirmed duel between pirate captains of the Golden Age. Again, the adversaries are Dutchmen. But their duel is not aboard

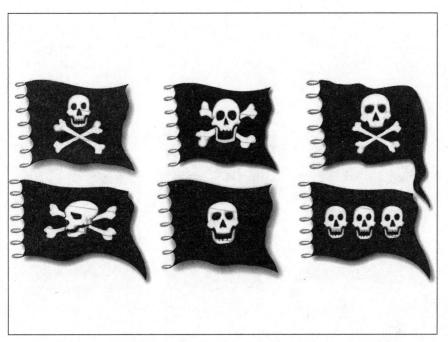

Possible likenesses of authentic pirate flags based on eyewitness descriptions. Top row: red flag of no quarter flown by filibusters at Acaponeta, Mexico (1688); common skull and bones with bones crossed behind; common skull and bones with bones crossed below. Bottom row: possible variation of skull and bones based on tombstone imagery; traditional death's head; two unidentified pirates (1718) at Barbados and Saint-Domingue flying multiple "death's heads" on a black field. Any pirate flag noted as flying a death's head could have looked like flags 2, 3, 4, or 5. Many pirates, including Blackbeard, were described as flying the skull and bones or death's head. (Original illustrations by Chad H. Scales.)

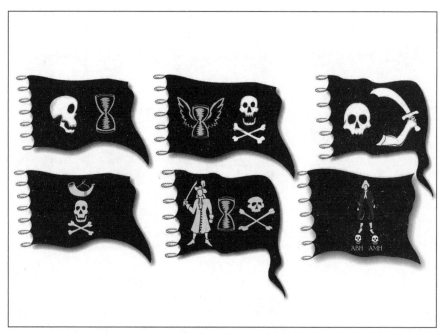

Possible likenesses of authentic pirate flags based on eyewitness descriptions. Top row: Capt. Napin (1717), version 1; Capt. Napin (1717), version 2, and Capt. Wynne (1700), shown with common winged hourglass variant; Capt. Roberts (1720). Bottom row: unknown pirates who attacked the Roggewein voyage (1721); Capt. Kennedy (1716); jack flown by Capt. Roberts (1720). (Original illustrations by Chad H. Scales.)

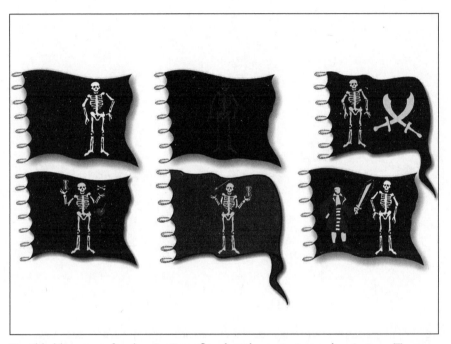

Possible likenesses of authentic pirate flags based on eyewitness descriptions. Top row: Capt. Worley (1718); Capt. Low aboard the *Merry Christmas* (1723); unidentified pirate off the coast of Brazil (1718). Bottom row: Capt. Roberts at Whydah (1722); Capt. Harris (1723); Capt. Skyrme at Whydah, 1722. (Original illustrations by Chad H. Scales.)

Possible likenesses of authentic pirate flags based on eyewitness descriptions. Top row: unidentified French pirate west of Madeira (1717); crossbones variant of the same unidentified French pirate (1717); unidentified pirate, probably French, among the Virgin Islands (1717). Bottom row: Capt. Dulaien (1728, based on a drawing reportedly made the same year); Capt. Dulaien (1728, based on a woodcut reportedly made in 1729); Barbary corsair flag of no quarter (1719, from a set of flag illustrations). (Original illustrations by Chad H. Scales.)

Five buccaneers and one *boucanier* from the 1680s. The image is based on eyewitness illustrations on French Caribbean charts drawn during this decade. (Original illustration by Chad H. Scales.)

A heavily armed Dutch-built Spanish *urca* similar to the "Honduras ship" *Gran San Pablo,* whose valiant captain and crew fought off both filibusters and Barbary corsairs in 1677. (Frontispiece from *Ordenanzas de la ilustre Universidad, y Casa de contratación . . . de 1737.* Bilbao: 1775.)

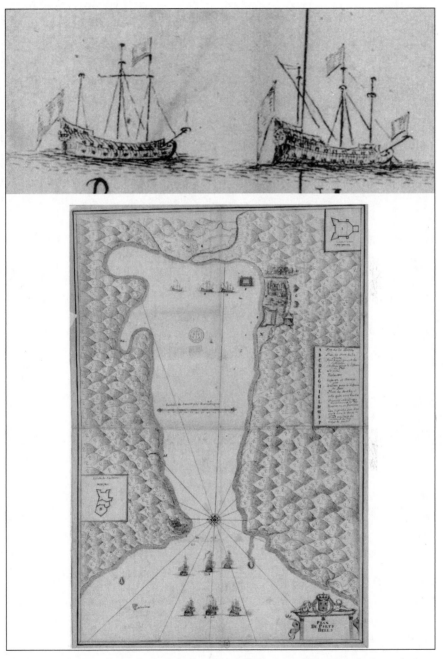

Portobello in 1682, showing the *Capitana* and *Almirante* of the *Armada de Barlovento*: the *Santo Cristo de Burgos* of fifty-six guns and the *Nuestra Señora de la Conceptión* of fifty-two. Filibuster Laurens de Graff commanding the *Neptune* will engage these two great ships in an epic sea fight three years later. (From a chart by Agarat, 1682. Courtesy of the French National Library.)

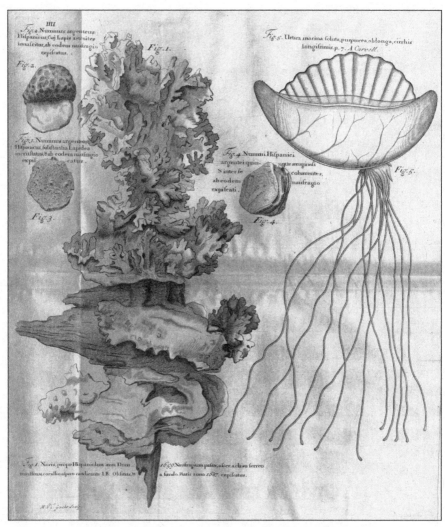

Coral-encrusted pieces of eight and timber salvaged in 1687 by William Phips from the Spanish treasure ship *Concepción*, sunk in 1641. (Originally published by Sir Hans Sloane in *A Voyage to the Islands Madera, Barbados, Nieves, S. Christophers and Jamaica*, volume 1, plate IIII. London: 1707.)

the confines of the deck of a small vessel, but ashore, as it ought to be, three and a half miles from Veracruz, Mexico, on the tiny Isla de Sacrificios (Sacrifice Island). Only two hundred by four hundred yards in size, it was named for the Native American sacrifices Spanish conquistadors found evidence of—in the form of five fresh human bodies—in the early sixteenth century.[36]

The adversaries are two of the three co-commanders of the only days-old sack of Veracruz: Laurens de Graff, tall, blond, swashbuckling, dashing, and known by the Spanish as Lorencillo, and Nicolas Van Horn, ostentatious but with much less flair than de Graff. Perhaps he is wearing the rich necklace of pearls and rubies he was known for. Both men are exceedingly proud. Both have short tempers, which, when circumstances force them to simmer, will eventually explode. Van Horn is also often insolent, and de Graff often impatient, at least with fools, and fond of cursing, a habit he perhaps picked up from the Spaniards whom he served as a gunner. Or perhaps he just understands the value of foul language in relieving anger, motivating men, and making oneself plain.

Surrounding them now are thousands of Spanish prisoners, plus a large number of their crews. These filibusters and buccaneers will not interfere, for duels are private affairs. Veracruz has already been sacked. The outcome will not affect the pieces of eight soon to overflow each man's cupped hands.

The origin of the duel is, at least according to several various accounts, uncertain. De Graff has despised Van Horn ever since he attacked the rich Honduras ships in the Bay of Amatique before they were loaded with goods. During the sack of Veracruz, de Graff has had de facto command, even though Van Horn is technically in command. In other words, de Graff considers Van Horn a fool unfit to command, and Van Horn resents de Graff for usurping him. This very morning an English buccaneer reported that Van Horn had insulted de Graff behind his back, calling him a coward.[37] But then, so has de Graff probably done to Van Horn, who is angry that de Graff would prevent him from decapitating a dozen prisoners in retaliation for Spanish soldiers from San Juan de Ulúa across the bay shooting at filibusters who were fetching cornmeal to feed prisoners. Some say there was an argument over what to do next: Van Horn wanted to wait for the treasure fleet to arrive and then attack it, but de Graff wanted to depart with what they had, rather than risk losing it. An English governor will believe they fought over the division of spoils.[38] Some Spaniards will later believe the men fought over who could choose how the spoils were divided, and thus over command—affirming what we all deep inside want to believe.

What matters is that the duel meets our expectations: pirate captains on a tropical beach, each man despising the other, each man ready to do violence to the other. Each unsheathes his bladed weapon—a cutlass or a more ornate hanger, although we imagine it might have been a smallsword of, to use a modern term, the "transitional rapier" sort, or even a light backsword or a cut-and-thrust sword of the sort the Scots called a shearing sword. Again, they probably do not use rapiers, although one might argue that de Graff, with his Spanish seafaring experience, might be inclined to. Even so, paintings of most fighting sea captains of the era show them with cutlasses.

De Graff, whose panache never leaves him at a loss for words, says as he draws his sword, or at least Alexandre Exquemelin says he does, "Voilà! With this I shall avenge the insult you have given me."[39]

There are but a few detailed accounts of the swordplay of specific duels of this era, and most are of what later would be, strictly speaking, affrays: two men agree to fight and simply do, with little of the formality mandatory in later centuries, and not uncommon even at this time. Most accounts do not describe the actual parries and thrusts. One reads of attacks, often called "pushing" if a thrusting sword is used, and of parries, ripostes, batters, and timings, but only rarely is the attack, parry, or other technique specifically identified. Occasionally there is mention of "commanding" (grasping the adversary's blade by the forte or shell), sometimes accompanied by grappling. Often enough, both fencers are hit. Records of sword duels suggest that most duels did not last long. In later centuries, two minutes was not uncommon, and many lasted as long as eight. Only rarely did duels last longer, although a few are known to have lasted hours. Most, however, were over in one, two, or three passes, as exchanges of attack, parry, and riposte were called. De Graff and Van Horn have plunder to load, prisoners to watch, guards to keep. They will not take all day.

Surely, we imagine, based on what we know of swordplay of the period, they make a trial pass. Their blades ring—sword blades, if of any decent quality at all, have a distinct peal that the fencer comes to eternally associate with his or her passion. The sound echoes across the small island. Surely some prisoners look up in fear, wondering if rescue is at hand, with all the dangers inherent of men fighting nearby. But the filibusters and buccaneers do not take up their arms. There is no rescue.

Probably they make a second pass. Perhaps Van Horn attacks, de Graff parries. So sharply do the blades strike each other that sparks fly; the adversaries might briefly note the metallic smell of ozone the sparks give off. The adversaries traverse. If it is morning, each tries to put the sun in the other's eyes, but both men are too smart to let the other get away with this.

De Graff, we imagine, now advances on Van Horn. The flamboyant swashbuckler, after all, is not a patient man, but one of action, and in attacking he feels he is in control, even if his attack is merely a feint. Yet perhaps he waits scornfully at first for Van Horn to attack, intending to cut him on his advance, or strike him with a riposte, hoping to heap even more scorn on Van Horn for being so foolish and so easily defeated. But, we imagine, Van Horn will not take the bait. De Graff attacks. He advances on Van Horn, shifting from an outside guard to an inside to a hanging guard—of which some say the Dutch are very fond—with each movement forward, even as he closes the distance. In range, de Graff suddenly presses lightly with his blade against Van Horn's, then, sensing no reaction, he presses strongly, binding Van Horn's blade and opening the line. Swiftly, his hand kept left to keep the line closed, he "throws an inside" at Van Horn's briefly exposed arm. Van Horn parries quickly, pushing hand and blade to his left, but de Graff's blade is no longer there. Expecting this, he has cut over sharply to the outside, to Van Horn's wrist.

Van Horn drops his blade. The fight is over, for Van Horn is now unarmed and also wounded, unable to hold his sword. To kill an unarmed man is to murder him, although, strictly speaking, so is killing a man in a duel, at least according to the law. It is best that Van Horn live, for even a "legitimate" death in a duel might fracture the bonds holding the several pirate crews together. Van Horn does not live long: gangrene or pestilence soon takes his life.

But this is only how we might imagine the duel might have gone, based on historical fencing texts, historical accounts of duels, related practical knowledge and experience of swordplay and personal combat, and what we know of buccaneers and filibusters. And certainly some duels might have gone the way just described. In this case, however, we have an actual account brought to us by Fray Juan de Avila, whose description of the sack and rape of Veracruz brings these horrors too sadly to life.

According to Fray Avila, "On Thursday afternoon Admiral Lorenzo [de Graff], seeing how we suffered [from thirst and hunger], told the General [Van Horn] that they should cast us ashore as I wanted them to do. The General grew angry and told me he would put us to the sword. At these words the Admiral drew his cutlass with such agility that before the General had put himself on guard Lorenzo had cut him in the arm and ear. They [the pirates] stopped them and I heard the admiral call his soldiers and send him [Van Horn] to his ship which was the *almiranta* [Van Horn's *St. Nicolas*], and from this day we saw him no more."[40]

The "stroke" de Graff used is unclear, but quite likely was as simple as a single movement: an upward cut as his cutlass cleared his scabbard, first striking Van Horn's hand or arm, then his ear, or a simple double movement, drawing and cutting to the head, perhaps inside to outside, high to low, hitting the ear then the arm. Certainly, de Graff made no more than three or four movements: draw, cut, recover, or draw, cut, cut, recover, all like lightning. Clearly, this was not Errol Flynn fencing Basil Rathbone in *Captain Blood* on the shore of Virgin Magra—novelist Rafael Sabatini's little joke on Virgin Gorda—which was actually filmed at Three Arch Bay just south of Laguna Beach, California. There appear to have been no noble words of honor and retribution suitable to a novel, there was no play of rapier on rapier from sand dune to sea foam—there were only angry words followed by a fight with cutlasses that lasted but seconds at most.

Soon enough the real pirates are back at sea and headed to Petit Goave, their headquarters on Saint-Domingue on the island of Hispaniola. But Van Horn dies en route, of complications of the minor wound, it is said, although disease does race through the ship before he dies. Due to Van Horn's death, de Graff must later seek a royal pardon in order to become a French naval officer.[41] Louis XIV grants the pardon. Thus ends the most famous pirate duel in history, fought between captains who crossed swords not over command but over private honor that derived from argument over command. Never had these men fought a duel for command, for they, like all pirates of their age, served at the pleasure of their notorious, sea-thieving crews.

CHAPTER 9

Titillation with a Cutlass

———✺———

"[S]oe that you shall see a common woman only in her smock ore linen peticote, barefooted, without shoo or stockins, with a strawn hatt and a red tobacco pipe in their mouths, and thus they trampouse about their streets in this their warlike posture, and thus arrayed they will booze a cup of punch rumby with anyone."[1]
—John Taylor, *Taylor's History of His Life and Travels*, 1687

Pirate democracy notwithstanding, piracy, like seafaring, was a male-dominated profession, so much so that it is fair to say it was for all practical purposes an entirely male profession. Nonetheless, in this modern era of female strength and intelligence un-reined, grand myths of pirate women have been un-reined as well. But there is more to the truths and myths of pirate women than mere revisionist history in light of modern women's rights and empowerment: they go to the very root of the nature and connection of the sexes.

By now, the pirates must have believed they would escape. It was four hours past sunset and the silver sliver that was the two-day-old moon had already followed the sun into the western Caribbean, leaving the Milky Way to ascend from the sea where they had disappeared.[2] On deck and below, most members of the pirate crew were damnably drunk.

All afternoon and evening, they had been drinking punch—a mixture of rum, sugar, and Key limes—and surely had even been quaffing rum straight as well, first in celebration at the signing of nine new men that morning, then to fortify themselves with "Dutch courage" when they realized a pirate hunter was in pursuit, perhaps by recognizing its "privateer jack"—a Union flag with a white escutcheon at the center, which Barnet had flown before.[3] And if the pirates were to be undone, it was probably rum that would do so, for only a crew of drunken fools in a swift sloop could not escape on a night so dark unless the wind had died.[4]

Aboard the sloop were nineteen pirates, although nine would later claim to have been forced aboard that morning, yet this attempt at saving their necks from the noose would not take. They were not a particularly notorious bunch, these pirates, and they should have been destined for a mere footnote in history. Mostly they cruised around Jamaica and among the Cuban cays, snatching up small trading and fishing sloops, looting their cargoes, and then sending their crews on their way.

Only three days before, on October 19, 1720, they had captured a small schooner, plundering her of fifty rolls of tobacco, nine heavy bags of "pimento" (allspice), and assorted sails and rigging. Two of the most vociferous of the pirates, brandishing arms, had cursed and screamed at the schooner's crew, putting them in fear for their lives. The next day, they did the same to the crew of a small sloop. They could not go after larger prey, for there simply were not enough pirates in the crew.

The sloop that struck so much fear into the pirates, and from which they had run after first firing a great gun and a musket or pistol in defiance, was a small, well-armed and well-manned trading vessel commanded by Jonathan Barnet, who was on a trading voyage to the keys off the south coast of Cuba, in company with a small trading sloop commanded by Captain Bonnevie. Previous to this, in November 1715, Barnet had commissioned for a period of no more than six months to "take and apprehend all Piratical Ships and Vessels."[5] Commissions were commonly renewed as necessary, and Barnet's apparently was, given his obvious willingness to chase a pirate, not to mention his behavior of authority under the King's colors, although, as already noted, many commissions had been revoked due to abuses. Barnet, a redoubtable seaman, had even been accused of doing his job too well by committing "hostilities upon the Cuba shore," for he had been one of those privateers whose pursuit of Spanish pirates may have gotten out of hand.[6] Barnet, however, did not turn to piracy.

He was not a man to be shaken off the trail easily, and tonight he would not be shaken off at all. He put his men to the oars, helping move the sloop along in the light airs. The pirates put their oars out, too, and slipped away from Point Negril on the western tip of Jamaica.

Barnet's sloop gained slowly on its prey, for the pirate sloop, of a mere thirty or forty tons, was reportedly "one of the swiftest sailors that ever was built of that kind."[7] In fact, it was nothing short of a miracle that Barnet's sloop still chased the pirate in the pitch-black darkness, unless the airs were still light. The standard tactic for a vessel chased was to do whatever necessary to escape until nightfall, then change course and run like hell into the darkness, leaving the pursuer to wonder which course to take. But the pirate crew was drunk; perhaps they even had lanterns lit. That was a rule when chased at night: dowse all lights.

Of course, there were other ways to chase in the darkness. If close enough, the hunters might have been able to follow the pirates by the noise they made. Or, if Barnet were fairly close to the pirate vessel and also between it and the shore, his lookouts might have been able to spot the sloop's great mainsail against the stars. Or, mighty Jupiter or Venus, if at their brightest, may have illuminated sea and sail enough for the pirate hunters to follow. Vessels could be pursued by this relatively small light: "But happening to be in the Wake of the Planet *Jupiter*, who then very much blazed, they again descry'd us . . ."[8] But neither Jupiter nor Venus was above the horizon during the chase.

Even so, if the sloop could gain some distance and slip between Barnet and the shore, it would be almost impossible to spot it against the great dark mass of the large island. The small-time drunken pirates, whether by leaving lanterns lit, or shouting too loudly and too often, or carelessly handling their sloop and oars, or simply not having enough men (or enough sober men) to row swiftly, gave the pirate-hunting sloop the opening it needed.

Around 10 p.m., a large form suddenly coalesced from bare hints of something unknown in the darkness. Barnet was alongside the pirate, well within the sixty-yard effective range of a swivel gun loaded with grapeshot or canister.[9]

"Ahoy!" came the hail from Barnet's sloop.

"John Rackam from Cuba!" came the reply.

"Strike immediately to the King of England's colors!" Barnet ordered.

"We will strike no strikes!" came the reply.[10]

A swivel gun, probably loaded with musket balls, cracked loudly in punctuation, sending a six-foot-wide swath of hot metal across the deck of the pirate hunter. Barnet would not stand for this. He ordered a broadside. His small cannon lit up the night, the fire from their muzzles reflecting briefly like liquid gold on the water, quickly shrouded by a great cloud of gun smoke. A round shot shattered the mainsail boom, carrying it away and crippling the pirate sloop. A musket volley followed: the red-gold of the fathom-long muzzle flashes looking like flaming death. The balls sped furiously on their way across the short distance to hammer timbers and, if they stood in the way, pirates.

The pirates panicked. Of those on deck, all but three fled below and cowered in fear or drunken stupor. Pirates of the early eighteenth century often flew into a panic at the sight of a man-of-war or other vessel capable of making a stout fight. "Hell was never in greater confusion than was then aboard," wrote a pirate prisoner of just such a situation.[11] These men, whose experience as pirates was mostly with merchant and fishing crews who did not put up a fight, and nine of whom probably had little or no experience at all as pirates, were no different.

But two of the three pirates on deck refused to surrender, at least according to pirate chronicler Charles Johnson. They would not retreat like dogs to closed quarters but would fight like men on deck. One of the vociferous pair—surely this must have been the pirate captain—fired pistols down the hatch into the mass of cowering pirates, killing one and wounding others, although Johnson may have been abusing his literary license and describing something that never actually happened.

Alas, the pirates on deck quickly realized there was little they could do to prevent their capture. They could not even manage the sailing of the sloop or man the small cannon, much less stand against a boarding party that surely would number two score or more. Cursing and swearing at both pirate hunter alongside and pirate crew below, they asked for "good quarter," which was granted. There was nothing immediately apparent to distinguish the two stout seamen who had been willing to fight the pirate hunters and certainly nothing that would suggest either was the captain. Doubtless they wore "men's jackets, and long trousers, and handkerchiefs tied around their heads." They were armed as usual among pirates, with cutlass and pistols.

Three weeks later the pirates were brought to trial and convicted, including the unfortunate nine turtle fishermen who had joined the pirates shortly before they were captured. When sentence was pronounced on the most valiant of the crew—". . . where you shall be severally hang'd by the neck, till you are severally dead . . ."—the two spoke up immediately, claiming to be "quick with child."[12] An inspection confirmed this, and their hanging was postponed.

The two pirates, of course, were Anne Bonny and Mary Read, the most significant female pirates of the Golden Age from 1655 to 1725. Mary Read was by reputation the warrior among the two, having served, according to Johnson, as a soldier, as a volunteer in the infantry at first, and later in a regiment of horse.[13] This is not far-fetched, for we know that other women had served similarly in disguise as men. But it's fiery Anne Bonny we invariably see in Hollywood films and television shows. She is always attractive, and always has the martial skills stolen by script writers from Mary Read and given to her. It is clearly not enough that there be a pirate woman; she must also be sexy.

According to Charles Johnson, Bonny was born in Kinsale, Ireland, Read in England. Bonny was apparently in her early twenties, Read well into her thirties. They were hellions, as pirates ought to be, brandishing pistols and cutlasses, and cursing and swearing, perhaps even more so than usual among pirates, for as women they may have felt they had to prove their worth. Yet they, at least according to Johnson, retained their feminine attractions as well: Bonny was the lover of John Rackam, alias Calico Jack. Johnson wrote that she told Rackam, just before he was hanged, that "she was sorry to see him there, but if he had fought like a man, he need not have been hanged like a dog."[14]

And Rackam was indeed hanged, and his body taken to Plumb Point, roughly four miles east of Port Royal, where it, and those of two of his companions, were "hung on Gibbets in Chains, for a publick Example, and to terrify others from such-like evil Practices."[15] Read was the lover of another of the crew, and reportedly even fought a duel on her lover's behalf, with pistol and cutlass, killing her adversary. A witness noted that the women dressed in pirate clothing only when chasing and attacking their prey. Otherwise, on board they went about dressed as women.[16]

In literature of the period, we often find adventurous women in disguise—in Shakespeare, for example, and in Restoration comedies and novels, some of them quite bawdy. The stories put women in strong masculine roles, yet the women retain their femininity, and thus titillate the audience or reader. For example, Meriton Latroon, the rakish hero of *The English Rogue*, published in 1665, is at one point held up by a highwayman. Victim and robber draw swords and fight, but the highwayman is a skilled swordsman and almost bests the merry rogue until they come to grips, whereby the hero discovers "him" to be a her. Even better, he soon discovers her two companion highway "men" are also in fact women. All soon retire to a room at an inn, where Latroon leaves the reader to imagine what their "nocturnal passages" were.[17]

Johnson recognized immediately that these women fit this literary bill, and if they did not, he rewrote history to ensure they did. Anne Bonny and Mary Read were perfect for myth and legend, a combination of violence and titillation—of woman freed of her restraints, yet woman still bound to and attractive to a man. Unfortunately, we do not know how much of the biographies of these two women was invented by Johnson.

Neither she-pirate was hanged. What happened to Bonny is unknown. Read died roughly nine months later, quite possibly of complications of childbirth. Were it not for these two women pirates, Calico Jack Rackam, whose other claim to fame was that he once served as quartermaster and consort pirate captain to the pirate Charles Vane, would almost certainly have been forgotten, and our swashbuckling cinema would be diminished. Above all, these two women are the source of our modern image of the woman pirate, most of whom are depicted as pirate captains—yet neither Anne Bonny nor Mary Read ever commanded a vessel.[18]

Picaresque Wives and Pirate Women

Indeed and unfortunately, we know of no women pirate captains, or even privateer captains, during the Golden Age from 1655 to 1725. In fact, there is only one other known female pirate of this era, at least that we know of, other than Bonny and Read: Mary Harvey, an Englishwoman tried in Virginia for piracy in 1726. Hers was a comical tale of a handful of clumsy, clueless oafs, one of whom was her husband, failing miserably at a brief stint at piracy. In 1729, Mary Crickett was tried and hanged for piracy, along with her several male companions. Neither of these women pirates, nor their male accomplices, were part of the great associated group of pirates who plundered from 1715 to roughly 1725. In fact, most of the women listed today as pirates during the period 1655 to 1725 were not pirates at all. Rather, their "piracies" are based on myth and hearsay, and in some cases, purported facts about these "pirate women" have been carved from thin air.[19]

Jacquotte Delahaye, for example, is said to have been a biracial female filibuster who cruised from Tortuga off the north coast of Saint-Domingue (modern-day Haiti) during the 1650s. An entire, if brief, biography has been written of her and repeated without question in books and online. She commanded a ship with a crew of a hundred men; she rejected a marriage proposal from filibuster Michel d'Artigue, known as "le Basque"; and she led the attack on Fort de la Roche on Tortuga in

1656 and recaptured it from the Spanish. But there is no evidence that she existed. Her life is a 1940s fabrication by French author Léon Treich.[20]

On the other hand, there are several real women whom popular histories claim as pirates, but in fact were not. The Marquise de Frèsne is often named as a female corsair of the late seventeenth-century Mediterranean, but the source for this myth is a slightly fact-based novel, perhaps better regarded as a novel masquerading as history, or a "pseudo-memoir," by French writer Gatien de Courtilz de Sandras in 1701, the same who wrote the *Memoirs of d'Artagnan,* upon which Alexandre Dumas based *The Three Musketeers.*[21] At one point the heroine, in classic best-selling-potboiler style, is sold to a Barbary corsair by her husband, who wants to be rid of her. And there really was a Pierre Hennequin, Marquis de Frèsne, and he did sell his wife, Marie-Elizabeth Girard du Tillay, to a corsair—a privateer, that is, not a pirate—named Gendron in the 1650s. Upon this fact, and an earlier published account, did de Courtilz de Sandras base his novel. But there is no record that the marquise participated in Gendron's sea roving as a member of his crew.[22]

Likewise is Ingela Gathenhielm often claimed as a female pirate of the early eighteenth century. As the wife of Swedish privateer and, later and far more profitably, wealthy privateer outfitter and financier Lars Gathenhielm, her participation appears to have been limited to playing a significant role in managing his lucrative privateering enterprise. His business was a lawful one, not a piratical one, at least not beyond the usual accusations all privateers were subject to—in his case, of his privateers attacking Swedish shipping at times.[23]

The most famous of these real women is Marie-Anne Dieu-le-veult (also Dieu-le-veut, "God-wills-it"). A large number of pirate history books and websites claim she was a seventeenth-century woman pirate, specifically a *flibustière.* Born in Normandy in 1654, she arrived in Saint-Domingue in the 1680s, quite possibly as one of the hundred women shipped there in 1685 as intended wives among the large, mostly male population.[24]

Saint-Domingue was a rough, rude, exotic world, especially to a young woman in her teens or early twenties. From the time her ship anchored at "Le Cap," as Cap François on the north coast was known, she would certainly have been amazed at the change from her native Normandy. Most likely greeted by a pirogue aboard which were two dozen or more armed men to ensure the ship was not a Spaniard bent on raiding the port, the women were eventually ferried ashore to a French colony carved by force from the Spanish Main.[25]

As she walked through the dirt streets of the richest town on Saint-Domingue, she surely thought she had come ashore at biblical Babel and not Le Cap. Although Le Cap was a French colonial town, Dieu-le-veult's ears tried to sort out the many languages she heard: French, Dutch, English, Portuguese, and Spanish, plus African and even Native American tongues, not to mention the beginnings of a French-African patois that would eventually become Haitian French.

Here at Le Cap were a few *boucaniers*, their long-barreled muskets and packs of hunting dogs keeping them company as they sold dried pork known as *boucan*. Nearby were filibusters, a motley crew of many nations and peoples, all armed with cutlass and pistol, some even with pet parrots and monkeys on their shoulders, loitering around a combination tavern and whorehouse. A few militiamen, whose dress might have indicated them as hunters, filibusters, or planters, stood guard at a small fort surrounded by hedges of lime trees and prickly pear cactus. Throughout the streets were merchants, planters, indentured servants, and slaves. There were whites and blacks, mulattos and *mestizos*, Native Americans and *zambos* or *alcatraces*, as people of mixed African and Native American blood were known.

And there were women, too—French women who dressed according to European custom, and African and mulatto women who went about topless, many of them the wives, mistresses, or slaves of the freemen of the colony. Of Saint-Domingue's population of seven thousand or so, only one in six were women. Among those entirely of European descent, only one in ten were women. Dieu-le-veult would find no scarcity of suitors.

Whether by dint of looks or spirit, she was quickly pursued by former filibuster Pierre Lelong. The leader of a dozen Frenchmen who left Tortuga and founded Cap François (modern-day Cap Haitian, Haiti) in 1670, Lelong was now one of the wealthiest men on Saint-Domingue. Alas, he died soon after marrying Dieu-le-veult in 1688 at Le Cap, the same year as a daughter, Yvonne, was born to them. Not too long in mourning, Dieu-le-veult married Joseph Cherel in 1691, surely also a filibuster or former filibuster, but he, too, gave up the ghost soon after, although his wife bore him a son. Life on Saint-Domingue was tough, with disease and violence taking the lives of many.

Enter Dutch filibuster Laurens de Graff. According to an early eighteenth-century history written after his death, de Graff, either visiting from Tortuga or by now posted at Le Cap, insulted Dieu-le-veult. Refusing to let the incident lie, Dieu-le-veult aimed a pistol at him and demanded to know the reason for the insult. This so impressed, infatuated, and inflamed de Graff, so the story goes, that he felt she was worthy of him and asked her to marry him. According to some later accounts, entirely without merit, she fought a duel with a hungover de Graff after he insulted her.

We do not know when de Graff first met the spirited Dieu-le-veult, but there is a good chance she was still married when he began to woo her. In 1685 he was seeking French citizenship for his wife, Francisca Petronila de Guzmán, who lived in the Canary Islands and whom he had not seen in years. However, in 1689 he suddenly changed his mind and made several appeals to the ecclesiastical courts at the Canary Islands and in Seville, Spain, for a divorce. It was eventually granted, and in 1693 he married the young widow of Saint-Domingue. Very likely the rich estate his inamorata controlled was an added inducement, quite possibly even the principal one.

Some twentieth-century legends pretend that Dieu-le-veult sailed with her husband on his cruises, but there is no evidence that she ever did. Had she done so, this would have been noted in at least one of the many records and journals of the period. With the exception of some occasional slave women and Spanish prisoners, filibusters and buccaneers typically did not permit women on their ships, at least while cruising for purchase. Their presence was considered divisive among the all-male crews. In fact, by the time de Graff was wooing the wealthy Dieu-le-veult, he was no longer an active filibuster, but a wealthy former filibuster now serving France as a military officer at Saint-Domingue, first at Tortuga in 1686, then at Le Cap in 1689. One imagines he met her in 1689 when he was first posted at Le Cap, fell quickly in lust or even love, then just as quickly sought a divorce from his wife. Perhaps Dieu-le-veult married Joseph Cherel because she grew tired of waiting for de Graff's divorce.

However, the fact that Dieu-le-veult was not a female pirate should not suggest that she could not take care of herself. She held her head high while she and her two daughters, one of whom was de Graff's, were held prisoner by the Spanish after a combined English-Spanish raid on Saint-Domingue. Almost certainly, she was one of the women of Saint-Domingue whom Father Lepers referred to romantically both as "female *boucaniers* and filibusters" and as "heroines and Amazons": women who could shoot as well as their husbands, even hunt as necessary, not to mention supervise the management of estates ranging from a few acres planted with tobacco to large sugar plantations built upon slave labor, while their husbands were away *boucan* hunting on Spanish lands or pillaging the Spanish Main.[26]

De Graff died in 1704 on Saint-Domingue, mythical claims that he died in Mississippi or Alabama notwithstanding.[27] He left his widow and their daughter, Marie-Catherine, an enormous estate, including a sugar plantation and more than 120 slaves.[28] But Marie-Anne Dieu-le-veult would survive her third husband by only six years. Their daughter lived much longer and had her mother's spirit. She reportedly once challenged a feckless man to a duel.

Given the strength and independence of these women of Saint-Domingue, there may indeed be much truth in the story that Dieu-le-veult pointed a pistol at de Graff after he insulted her. For all we know, the insult was de Graff's way of flirting with her. De Graff was tall, handsome, adventurous, wealthy, famous, and now an important officer on

Saint-Domingue; Dieu-le-veult was wealthy, strong-willed, and independent; could handle a pistol and probably a musket and cutlass as well; and was certainly very attractive in character and quite probably in appearance. It was a match made in pirate heaven.

It is easy to see how Dieu-le-veult, the three-time wife of filibusters or former filibusters, would come to be seen in later ages as a female pirate. After all, she married pirates, so obviously she must have been one herself, or so the logic goes. Surely, according to this romantic reasoning, de Graff would have taken her to sea, where she would have stood on the quarterdeck, dressed in tight-fitting men's clothing, her hair blowing in the wind, a cutlass in one hand and a pistol in the other.

Women Swashbucklers and Real She-Captains

Although many pirate marriages and couplings are documented, we so far know of only two male pirates who took their wives or inamoratas to sea in men's clothing—effectively making subject to the accusation, if not conviction, of piracy—during the Golden Age. Probably a few wives traveled with their husbands at sea on rare occasions. The wife of Henry Every's quartermaster sailed with Every to Ireland aboard the *Sea Flower* sloop from New Providence, after the pirate crew's return from the Red Sea. She was, according to a witness, not in her husband's company, but in Every's.[29] Of the two wives or lovers who dressed, at least some of the time, in men's clothing, there was foremost Anne Bonny, who went to sea with Calico Jack Rackam. One might argue that Mary Read falls into this category, for she reportedly took a lover aboard Rackam's sloop, although this is not the same as running off to sea with one's husband or lover. The third is an unnamed woman from Port Royal, Jamaica.

In 1686, Captain John Beare had two loves: robbing ships at sea, and the daughter of a "rum-punch-woman" from a Port Royal, Jamaica, tavern.[30] Port Royal, the notorious former haven of buccaneers, was even now a haven for former buccaneers as well as those still secretly engaging in the trade of plunder by force of arms, and of smugglers as well.[31]

Granted a privateering commission by deputy governor Sir James Russel of Nevis, Beare could not contain his enthusiasm. Instead of hunting pirates—which was not very profitable, not to mention often dangerous—he attacked Spanish ships, even though England was not at war with Spain. In the course of these illegal pursuits, he often took the woman he loved with him, dressing her up in men's clothes, where she surely stood on deck, as picaresque as Joan Fontaine in the film *Frenchman's Creek*, based on the novel of the same name by Daphne du Maurier. But, like Fontaine's character, the Lady Dona St. Columb, the "strumpet," was not a pirate except perhaps briefly as an exciting diversion.[32]

The Royal Navy, of course, had no intention of letting Beare's piracies go uncontested. Beare knew his days were numbered. He fled to Havana with the woman he loved and offered his services to Spain. He and his fiancée became Catholics and were married at a grand wedding attended by the governor of Havana and the grandees of the city. The governor even ordered the cannon of the great fort, El Morro, fired in celebration. As for Beare's English crew, he gave them two choices: sail with him or go to prison. When England and Spain became allies against France in 1688, Beare took service with the French. We do not know whether his wife ever went to sea with him again after their wedding day—or what the grand Spanish ladies of Havana would have thought of this!

However, the fact that we do not have much evidence for women pirates should not discourage us from looking for them. Indeed, women were often found at sea, especially in navies when squadrons cruised close to home. The wives of petty officers, warrant officers, and even commissioned officers were sometimes found at sea and even assisted in battle.

If a woman wanted to serve at sea in the same capacity as a man, or even ashore, swashbuckling her way through the countryside, she invariably had to do so in disguise. There are numerous other accounts of real cross-dressing, swashbuckling women in the seventeenth and eighteenth centuries. Catalina de Eruaso, also known as La Monja Alférez—the

Nun Lieutenant—swashbuckled her way through early seventeenth-century Spain and the New World, sword in hand and dressed and living as a man.[33] According to Bartolomé Arzáns de Orsúa y Vela, in Potosí (in modern-day Bolivia), during the 1650s the apparent lovers Doña Ana Lezama de Urinza and Doña Eustaquia de Souza dressed themselves as hidalgos or caballeros (gentlemen, in other words) and swashbuckled, brawled, and dueled through Chile and Peru.[34] In late seventeenth-century France, opera singer and superb swordswoman Julie d'Aubigny, better known as Mademoiselle de Maupin, often took to the road dressed as a man, fought and won duels against men, and took both men and women as lovers.[35]

Unfortunately, it was probably far easier for women to get away with this behavior ashore than it was in the confines of a ship at sea. Disguise of one's sex—not merely dressing in a man's clothes—was mandatory, for women were not permitted as members of a ship's crew. Urination, menstruation, and breasts must be hidden, not an easy thing to do in the close confines of a vessel at sea, yet this clearly was managed well by some women in disguise. Famous libertine and memoirist Giacomo Casanova provides part of a possible solution, for example, when he describes how a woman pretending to be the *castrato* Bellino used a fake yet apparently lifelike penis, which she attached with glue, to facilitate her deception.[36] Both Mary Read, who had indeed served as both soldier and sailor, and Anne Bonny first went to sea in disguise and shifted to female clothing apparently only after Rackam's crew accepted the notion of women aboard.

This acceptance of women as part of a pirate crew was highly unusual and probably due in large part to the very small size of the crew. Pirates of this era were highly sexist, as nearly all men were at the time, and largely heterosexual, probably to the same degree as the population as a whole, and not gay communities, as has been occasionally proposed.[37] Even so, there is evidence to suggest that some pirates might have had a "don't ask, don't tell" policy regarding gay or bisexual pirates, or at least a more progressive attitude than was common at the time. The evidence is not conclusive, however.[38] Articles prohibiting women aboard were intended to prevent disruptions among the male crewmembers—to prevent fights over women, in other words, and not necessarily to protect women, although there is evidence that not all women prisoners were raped, although they were always to some degree in danger of it.

Elizabeth Trengrove, a passenger aboard the *Onslow* when it was captured by Bartholomew Roberts, gave testimony that a pirate named William Mead "was very rude to her, swearing and cursing, as also forcing her hoop'd Petticoat off; and to prevent more of his Impudence, which she was afraid of, went down into the Gunner's Room by Advice of one Mitchel a Pyrate." It is all too easy to imagine how captured women slaves were treated by pirate crews.[39]

The fact that both Bonny and Read wore women's clothing except when attacking and capturing prey suggests, first, that the men's clothing they wore was partly for disguise, and, second, that their dressing otherwise in women's clothing was meant to maintain a separation between the sexes. We do not even know for certain to what degree the women were incorporated as members of Rackam's crew. Did they, for example, have a vote and a share each along with the rest of the crew? Was there a "pirate women's suffrage" aboard Rackam's ship? Probably there was, but perhaps not.

Still, such difficulties of disguise and acceptance did not deter women from going to sea. The historical record contains numerous accounts of women discovered in disguise aboard ships, everywhere from Dutch East Indiamen to the Spanish treasure fleets. Surely many more were never caught. One woman, bearing the name of John Brown, enlisted with the Royal African Company as a soldier and was shipped to Africa aboard the slave ship *Hannibal* in 1693. Unfortunately, she became ill and her sex was discovered, as many women in her situation were. Medicine was often given via a clyster (enema) pump via the rectum, making it likely that any seriously ill woman in disguise would be found out. Female soldier John Brown had done the same work as any man and as well, yet, when she was found to be a woman, the captain of the *Hannibal* ordered her into a dress, gave her private quarters, and put her to work washing his clothes. He thought he was doing her a favor.[40]

So where does this leave us? Were there any she-captains among the pirates of the Golden Age? Alas, no, myth and even a bit of shoddy scholarship that claims Bartholomew Roberts was a woman notwithstanding. The closest we can come is Hollywood, where we put women in roles any feminist would be proud of, yet simultaneously turn them into titillating "eye candy."[41] Not for historical accuracy do we usually find cinematic women pirates in thigh boots! We see Jean Peters in *Anne of the Indies* fencing skillfully in boots against Blackbeard; Maureen O'Hara in *Against All Flags* in black thigh boots as a captain among the "Brethren of the Coast"; Gianna Maria Canale in *The Queen of the Pirates*, also in thigh boots, avenging the death of her father; and Geena Davis in *Cutthroat Island*, in boots of course, swinging her cutlass, commanding men, and likewise avenging the death of her father. Even Keira Knightley in *Pirates of the Caribbean: At World's End* has a brief stint as a pirate captain, but without the thigh boots. Nonetheless, not long before becoming a pirate captain, she is titillatingly forced to strip down to nearly nothing. But this is nothing new: an early eighteenth-century depiction of Anne Bonny and Mary Read shows them as bare-breasted.

Sexism both obvious and subtle also reigns in these films, in spite of the positive elevation of women to the strong role of pirate captain. All of these Hollywood women pirates became pirate captains via the patronage, one way or another, of men, often their fathers. To be fair, given the male dominance and chauvinism of most professions at the time, it would have been difficult for a woman to become a pirate captain without some form of male support, no matter her ability.

Our modern idea of the woman pirate originated largely with Charles Johnson's descriptions of Anne Bonny and Mary Read. Add to this the tales of a handful of women pirates before and after, the pro-woman desire to show women in strong, active roles, and sex appeal, and we have the female pirate captain, Hollywood style—our myth of the she-captain, in other words. But rather than accept at face value the Hollywood-style woman pirate, we should look instead to the sort of women described in the opening quotation to this chapter, to the common yet uncommon women of Port Royal in the late seventeenth century: forward, unrestrained by conventional ideas on dress and deportment, independent, the social equals of the mariners and buccaneers who resorted to the most infamous of pirate ports. These would have been our true pirate women. And perhaps indeed some of them did go to sea to plunder.

Yet there were real women pirate captains. Although, sadly, the reality of these women sea thieves may have had little to do with the creation of the myth, their deeds still resonate on wind and wave. These she-captains were not queens who commanded pirate fleets yet seldom or never went to sea, like Queen Teuta of Illyria in antiquity, who sent her vast fleet to plunder anyone and everyone.[42] Teuta was not a she-captain any more than was Queen Elizabeth I of England, who also sent ships to sea to plunder, but on a much smaller scale. No, the real she-captains were real pirates who went to sea in command, led crews into battle, and stood on deck as the shot whistled through the air.

The two we know the most about are Grace O'Malley, the daughter of a noted Irish clan leader and pirate, and Cheng I Sao, a former prostitute who married a rising pirate captain. O'Malley commanded Irish pirate galleys in action at sea and their crews in action ashore and effectively led her Irish clan in the late sixteenth century. She threatened shipping from Scotland to Spain, and she also came to be recognized as a powerful leader by Queen Elizabeth I herself, with whom she even had an audience. Cheng I Sao, the power and mind behind both her husband and son, and the de facto pirate admiral, commanded five hundred pirate junks and as many as sixty thousand pirates, both men and *women*, in the early nineteenth century and led them on a famous, brutal, bloody raid up the Pearl River. She threatened the waters from northern China south to Vietnam. Both women were masterful leaders and incredibly effective marauders.[43]

Surely, though, there are others out there whom we know nothing of. Certainly the idea of the woman pirate is nothing new. Roughly thirty-three hundred years ago, Jason and the Argonauts, or men like them—plainly pirates, although in this ancient era piracy was practically indistinguishable from common warfare—put to sea to seek and steal the Golden Fleece. In some accounts, the fifty Argonaut heroes included a woman: Atalanta, the fierce virgin huntress raised in the wilderness. By any reckoning, here is the first-known woman pirate, if perhaps only a mythical one. Still, given that humans or their cousins may have first taken to the sea 130,000 years ago or more, pirates surely followed soon in their wakes.[44]

Among these ancient mariners must have been some women pirates, not to mention at least a few pirate she-captains. After all, as Arzáns de Orsúa y Vela wrote in the early eighteenth century about the *picaras* Doña Ana Lezama de Urinza and Doña Eustaquia de Souza, "Those who do not think that it is easy for a woman to succeed in whatever she attempts are mistaken, for many women have surpassed men in valor, in the use of arms, and in knowledge."[45]

CHAPTER 10

Not Every Man Created Equal

—⊙∞⊙—

"This Mulatto proved so true and faithful in his good services unto the Hollanders, that they esteemed much of him, married him to one of their Nation, and made him Captain of a ship under that brave and gallant Hollander whom the Spaniards then so much feared, and named, Pie de Palo, or Wooden Leg. This famous Mulatto it was that with his Sea Souldiers borded our Frigat . . ."[1]
—Thomas Gage, *A New Survey of the West Indies*, 1677

*V*aliente soldados, buen valiente soldados!" the Spanish governor had shouted high above the fray: "Valiant soldiers, good valiant soldiers!"[2]

He had waved his large handkerchief to get their attention as he called to the defenders in the town of Arica immediately below, certain that if they saw him they would fight even harder, not to mention that he could direct them to cut off the attackers as they moved from street to street. From his perch on the Morro, a great hill more than four hundred feet high, he could see the entire field of battle. It ranged from the barricaded streets of the town at the base of the Morro to the nearby fort built to protect the silver of Potosí (in modern-day Bolivia)—the richest vein in the world—as it passed through Arica, Chile, en route to Panama and thence, via the Isthmus of Darien and the Caribbean, to Spain.[3]

What the wounded buccaneer, now surrounded by Spaniards— white, black, mulatto, *mestizo*—in the town below thought of the governor's distant courage is unknown. His thoughts were on the men around him, and on the offer of "good quarter" they beckoned him with.

The governor on the hill had been in little, if any, danger, mounted as he was and just beyond the effective range of the buccaneers' muskets. Even so, several buccaneers sent musket balls his way, yet all missed. Below, however, the governor's men were fighting fiercely for their lives, doing all they might to beat back the buccaneer attack. Most of these fearful yet valiant defenders were volunteers, and among the stoutest and most numerous were free blacks, mulattos (persons of both white and black ancestry), *mestizos* (persons of both white and Native American ancestry), and Native Americans, the backbone of the governor's force. With coca leaves tucked between cheek and gum, and lance or harquebus in hand, they stood their ground before the onslaught. They were not expert soldiers, and many had little experience in battle. But they had courage and courageous officers, and they could fight all day, for the coca leaves would diminish their hunger and give them "strength and vigor."[4]

To the wounded buccaneer, his leg shattered, the past four hours had seemed an eternity of violent give-and-take. It was January 30, 1681, better known as King Charles Day, a holiday set aside in memory of the martyrdom of Charles the First of England. Charles was long dead, but all around the wounded buccaneer lay fresh martyrs to their own causes, one of greed, the other of defense of home and family.

These buccaneers were a motley bunch of bloodied veterans, mostly white men of various English extraction, but with a sprinkling of Irish, French, and Dutch, and even of a few free Native Americans and blacks, and perhaps a few *mestizos* and mulattos as well. Pirates of European origin often took men of other races into their crews, and these attackers were no different. Surely such egalitarian men had an enlightened view of mankind, even as they robbed and murdered them.

Today, though, neither equality nor enlightenment was foremost on their minds, for they were desperate men making a desperate attack on a town that had once before repulsed them. Embittered and divided by political strife, they were led by the recently elected John Watling, a veteran buccaneer who intended to prove his worth by capturing Arica. Unfortunately, his worth as a leader had just become apparent: Watling had ignored intelligence that Arica was well prepared for the buccaneers, even murdering the old *mestizo* prisoner who had told the truth about the city and its defenses. He now had but one way to redeem himself, but it would not be easy. Capturing Arica would require skill with arms of steel and fire, as well as an extraordinary display of courage.

Surging ashore, leaving ten men behind to guard their canoes, the eighty-two buccaneers had marched quickly to Arica, then divided into two companies of roughly forty men each and raced respectively toward the fort and town. A large party of defenders waited on the northern outskirts of Arica and opened fire on the buccaneers as they drew near. The attackers returned their fire with devastating accuracy, but the Ariqueños—whose firearms were a variety of heavy *mosquetes* that required forks to prop their barrels up; lighter *arcabuces*, short-barreled *carabinas* with bandoleers of Russian leather; and doubtless a few *escopetas,* used only for hunting—held their ground. Only 110 military long arms were available for the city's defense.

Realizing their Brethren of the Coast might be in trouble, the buccaneers heading along the shore toward the fort altered course, swept around the flank of the Ariqueños, and opened their own withering fire, shouting, "They run! They run!" as they did.[5] Caught in a crossfire, the defenders quickly retreated to the stout barricades in the streets. Here, behind these rude, hastily assembled walls of timbers, hides, and anything else that might help stop a bullet, they would make their stand.

Then *crack!* came the sound of some of the fort's eleven brass cannon, of various calibers and all in poor condition, firing upon the buccaneers left in the open. All of the pirates now hastened toward the barricades of the town, where the cannon could not reach them. But here the defenders—a large but unknown number, certainly fewer than the seven hundred estimated by the buccaneers—again stopped the buccaneers in their tracks with a tremendous volume of musketry. In the air was the loud crack of cannon and the nearby whizzing of musket balls as they sped past ears, just barely missing the heads they were mounted on. Buccaneers, firing in pairs, peered through the smoke to pick out their targets, but the defenders were well protected behind their barriers and killed several of the pirates, unprotected as they were on the open ground.

But these sea-roving fighting men were not amateurs. A party of buccaneers, under heavy fire, flanked the main barricade, then fired their muskets at close range, the loads of musket ball topped with seven or eight "swan shot" (similar to buckshot), making quick, bloody work of the defenders.

The Spaniards behind the barricade quickly cried for good quarter. Captain Watling granted it, over the complaints of many of his men. But in battle his word was absolute; his buccaneers obeyed. They herded the prisoners away, but the fight was not over. Three barricades remained, their defenders sniping constantly at the pirates. A party of buccaneers turned on the enemy, laying down a constant, accurate fire while others swept around the flanks. Again they fired their muskets at close range, slaughtering their enemy with loads of ball and shot. But when these defenders cried for good quarter, the buccaneers ignored them and instead put cutlass and pistol to use. They killed all who still stood to their arms and all who threw down their arms as well. The defenders were "Creolians, a people half Spaniards and half Indians, of a Copper-colored complexion and men that never gave [quarter] themselves."[6] In fact, most who lived in Arica were nonwhite. Their skin color was a convenient excuse to murder men so that they might not be bothered with managing them as prisoners.

Now the town belonged to the buccaneers. They seized the nearby church of San Marcos and put their surgeons to work, sawing off limbs and dressing the wounds of injured buccaneers. But still the battle was not over. Many of the townspeople had rallied to the fort, and the pirates had their hands full managing their prisoners, who indeed outnumbered their captors.

The buccaneers attacked the fort again. They wanted its cannon for their ship, but the defense was fierce. Quickly, Watling ordered his men to round up some prisoners and march them in front of the buccaneers as they advanced on the fort. But the defenders began to fire on both Spaniard and buccaneer. Then, at a signal from the fort, the Spanish prisoners leapt away, sprinted to a sally port at the fort, and slipped inside. The buccaneers shot dead the few who did not make it.

In spite of the cannonade and fusillade arrayed against them, the buccaneers stoutly fought their way to the walls. Now they could hurl their grenades onto the ramparts and clear them, then climb over the walls and seize the fort! But their grenades were bad; the powder or fuse was damp. Back to the town they retreated, only to find that Arica had been reinforced.

Beaten from the fort, the buccaneers were now being beaten from the town. Captain Watling was shot through the loins and quickly bled to death. The quartermasters who should have stepped up to take his place were also dead or captured, as were fifteen or twenty more buccaneers. Chaos, breeding panic, now threatened the buccaneers, too. Soon, though, after several buccaneers begged him to do so, Captain Bartholomew Sharp took command and rallied the survivors for an organized retreat in which they might yet survive. All around him lay men dead and dying, the color of their skins black, white, and brown— not to mention a sticky scarlet hue that, after it slipped to the ground, turned purple and then soon black. The flies and vultures that would soon seek the dead would not distinguish among the various colors of the corpses.

The Color of Courage

Here now we find the wounded, surrounded buccaneer. The decision to surrender or not was his alone. Nearby, the Spaniards—whites, blacks, Native Americans, *mestizos*, mulattos, and other mixed bloods—were "knocking" captured pirates in the head. With muskets and pistols they shot them. With lances and swords they stabbed them, leaving gaping wounds from which the pirates quickly bled to death in bloody pools. Some pirates literally had their skulls crushed with musket and pistol butts. Only the surgeons, whom the Ariqueños would keep prisoner and put to work, were exempted. Any other buccaneers who were not killed outright would later be hanged.

By now the survivors, including one or two injured buccaneers who had fled under fire from the buccaneer hospital in the church, had grouped for a retreat from Arica. In a large circle, they would soon fight, their wounded at the center, keeping up a constant, accurate fire so that the Spaniards afoot or on horse dared not approach too closely. Under fire these buccaneers would retreat, their throats clogged from several hours of dust, gunpowder smoke, and, worst of all, rabid thirst. Some would drink their urine in hopes of fending off the raging, lunacy-inducing sensation.

But the wounded buccaneer could not go with them. We can never know what went through his mind as he stood on one leg, the other shattered, the ground beneath now a purple mud. Did he consider surrendering, of asking for good quarter? Many may claim that they will never surrender, but far fewer actually refuse to do so under any circumstances. The strength of will required to refuse quarter in the face of certain death is extraordinary.

The wounded man's shipmates, except for the captured surgeons, were either dead in the streets or beginning their retreat under heavy fire. No one could know whether these men would even make it back alive to their canoes drawn up on the shore and under guard. Perhaps by now the Spaniards had even captured this last avenue of escape, and there would be no retreat for the buccaneers, only an eventual slaughter by hot lead and cold steel, or, if they surrendered and were not killed out of hand, by strangulation.

Why, then, should he not surrender? Did he fear the Spaniards were lying to him, that they would kill or torture him after he surrendered? But in that case they could have killed him already. Perhaps he feared they would enslave him after he surrendered, and this freeman would be a slave to no man.

The Spaniards crowded close to the buccaneer. Perhaps shock, endorphins, and stoic control of his pain kept him on his feet. Later would come greater pain, but likely he would bear it then as well—if he were still alive, for he refused their offer of good quarter. He made this quite clear by killing one Spaniard, and then another, and then two or three more. Surely with musket, then pistol, then musket butt or cutlass blade, he swept aside the enemy. Most of them were armed only with lances and machetes and had to come close to give him the coup de grâce. Several Spaniards now lay dead or dying at his feet, and the rest had learned their lesson. They kept their distance, surely no closer than ten yards. They would not offer him good quarter again, nor could they permit him time to reload.

The wounded buccaneer heard his shipmates calling, shouting that anyone who still lived must run to them, no matter the risk. But he could not run. Perhaps he raised his cutlass and hobbled forward to kill more Spaniards. Perhaps he began to swiftly reload his musket or pistol. It would not matter. His enemies, some now armed with *arcabuses* and pistols, shot him dead from a safe distance.

A buccaneer present at the attack later learned from Spanish prisoners how the man died, and in his journal he described the brave buccaneer's end: "[O]ne Negro, who had his leg shot off, being offered quarter, refused it, and killed four or five of their men, before he was shot dead on the spot. This fellow had been a slave, whom our commander had freed, and brought from Jamaica."[7]

This instance—of a buccaneer's buccaneer, of a courageous pirate fighting to the last, yet of a sea rover not white but black—appears to prove the modern myth that pirates commonly freed slaves and took them into their crews. And so they often did, caring more for merit than color, at least in their own ranks. By inference, the myth has expanded beyond this, claiming that pirates not only were more egalitarian than most of their contemporaries, but also were at least to some degree anti-slavery. But the myth is only partly true. Pirates indeed were generally more egalitarian than many of their contemporaries, for a strong sense of common cause—including greed—is a powerful force that can unite men and women of different beliefs, cultures, and races.

But here the truth of the myth ends. For every slave whom Golden Age pirates freed and brought into their crews, they had surely sold at least ten, and perhaps even as many as a hundred. Humans—Africans, and often Native Americans, mulattos, *mestizos*, indeed any person of color—were valuable plunder, and no pirate's sense of morality was strong enough to override his lust for riches. Pirates have engaged actively in the slave trade since the earliest recorded days of sea thieving, and in antiquity, humans, to be sold as slaves or, if they were rich enough, ransomed, were the principal source of plunder.

When People Were Property

Simply because pirates of the Golden Age operated as functioning democracies is no reason to assume that they believed in, granted, or accepted equality across the board. The process of democracy, after all, does not of itself guarantee equal rights. It took the United States, for example, almost a century to outlaw slavery, then a century afterward to grant full civil rights to its citizens of all races and ethnicities. Such rights require either the will of the people or the adjudication of the laws of the people.

Golden Age pirates functioned as democracies, yet they chose to engage in the slave trade and treat most members of several peoples as worthy of nothing more than slavery. Only the few free blacks, mulattos, *mestizos*, *zambos* (mixed African and Native American), and Native Americans whom pirates permitted into their crews were granted the same rights and respect they accorded to themselves. The rest they regarded as property, whether free or already enslaved.

There were, of course, more than a few men of color among the crews of the Golden Age pirates who sacked the Spanish Main in the late seventeenth century, as well as among those who turned against all flags in the early eighteenth. According to Charles Johnson, half of the crew

of the pirate Oliver La Bouse in 1719 was African.[8] In 1722, at the time
he was killed in action, fifty-two of Bartholomew Roberts's crew of 152
were Africans from the Guinea Coast.[9] In 1721, a "sloop with 50 negroes
commanded by a white person was lately run away with from Martinique
on the pirating account as is supposed," although it is not quite clear
who ran away—mutinied, that is—with what, and whether they actually went pirating. Nothing was heard of them afterward.[10]

Most Golden Age pirates and privateers had Africans in their crews,
and often other races and ethnicities as well. The early eighteenth-
century pirates tended to have a much larger proportion of nonwhites,
especially Africans, among their crews for the simple reason that they
needed recruits. Because they were complete outcasts and outlaws,
unlike the buccaneers and filibusters of the late seventeenth century,
recruiting was much more difficult. Again, greed and need can tear down
many barriers. The men of color in these crews were of two sorts: freemen
who functioned as equals in the pirate crews, and slaves who were kept
to do "drudgery."[11]

The problem lies in the fact that we do not always know to what
degree these black men, and other men of color, were integrated into
pirate crews. When one reads the trial record of Bartholomew Roberts's
men, there is a distinct sense that the Africans aboard were treated at the
very least as second-class citizens, and perhaps even as slaves. A "Negro,"
not a white pirate, was sent whenever Roberts and his crew needed a
boat fended off or bailed out. Roberts even gave "eight or nine Negroes
a-piece" to the captains and crews of two down-on-their-luck pirate
sloops who came seeking "Charity," for they were "in want of every
thing." Roberts received some seamen, apparently white, in their place.[12]

Still, some men of color were fully integrated into these crews, even
as captains. Diego the Mulatto, a "runnagate [renegade] mulatto"
Spaniard born in Havana and raised in Campeche, Mexico, cruised,
often with a largely white crew, from the 1630s until his reported
death—assuming this was the same person—at the hands of Spaniards
in 1673.[13] The mulatto "Captain Francis" was a Dutch privateer in 1674
and almost without doubt a piratical freebooter at times as well.[14]

Another Caribbean sea rover of African ancestry was Francisco Fernando, a mulatto privateer captain and Jamaica property owner accused of piracy in 1716—one more who fell afoul of English authorities while hunting Spanish pirates.[15] All of these men plundered the Spanish Main.

However, no pirate captains of full African blood have yet been positively identified among the Golden Age pirates. Racism may have precluded this, even among "egalitarian" crews, the courage and ability of black pirates notwithstanding. We cannot forget the incontrovertible fact that pirates were products of their age and were heavily engaged in the slave trade as purveyors of humans, primarily African. Not only that, but like many of their contemporaries, most would have regarded blacks as inferior to whites. As already described, Bartholomew Roberts might have thought twice about burning a white crew to death, but he thought nothing of letting black slaves burn to death or drown. The filibusters in chapter one thought nothing of murdering African slaves aboard a pair of Portuguese ships in revenge for an attack by free Africans, although in this case the pirates changed their mind about killing innocent men, but solely because they were not from the same tribe as those who had attacked.[16]

Some historians claim there were even more free men of color among French, English, and Dutch pirate crews of the Golden Age than there is solid evidence for, which quickly imbues the myth with even greater credibility. It is natural to want to paint our heroes as socially progressive and to include all races and ethnicities among their ranks. All too often, though, some of the evidence for black and mulatto pirates is highly speculative or even entirely misread or misinterpreted.

For example, since the nineteenth century, a few historians have suggested or even stated categorically that Laurens de Graff, one of the great sea rovers in history, was not a white Dutchman, but a mulatto and even a former slave. However, every seventeenth-century document that describes him, including those written by men who knew him or had seen him, notes that he was a Dutchman, and none notes that he was a mulatto or a former slave.[17] Most period documents give his birthplace as Doort (Dordrecht) in the Netherlands. The error can be traced back to the late seventeenth century, during de Graff's lifetime, in which his name is confused with Lorenzo Jacomé, a mulatto Spanish pirate of the early 1650s. Fray Juan de Avila, in describing the sack of Veracruz, describes "el Almirante Lorrenso de Xacome Alias Lorencillo," and Agustín de Vetancurt, author of a 1697 history of the province of Santo Evangelo of Mexico, describes de Graff as Lorenzo Jacomé—but both (and Avila was an eyewitness) also describe him as a Dutchman.[18] Both Jacomé and de Graff were commonly known among Spaniards as Lorencillo, thus the likely error.

Part of the problem is the incorrect assumption that the name de Graff derives from *griffe*, a word used in some New World localities for the offspring of an African and a Native American—but not for a mulatto. De Graff was actually a fairly common Dutch name, and could also mean "count." De Graff apparently appended it to his name much as some French filibusters appended "sieur" (sir). The myth that de Graff was a mulatto ex-slave was propagated by mistaken nineteenth-century historians and wishful twentieth-century thinking that wants to see pirates as less bigoted than their contemporaries (and in some ways, they really were) and as somewhat antislavery (which they were not at all). In fact, de Graff's origin and race have been definitively traced to the Netherlands, and a physical description of him, published in 1699 while he still lived, is of a blond Dutchman.[19]

In some quarters, it is claimed that Captain William Kidd's quartermaster was a black man, and therefore may have been second-in-command, according to the common practice of colonial English privateers. Their standard articles, which would come to be known as the "Jamaica Discipline," were derived from those of the buccaneers whose era had just ended.[20] And in fact, Kidd's articles were written upon these lines, and were signed by the original quartermaster, John Walker (or Warker), on behalf of the crew. If Kidd's quartermaster were indeed black, he may have held the highest known position of a black man among the pirates of the Golden Age.

The claim is based on a single written description: "[H]is mate was a little black man, unknown to the narrator by name, who, as it was said, had been formerly Captain Kidd's quartermaster."[21] The man, Hendrick van der Heul, would have been named quartermaster later in the voyage, although his name as given here is not on the original ship's watch bill. However, the name "Yoer Oovrall" is probably his.[22]

But there may be a problem with this argument, and it lies in the term "black man." It could mean a black man of African origin.[23] However, the term was also used when describing a white male with black hair or dark complexion—pirate Bartholomew Roberts was described as a "black man," as already noted. Further, both Hendrick and van der Heul were common Dutch names, and there are birth records for at least two men christened as "Hendrick van der Heul" among the Dutch descendants of New York in the late seventeenth and early eighteenth centuries, for example. Given the name and the pirate-hunting voyage's New York origin, van der Heul was *probably* a white man with black hair and perhaps dark complexion. It is worth noting that Kidd's original watch bill lists "John Parerick, negro," strongly suggesting that a crew member of African descent would have been so noted.[24]

A perhaps more likely candidate is a black filibuster named Diego who was hanged or garroted at St. Augustine, Florida, in 1686 alongside Captain Nicolás Brigaut for their part in an attempted assault on the old Spanish city: they were two of only three who survived a counter-attack after being stranded ashore. In those days the Spanish usually put only pirate officers to death, and sentenced the rest of the captured crew to, in essence, slavery in the New World or Spain. It is therefore possible that Diego was Brigaut's quartermaster—his second-in-command, that is. Thus to date, Diego, who served under Brigaut, may be the most likely candidate for the highest-ranking Golden Age pirate of full African ancestry we know of among the English, French, and Dutch rovers. Almost certainly there were others like him of his rank, and perhaps even some captains.[25]

More critically, though, the assumption that one or two black quartermasters held the highest rank among black members of the pirates of the Caribbean misses an entire class of these Golden Age pirates whose crews were often composed of men of color, including many of their captains and officers. Yet we never hear much about these pirate crews. Why? Because they were Spanish.

In fact, the majority of the population of the Spanish Main was not white at all, but brown and black. It was very much a population of Native American, *mestizo*, African, mulatto, and *zambo*. Spanish-born whites known as *Peninsulares* and New World–born whites known as *Creoles* were the minority. Spanish pirate and privateer crews—often one and the same, at least in English, French, and Dutch eyes—reflected this diverse population. Indeed, in many ways New World Spain was more tolerant of nonwhites than were the English, French, and Dutch colonies.

If we want to find crews largely or even entirely composed of men of color, we need only look at the Spanish pirates of the Golden Age. Here were far more pirates and privateers, even pirate and privateer captains, of color than were found among the Spaniard-plundering English, French, and Dutch pirates of the Caribbean. For certain, although there were Spanish, Portuguese, Italian, Dutch, Irish, and even English captains among the Spanish pirates and privateers, there were also many mulattos among them. Likely some were of full African blood as well.

Men of color were well known for their fighting prowess in the New World, and not only among sea rovers. Although often—but by no means always—under the command of white Spaniards, men of color were the backbone of Spanish defenses throughout the Spanish Main. They repulsed the English at Santo Domingo (modern-day Dominican Republic) in 1655 and carried on a guerrilla war against the English on Jamaica for several years after the English captured the island in the same year. Escaped African slaves formed independent colonies, including two on Jamaica. The most valiant of the Spaniards who attacked the buccaneers at the battle of Perico near Panama in 1680 was the black crew of an *armadillo*.[26]

Also here, though, the racism of Spain's enemies shows through. Sir Thomas Lynch, lieutenant governor of Jamaica, wrote in 1683 that the

Spanish pirates were "Corsicans, Slavonians, Greeks, mulattoes, a mongrel parcel of thieves and rogues that rob and murder all that come into their power without the least respect to humanity or common justice."[27] Former buccaneer William Dampier wrote that they were "the soldiers and rascality of the people; and these do commonly consist of mulattos or some other sort of copper-color'd Indians, who are accounted very barbarous and cruel."[28] But then, many of the buccaneers with whom Dampier sailed were also barbarous and cruel. With these mixed Spanish crews were also many Africans, both slave and free.

Pirate equality toward crew members of color notwithstanding, the fact remains that the majority of blacks, and probably mulattos as well, dealt with by pirates of the Golden Age—including by Spanish pirates— were dealt with as slaves. There were even occasional slave rebellions against pirates. Unfortunately, in most instances we know of, the rebellions were suppressed by the pirates.[29]

The myth of Golden Age pirates as colorblind is fairly recent and has two origins. First, many scholars have promoted pirates of color to their rightful place in history. However, in doing this, they have often sought to diminish the role of the pirate as slaver, in order to improve the pirate's image—less racist and more egalitarian, in other words. Second, Hollywood and popular fiction have also had a strong role, primarily by ignoring slavery as a critical aspect of piracy.

In fact, Hollywood and many historical novelists—the sources of most of our pirate mythology—have tiptoed around the subject of pirates and slavery or have even blatantly rewritten history to make it more palatable. Rarely are African slaves depicted extensively in swashbuckling novels and film, and seldom as part of pirate cargo or booty, and even then only in cursory fashion. Swashbuckling derring-do, titillation, and even graphic violence help sell books and films, but only seldom does slavery, and never, at least in our modern age, when our heroes are depicted as slave traders, even if only part-time ones.

Authors and screenwriters have long realized that accurate depictions of how pirates treated slaves might put off much of the audience. The pirate as slaver does not fit the modern myth of the pirate as a social and political rebel—as a colorblind Robin Hood, so to speak. Even when Hollywood depicts pirates freeing oppressed populations (something pirates never really did), the populations are usually white. The Hollywood and video game ideals, seen for example in *Rage of the Buccaneers* and "Assassin's Creed Freedom Cry," of pirates freeing slaves out of a sense of moral obligation derived from anti-slavery beliefs, has no basis in fact, no matter how appealing these ideals are.

We also need to remember that pirates of the Golden Age changed over time. In the late seventeenth century, buccaneer and filibuster ships never forced men to join their crews. They might force a captured Spaniard to serve as a pilot, and captured slaves to work for them, but they did not force free men or slaves to become members of their crews. The early eighteenth-century pirates, who were always in need of recruits, routinely did. And just how did these latter pirates, whose ranks include Blackbeard, Stede Bonnet, Calico Jack Rackam, Bartholomew Roberts, and Ned Low, and whose crews often included many Africans, really regard the men of color they captured?

The Noose or the Shackle

On Saturday, September 27, 1718, Major Stede Bonnet, the dilettante gentleman pirate from Barbados who had once been relieved of his command by Edward Teach, better known as Blackbeard, and left to walk the great pirate's deck in his nightclothes, finally proved his mettle, at least for a few hours. He had no other choice, unless he wanted to hang, and even then he might not escape the bight of hemp intended to strangle him, parting flesh from soul.[30]

Bonnet's pirate sloop the *Royal James*, along with two sloops he had recently captured, had been discovered the day before by two pirate-hunting sloops outfitted in Charlestown, South Carolina, under the command of Colonel William Rhett, a seasoned pirate hunter. In the darkness, Bonnet sent three canoes to attack the pirate hunters, but to no avail. Colonel Rhett was no amateur, and had kept his men on watch and under arms all night. Now there was nothing left to do but wait until morning and attempt a running fight against the men who intended to end the depredations—not to mention the lives—of Bonnet and his pirate crew.

Bonnet had his work cut out for him. Arrayed against him were two small sloops with large crews: the *Henry* of eight guns and seventy men, and the *Sea-Nymph* of eight guns and sixty men. Quickly he set sail down the Cape Fear River in North Carolina, intending to force his way past the pirate hunters and to the sea, where freedom awaited. He left the captured sloops behind.

But it was not to be so easy. Rhett's sloops set after Bonnet in close pursuit. They closed quickly, one on each quarter, intending to board. The 130 men would easily overwhelm Bonnet's crew of 40 in a matter of minutes.

Suddenly, the *Royal James* ran aground on a river shoal, losing way immediately. The pirate-hunting sloops, unable to take in sail so quickly, shot past him, then grounded too. The *Henry*, with Colonel Rhett aboard, lay within pistol shot—variously given as from 70 to 150 yards—just off the bow of the *Royal James*, but the *Sea-Nymph* had sailed far beyond, almost out of gunshot, and would have no great role in the fight.

Worse than the loss of the *Sea-Nymph* for the pirate-hunting Colonel Rhett was the position of his sloop. Although he was well placed to batter the pirate, his sloop was heeling—tilted, that is—toward the *Royal James*, but the *Royal James* was heeling away from the *Henry*. In other words, the *Henry*'s deck was exposed, but the *Royal James*'s was not. Bonnet's pirates opened fire, and Rhett's pirate hunters in return. The only way for the pirate hunters to protect themselves was to fire constantly at the pirates, preventing them from firing effectively. And this the pirate hunters did with a vengeance.

But the pirates were undaunted. They flew the red flag of defiance, and at one point tied a bit of line around its center, making a "wiff," and hoisted it back up, shouting as they did for the pirate hunters to come board them.[31] A wiff in a flag was the common signal for a pilot to come aboard, thus the pirates were humorously encouraging the pirate hunters to board them, if they dared. But it was not much of a brave joke, for

Rhett's men could not board. Had they been able to, they would surely, given their large number, have wiped the smug smiles and jests from the pirates' faces. The pirate hunters indeed were undaunted, shouting "Huzza!" in return and letting the pirates know that "it would soon be their turn."[32]

For five hours, pirate and pirate hunter blazed at each other with small cannon and much musketry. In the air lay thick smoke twisted into wispy tendrils by the breeze, the smell of burned powder and fear, and the sounds of men proclaiming in triumph and agony. Aboard the *Henry*, ten men were dead and fourteen wounded; aboard the *Sea-Nymph*, two and four.

But tides turn, and fortunes too. Colonel Rhett's sloop soon floated from the shoal. He brought it out of range, knotted his damaged rigging, prepared his crew, and then made directly for Bonnet. Rhett intended to board, and there would be the end of Bonnet and his pirate crew.

Suddenly, up went the white flag! Bonnet would now rather talk than fight. After a brief negotiation, Bonnet and his crew surrendered. Here would be no famous fight to the finish. In fact, such fights among pirates and their enemies were rare. The pirates were quickly brought to trial, although the proceeding was briefly delayed by the escape of Bonnet. But his freedom—if a hunted man can truly claim he has his freedom—was not for long, and soon he was bound to trial with his crew. Most were plainly guilty and could put up no defense. They knew they would hang, barring some unlikely act of God. But a few of his crew pleaded that they were "forced men" and therefore innocent. In other words, the pirates had forced them to join their ranks. One of them was Thomas Gerrard, a free mulatto mariner from Antigua.

Gerrard's experience was surely typical of mulattos and blacks captured by pirates during the early eighteenth century. In his words, "Some time after we were taken, one of the men [pirates] came and asked if I would join with them? I told them, 'No.' He said I was but like a Negro, and they made slaves of all of that color, if they did not join."[33]

For Gerrard—notwithstanding that he was a free mulatto, not an African slave—it was a simple choice: join or be enslaved. In a way, he was lucky, for when these pirates did not need to add to their crews, they simply sold captured Africans, and often any person of color, into slavery. He joined the pirate crew under duress and even signed their articles. But he refused to share in their plunder, and intended "to get clear of them at the first opportunity."[34]

Gerrard was indicted on two counts of piracy, specifically that he had boarded and plundered two sloops, the *Francis* and the *Fortune*. Witnesses attested to his character, to the fact that he would be enslaved if he did not join, and that he never shared in the plunder. He was acquitted of all charges, and even Judge Nicholas Trott considered him innocent, although he did acerbically note that "he had better been made a slave than go a pirating," a sentiment many slaves would probably not have agreed with.[35]

The fact is, Gerrard was treated better by a white judge and jury imbued with the common racism of the age than he was by pirates, who took men of color into their crews and who are believed today to have been ahead of their time in regard to race. The former gave Gerrard his freedom; the latter offered him only a choice between slavery and crime—with a noose waiting at the end.

For actual slaves, though, the choice may have been clearer, with piracy preferred to slavery. Some historians have even compared oppressed seamen, many of whom turned pirate, as being in similar circumstances as slaves. But no one was physically forcing seamen to become slaves any more than they were forcing most of them to become pirates. For certain, no one was going to force a merchant seaman over the side because he was seriously ill and might infect the rest of the crew and damage the profitability of the voyage. But for a slave crammed between the decks of a ship, this was a very real possibility. Piracy, in its peculiar way, was seen as a form of freedom, by both a fair number of slaves and oppressed mariners.

If pirates were truly antislavery, they would not have sold so many as slaves, including freemen and women of color, as they all did. They would not have ransomed slaves back to their slave ship captains, as many did. And they would never have burned a cargo of slaves to death, or let those who jumped overboard drown, because they were in too much of a hurry to unshackle them, as Bartholomew Roberts did—and Roberts is the pirate often noted as hating slave-ship captains, and thus by inference making him an antislavery pirate.

But Roberts and his ilk were nothing of the sort. They were somewhat ahead of their time, as compared to their fellow men and women in the English, French, and Dutch colonies, in that they sometimes freed slaves and brought them into their crews as equals. In no way, however, did they oppose the slave trade. Rather, they engaged in it extensively because it was profitable to do so. Profit, after all, was the pirate's ultimate motivation.

CHAPTER 11

Pirate Heaven

———⊗⊗⊗———

"'Tis the most beneficiall trade that to Madagascar with the pirates; that was ever heard of, and I beleive there's more got that way than by turning pirates and robbing. I am told this Shelly sold rum which cost but 2ˢ per gallon at New York, for 50 shillᵍˢ and £3 pʳ gallon at Madagascar, and a pipe of Madera Wine which cost him £19. he sold there for £300. Strong liquors and gun powder and ball are the commodities that go off there, to the best advantage, and those four ships last summer carried thither great quantities of those things."[1]
—The Earl of Bellomont to the Lords of Trade, 1699

One of the enduring myths of Golden Age piracy incorporates those of colorblindness, egalitarianism, and revenge against economic and social injustice, and raises them to the obvious extreme, that of an independent pirate state, and even beyond this, to a pirate utopia where democracy reigns and the common pirate makes good on the words purportedly spoken by the ancient pirate Dionides to Alexander the Great, and paraphrased by pirate chronicler Charles Johnson into the mouth of pirate Samuel Bellamy.

"What thou meanest by seizing the whole earth; but because I do it with a petty ship, I am called a robber, while thou who dost it with a great fleet art styled emperor," reportedly demands Dionides.[2] "I am a free prince, and I have as much authority to make war on the whole world as he who has a hundred sail of ships at sea, and an army of 100,000 men in the field, and this my conscience tells me," reportedly rants Bellamy.[3] But St. Augustine, repeating an old story, was not favorably comparing pirates to princes. Rather, he was chastising unjust princes, comparing them to pirates. The comparison was probably lost on both Dionides and Bellamy, assuming the latter actually made the comment ascribed to him. Pirates considered themselves as princes, as kings even, and it is but a small step from here to the idea of a pirate kingdom.

The first and second captains and the first three lieutenants of the *Victoire* lay dead or dying, killed by the English man-of-war's first broadside, surely of round shot topped with bags of scrap metal or cans of musket balls. It was a powerful combination that cut sails, rigging, torsos, and limbs, shattered masts and timbers, and sent splinters through the air and into the unprotected flesh of men. The ship's master fearfully, urgently shouted orders to strike the colors and lower topsails—to surrender, in other words.[4]

But the former French musketeer, a volunteer among the crew, would have none of this. Surely damning the master for his cowardice, he appointed his Italian companion as the ship's lieutenant with a word and a nod, then took command of the chaos that reigned aboard the French man-of-war. Sword in hand, he restored order and by his example encouraged the crew. For six glasses—three hours—Frenchman fought Englishman, broadside after broadside, leaving decks awash in splinters and blood. Since 1688—for nearly five years—England and France had been at war, and this brutal sea fight was but a common one, except, of course, to those in its hellish midst.

Suddenly, by a stroke of terrible, tragic fortune, the English man-of-war blew up, leaving only one survivor. It was a horrible thing to witness so close, at the range of one or two hundred yards: the great sudden fiery flash and the ear-splitting, tooth-rattling crack that followed; the sight of men blown up into the air; the gross, hellish heat of the remainder of the ship as it burned to the waterline, if by some strange chance it did not sink soon after; the smell of burning timber, flesh, and tar; and the sight of dead bodies floating in the water, some mangled, some dismembered, some entirely intact.

The victory belonged to the French, although, sadly, none of the senior officers had survived to see it—and obviously none could give orders now. The Italian, a man for whom freedom and rebellion were watchwords, took the arm of his French friend and whispered what he must do. He was a man of solid, unwavering principles, this Frenchman named Misson. Some might have called him severe but fair. Misson's Italian friend, named Caraccioli, was likewise so, yet more liberal—a freethinking former priest who had tired of what he saw as papal hypocrisy and who now no longer needed religion. Men, he believed, should be free of both state and religion. Misson listened well to Caraccioli. Misson had a following among the crew, and now he also had a ship. He took the Italian's advice: they would "reign sovereign of the Southern Seas, and lawfully make war on all the world, since it [the world] would deprive him of that liberty to which he had a right by the laws of nature."[5]

From the Caribbean, they made their course around the Cape of Good Hope, first plundering several vessels. Misson was highly unusual not only among the pirates of his age but also among the men of his age. He did not tolerate slavery. He routinely freed slaves aboard the ships he captured and brought them into his crews as equals. He governed by reason, not according to the dictates of religion or other tradition.

As Misson made his course, he engaged any rich ship if it would not surrender. A pair of Dutch merchantmen fought the *Victoire* ruthlessly and might have gained the upper hand had not Misson directed his guns in such a way that they breached the hull of one at the waterline. Seeing its consort sink into the deep, the other Dutchman surrendered. As Misson and his crew of mutineers headed south along the African coast, they fell in with an English ship that they fought just as obstinately as they had the Dutchman, captured it, and kept it as a prize. The English captain was killed in action; Misson rendered all honors to him and had him buried ashore. Now Misson had a pair of ships fitted as men-of-war.

Sailing around the Cape of Good Hope, the Frenchman directed the *Victoire's* course into the Indian Ocean. Adventure followed adventure; theirs was the reality that writers of fiction believe should always have been. At Johanna (modern-day Anjouan in the Comoros Islands, near Madagascar), they defended the local queen against an invasion from the neighboring island of Moheli. Misson and Caraccioli also took Johannan wives. These were both practical moves: Johanna was an important stop for ships en route to the Indies.

Heading north, on the coast of Mozambique, the *Victoire* engaged a Portuguese merchantman of sixty guns for eight hours until her Portuguese captain was killed and the crew struck. The ship was rich in gold dust, but the capture came at a high cost. Thirty of Misson's pirates lay dead, and Caraccioli had lost a leg. While his Italian lieutenant recovered, Misson cruised along the north coast of Madagascar and sailed into Diego Suarez Bay. Realizing the great bay was ideal for a pirate base, he immediately recruited inhabitants of Johanna to help him, promising their queen he would keep them for no more than four months and would aid her in her wars against the Moheli. Misson directed the building of two forts in Diego Suarez Bay, mounted them with forty guns taken from the Portuguese prize, then supervised the construction of a small town. With his fortified harbor and powerful ship, he could easily seize a share of the great East Indian trade.

And he set about to do this. He cruised along the Zanzibar coast, off modern-day Tanzania, and espied a stout Portuguese ship. Quickly he engaged her, but she mounted fifty guns and had a crew of three hundred. For four hours they fought, until the *Victoire* was in danger of being captured. Misson knew he had but one option, a desperate one: he grappled the Portuguese and shouted for his men to board her. At the cry of "*À l'abordage!*" nearly all of his crew followed him into the waist of the Portuguese ship.[6] "Death or victory!" Misson cried, sword in hand.[7] Many of the Portuguese fled belowdecks to closed quarters as their captain did his best to stop them. Misson raced over to the captain and fought him, man to man, sword to sword, even as his own men engaged the Portuguese with cutlasses. The former musketeer deftly slipped his sharp blade into the Portuguese captain's neck. The Portuguese fell; the battle was over.

Misson sailed back to Madagascar with his prize, both ships and crews badly battered. At the coast, the *Victoire*'s lookout espied an approaching sloop. Coming into range, the sloop fired a gun and hoisted black colors. It was an order to surrender or face death. The sloop knew not whom she was threatening. Yet the *Victoire* did not reply with a bloody broadside. Instead, she "lay by" and invited the sloop's captain, Thomas Tew, aboard. Tew was a noted Red Sea pirate, and quickly he and Misson realized the value of an alliance.

Together the two crews established a colony of sorts in Diego Suarez Bay. They made alliances with Madagascan kings, freed captured slaves and brought them into their crews, and captured ships, using the spoils to enrich their burgeoning pirate empire.

But government is a difficult thing. Soon, nationalistic differences emerged between Misson's largely French crew and Tew's largely English one. Some believed their differences should be settled captain to captain, sword in hand, but this was rejected as too divisive. Caraccioli appealed for unity between the crews, and the crews let bygones be bygones. Soon after, they established a democratic government, based in many ways on their own pirate articles. Treasure and cattle would be divided equally, for example, and a man could own the land he himself enclosed. It was, by the standards of the day, a social and political utopia—not to mention a place where piracy would be protected not by complicit, greedy nations, but by pirates themselves.

But it was not to be. One night, without warning, Madagascan natives surged down upon the European intruders, slaughtering as many as they could, including Caraccioli. Misson barely escaped with his life. By good fortune, Tew had been away on a piratical cruise. The men set sail in consort for other profitable shores, but they were overtaken by a storm off Cape Infante on the southern coast of Africa. Misson's vessel foundered. He and all his crew were taken to Davy Jones.

The name of the freethinking, forward-looking pirate settlement was Libertalia, sometimes called Libertatia—Liberty, in other words. Considering the source, it was an extraordinarily noble effort. A few historians have even claimed that Libertalia helped inspire both the American and French revolutions. And perhaps in some very small way it did.

Unfortunately, there is a problem with this fascinating tale: Libertalia never existed. Nor did its two principal founders, Misson and Caraccioli. Pirate author Charles Johnson made up the entire story.

Sacrificing Truth for a Good Story and Allegory

Most scholars have long admitted that Libertalia is a myth. Even so, the myth persists in the general public and among a fair number of pirate fans. Significant elements of it even endure among some scholars, who argue that pirates were more than mere thieves wanting foremost to make themselves rich: they were also freethinking rebels. Some historians, acknowledging that Libertalia was a tall tale largely invented by Charles Johnson, still believe that something similar may have existed briefly on Madagascar, but on a smaller scale. Johnson's story is something they want to believe.[8]

And indeed, Libertalia is an appealing myth of rebellion and of living outside the norm, and Johnson's convincing writing, coupled with our need to believe in utopias in some form, has kept it alive. After all, Johnson was a good writer and no fool. He knew what his readers wanted, and he gave it to them. Unfortunately, this led him occasionally—perhaps often—to consider the truth as secondary to a good story. Although most of his pirate biographies are largely factual, he sometimes invented facts to fill in the empty places in his descriptions, and he even altered facts to make his stories more interesting. Much of his dialogue is suspect, for example. In the case of Libertalia, he went far beyond this and invented an entire chapter.

Like any good storyteller or liar, Johnson knew that facts in the right places make a story more believable. People are more likely to believe a lie, for example, if it's found amid a bundle of truth. After all, the best liars tell the truth ninety-nine percent of the time. Johnson put his story of Libertalia in the middle of a book filled with largely factual pirate biographies, lending it credibility. And he did something else just as important with his tall tale of Libertalia: he mixed some facts into it, making it seem even more believable.

There really was, for example, a privateer-turned-pirate captain named Thomas Tew. A successful Rhode Island privateer, Tew turned sea thief and sailed the sloop *Amity* of seventy tons, eight guns, and sixty men on a piratical voyage illegally funded by New York investors, including Governor Benjamin Fletcher, a man who had no qualms about investing financially in anything that would make money for him and his colony, including piracy and smuggling.[9]

Tew did indeed visit Madagascar and briefly use it as a base. He was killed in action in 1695 as the captain of one of five vessels, including famous pirate Henry Every's, trying to capture two of the Great Mogul of India's ships, the *Fateh Mohammed* and the *Gang-i-Saway*, or *Gunsway*, as it was called by the pirates. A "great Shott"—a cannonball, that is— from the *Fateh Mohammed* "carried away the rim" of his belly.[10] The wound might have disemboweled him entirely had he not held his intestines in as he bled to death. But he never helped found a pirate utopia on Madagascar. Even had he wanted to, he did not live long enough to have done so.

Likewise, there was another privateer-turned-pirate, Captain William Mason or, important to this story, Masson. In 1690, the English Masson led a mutiny against privateer captain William Kidd, who would later become the famous failed pirate hunter and pirate who ended his life hanged in London. Masson relieved Kidd of his ship, the *Blessed William*, then sailed to New York, where he received a privateering commission from New York Lieutenant Governor Jacob Leisler. In 1688, King James II was deposed in England, but the New York aristocracy and government still supported him. Leisler had led a brief successful rebellion against them, supported by the poor and middle class.[11]

Masson changed the name of the *Blessed William* to the *Jacob* and set sail for the Indian Ocean to plunder the Mogul's ships rather than the much poorer French trading and fishing vessels of Canada. Leisler was soon afterward captured, condemned for treason, and put to death or, as Governor Bellomont would soon write, murdered. Like Tew, Masson visited Madagascar only to refit and trade. But he built no utopia, nor even a pirate port.

The priest Caraccioli, so inflamed with what he saw as papal hypocrisy, is fictional and based entirely on the character of a priest of the same name in a popular sixteenth-century book, *Mery Tales*. The priest scorns the behavior of pompous church hierarchy—he is a rebel, in other words. Charles Johnson's description of the philosopher-pirate Caraccioli's behavior is so similar to that of Caraccioli in the storybook that the two can be considered identical. Educated readers of Johnson's day must surely have recognized the substitution and knew the story was intended as a hoax, a joke, or an allegory.[12]

As with a more modern hoax, that of the entirely fictional memoirs of the entirely fictional filibuster Louis Adhémar Timothée le Golif, known as Borgnefesse (Half-Ass), Charles Johnson began his story of Libertalia with the lie that he possessed a "French manuscript" that had been found among Captain Tew's papers.[13] The manuscript was Misson's own journal, or at least so Johnson claimed. Many readers never look for the actual evidence when reading a good story purportedly based on fact. All they need is for the author to assure them that he has seen the original manuscript—or treasure map, or letter, or whatever—and they will believe the story and look no further. No journal has ever come to light, nor has other evidence backing Johnson's tale. Overwhelming evidence to the contrary ensures that they never will, for they do not exist.

What Johnson was really doing was expanding on pirate rhetoric similar to that of political rebels and freethinkers of the time. He used it to tell a story that would doubtless get his readers' attention. It was easy to get people to believe there was a pirate empire at Madagascar. Tales of such abounded after pirate Henry Every, who had used Madagascar briefly as a base, captured the *Fateh Mohammed* and the *Gunsway* in 1695 and became famous worldwide for the gold and jewels he had plundered. The fact that believable accounts claimed his crew had raped all of the many women aboard the *Gunsway* did not impinge on his fame. Years later, people would believe that the ruins of the small fort at Madagascar had belonged to Every, although they never did.[14]

But there are plenty of small telltale giveaways in the story, not to mention common literary devices, most of which we have already discussed: pirates of the late seventeenth century did not fly the black flag; they sold far more slaves than they ever freed; they almost never saw themselves as a nation or people unto themselves, but instead retained a sense of loyalty to their native or adopted country; and although it made for excellent drama, captains of ships rarely engaged each other in sword fights in battle. In fact, the storybook narrative style may be the biggest telltale of all.

Although Johnson made the story of Libertalia up, he was probably inspired by the fame of Henry Every and other Red Sea pirates who visited Madagascar, as well as in general by the community of pirates and the claim of a small number of them that they were rebelling against cruel masters and others. And in fact there were small communities of pirates, former pirates, and maritime drifters who had settled on Madagascar, often among the local peoples.

But he also surely had inspiration from travel writers and philosophers. Seventeenth-century travel writer François Leguat, who some scholars claim was travel writer François Maximilien Misson (and some claim Misson was an invented name), wrote a book about a voyage to the East Indies, including to the island of Mascaregne (Mascarin, modern-day Réunion), east of Madagascar.[15]

Very likely, Johnson was also inspired by a novel written by freethinker Symon Tyssot de Patot, titled *Voyages et Avantures* (*Voyages and Adventures*), published in either 1710 or 1717. In the book, travelers visit Madagascar and then are shipwrecked on Australia, where they discover a utopia in which all the men are equal and all are atheists who govern themselves via reason. Tyssot de Patot wrote the novel under a pen name: Jaques Massé. Johnson was surely inspired by the coincidence of names: Mason or Masson, Misson, Massé. The similarity made his tale more credible, and he was probably making another small inside joke. Johnson's inspiration was doubtless aided by the fact that Captain Mason or Masson had been commissioned by the anti-elite rebel Jacob Leisler. Educated readers probably spotted these telltales.[16]

Charles Johnson surely had fun inventing his mythical pirate utopia Libertalia or Libertatia and using it to challenge established beliefs about government and equality. He may even have intended it as an allegorical warning of what might happen if pirates actually did band together and form their own country. All of this having been said, there really were small pirate settlements at Madagascar, and they are probably the ultimate inspiration for Johnson's pirate utopia. As there is with nearly all myths, there is a kernel of truth behind the myth of pirate utopias, more interesting even than the myth itself. It describes what pirate heaven was really like.

The Pirate Factor of St. Mary's

Whether the deed was committed in hot or cold blood, there were two incontrovertible facts: a man was dead, and Adam Baldridge had killed him. Perhaps, though, there were extenuating circumstances, and a court might rule the death as manslaughter instead of murder. Whatever the truth, Baldridge was no fool. He preferred neither to hang nor even to risk it by standing trial. He chose wisely, at least for a certain sort of man, and quickly, slipping away to do what many in Jamaica did in those days when they grew tired of tilling the soil, overseeing slaves, and serving planters and other wealthy men, or when they had committed a crime or simply needed to put food in their bellies: he joined the buccaneers.[17]

The year was 1685 or thereabouts. It was easy enough for Baldridge to get away. Although active buccaneers no longer truculently walked the streets of Port Royal, they still visited the island routinely, and it was not difficult to join one of their crews when they anchored in one of the many Jamaican coves to offload stolen goods and take on supplies. And if the timing were bad for Baldridge—if there were no buccaneer vessel at Jamaica—he only had to join the crew of a smuggling or turtle-fishing sloop or sign onto a ship trading for logwood at Campeche, Mexico. Soon enough, he would find a buccaneer crew.

Possibly he joined the second great buccaneer expedition to the South Sea, which was recruiting men to pillage again the Pacific coast of the Spanish Main. More likely, he joined some of the pirates who were going back and forth between cutting logwood at Campeche or the Mosquito Coast of Nicaragua, kidnapping Native American divers and using them to "fish" for silver on Spanish wrecks, and pirating in the Caribbean.

Eventually, Baldridge made his way to New York or Rhode Island, a pair of the great new havens for pirates and pirate goods—at least as long as pirates kept a reasonably low profile. He was a bright man who, along with his skill at piracy, knew how to keep books and make business deals. Whatever he may have done for his first five years as a pirate, in early 1690 he set sail for Madagascar aboard the *Fortune*, commanded by Richard Conyers. The *Fortune* was probably a slave ship intending to trade legitimately for slaves and illegitimately with pirates, but it may also have been a pirate masquerading as a slaver—or both. Almost certainly the ship had been fitted out and "cleared" for the voyage with the blessing of New York's governor, Benjamin Fletcher. The fact is, many of the pirates who sailed to the Indian Ocean were outfitted by investors in the North American colonies.

Beginning in the late 1680s, the Indian Ocean had quickly become the great new pirate cruising ground. Governments had started chasing pirates out of business in the Caribbean in the 1680s, and they were supposed to be doing so in the North American colonies. It certainly did not help that after 1688, when Europe went to war, the Spanish Main suddenly abounded with men-of-war and privateers, making the pirate's life even more difficult. The Indian Ocean, with its Moslem shipping, was now the place to be—surely the English authorities would turn an even greater blind eye to attacks on the vessels of the Islamic "Great Mogul" of India than they once had to attacks on those of Catholic Spain. The Mogul's ships were not "Christian" ships, so European pirates had no qualms about attacking them. As they rationalized it, there was no sin in stealing from a "heathen." Here was the new "pirate heaven."

When the *Fortune* anchored at St. Mary's Island (modern-day Île Saint-Marie) on July 17, 1690, only a few miles off the northeast coast of Madagascar, her crew surged ashore for fresh food to relieve palates savaged by months of salt beef, salt pork, rock-hard bread, dried peas, and probably rancid butter and cheese. Doubtless some of the crew were savaged by scurvy as well, and the island's oranges and limes stymied the disease and healed the sick bodies. The *Fortune* refitted, repaired, and refreshed as necessary, then put back to sea. If she were a pirate, she sought the ships of the Great Mogul of India, probably in the Red Sea, where they were most easily found.

By January 1691, whatever she had been doing in the Indian Ocean, the *Fortune* with Adam Baldridge aboard—yet neither as captain nor as crewman—was anchored once more at St. Mary's. But long before the *Fortune* had even set sail from New York, Baldridge had espied a much better prospect than mere piracy or trading in slaves or other goods. In fact, he had probably already made one voyage to St. Mary's as a pirate and found his inspiration there.

The Madagascar ports of Charnock's Point at St. Mary's, plus St. Augustine, Fort Dauphin, and Antongil Bay, had long been used as way points for travelers between the Atlantic and the Indian Oceans, including pirates. Madagascar was ideally located, just far enough away from India to make pirate hunting difficult, and close enough to the Cape of Good Hope, Africa, to serve as a resting place after making the rough passage from the Atlantic or when preparing for it. Pirates were flocking to the Indian Ocean from the Caribbean and North America, and merchantmen had long been stopping there.

Always looking for a deal, many merchant captains and their supercargoes—the owners' business agents—were more than willing to look the other way and trade with pirates. But there was no organization to the refreshing and trading that went on at Madagascar. What the pirates needed was a real pirate port to serve them. Adam Baldridge was determined to make that happen.

He took his sea chest and, along with two companions and his apprentice, John King, went ashore at St. Mary's on January 7, 1691. Madagascar is an enormous island, almost 1,000 miles long and roughly 350 miles wide at its widest point. Numerous competing peoples lived there at the time, and they were often at war. It was no different on St. Mary's. A long, skinny island more than 30 miles long, its inhabitants were often at war with their neighbors on the mainland. Baldridge knew the value of St. Mary's. The first thing he had to do was get the local people on his side, and the best way to do that was to settle among them—and then go to war with them. He would get rich, if he could, by political, piratical manipulation.

Baldridge did not waste any time. He married a native woman, then offered himself to the local Malagasy king as a military commander. This was a lucrative position, for an Englishman who went to war as a commander with a Madagascar king would be rewarded with half the slaves captured. Although Baldridge probably had but few muskets, they surely still gave his force something of an advantage, for the various tribes of Madagascar were not yet armed with firearms. In March, Baldridge and the warriors of St. Mary's went to war—and to pillage. They sailed to the mainland aboard canoes made from hollowed-out trees and aboard pirogues made of planks sewn together so tightly that little if any water leaked inside.

Baldridge and the Malagasy marched to the enemy's country, then attacked. Fighting on foot, warriors charged forth and darted their *zagayes*—a dart or spear with a poisoned iron tip—with extraordinary accuracy, then closed with the enemy. At hand-to-hand range, the armies fought with "half-pikes," or short spears they used for thrusting, while they defended themselves with shields.[18] Any muskets Baldridge brought along might have made the difference in the battle. Madagascar armies sometimes numbered in the thousands, and both the battle and the aftermath could be horrific.

As the enemy fled from the field of battle, the victors from St. Mary's stormed into the unknown enemy town. They plundered the defeated. They took many of them as slaves, rounded up their cattle, and probably murdered many of the vanquished whom they could not or did not want to take as slaves. One visitor reported that at times the victors would snatch infants from their mothers' breasts and "dash out their brains against the rocks," excusing the act as a practical means of preventing revenge.[19] This was hardly a novelty in warfare: many peoples across the world have done the same.

Baldridge returned to St. Mary's with his king in May. For his pains, the pirate now had seventy head of cattle and some slaves. He built a great house, lived "quietly" for a while, or so he said, spending much of his time helping to recover "wives and children that were taken before my coming to St. Maries by other Negroes to the northward of us about 60 leagues."[20] He never said how much he charged for this noble deed.

All the while, though, he was really preparing his "factory." In October 1691, a pirate ship arrived. Baldridge traded beef cattle for cannon, powder, shot, and various sundries. He built a fort and mounted the cannon there, and as other pirates came to trade, he added more. One witness claimed he had seven or eight cannon, another as many as twenty-two. For certain, by the end of 1692 he had at least a dozen cannon mounted and was prepared to fight friend or foe as necessary— pirate, Madagascar native, or pirate-hunting man-of-war.

By now, Baldridge had made a deal with the wealthiest man in New York, Frederick Philipse. Indeed, Philipse might even have been the owner of the *Fortune*, the ship that brought Baldridge to Madagascar. The rich businessman shipped Baldridge the stores and provisions the pirates—most of whom were outfitted in New York and Rhode Island, many by Philipse himself—needed, everything from powder and shot to rum, including shirts, stockings, breeches, shoes, Madera wine, stills to distill hard liquor, books, seed, carpenter tools, and other sundries. Baldridge paid in pieces of eight, slaves, cattle, and iron bars. He even offered credit to pirates, and he could arrange passage home for pirates and deserter seamen who had tired of the Indian Ocean.

Pirate ships and crews needed such a base. The ships were often in a sad state after months cruising for the Mogul's ships. Some were reported as "for want of a new suit of sails, they were forced to employ double silk instead of canvas."[21] The silk, of course, was provided from their plunder. Pirates, too, were often in need of rest and repair. At St. Mary's, they could buy almost anything they needed, and at a fairly reasonable price. Baldridge wanted to ensure a monopoly, and to do this he had to get pirates to do business with him.

And what a list of pirates it was! Edward Coates, Thomas Wake, Thomas Tew, Richard Glover, John Hoar, and Dirk Shivers, all of them notorious. Henry Every also visited, but Baldridge conveniently forgot to mention this in his deposition. At one point there were hundreds of pirates in St. Mary's: Captain Giles Shelly carried about fifty from Madagascar to New York, along with their riches, after they had "made their voyage."[22] Captain Kidd should have gone there as a pirate hunter, before he turned pirate, but he decided this was either unprofitable or dangerous, or both. Perhaps the idea of two or three dozen cannon, plus whatever pirates might have been there at the time, not to mention the many warriors Baldridge could summon, not to mention his own potentially mutinous crew, made him think twice. He would, however, later visit St. Mary's as a de facto pirate, as would the pirate Culliford.[23]

Soon, the enterprising former pirate, now a pirate "factor" (a company agent who worked at a "factory" ashore) Baldridge was joined by another factor, Lawrence Johnston. Pirates traded stolen goods to the factors, who also had ready cash and slaves with which to buy them. Baldridge then shipped the stolen goods—always with a full load of slaves—back to New York aboard ships that pretended to have sailed to Madagascar solely for slaves. Philipse even had a sloop, the *Frederick*, that on at least one occasion, after receiving word of their arrival, met a contraband ship at sea off the coast of New York, offloaded its suspicious East Indies cargo, and sailed to Hamburg, where it sold the goods. Slaves, however, were left aboard the Madagascar ship and were sold in New York.

For Baldridge, it was the best of all possible worlds. At St. Mary's, pirates could careen, repair, and provision their ships, get new clothes, not to mention get drunk and have sex with women. They paid well and made Baldridge rich. He was treated as a king! He had many slaves, many head of cattle, doubtless a rapidly growing sum of money waiting in New York, and the regard of both the people of St. Mary's and the Red Sea pirates. Here was pirate utopia! It was a place where a man could get rich, where he could have all the women he wanted, where no government would interfere with his theft! Pirate utopia was not a freethinkers' paradise, but a free traders' paradise and a hideout for those for whom the noose might await.

In 1697, he decided it was time to return to New York, or he had no choice, depending on whom you believe. According to Captain Kidd, Baldridge persuaded a large number of St. Mary's inhabitants, men, women, and children, all longtime allies and friends of his, to board a brigantine and then he sailed to Mascaregne and sold his passengers as slaves. And why not? He wasn't coming back. But when the inhabitants at St. Mary's discovered his heinous trick, they turned on the white men there, most of whom were pirates or former pirates, and slaughtered thirty. They burned Baldridge's house and fort and stole his goods. Of course, Baldridge laid the blame on the massacred white men themselves, claiming they had abused the natives and stolen their cattle, which may also have been true.

Baldridge returned briefly to Madagascar, rescued some of the survivors of the massacre, then headed home. He was replaced by Edward Welsh—in no case was a lucrative pirate factory to be abandoned!—was not as successful as Baldridge had been. In New York, Baldridge was received for a time as a respected citizen, such as such are. Indeed, he was said "to be a sober man and reported wealthy."[24] But as word came to light of his pirate trading, he was indicted for piracy. Richard Coote, Earl of Bellomont, who succeeded Governor Fletcher of New York and who claimed to be a hater of pirates and of those who consorted with them, would have tried Baldridge for piracy had there been an honest prosecutor and judge or two in New York. Unfortunately, for "ten pieces of eight" (roughly $500 to $600 today) a man could bribe the "honest" officers of the court.[25] Baldridge never stood trial, but, ever with an eye for profit, he tried to persuade Governor Bellomont to establish a substantial trading post on Madagascar—a legal post with an illicit pirate trade on the side, naturally, and surely with Baldridge running it.

Soon, the former pirate factor married the wife of Edward Buckmaster, who had sailed with Captain Kidd on his voyage of pirate hunting and piracy. But Baldridge, as we know, was still a thief at heart: Buckmaster was still alive, and the man who married Baldridge to Buckmaster's "widow" had no authority to do so, not to mention that he had obtained the license under the pretense of two people in love who needed to conceal their identities—but this probably mattered not at all to the pirate factor. Almost certainly he was the instigator, at least at his fiancée's request.

Realizing his days in New York were probably numbered, Baldridge provisioned a brigantine, persuaded Governor Bellomont to provide him with a pass to trade at Antigua, persuaded the brigantine's owners that he was sailing to Madagascar or the Guinea Coast of Africa for slaves—and instead turned pirate and attacked ships off the coast of Newfoundland. Doubtless he was looking for a ship suitable for piracy in the Indian Ocean. But we do not hear of him again.

Baldridge, the "chief transactor and manager in carrying on that mischievous trade" at St. Mary's, had made the Grand Tour, so to speak, from murderer to pirate to pirate factor—even pirate prince!—to wealthy New York gentleman to pirate once more.[26] Or perhaps it was not much of a grand tour after all, but rather the same wolf in different clothing. Baldridge's fort at St. Mary's was the real pirate "utopia" that inspired Charles Johnson's mythical one. His was the "utopia" that actually existed on Madagascar during the years Johnson placed his imaginary one there. But here the resemblance ended—Baldridge's "utopia" was purely a business proposition.

Yet good ideas are seldom retired. By 1699, Abraham Samuel, a mulatto pirate, had established a similar "utopia" at Fort Dauphin, Madagascar (modern-day Tolagnaro), and within two decades another pirate would do much the same as Baldridge had, but on an even grander scale.[27]

The King of Ranter Bay

In many ways it had been a successful cruise. The pirates had defeated and captured the Honorable East India Company ship *Cassandra* in July 1720, in spite of a valiant defense by Captain Mackra and his crew, who had fought two pirate ships at once. Truly, had their companion ship come to their aid, they might well have sent the pirates flying. But now the *Cassandra* was mounted with forty great guns—a formidable pirate ship indeed!

A great lumbering Portuguese East Indiaman had also fallen to their hands, and the pirates had mounted her with seventy guns, or so John Plantain, a former member of the pirate crew, reported to East India naval officer Clement Downing. We must be a bit suspicious of Mr. Plantain, for it was no easy task to corroborate all that he claimed, and some of his statements were indeed untrue. Even so, Plantain's most significant claims were corroborated by Downing's own eyes.[28]

The pirate crews gathered in council at Charnock Point, Madagascar, and voted on their next course. As was usual among pirates whose booty had been good, some "were for leaving off, and living on what they had; others of a more covetous disposition, were for still continuing their unlawful practices."[29] Most of all, they knew of and feared a pirate hunting squadron under the command of Commodore Thomas Matthews. Many of the pirates considered sailing to Veracruz on the Spanish Main and accepting a Spanish amnesty and Spanish service as *guardas costas*. Soon enough, the pirates sailed away to the African coast, refitted, then put to sea again and eventually dispersed. However, sixty or seventy of the pirates, including their former captain, Edward England, who either voluntarily stepped down after a dispute or had been voted from office, remained behind. Some pirates settled quietly, but others intended to build their own small empires.

John Plantain was one of the latter. Born at Chocolata Hole, where ships careened at Port Royal, Jamaica, at thirteen he turned to privateering and logwood cutting, and at nineteen to piracy at Rhode Island. He was no more than twenty-five, and probably younger, when, along with Scotsman James Adair and Dane Hans Burgen, he insinuated himself into the local inhabitants at Antongila Bay, known then as Ranter Bay, a grand harbor roughly fifty miles deep and twenty-five miles at its greatest width.

With the help of the inhabitants, and especially with Plantain's stolen wealth, a sum far greater than that of his companions, they built fortifications, hired warriors, and set themselves up as kings, Plantain above the other two. They made war on their neighbors, stole their cattle, made slaves of their people, and demanded tribute. Plantain ruled with an arbitrary hand, yet his adopted subjects sang songs and danced in great numbers in his praise, inspired by his victories and the wealth they brought. Nearly every verse of their songs ended with "Plantain King of Ranter Bay."[30] Or at least so he said.

The pirates at Ranter Bay were well outfitted with supplies and goods, all via their piracies against the English and Portuguese East India companies and the Great Mogul. Passing ships, ranging from merchantmen to pirates, stopped at Plantain's pirate utopia for refreshment and repair, and he gladly accommodated them. He even sold slaves to passing slave ships. Ranter Bay was what we imagine an independent pirate haven to have been: a tropical paradise where rum was plentiful and women were willing.

But Ranter Bay was no thinker's utopia. The pirates swaggered around, a brace of pistols in each of their belts and a cutlass in hand, ready to fight the enemies they had made among the various peoples of Madagascar—and among their brethren. They quarreled constantly among themselves, their riches and power having made them even more greedy, not to mention fearfully paranoid of losing their ill-gotten gains in the same way as they had seized them.

Plantain, who had many wives and women servants to whom he gave names like Moll, Kate, Sue, and Peg, learned of the beautiful granddaughter of a local king known as Long Dick by the English on the island. Earnestly he desired her, for she was of part English extraction. He demanded her hand. Long Dick refused. John Plantain had no choice: he declared war. Arming a small number of his men with muskets—as few as thirty among a thousand men—he marched to battle.

But Long Dick was similarly advised and armed by former pirates, and sent word he would meet Plantain on the field of battle.

With his general, Mulatto Tom, who claimed to be the son of famous pirate captain Henry Every, and four or five allied Madagascar kings, Plantain set forth to battle. He fought under English colors, his ally Adair under Scottish, and his ally Burgen under Danish—and, notably, not under the piratical black flag. Long Dick was as good as his word, and met Plantain halfway. The forces joined battle, the enemy darting their lances effectively. But Plantain's superiority in firearms won the day. His men routed Long Dick's, who took to their heels, knowing well what was in store for those who were captured. Plantain captured several pirates, mostly English and Dutch, who had allied themselves with Long Dick. These he forced to run barefoot over hot coals while his allies hurled lances at them until all were dead. Surely many fell, still alive, onto the searing hot coals, their blood literally boiling as they bled to death in agony.

But alas for Plantain's great love! She was pregnant by one of the pirates he had tortured to death. Furious, he tortured Long Dick to death, damning him for letting another man have her when he knew Plantain desired her. Plantain continued to make war for two years, torturing captured pirates and captured kings to death. Yet he doted on his favorite wife, Long Dick's granddaughter. Her name was Eleanor Brown. Plantain fathered several children with her, and gave her "twenty girl slaves to wait on her." One day, a deserter from an East Indiaman made plain his desire for Eleanor; Plantain shot him dead.

By now Plantain believed he could make himself king of all Madagascar. But such grand deeds do not come easily when you have made enemies of nearly everyone. After all, "the enemy of my enemy is my friend," as the common saying goes. Plantain had become a rich, powerful man, with more than a thousand slaves, with cannon-mounted forts, with an army of at least hundreds of warriors. Plantain's wars grew even uglier. He attacked with an even greater viciousness, butchering five hundred prisoners on one occasion and putting all of the men, women, and children of several towns to the sword on another. In the brief, ugly peace that followed he was proclaimed "The Great King of Madagascar."[31]

Still, Plantain was no fool. He knew the peace he maintained by the sword had come at the expense of great bloody plundering slaughter. He could never live in peace, for he had made too many enemies, and sooner or later his own allies—even the English and Dutch pirates among them—would turn on him and murderously torture him as he had tortured so many. The native peoples had come to distrust their European pirate allies, given their brutalities. Half of the pirates who had settled on the island were dead of wars and disease.

Venturing with his wife and treasure to India, Plantain entered the service of the great Kanhoji Angria at Alibag, as other pirates and adventuresome spirits had done. Kanhoji entertained him in a grand manner, with dancing girls and great food. Here was what Plantain had lived to become! He entered the service of the great Indian naval-privateer-and-pirate admiral. What eventually became of him we do not know, but if he served Kanhoji well, then John Plantain, the piratical king of Madagascar, likely ended his days as a great lieutenant of one of the greatest sea-roving admirals in history.

Utopias for Greedy Men

The great "pirate" settlements at Madagascar were remarkable bases for a greedy sort of laissez-faire capitalism combined with a liberal democracy, of a transient population of men who managed to work together for a common purpose of profit by force of arms. But they were hardly utopias, unless a utopia is a place where you can get rich via theft, murder, and slavery. Many pirates mistreated the members of the various native tribes on the island, causing them to make war on the pirates.

We cannot forget why pirates stopped there: to refresh themselves, to refit their ships, and to sell stolen goods to passing merchantmen or pirate businessmen. Pirates were thieves who often in the process tortured, raped, and murdered. Baldridge's settlement at St. Mary's was a pirate trading station. Plantain's was a murderous petty empire of the worst sort. These were the real Libertalias. They were built upon theft, murder, and Machiavellian manipulation, not upon grand ideals of liberty and equality. If there ever were any real "Libertalias" on Madagascar, they were small, did not last long, and never foreswore slavery.

There were, of course, small settlements of former pirates and occasional pirates, where all lived fairly quiet, harmonious lives, indulging in piracy or similar activities only rarely. Some of these men settled among the Miskito Indians on the Mosquito Coast of Nicaragua, others along the west coast and islands of the Bay of Honduras (modern Belize), and still others among the Cuna on the Darien coast. Some cut logwood at small transient settlements at Campeche, Mexico, at least until the next time Spanish *guardas costas* ran them off or enslaved them. Others settled in small numbers on the Guinea Coast of Africa and some quietly at various places at Madagascar. Most typically married and lived among the local peoples.

For a while at least, a few probably settled in small numbers in the Carolinas and at Accomac, Virginia, carefully hiding their piratical pasts, as did a perhaps larger number in New York and Rhode Island. A few scrounged out a living at New Providence, several times a short-lived Caribbean pirate capital in the late seventeenth and early eighteenth centuries, and a few others sought piratical shelter at the Danish Caribbean "freeport" at St. Thomas. Of course, we cannot forget the great buccaneer and filibuster bases at Tortuga and Petit Goave at Hispaniola, and of Port Royal, Jamaica, but they were always under a government's thumb. Tortuga went first, largely replaced by Petit Goave in the 1670s. By the early 1680s Port Royal was finished as a pirate port. Petit Goave lasted until the turn of the new century.

Perhaps for pirates who lived long enough to retire but had squandered most of their ill-gotten gains, the small, quiet, secluded places were indeed utopia or "pirate heaven." For most, though, utopia was little more than fistfuls of plunder from the seas and the ability to squander it as pirates most often did: on rum, dice, and women. In general, to a pirate, hell was surely not the hangman's noose or a lingering, suffering death from marooning on a desert isle devoid of food, water, and shelter, but a lifetime spent among timid, lubberly souls.

CHAPTER 12

Buried Treasure, Sunken Treasure

—∞∞∞—

"But above all, in the great cabbin, was a large chest, so heavy, that five or six men could be just draw it along the deck, full of pigs of silver, bags of pieces of eight, and some gold. This treasure brought us into some danger . . ."[1]

— Charles May, *An Account of the Wonderful Preservation of the Ship Terra Nova*, 1688

"The next thing they did was, with madness and rage to tare up the Hatches, enter the Hould like a parcel of Furies, where with Axes, Cutlashes, etc., they cut, tore and broke open Trunks, Boxes, Cases and Bales, and when any of the Goods came upon Deck which they did not like to carry with them aboard their Ship, instead of tossing them into the Hould again they threw them over-board into the Sea. The usual method they had to open Chests was by shooting a brace of Bullets with a Pistol into the Key-hole to force them open."[2]

— *The Boston News-Letter*, August 22, 1720

The great raid—or murderous assault—had gone well. Veracruz, the rich Spanish port on the Gulf Coast of Mexico, had fallen easily, far more so than anyone could have expected. The city, home of the pirate-hunting Armada de Barlovento and protected as well by the powerful fort of San Juan de Ulloa a mile and a half away across the bay, was expecting nothing but the arrival of the treasure fleet known as the Flota. Through the low walls of Veracruz passed tons of Mexican silver and goods that were loaded every two or three years aboard the Flota that anchored in its harbor. But the Armada de Barlovento was away, and the filibusters had ignored the fort across the harbor and attacked by land instead, where defenses were weak.[3]

The fourteen hundred pirates, under the command of a Frenchman, the Sieur de Grammont, and of Dutchmen Laurens de Graff and Nicholas van Horn, hit the city hard and with overwhelming surprise in the early hours of May 18, 1683. It was a pretty city, with straight streets in the Spanish style, handsome houses enlivened by caged cardinals, and haughty hidalgos and their richly clad wives. But its walls were so low that they could be climbed in many places without ladders, and its landward defenses were almost nonexistent.

Several of the filibusters, including de Graff, had been to the city before—some had lived in it—and knew its streets and lanes well. They easily captured the seaside bastions. In one, the sentries were asleep. The other they took by deception. A Spanish-speaking filibuster, dressed as a local Spaniard, asked the sentry for fire to light his pipe. Then he shot the sentry dead and fired two more shots in quick succession, the signal for the attack to commence.

Quickly, the pirates charged through Veracruz. The Sieur de Grammont led his force into the plaza at the city's center, easily thrusting aside any resistance they met. In the plaza a few Spaniards, doing their best to keep their calm among the disorder, stood ready to defend the lives and riches of Veracruz. Grammont—an expert in land warfare, equal even to Henry Morgan—drew his filibusters up in line of battle. They fired three successive volleys. Through the great cloud of gun smoke the filibusters now surged, cracking Spanish heads with musket butts, wielding bloody injury and painful, cruel death via cutlass and pistol. In moments, the plaza was cleared of those who had dared defend it.

Having secured the city, the filibusters plundered from house to house, taking prisoners and looting valuables. No one had had time to hide much of anything. In the chaos, a few pirates settled private scores with Spaniards who lived there. One murdered his wife, another a priest of the Holy Inquisition. The pirates locked their prisoners in the great church, La Merced, with barrels of gunpowder placed at the entrances, accompanied by a stern warning that they would blow up the church if the prisoners did not behave themselves. There, for three days, they were left to suffer from thirst and hunger, and the women from rape as well. In the meantime, the pirates continued to plunder and vandalize.

After four days the filibusters, alerted to the presence of the well-armed Flota, ferried their plunder and all four thousand prisoners to nearby Sacrificios Island, making any rescue attempt virtually impossible. By the end of the day, three hundred prisoners still remained ashore on the mainland. Not wanting to ferry them by night, Grammont would have murdered them all had de Graff not prevented him by sending them back to Veracruz.

Grammont was a famous filibuster, and although he was an adequate seaman, he was best known for his prowess at fighting on land, where he invariably led from the front. He was a gouty, black-haired, olive-skinned pirate between forty and fifty years of age who, when young, had killed one of his sister's suitors in a duel and then entered the French "Régiment Royal des Vaisseaux" as a cadet before becoming a filibuster.[4] Irreverent and with a passion for wine, women, and dice in no certain order, he was as highly regarded by his crew as he was cold-blooded to his enemies.

For more than a week, the pirates tarried on Sacrificios, dividing their plunder, planning their escape, and almost certainly sobering up. After a disagreement over whether to fight the now nearby Flota and steal its riches or return to Petit Goave on Saint-Domingue (modern-day Haiti), the pirates set sail, leaving a city in ruins and its population brutally traumatized.

Van Horn, wounded, as already described, in a duel with de Graff on Sacrificios, took sick and died. Grammont was awarded his ship, the *Saint Nicolas*, which he renamed the *Hardy*, and set a course for Petit

Goave. But to sail from Veracruz, located on the southeast coast of Mexico, was not an easy task. The winds in the Caribbean and the Gulf of Mexico generally blow from east to west. Grammont's course, and surely the Gulf "loop" current, took them too far north into the Gulf, forcing them to beat—sail a zigzag course against the wind—their way south between Mexico and Cuba, or southwest between Cuba and Florida.[5]

Of course, if we believe the myth of pirates burying their treasure, Grammont and his crew should have set a course for a desert island somewhere, and when they arrived, they should have gone ashore with chests of treasure and picks and shovels to bury it with. Yet they did nothing of the sort.

Doubloons and Pieces of Eight

And just what was this rich treasure they might bury? The most common plunder on the Spanish Main was silver coins. Known as pieces of eight, they were crude, irregular coins weighing almost one ounce (27 grams, to be more accurate) apiece and measuring roughly one and quarter to one and a half inches in diameter. Each coin was unique in shape. Three sorts were noted in the English colonies: Seville (minted in Spain), Mexico (minted in Mexico City), and "pillar" (minted in Potosí in modern-day Bolivia and in Lima, Peru).[6] Coins from Mexico, Potosí, and Lima mints were the most common on the Main. But there were other coins as well, especially Spanish doubloons, or double escudos, from the Spanish word *doblón*, worth two pieces of eight. There were even double doubloons. Most doubloons were fairly small, crude gold coins ranging in size from that of a nickel to that of a quarter—not the much larger gold coins we are accustomed to seeing in Hollywood films.

Pirates also stole other plunder, including pearls; emeralds; silver and gold jewelry, decorations, and utensils; and valuable cargo such as cochineal, logwood, brazilwood, and indigo and annatto dyes; tobacco; cacao (chocolate); hides; ambergris; tortoiseshell; Jesuit's bark and other medicines; sugar; valuable seasonings such as vanilla, ginger, and allspice; and slaves, who were generally valued at one hundred pieces of eight apiece. Grammont had two hundred African, mulatto, and other men, women, and children of color as slaves aboard the *Hardy*.

The large chests of gold and silver we associate with pirates were fairly rare. Most treasure chests were small, and for good reason: coins were heavy. The typical Spanish merchant treasure chest held two thousand pieces of eight, and those of the king, three thousand. Each of the royal chests was roughly ten inches high and deep, and twenty inches wide. Its coins divided equally into three linen bags called *talegas*. The silver alone in each chest weighed almost 180 pounds. Add to this the weight of the wooden chest, and it is easy to see that such chests were not easily moved, even by two strong men. Only occasionally was treasure shipped in a larger chest, as in the quotation at the beginning of this chapter.[7]

Unfortunately, even if Grammont had so intended, he was by now in too much trouble to sail to a small island or inlet, bury the ill-gotten loot, and make a map showing the exact route to the buried treasure, with an X to mark the spot. If he had, he might also have shot the witnesses and buried at least one of them with the treasure, for, being a superstitious lot, he and his pirates believed that the dead man's ghost would help protect the chest of doubloons and pieces of eight from any beachcomber who might inadvertently stumble across it. Some might even have buried a Bible with the treasure, superstitiously believing it would earn them the devil's help in protecting the riches.[8] The pirates would then sail away and return on some future date to dig up their loot and spend it.

Of course, this is all arrant nonsense. With only a rare exception or two discussed next, pirates had no reason to hide—or necessarily bury—their plunder. Besides that, what fool would leave a fortune buried somewhere in the sand where it might later be accidentally discovered? Or where one pirate might slip away later and dig it up, keeping it all to himself and a few cronies? As for superstition, pirates did not believe that buried Bibles or corpses would protect anything. Most of all, though, what pirate crew would trust its booty solely to the captain and quartermaster? Or to anyone, for that matter?

Pirates had no need to bury their treasure, and no desire to. They "shared" it as soon as practical after they plundered a vessel or sacked a town. Most received a single share, boys a half share, some officers one and half shares, and captains from two to six shares. Each man took his share and did with it as he pleased, although at sea the plunder might be kept in a central location, in a pirate bank, so to speak, with the quartermaster keeping record. Still, each pirate could withdraw his shares as he pleased.[9]

Pirates were scrupulous about their calculations and made sure each man received his fair division. They did not consider their plunder to be owned in common, except to pay disability, the surgeon, and often the carpenter who had prepared their vessel for sea. As soon as these payments were made, the rest was shared among the crew and investors (if there were any), according to the articles. And this is what Grammont's crew had already done, although the profit from any goods and slaves aboard would have to be shared after they were sold.

The problem was, they might never get to do what both pirates and sailors in general have done for millennia when they returned from a cruise. Gulf winds and the powerful "loop" current had forced the *Hardy* far north into the Gulf of Mexico, upon whose shores there was nothing to be had but shipwreck followed by death from disease or at the hands of Native Americans, something both the famous French explorer René-Robert Cavelier, Sieur de la Salle, and the Spanish pirate Juan Corso would experience within two years. Grammont and his pirate crew, now at sea for weeks, suffered severely from thirst and hunger. Many crews might have considered mutiny in such dire straits, but Grammont was a strong leader who "knew how to win men's hearts."[10] It helped that the pirates were rich with plunder. They kept their faith in their captain, just as they had at Veracruz.

The starving, dehydrated pirates, fearful that their golden dreams come true were about to vanish before their eyes, arrived along the Florida Keys, a string of islands littered with wrecks of Spanish treasure ships and others. But for the lack of food, they were in better straits now, sure to eventually arrive at home—provided they didn't starve to death.

So far east were they that their best course was now to sail to South Carolina, sell their cargo and refit, then return to Petit Goave. Among the Keys, their lookouts kept an eagle-eyed watch not for small islands on which to bury their treasure—there were plenty of them here—but for a sail, any sail, whose hold they might plunder of food and water.

By a miracle, there she was, a small, light grayish brown spot on the horizon at first, then a hull. Grammont's *Hardy* quickly ran the *Nuestra Señora de la Candelaria* down near Key West. The Spanish ship immediately struck her colors, for the *Hardy* carried fifty-two guns. The haggard pirates boarded the ship, ravenously seeking sustenance of any sort. When the pirates inspected the ship's cargo, they discovered a miracle upon a miracle: the *Candelaria*'s hold was filled with grain destined for Veracruz, and she had plenty of jars of water as well. The pirates would neither starve nor die of thirst.

They set a course north, to South Carolina, sold their two hundred slaves, then turned south for Petit Goave, arriving in December 1683, after a voyage of more than six months. Never did the pirates stop to bury their treasure, not at the Florida Keys, nor among the barrier islands off Georgia and the Carolinas, nor among the many islands of the Bahamas. Grammont's *Hardy* anchored off Petit Goave, a narrow sliver of a town that was now the most notorious pirate haven in the Caribbean. With bags of silver his crew surged ashore to do what pirates really did with their plunder.

Rum Punch and Naked Women

Grammont's filibusters hit Petit Goave—and probably Charlestown, South Carolina, previously as well—almost as fiercely as they had hit Veracruz, but with a far different purpose and attitude. They boarded local canoes and pirogues that ferried them the five hundred yards to shore. In Carolina they had not yet recovered from their starving voyage, but here they would celebrate.

On their shoulders were sacks of pieces of eight with which they would redeem their spirits and appearance. If they behaved as buccaneer-surgeon Alexandre Exquemelin says buccaneers did, then directly to the taverns they went, where prices suddenly surged upward. Rum they ordered, and rum punch, and wine, and after they emptied each glass or bottle they flung it into the air or against the walls or onto the floor. They tossed some glasses and bottles into the air and swung at them with sticks instead, smashing them midair—if the pirates were sober enough or lucky enough to actually hit the glassware, that is. Next they ordered food: sea turtle, fresh beef and pork, roast chicken, and condiments of allspice, salt, pepper, and crushed hot pepper to season them all, and even oranges, pineapples, and other tropical fruit. Soon the tavern floor and tables were strewn with broken glass, turtle bones, and other remnants of drunken revel.[11]

From the taverns they staggered to the haberdashers, buying new clothing, all overpriced and which they all too quickly changed into—for the women were waiting. A well-dressed man with money in his pockets is invariably more appealing than a poorly dressed one with money in his pockets. Back to the taverns or bawdy houses they went, wherever there were women for sale. The pirates paid richly for sex with women who drank and swore as much as they did. Some pirates paid small fortunes just to watch one strip and dance on a table. Doubtless there were displays such as the "burning shame" described in a late eighteenth-century dictionary: "a lighted candle stuck into the private parts of a woman."[12] Similar displays are seen in the more notorious seaports and border towns of the world today.

By now, many pirates were drunk and exhausted, having imbibed too much rum and wine much too quickly, having eaten too much turtle and pork and vomited it and the alcohol up at least once, having shouted and caroused too loudly for too long, and having had sex as often as they could—or at least as often as their drunken states allowed. Surely many now lay passed out on tavern floors or tables, in streets or alleyways, or on backroom floors, shoved there by strumpets and prostitutes after they passed out in their beds.

Their thirst and lust sated for the moment, those who had not passed out hastened immediately to the gambling pits, followed not long after by their seriously hungover brethren, where they played a dice game called *passe-dix* ("passage" in English) or a variety of card games or placed bets on cockfights or the outcome of a billiard game.[13]

Many spent and lost a fortune here in a short time, leaving them soon in debt to tavern keepers, with nothing left to their names but their weapons and the clothes on their backs, and now desperately in need of a new voyage so that they might binge in wanton debauchery again. However, some pirates, wiser than their other Brethren of the Coast, invested part of their booty in land or in goods from Europe to trade in the New World. After all, one could not rove the seas forever. One day they must retire—if they lived so long. The myth notwithstanding, buried treasure was not a means of securing a pirate's retirement from the roving seas.

Captain Kidd's Buried Treasure

The origin of the myth of pirates burying their treasure is a simple, not particularly noteworthy, act of the unfortunately infamous Captain William Kidd, erstwhile pirate-hunting-privateer-turned-pirate. Sent to the Indian Ocean to pursue sea thieves, he failed miserably at the task, killed his back-talking and therefore mutinous gunner by cracking his skull with a wooden bucket, and, under pressure from his crew, engaged in piracy. To be fair, Kidd never considered himself a pirate and hoped his depredations might have enough color of legitimacy that accusations of piracy might not be leveled.[14]

But it was not to be. By the time Kidd returned to New York in 1699, he was already considered an infamous pirate, convicted in the public mind and ready to be made a scapegoat for the wealthy men who had invested in the failed pirate-hunting scheme. He well knew he might be arrested and indicted. More important, he also knew that money—coins of silver and gold, as well as goods and jewelry that could be converted into silver and gold—would be the only means of his salvation. The truth would not suffice, not to mention that he was guilty of both manslaughter and piracy, or at least manslaughter and attempted piracy. With money, he could bribe men to look the other way, he could hire an attorney to help prepare his case (lawyers were not yet permitted to represent their clients in court in criminal cases), and, if it came to it, he could use it to help him escape.

In late July 1699, Kidd's small, six-gun sloop lay at anchor off Gardiner's Island, three miles off the far eastern shore of Long Island, New York. The skinny island, whose name was probably pronounced as "Gar'ner's," was roughly five miles long and three and a third miles wide and named for its proprietor, John Gardiner.[15] Kidd's sloop was first noticed in the evening light, a solitary vessel quietly riding at anchor, lending a mysterious and surely somewhat menacing air to the island's secluded atmosphere. New York, after all, was a pirate haven, and its capital one hundred fifty miles away by sea was filled with rich merchants who invested in pirate enterprises meant to plunder the Mogul's ships in the Indian Ocean and Red Sea, and with many pirates and former pirates to be found among the seamen who frequented the taverns and bawdy houses on the waterfront. A sloop riding unobtrusively at anchor in an isolated cove or anchorage might well have been up to no good.

Three days after he first anchored off the island, Kidd sent two of his men to fetch Mr. Gardiner to the sloop. According to Gardiner's deposition, the accused pirate asked him to "take on shore for him and keep for him . . . a chest, and a box of gold and a bundle of quilts and four bales of goods."[16] Kidd's men also delivered two bags of silver of thirty pounds weight, a small bundle of gold, and a pound of gold dust to Gardiner for safekeeping. Naturally, the proprietor later claimed to know nothing of Kidd having been "proclaimed a pyrate."[17] Added to the gold and silver he would later hide in his lodging, the value of this treasure might have been as much as £14,000 at the time—or more than $2.5 million today.

This treasure belonged to Kidd alone and was hidden for brief safekeeping. He needed it for bribes, legal defense, and escape should it come to that. Of course, he also needed it in order to live well. The division of spoils had already been made. This was not a pirate treasure belonging to a pirate crew, but that of a single individual who knew it would be confiscated immediately.

And indeed it was. Richard Coote, governor of both New York and Massachusetts and better known by his title, Lord Bellomont, was one of the partners in the disaster. He quickly committed Kidd to jail. The same day, quite by accident, he heard that one of Kidd's former crewmen was willing to pay £30 to engage a sloop to carry him to Gardiner's Island, "Kidd having owned he had buried some gold on that island" so he could carry away the treasure Kidd had buried there.[18]

Bellomont immediately issued "a peremptory order to Mr. Gardiner in the King's name to come forthwith and deliver up such treasure as Kidd or any of his crew had lodged with him, acquainting him that I had committed Kidd to Goal [jail] as I was ordered to do by the King."[19]

Gardiner, of course, complied immediately and turned *everything* over to the governor and his committee, excusing his willingness to assist Captain Kidd by noting that he had been threatened by "privateers"—pirates, in other words—before.[20] Kidd would not have his money after all. Instead, he was now jailed, friendless, and penniless. Eventually he was carried to London, where he was tried for piracy and murder, convicted of murder, and hanged. Unbelievably, the rope broke the first time he was pushed off the ladder. It was fortune's last cruel joke at Captain Kidd's expense, dragging out his pain and anger a few minutes more while thieves greater than he went free. The rope did not break the second time.

While Kidd's sloop had lain at anchor at Gardiner's Island, other small sloops had come and gone as well, transferring plundered goods from one sloop to another, then sailing quietly away. The mysterious comings and goings—obviously a secret means of hiding booty—lent credence to the idea that pirates were sneaking about at night and hiding their treasure.

The tale of Captain Kidd at Gardiner's Island is the ultimate origin of our myth of pirates secretly burying their treasure. Yet it is not even certain that any of Kidd's treasure was actually buried. Instead, it may simply have been in Gardiner's and others' keeping until called for. Even so, rumors by now ran their course: Kidd the pirate had buried his treasure on Gardiner's Island!

We cannot know for sure how quickly these rumors spread or how far, but they were well known locally. Charles Johnson, in his pirate chronicle, did not mention Kidd's "buried treasure," so we cannot blame him for spreading the myth beyond New York and Massachusetts. Nor can we blame the writer of the popular lyrics to "Captain "Kid's Farewell" to the Seas" in 1701, for the verses mention nothing about burying or hiding treasure or anything else.[21] Who, then, can we credit? Or is it simply natural to assume that anyone who steals treasure must therefore bury it?

Iron-Bound Chests and Pirate Ghosts

After Kidd's death, rumors of buried treasure associated with pirates began to spread far and wide. In 1722, Clement Downing, an officer of the Honorable East India Company, visited Madagascar and met the infamous John Plantain, the King of Ranter Bay. Plantain, the former pirate whose history has already been described, amassed a fortune helping one Madagascar tribe raid another, which facilitated his trade in slaves. Downing noted that Plantain concealed treasure as a means of safekeeping, especially when he went to war, this being the only way he had to protect it while he was gone.[22]

Burying treasure chests, particularly during invasions, was a common means of protecting wealth. The Spanish inhabitants of Jamaica had done so when the English invaded in 1655, and for years afterward were told tales of secret and at times "inchanted" caves in which were hidden iron-bound chests and earthenware jars assumed to be filled with treasure.[23] Similarly, British forces in India, engaged in local wars for the sake of commercial enterprise in the seventeenth and eighteenth centuries, often dragged ponds for treasure chests after they and their local allies captured a town.[24]

So here at least is an example of a former pirate, who would soon serve one of the great sea rovers of history, the Indian admiral Kanhoji Angria, actually burying his treasure for protection—but not at the end of a pirate voyage.

In 1687, three of the buccaneers Henry Pitman met on Salt Tortuga Island—"ill principled and loose kind of Fellows"—robbed their several brethren of arms, food, and personal goods at point of pistol. They captured two of their companion buccaneers, then a third whom they bound, then waited to capture the remaining two upon their return. "The reason why they endeavoured to take them, was because they had hid their Monies in the Sand, and did not keep it in their Chests." Here indeed is buried treasure—but only a little bit, and only to keep it safe from fellow pirates. So much for honor among thieves![25]

There is at least one more authentic account of hidden, if not buried, pirate treasure. In 1729, French pirate Jean Thomas Dulaien and ten of his pirate crew arrived in Nantes with a rich cargo of goods and money. For several weeks, while waiting for official word from Versailles regarding their pardon, they secretly sent their booty ashore in small packages and hid it from the search the French admiralty's inspectors would soon make.[26]

The inspectors, despite their diligence, were at first able to locate only a small part of the treasure—some in Dulaien's mother's tiny cottage, some in his mistress's lodging house—after local priests inveighed against the pirates and threatened to excommunicate anyone who aided them. But the inspectors were never able to recover all of the treasure nor even calculate what its exact value was. Dulaien, with money at hand to grease the necessary palms, largely succeeded in doing what Kidd had intended: his crew received an amnesty, albeit after a brief stint in prison, and kept much of their booty. Dulaien's amnesty, however, was refused. No one knows whether he was released or committed to an oubliette in a French prison, leaving him to die a forgotten man.

But none of these instances are what we think of when we think of pirates burying their treasure. Clement Downing, however, comes to the rescue. Captured at one point and held prisoner in Gujarat, India, he chanced to meet two Dutchmen and three Portuguese who had come to seek service in the Mughal Empire, as many Europeans did. One of them, Anthony de Silvestro, claimed to have a member of one of the crews of the two pirate-hunting sloops that trapped Blackbeard in his lair and killed him. He told Downing that if he were ever at the "York River or Maryland, near an Island called Mulberry Island, provided we went on shore at the watering place, where the shipping used most commonly to ride, that there the pyrates had buried considerable sums of money in great chests, well clamp'd with iron plates."[27] De Silvestro gave directions in great detail, including mentioning the five trees near where the treasure was hidden.

Of course, in reality de Silvestro was "pulling Downing's chain," so to speak, and Downing was well aware of this. There was no treasure, and if there were, it would have long ago been dug up and hidden elsewhere, and surely spent as well, by de Silvestro if not by the hundreds of others who had heard the tale. Downing amusingly suggested that if "any body should obtain any benefit by this account, if it please God they ever come to England, 'tis hoped they will remember the author for his information."[28] The myth was probably inspired by the tales of Kidd's treasure.

Downing's book was published in 1737 and was widely read, as it gave an often firsthand account of the wars between the Honorable East India Company and the Indian sea rovers, especially the famous "pirate" admiral Kanhoji Angria. The myth of pirate treasure continued to grow for the rest of the century. In 1767, a play, *Disappointment; or, the Force of Credulity* by Andrew Barton, was published in New York, its plot mocking those who searched for easy riches, in this case Blackbeard's buried treasure, which is, of course, a hoax. The perpetrators create false documents belonging to Blackbeard's imagined granddaughter, including a "weather-beaten . . . draught of the place where the treasure lies"—a treasure map, in other words. They even fashion "Blackbeard's Ghost," who attempts to protect the treasure with a supernatural display of manmade fireworks. The play was rehearsed in Philadelphia but closed before its first performance due to a variety of opposition, including anti-intellectual, anti-British rabble-rousers, the local ministries, and a few local personages who felt the play was written to mock them. Yet buried treasure as a pirate myth does not show up in its grandest force until the early nineteenth century.[29]

The real source for our myth—at least in the sense of its explosion into literature and ultimately into film—is Washington Irving's "Kidd the Pirate" and "The Devil and Tom Walker" in his *Tales of a Traveller* published in 1824. Irving, best known as the author of *Rip Van Winkle* and "The Legend of Sleepy Hollow," collected many folktales and turned them into stories and anecdotes. "There were rumors on rumors of great sums of money found here and there," he writes in "Kidd the Pirate" of the treasure locals believed Kidd had buried somewhere.[30] Treasure seekers told of strange carvings and signs in the woods, surely meant as signs to aid pirates when they returned for their treasure. Yet when they went looking for it, it was never there! It must have been the devil who carried it away, for what other supernatural power would strip a treasure from its grave just before it was discovered?

From a sea chantey sung by an "iron-faced" Cape Cod whaling man, Irving gives us new lyrics about Kidd burying a Bible to get into the devil's good graces—and thus prevent anyone not so evil from finding it, leading into the tale of "The Devil and Tom Walker," in which the devil knows the whereabouts of Kidd's treasure.[31] In his "Wolfert Webber, or Golden Dreams," an old unknown and mysterious old buccaneer, holding rude, loud court among armchair adventurers in a tavern, puts his "iron fist" down and with a "quiet force" notes that buccaneers "fought hard for their money, they gave body and soul for it, and wherever it lies buried, depend upon it he must have a tug with the devil who gets it."[32]

Here now we also begin to see ghosts and demons associated with buried treasure. If burying a Bible would earn the devil's protection, would not a man killed with the treasure leave a ghost to protect it? Victorian Gothic literature soon came of age, and suddenly pirates haunted lost ships and buried treasures—and those who boarded these ships or found these treasures. Ghost stories with pirates and buried treasure at their core became a small new genre. Howard Pyle would later paint the ghost of a pirate captain beneath the sea.

In the popular view, pirates suddenly became extraordinarily superstitious, which they in fact were not much at all, no more than seamen in general. Although they might at times see specters upon the sea at night, as many seamen did (even today many sailors have seen unknown phenomena at sea), and might see unknown sea creatures that must surely be monsters, they were a practical lot. Superstition did not usually interfere with ship handling and probably never with plundering. A buccaneer crew might refuse to permit one of their educated shipmates from bringing a mummy aboard—as one crew actually did so refuse buccaneer-surgeon Lionel Wafer—out of fear it would affect the compass, but it is doubtful they would have let their superstition stop them from looking for treasure.[33]

Francis Marryat, novelist and captain in the Royal Navy, put the words perfectly in the mouth of one of his characters in his 1839 *The Phantom Ship*, a romantic melodrama of love, the Flying Dutchman, buried treasure, and a spectral character: "[H]e must be a bold specter that can frighten me from doubloons."[34]

In 1843, Edgar Allan Poe wrote "The Gold Bug," a tale of secret mystery, including a gold "bug" or scarab, a parchment with a skull depicted on it, and a secret code, all related to Captain Kidd's buried treasure—now on Sullivan's Island, South Carolina, where by rights should be Blackbeard's imaginary treasure—and all much inspired by Washington Irving's short tales. A year later, Alexandre Dumas published *The Count of Monte Cristo*, in which a great treasure is discovered, via a scrap of burned paper written with coded instructions in Gothic characters, in a hidden grotto on an island—surely the origin of every treasure grotto in every pirate novel and film that followed.[35]

In 1849, James Fenimore Cooper published *The Sea Lions*, in which a dying seaman holds maps and other information not only to a secret island where sea lions are abundant, but also to an island where pirate treasure is buried. In the nineteenth century, the public was struck with a number of manias, ranging from secret codes to spiritualism to buried treasure (not that imagined lost treasures have ever been unpopular), and writers were sure to capitalize on them.

And not only writers. In 1868, in one example of many, A. D. Putnam, a descendant of the famous Revolutionary War hero Israel Putnam, arrived in Hazardville, Connecticut. He claimed that the spirit of Benjamin Franklin had sent him there from California to unearth a great treasure buried by Spanish pirates three centuries before. Of course he found no treasure, but visitors paid well to watch the digging and hear the tale. Doubtless, Putnam split the profits with the owner of the land, Thomas Barrett.[36]

From Poe's story it was but a short leap to the final form of the myth, including a treasure map, dead men's bones, and clues for finding the treasure. In 1881, Robert Louis Stevenson began publishing *Treasure Island* as a serial, and in 1883 as a book. He took his inspiration for the treasure map, skeleton, and buried treasure largely from Poe's story as well as from James Fenimore Cooper's *The Sea Lions*, and he also unwittingly plagiarized Irving's old buccaneer from "Wolfert Webber, or Golden Dreams," turning him into Bill Bones, the "old sea dog at the Admiral Benbow."[37]

The famous "dead man's chest" of Stevenson's *Treasure Island* actually has nothing to do with a buried treasure chest, nor even a seaman's sea chest, nor is it even a mystery, although many have made it out to be. Stevenson discovered the romantic, piratical-sounding place-name in *At Last: A Christmas in the West Indies*, a travelogue by Charles Kingsley, author of *Westward Ho!*, a tale of Elizabethan sea dogs.[38] Kingsley noted the romantic names of several small islets in the Virgin Islands, including Dead Man's Chest.[39] Known today as Dead Chest Island, it looks from a distance like a coffin.[40] There is a similar island off Puerto Rico, known as Caja de Muerto (Coffin Island).[41] Isla de Muerto, also known as Isla Santa Clara, in the Bay of Guayaquil, Ecuador, was likewise described in the seventeenth century as appearing "like a dead Man stretched out in a Shroud," and not for any colorful yet mythical reason such as a pirate massacre of a shipwrecked crew, although the story remains a popular one.[42]

With the publication of Stevenson's book, pirates now invariably buried their treasure, at least in most fiction and film. Illustrator Howard Pyle contributed significantly to the myth, painting or drawing Captain Kidd and others burying treasure. In his story about Kidd's treasure, "Tom Chist and the Treasure Box," Pyle realizes the modern myth, with its steps and bearings paced out, the burying of the treasure itself, the murder of a witness. The story was printed, along with Pyle's famous illustrations of pirates and buried treasure, in *Howard Pyle's Book of Pirates*. It was read by millions. Other illustrators showed Kidd burying treasure, and some illustrated him burying a Bible as well.[43] The image was fixed. It became so obvious that there was no need to question its authenticity. Of course pirates buried their treasure! Yet seldom is asked the question: Why would they bury it when they could spend it?

Among pirate films, the myth was originally fueled by *The Black Pirate* in 1926, itself inspired not only by best-selling swashbuckling romances like Mary Johnston's 1900 *To Have and to Hold* and Rafael Sabatini's 1922 *Captain Blood* (and probably the 1924 film of the same name), but also by *Howard Pyle's Book of Pirates*. In *The Black Pirate*, pirates carefully step out distances according to a treasure map, then bury the richest part of their treasure in an underground vault. The captain and his quartermaster prepare to murder the witnesses, but they are stymied by the arrival of Douglas Fairbanks, the dashing, athletic, swashbuckling hero. The film is the true progenitor of the modern pirate swashbuckler.

These film myths surely helped inspire twentieth-century myths of buried treasure, such as that of Olivier Levasseur, also known as La Bouse, who purportedly flung to the crowd coded directions to his buried treasure just before he was hanged in 1730. Some, in attempting to decode these almost certainly forged instructions, have suggested that Levasseur's treasure was buried in a secret grotto, perhaps resembling that of Oak Island—or of Hollywood film, one might add.[44] These treasure hunters, not to mention magazines and Internet sites that run articles on the richest pirate captains in history, make a critical mistake when they suggest a buried treasure or pirate captain's wealth is equal to the amount of the wealth plundered by the pirates in question.

What they ignore is the reality that pirate captains typically received only two to six shares for each common pirate's single share. In other words, out of one hundred thousand Spanish dollars and a crew of seventy-five, there might be a division of one hundred shares, including disability and so forth. Each pirate received one thousand pieces of eight, and the captain two thousand, or perhaps a few thousand more if he owned the ship. Tidy sums, but nowhere near the amount actually captured. Pirate treasure hunters typically assume the entire treasure was buried, but this would never be the case even if a pirate actually did bury his own treasure. At most, a pirate captain who had set himself up as a petty prince and slaver on Madagascar and buried his personal fortune nearby for security, for example, would have hidden only a percent or two of the entire booty he and his crew had captured.

Even so, the myth is obviously here to stay. James Fenimore Cooper, author not only of *The Last of the Mohicans* and many other tales, but of a pirate novel as well, *The Red Rover*, put it best in his 1839 history of the US Navy: "With the blindness usual in matters of this sort, it was believed that he [Captain Kidd] secreted his gold in spots that he had probably never visited, and to this day it is not an unfrequent thing for diggings to be made on the coast, under the influence of dreams that have been occasioned by meditating on the subject, and in the hope of finding some of the long lost riches."[45] Novelists of this era—including Cooper himself in *The Sea Lions*—ignored fact and, as necessary to tell a good tale, devised unlikely reasons and means for pirates burying their treasure, and in doing so helped incite past treasure hunts.

Such treasure hunts continue even today, often based on hoaxes of treasure maps, especially of Captain Kidd's, spread in the early to mid-twentieth century. There is almost no arguing with "treasure fever" once it takes hold—this the author knows from personal experience, having been consulted by seekers of purported buried pirate treasure, including one who indeed believed he had found the site of a famous pirate's treasure.[46]

Cooper commented on the lasting effects of the love of gold: "Of all the passions to which poor human nature is the slave, the love of gold is that which endures the longest, and is often literally carried with us to the verge of the grave."[47] When this overwhelming greed is attached to treasure fever, it is a double obsession, an ancient, often incurable disease.

One seventeenth-century treasure hunter devoted much of his life to digging up Anegada Island, also known as Drowned Island because it was mostly covered by the sea at spring tides, among the Virgin Islands in the Caribbean. He believed a Spanish galleon had wrecked at the island, and that the treasure had been carried ashore and buried. How the treasure hunter rationalized the apparent fact that no one survived to recover the treasure, yet still the story was known, is unclear. The southwestern point of the island was once known as Treasure Point, from a Spanish galleon's "Gold & Silver" believed buried nearby.[48] One easily imagines the film *Cutthroat Island*.

So pirates did not really bury their treasure after all. Of course, we wish they did, for it is quite a romantic notion, of mystery, adventure, and skullduggery with a fortune waiting at the end. Yet, while pirates did not bury their plunder, nor obviously did they go ashore with picks and shovels to dig up buried treasure, this does not mean they did not look for it. They did. But not on land did they seek it.

Sunken Ships and Spanish Silver

In January 1656 during the darkness of storm and night, the *Nuestra Señora de las Maravillas* collided with the flagship of the Spanish treasure fleet and settled quickly beneath the sea on Matanilla Shoal in the Bahamas, roughly seventy miles west of modern-day Fort Pierce, Florida. Only fifty of her seven hundred passengers and crew survived.[49]

Lives, of course, could not be recovered, but cannon, gold, and silver could. Within three years, a Spanish ship and diving crew were on the wreck, salvaging what they could, not to mention fighting wind and wave and watching for sharks and other dangerous denizens of the deep. Native American and African divers descended in "diving bells" or simply leaped over the side with large stones in their hands, which sent them quickly to the bottom. There they used crowbars and grappling hooks to tear apart timbers, then loaded silver and gold coins into baskets that were ferried to the surface via a crane.

In 1676 Captain Martín de Melgar, a Basque originally from Guipúzcoa, Spain, began to work the "Wrack," as it was now known to the English of Port Royal, the buccaneer capital at Jamaica.[50] He came annually from Havana, Cuba, "fishing" for silver on the wreck during the months when it was not hurricane season.

In late April 1679 Melgar "showed up again, this time" aboard a tiny frigate or bark. Accompanying it was a salvage barge mounted with a crane and diving bell. The expedition was well manned, with sixty Spaniards of various races and ethnicities and twenty-five Native American divers hired for the purpose.

Not long after they began to work the site, Melgar's lookout espied a sail on the horizon. It soon became clear that the small vessel was standing directly toward the site of the wreck. Melgar, no fool, ordered his frigate to clear for engaging. The approaching vessel was filled with filibusters looking for easy pickings. The Spaniards, however, were in no mood to give up easily.

As soon as the filibuster vessel was in range, Melgar's small frigate opened fire. His guns were small, but he had ten or twelve, more than most small pirate vessels carried, and he had plenty of men to work them. The pirates turned and fled, Melgar's frigate in fast pursuit. Pirates, however, did not give up easily either, and they fought back as was their wont: with a blaze of accurate fire from their long-barreled muskets.

Melgar was doubtless certain that the day was his. Suddenly, however, one of Melgar's cannon exploded. The flame from the exploding powder ignited a small chest of cartridges, whose flame raced across the deck and ignited others. Fire and explosion filled the air, burning flesh to the bone and killing thirty-six of the sixty-man crew, including Captain Melgar.

The filibusters quickly boarded and captured the frigate, then the barge. They kept the Spanish pilot and divers, but anyone who was not a diver or was not associated with them they marooned ashore on Sandy Cay some thirty-five miles to the south, leaving them to suffer for two months with little water and provisions. The pirates put the Native American divers to work and worked them from dawn until dusk, threatening to murder them if they did not bring sufficient silver to the surface. It was arduous labor among the sharp coral and rotting timbers, and the divers were probably often injured and ill. Some may have had decompression sickness, commonly known as the bends, for even breath-hold divers can get the disease if they dive underwater often enough, deep enough, and stay there long enough. Divers working from bells would have been especially vulnerable.

When the pirates had their fill of treasure from the wreck—several tons of silver bars, plate, and coins, as well as silver in the form of cones, planks, "pigs," and "sows"—they gave the Spanish pilot a receipt for the silver, thanked him for his help, and suggested they cooperate again soon. The pirates then weighed their anchors and set sail for Petit Goave, and some of them for Port Royal as well, where doubtless they reveled in drunken debauchery and soon squandered all they had stolen. Throughout the Golden Age from 1655 to 1725, pirates often stole wrecked silver or kidnapped divers and forced them to work the Spanish wrecks. Here was the real "buried" treasure of pirates.

Pirates did not bury their treasure on sandy shore or in hidden grotto, nor did they draw maps or "draughts" to find it. The real treasure maps were those that gave directions to the rich wrecks of Spanish galleons, wrecks that pirates sometimes sailed over by accident and spotted beneath the azure surface of the Caribbean. Here, among the corals and fishes of the sea, also lie the last pieces of the puzzle of all pirate myths: the bones of pirate ships and of those who sailed them along the Spanish Main.

Still, the truth will never stop the hunt for buried pirate treasure, for the entwined twain of romance and riches will forever reign in the minds of many. Perhaps Andrew Barton put it best, presaging Francis Marryat:

> *Enchanting gold! that doeth conspire to blind*
> *Man's erring judgment, and misguide the mind;*
> *In search of thee, the wretched worldling goes;*
> *Nor danger fears, tho' FIENDS of night oppose.*[51]

Bibliography

———∞∞∞———

Abbreviations:

ANF: Archives Nationales (France)
ANOM: Archives Nationales d'Outre-Mer
BNE: Biblioteca Nacional de España
BNF: Bibliothèque Nationale de France

Agarat. "Plan de Porto Bello." 1682. BNF, ark:/12148/btv1b59708181.

Alaux, Gustave, and Albert t'Serstevens [le Golif, Louis Adhémar Timothée]. *Cahiers de Le Golif, Dit Borgnefesse, Capitaine de la Flibuste*. Paris: Grasset, 1952.

_____. *Memoirs of a Buccaneer*. New York: Simon and Schuster, 1954.

al-Mûsili, Elias. *An Arab's Journey to Colonial Spanish America: The Travels of Elias al-Mûsili in the Seventeenth Century*. Translated and edited by Caesar E. Farah. Syracuse, NY: Syracuse University Press, 2003.

Alonso, Carmen Marcos, Paloma Otero Morán, and Paula Grañeda Miñón. "Las Monedas de la Fragata Nuestra Señora de las Mercedes." Museo Arqueológico Nacional, Madrid. www.mecd.gob.es/fragatamercedes/bienes-culturales/material-numismatico.html.

Al-Shaṭi, Bint. *The Wives of the Prophet*. 1971. Translated by Matti Moosa. Facsimile reprint, Piscataway, NJ: Gorgias Press, 2006.

Anon. *An African with a Sword*. Mid-seventeenth century. Oil on canvas. 29 5/8 by 24 3/8 in. Collection of Saam and Lily Nijstad.

Anon. *The Arraignment, Tryal, and Condemnation of Captain William Kidd, for Murther and Piracy.* London: J. Nutt, 1701.

Anon. *Articles Exhibited Against Lord Archibald Hamilton, Late Governor of Jamaica; with Sundry Depositions and Proofs Relating to the Same.* London: 1717.

Anon. *Captain Kidd Burying His Bible.* Illustration for *The Pirates Own Book, Or Authentic Narratives of the Lives, Exploits, and Executions of the Most Celebrated Sea Robbers by Charles Elms.* Portland, ME: Sanborn and Carter, 1839.

Anon. "Captain Kid's Farewel to the Seas; or, the Famous Pirate's Lament." London broadside, 1701.

Anon. [Philip Ayers?]. *Captain Van Horn's Taking of la Vera Cruz.* In *The Voyages and Adventures of Capt. Barth. Sharp, and Others, in the South Sea.* London: P. A. Esq. [Philip Ayers], 1684.

Anon. "Diseño ó plano del Fuerte y Plataforma de San Vicente, en Santa Marta," June 16, 1667. AGI, MP-PANAMA,82.

Anon. *A Full and Exact Account, of the Tryal Of all the Pyrates, Lately taken by Captain Ogle.* London: J. Roberts, 1723.

Anon. *Journal historique et littéraire.* Paris: Etienne Ganeau, 1718.

Anon. *The Importance of Jamaica to Great-Britain.* London: A. Dodd, 1741.

Anon. "The Jolly Roger: Origin of the Appellation." *Sea Breeze*, vol. 3 (1921), reprinted from *Lloyd's List.*

Anon. "The Last Pirate Treasure Delusion." *The Hartford Times*, January 1, 1868.

Anon. "Letters Concerning the English Expedition into the Spanish West Indies in 1655." In *The Narrative of General Venables* by Robert Venables, edited by C. H. Firth. London: Longmans, Gree, and Co., 1900.

Anon. *Mery Tales, Wittie Questions and Quicke Answeres, Very pleasant to be Readde.* 1567. Reprinted in *Shakespeare Jest-Books.* 2 vols. Edited by W. Carew Hazlitt. London: Willis & Sotheran, 1864.

Anon. *A New Canting Dictionary.* London: Booksellers of London and Westminster, 1725.

Anon. *A Pacquet from Parnassus: or, a Collection of Papers*, vol. 1, no. 1. London: J. How and J. Nutt, 1702.

Anon. *The Present State of Europe, Or, The Historical and Political Mercury.* Vol. 35. London: Jane Rhodes, 1723.

Anon. "Principal Characters in the Seven Wonders of the World or Harlequin Colossus." 1812. Advertising illustration from a stage production in Covent Garden. British Museum, 1886,0513.1838.

Anon. "Relation du voyage des Flibustiers aux Andoures et Nove Espagne," 16 November 1683, ANF, CHAN MAR-B4 9, fol. 389, reprinted in Les Archives de la Flibuste, http://www.geocities.com/trebutor/ADF2005/1680/16831116veracruz.html.

Anon. *Remarks on the Life and Death of the Fam'd Mr. Blood.* 2nd ed. London: Richard Janeway, 1680.

Anon. "Ring Mottos." In *Notes and Queries: Medium of Inter-Communication for Literary Men, General Readers, Etc,* ser. 3, vol. 3 (January–June 1863): 503–4. London: Bell & Daldy, 1863.

Anon. *Sad and Dreadful News from New England.* London: Langley Curtis, 1684.

Anon. "A Sailor's Definition of Drunkenness." In *The New Bon Ton Magazine; or, Telescope of the Times,* vol. 1 (May–October): 356. London: J. Johnston, 1818.

Anon. "Statuts d'un Navire Forban, Nommé le Sans-Quartier." In *Le Magasin Pittoresque,* edited by Édouard Charton, 223–24. Paris: Aux Bureaux d'Abonnement et de Vente, 1842.

Anon. *The Trials of Eight Persons Indited for Piracy &c.* Boston: B. Green, for John Edwards, 1718.

Anon. *The Tryals of Captain John Rackam and Other Pirates.* Jamaica: Robert Baldwin, 1721.

Anon. *The Tryals of Joseph Dawson* [et al] *for Several Piracies and Robberies.* London: John Everingham, 1696.

Anon. *The Tryals of Major Stede Bonnet, and Other Pirates.* London: Benj. Cowse, 1719.

Anon. *The Whole Tryal, Examination & Condemnation of All the Pirates.* London: Robert Brown, 1725.

Anon. *Voyage to the Mississippi through the Gulf of Mexico ("The Talon Interrogations").* In Weddle, *La Salle, the Mississippi, and the Gulf,* 1987.

Apestegui, Cruz. "La Arquitectura Naval Entre 1660 y 1754: Aproximación a los Aspectos Tecnológicos y Su Reflejo en la Construcción en Guipúzcoa." *Itsas Memoria: Revista de Estudios Marítimos del País Vasco*, no. 2 (1998): 237–66.

_____. *Pirates of the Caribbean*. Translated by Richard Lewis Rees. Edison, NJ: Chartwell Books, 2002.

Appleby, John C. *Women and English Piracy, 1540–1720: Partners and Victims of Crime*. Woodbridge, England: Boydell Press, 2013.

Arnoult, N. *Portrait de Jean Bart, en Pied: [Estampe]*. Paris: N. Arnoult, [1701–1702], ark:/12148/btv1b8407615r.

Arzáns de Orsúa y Vela, Bartolomé. *Tales of Potosí*. Edited by R. C. Padden. Translated by Frances M. López-Morillas. Providence, RI: Brown University, 1975.

Ashton, Philip, and John Barnard. *Ashton's Memorial*. 1725. Reprinted in *In the Trough of the Sea*, edited by Donald P. Wharton. Westport, CT: Greenwood Press, 1979.

Atkins, John. *A Voyage to Guinea, Brazil, and the West Indies*. 1735. Facsimile reprint, London: Frank Cass, 1970.

"Au Marquis d'Harcourt au Sujet de rapatriement de Madame *de Graff* (16 septembre 1698)." ANOM: FR ANOM COL B 21 F° 186.

"Au Marquis d'Harcourt au Sujet du Retour des Prisonniers Faits par les Espagnols à *Saint-Domingue* (Madame *de Graff*) et de la Prise d'une Barque de *Marseille* par une Galère de *Sardaigne* (23 juillet 1698)." ANOM: FR ANOM COL B 21 F° 107.

d'Auger, Charles. "Analyse d'une lettre d'*Auger* (Charles), Gouverneur de *Saint-Domingue* (24 juin/18 août 1704)." ANOM: FR ANOM COL C^{8A} 15 F° 259.

Augustine, Saint. *The City of God*. Translated by Marcus Dods. In *Great Books of the Western World: 18. Augustine*. 1952. Reprint, Chicago: Encyclopedia Britannica, 1982.

Avila, Juan de. "Pillage de la ville de Veracruz par les pirates le 18 mai 1683 (Expedition de Lorencillo)." Amoxcalli manuscript no. 266, http://amoxcalli.org.mx/paleografia.php?id=266.

Baker, William A. *Sloops & Shallops*. 1966. Reprint, Columbia, SC: University of South Carolina Press, [1986].

Baldæus, A *True and Exact Description of the Most Celebrated East India Coasts of Malabar and Coromandel, and also of the Isle of Ceylon*. 1672. Reprint, London: Awnsham and John Churchill, 1703.

"Baldran de Graff (Laurent Corneille)." ANOM: FR ANOM COL D2C 222, pg. 41.

Barlow, Edward. *Barlow's Journal*. 2 vols. Edited by Basil Lubbock. London: Hurst & Blackett, Ltd, 1934.

Barlow, Jonathan. "A Memorandum of the Transactions of me Jonathan Barlow Since sail'd out from London." In *Captured by Pirates: Two Diaries of 1724–1725*, edited by Robert Francis Seybolt. *The New England Quarterly*, vol. 2, no. 4 (October 1929): 658–63.

Barroto, Enríquez. "The Enríquez Barroto Diary." In Weddle, *La Salle, the Mississippi, and the Gulf*, 1987.

Barrie, J. M. *Peter Pan and Wendy*. 1906. Reprint, illustrated by Edmund Blampied. New York: Charles Scribner's Sons, 1940.

Barton, Andrew [Thomas Forrest?]. *The Disappointment, or, the Force of Credulity*. 1767. Reprint, edited by David Mays. New York: University Presses of Florida, 1976.

[B. E. Gent.] *A New Canting Dictionary*. London: W. Hawes et al, [1699].

Beal, Clifford. *Quelch's Gold: Piracy, Greed, and Betrayal in Colonial New England*. Westport, CT: Praeger, 2007.

Beeston, William. "A Journal Kept by Col. William Beeston, from His First Coming to Jamaica." In *Interesting Tracts, Relating to the Island of Jamaica*. St. Jago de la Vega, Jamaica: Lewis, Lunan, and Jones, 1800.

Behlmer, Rudy. Audio commentary for *The Black Pirate* (United Artists, 1926), Kino International DVD, 2004; Kino International Blu-Ray, 2010.

_____., ed. *The Sea Hawk*. Published screenplay. Madison, WI: University of Wisconsin, 1982.

_____. "Swordplay on the Screen." *Films in Review*, vol. 16, no. 6 (June–July 1965): 362–75.

Benevides C., Antonio, and Antonio P. Andrews. Ecab, *Poblado y Provincia del Siglo XVI en Yucatán*. México: Instituto Nacional de Antropología e Historia, 1979.

Bes, Lennart, Edda Frankot, and Hanno Brand. *Baltic Connections: Archival Guide to the Maritime Relations of the Countries Around the Baltic Sea (Including the Netherlands) 1450–1800*. Vol. 1. Leiden: Brill, 2007.

Besson, Maurice. *The Scourge of the Indies*. Translated by Everard Thornton. London: George Rutledge & Sons, 1929.

Bialuschewski, Arne. "Daniel Defoe, Nathaniel Mist, and the General History of the Pyrates." In *Papers of the Bibliographical Society of America* 98 (March 2004): 21–38.

Blunt, Edmund M. *The American Coast Navigator*. 11th ed. New York: Edmund and George W. Blunt, September 1827.

Botting, Douglas, and the editors of Time-Life Books. *The Pirates*. Alexandria, VA: Time-Life Books, 1978.

Bradley, Peter T., editor and translator. *The Last Buccaneers in the South Sea 1686–1695: Diary and Texts*. N.p.: lulu.com, 2011.

Brandes, Jan. "Dekzicht van een Oostindiëvaarder met stuurman aan het roer, Jan Brandes, 1779–1787." In the Album van Jan Brandes, deel 1 (NG-1985-7-1). Rijksmuseum.

Breverton, Terry. *Black Bart Roberts: The Greatest Pirate of Them All*. Gretna, LA: Pelican Publishing, 2004.

"Brevet de naturalité pour le nommé Laurens de Graff et sa femme," 5 August 1685, ANF: CAOM COL-B 11, folios 193—94.

"British Newspaper Accounts of Blackbeard's Death." Arthur L. Cooke. *The Virginia Magazine of History and Biography*, vol. 61, no. 3 (July 1953): 304–7.

Brodhead, John Romeyn, Edmund Bailey O'Callaghan, eds. *Documents Relative to the Colonial History of the State of New-York*. Vol. 4. Albany: Weed, Parsons, and Company, 1854.

Brooks, Baylus C. ""Born in Jamaica, of Very Creditable Parents" or "A Bristol Man Born"? Excavating the Real Edward Thache, "Blackbeard the Pirate."" *The North Carolina Historical Review*, vol. 92, no. 3 (July 2015): 262–304.

Brookes, Richard. *The Art of Angling, Rock and Sea-Fishing*. London: John Watts, 1740.

Brown, Thomas. *The Works of Mr. Thomas Brown, Serious and Comical, In Prose and Verse*. 4 vols. London: Sam. Briscoe, 1715.

Bruchius, Joannes Georgius. *Grondige Beschryvinge Van de Edele ende Ridderlijcke Scherm-ofte Wapen-konste*. Leyden: Abraham Verhoef, 1671.

Bruckheimer, Jerry. *MTV News* interview, March 19, 2010.

Buisseret, David. "The Loss of H.M.S. *Norwich* off Port Royal in June 1682." *The Mariner's Mirror*, vol. 54, no. 4 (1968): 403–7.

Burg, B. R. *Sodomy and the Pirate Tradition: English Sea Rovers in the Seventeenth-Century Caribbean*. New York: New York University Press, 1984.

Buti, Gilbert, and Philippe Hrodej, eds. *Dictionnaire des Corsaires et Pirates*. Paris: CNRS Éditions, 2013.

Caille, Jean de la. *Histoire de l'Imprimerie et de la Librarie*. 2 vols. Paris: Jean de la Caille, 1689.

Calendar of State Papers, Colonial Series, America and West Indies, 1574–1738. 44 vols. Edited by Noel W. Sainsbury, J. W. Fortescue, et al. London: H.M. Stationery Office, 1860–1969.

Calendar of State Papers, Domestic, of the Reign of William III. Vol 11. Edited by William John Hardy and Edward Bateson. London: H.M. Stationery Office, 1937.

Camus, Michel Christian. *L'Île de la Tortue au coeur de la Flibuste Caraïbe*. Paris: Éditions L'Harmattan, 1997.

[Care, Henry]. *English Liberties: or, the Freeborn Subject's Inheritance*. London: G. Larkin [1680].

Carr, John Dickson. *The Devil in Velvet*. New York: Harper & Brothers, 1951.

_____. *The Murder of Sir Edmund Godfrey*. London: Hamish Hamilton, 1936.

Cartas del Virrey Marques de la Laguna. AGI, Mexico, 52, no. 10.

Casanova, Giacomo. *History of My Life*. 2 vols. Translated by Willard R. Trask. New York: Harcourt, Brace & World, 1966.

Castille, Hippolyte. *Histoire de la Seconde République en Française*. 2 vols. Paris: Libraire de la Société des Gens de Lettres, 1854.

Cauna, Jacques de. "Flibustiers Basques et Gascons de la Caraïbe." In *Les Tyrans de la Mer: Pirates, Corsaires et Flibustiers*, edited by Sophie Linon-Chipon and Sylvie Requemora, 145–62. Paris: Presses Paris Sorbonne, 2002.

Chambers, Anne. *Ireland's Pirate Queen: The True Story of Grace O'Malley*. 1998. Reprint, New York: MJF Books, 2003.

_____. "'The Pirate Queen of Ireland': Grace O'Malley." In *Bold in Her Breeches: Women Pirates Across the Ages*, edited by Jo Stanley. London: Pandora, 1995.

Chapin, H. M. *Privateer Ships and Sailors, the First Century of American Colonial Privateering 1625–1725*. Toulon: Imprimerie G. Mouton, 1926.

Charlevoix, Pierre-François-Xavier de. *Histoire de l'Isle Espagnole ou de S. Domingue*. 2 vols. Paris: Hippolyte-Louis Guerin, 1730–1731.

Chaucer, Geoffrey. *The Canterbury Tales*. Translated by J. U. Nicolson. Garden City, NY: Garden City Books, 1934.

Cleve, Per Teodor. *On the Geology of the North-Eastern West India Islands*. Stockholm: P. A. Norstedt & Söner, 1871.

Clifford, Barry, and Peter Turchi. *The Pirate Prince*. New York: Simon & Schuster, 1993.

Cochran, Hamilton, and the editors of American Heritage. *Pirates of the Spanish Main*. New York: American Heritage Publishing, 1961.

Coke, Edward. *The Third Part of the Institutes of the Laws of England*. London: M. Flesher, 1648.

Coke, Roger. *A Detection of the Court and State of England*. 2 vols. 4th ed. London: J. Brotherton and W. Meadows, 1719.

Collombon, Jacques. *Traité de l'Exercice Militaire, où est l'Instruction des Jeux de Toutes Sortes d'Armes, & Celuy du Drapeau*. Lyon: Pierre Anard, 1650.

Commission Départementale des Antiquités. *Mémoires de la Commission des Antiquités du Département de la Côte-d'Or*. Dijon: Commission Départementale des Antiquités, 1878.

Cooke, Edward. *A Voyage to the South Sea and Round the World in the Years 1707 to 1711*. 1712. 2 vols. Facsimile reprint, New York: Da Capo Press, 1969.

Cooper, James Fenimore. *The History of the Navy of the United States*. 2 vols. Philadelphia: Lea and Blanchard, 1839.

_____. *The Red Rover: A Tale*. 3 vols. London: Henry Colburn, 1827.

_____. *The Sea Lions: or, The Lost Sealers*. 2 vols. New York: Stringer & Townsend, 1849.

Cordingly, David. *Pirate Hunter of the Caribbean: The Adventurous Life of Captain Woodes Rogers*. New York: Random House, 2011.

_____. *Under the Black Flag*. New York: Random House, 1995.

_____. *Women Sailors & Sailors' Women: An Untold Maritime History*. New York: Random House, 2001.

Cornuau, Paul. "Plan de la Petite-Rivière de Léogane." 1685. BNF, ark:/12148/btv1b53103579b.

_____. "Plan des Passes et du Bourg du Levé et Dessigné par Ordre de Mr. De Cussy, Gouverneur pour le Roy de l'Isle de la Tortue et Coste St. Domingue." 1685. BNF, ark:/12148/btv1b59727137.

_____. "Plan du Cap et de Son Entrée," 1684. BNF, ark:/12148/btv1b5972714n.

_____. "Plan du Cul de Sac de Léogane." 1685. BNF, ark:/12148/btv1b53103721f.

_____. "Plan du Petit Goave et de l'Acul, avec le Figuré du Fort du Petit Goave tel qu'il a été Reformé, avec Deux Autres Plans de ce Même Fort." Circa 1688. FR ANOM 15DFC696B.

_____. "Plan Ignographique du Fon et de l'Isle à Vache," 1686. BNF, ark:/12148/btv1b53103834k.

_____. "Plan Ignographique du Fon et de l'Isle à Vache," 1686 (second chart bearing this title). BNF, ark:/12148/btv1b53103356d.

Courtilz de Sandras, Gatien de. *Memoires de Madame la Marquise de Fresne*. 2nd ed. Amsterdam: Jean Malherbe, 1702.

[Cox, John]. *The Voyages and Adventures of Capt. Barth. Sharp, and Others, in the South Sea*. In London: P. A. Esq. [Philip Ayers], 1684.

Crane, Verner W. *The Southern Frontier 1670–1732*. 1929. Reprint, Ann Arbor: University of Michigan Press, 1956.

Creighton, Margaret S., and Lisa Norling, eds. *Iron Men, Wooden Women: Gender and Seafaring in the Atlantic World, 1700–1920*. Baltimore: Johns Hopkins, 1996.

Crisp, Edward, et al. Map, "A Compleat Description of the Province of Carolina in 3 Parts."
[London]: Edw. Crisp, [1711?].

Crowne, John. *The Ambitious Statesman, or The Loyal Favourite.* 1679. Reprinted in *The Dramatic Works of John Crowne*, vol. 3, edited by William Hugh Logan. Edinburgh: William Paterson, 1874.

Cruikshank, E. A. *The Life of Sir Henry Morgan: With an Account of the English Settlement of the Island of Jamaica (1655–1688).* Toronto: Macmillan Company of Canada, 1935.

Cruzado y Peralta, Manuel. *Las Tretas de la Vulgar y Comun Esgrima, de Espadas Sola, y Con Armas Dobles.* Saragossa, Spain: 1702.

Dagnino, Vicente. *El Correjimiento de Arica: 1535–1784.* Arica, Chile: La Epoca, 1909.

Dampier, William. *A New Voyage Round the World.* 1697. Reprint, New York: Dover, 1968.

_____. *Voyages and Discoveries.* 1729. Reprint, London: Argonaut Press, 1931.

Dan, Pierre. *Histoire de Barbarie, et de Ses Corsaires.* 2nd ed. Paris: Pierre Rocolet, 1649.

Danet, Pierre. *A Complete Dictionary of the Greek and Roman Antiquities.* London: John Nicholson, 1700.

Davis, Nathaniel. *The Expedition of a Body of Englishmen to the Gold Mines of Spanish America, in 1702.* In Wafer, *New Voyage & Description.*

de Lussan, Raveneau. *Journal du Voyage Fait a la Mer de Sud, avec les les Flibustiers de l'Amerique en 1684. et Annés Suivantes.* Paris: Jean Baptiste Coignard, 1690.

_____. *Journal of a Voyage into the South Seas in 1684 and the Following Years with the Filibusters.* 1689. Reprint, translated and edited by Marguerite Eyer Wilbur. Cleveland: Arthur C. Clark Company, 1930.

_____. *Journal of a Voyage Made by the Freebooters into the South Sea, 1684, and in the Following Years.* 1699. In *The History of the Buccaneers of America* by Alexandre Exquemelin [Joseph Exquemelin]. Reprint, Boston: Sanborn, Carter and Bazin, 1856.

_____. *Les Flibustiers de la Mer du Sud.* 1695. Reprint, edited by Patrick Villiers. Paris: Éditions France-Empire, 1992.

Dellon, Gabriel. *Nouvelle Relation d'un Voyage Fait aux Indes Orientales.* Amsterdam: Paul Marret, 1699.

_____. *A Voyage to the East-Indies: Giving an Account of the Isles of Madagascar.* Translated by Jodocus Crull. London: D. Browne, 1698.

del Monte y Tejada, Antonio. *Historia de Santo Domingo.* Vol. 3. Santo Domingo: Garcia Hermanos, 1890.

"Demande de pardon du capitaine Laurens De Graff," 25 January 1685, Archives Nationales, CAOM COL-F3 164, f. 401.

de Pouançey, Jacques Neveu. "M. de Pouançey M. [au comte d'Estrées]," 1 April 1677, ANF, Colonies, C9 A, rec. 1.

Díaz del Castillo, Bernal. *Historia verdadera de la conquista de la Nueva España.* 2 vols. Madrid: Don Benito Cano, 1795.

[Dick, William]. "A Brief Account of Captain Sharp . . ." In *The Buccaneers of America* by Alexander Exquemelin [John Esquemeling], 257–83. 1684. Reprint, New York: Dorset, 1987.

Dickens, Charles. "The Perils of Certain English Prisoners." 1857. Reprinted in *Charles Dickens's Stories from the Christmas Numbers.* New York: MacMillan, 1896.

Diéreville, Sieur de. *Relation of the Voyage to Port Royal in Acadia or New France.* 1708. Reprint, edited by John Clarence Webster, translated by Mrs. Clarence Webster. Toronto: Champlain Society, 1933.

Disney Enterprises. Pirates of the Caribbean attraction soundtrack. Audio CD. N.d.

Dow, George Francis, and John Henry Edmonds. *The Pirates of the New England Coast 1630–1730.* 1923. Reprint, New York: Argosy-Antiquarian, 1968.

Downing, Clement. *A Compendious History of the Indian Wars; with an Account of the Rise, Progress, Strength, and Forces of Angria the Pyrate.* London: Printed for T. Cooper, 1737.

Druett, Joan. *She Captains: Heroines and Hellions of the Sea.* New York: Simon & Schuster, 2000.

Drury, Robert [Defoe, Daniel?]. *Madagascar: or, Robert Drury's Journal, During Fifteen Years Captivity on That Island*. London: W. Meadows, 1729.

du Maurier, Daphne. *Frenchman's Creek*. New York: Literary Guild, 1942.

Dugaw, Dianne. *Warrior Women and Popular Balladry, 1650–1850*. Chicago: University of Chicago, 1996.

Duguay-Trouin, René [M. du Gué-Trouin]. *The Memoirs of M. du Gué-Trouin*. London, J. Batley, 1732.

Dulaien, Jean Thomas, et al. "Liste charte partie ès règles que doivent suivre les braves gens de la mer." In Vignols, *Piraterie Sur l'Atlantique*, 106–7.

Earle, Peter. *The Pirate Wars*. New York: Thomas Dunne Books, 2003.

Eastman, Tamara J., and Constance Bond. *The Pirate Trial of Anne Bonny and Mary Read*. Cambria, CA: Fern Canyon Press, 2000.

Enfield [Connecticut] Historical Society. "A Ghost Story." Newsletter, September 2008.

Eruaso, Catalina de. *Lieutenant Nun: Memoir of a Basque Transvestite in the New World*. 1829. Reprint, translated by Michele Stepto and Gabriel Stepto. Boston: Beacon Press, 1996.

Ettenhard, Francisco Antonio de. *Compendio de los Fundamentos de la Verdadera Destreza y Filosofia de las Armas*. Madrid: Antoni de Zafra, 1675.

Evans, Amanda M. "Defining Jamaica Sloops: A Preliminary Model for Identifying an Abstract Concept." *Journal of Maritime Archaeology*, vol. 2, issue 2 (December 2007): 83–92.

Everard, Robert. *A Relation of Three Years Sufferings of Robert Everard, Upon the Coast of Assada Near Madagascar, in a Voyage to India, in the Year 1686*. In *A Collection of Voyages and Travels*, vol. 6, edited by Awnsham Churchill and John Churchill. London: John Walthoe et al, 1732.

Exquemelin, Alexandre [John Esquemeling]. *The Buccaneers of America*. Crooke, 1684. Reprint, New York: Dorset Press, 1987.

———. [A. O. Œxmelin]. *Les Flibustiers du Nouveau Monde*. 1699, with additional passages from the 1688 edition. Reprint, edited by Michel Le Bris. Paris: Éditions Phébus, 1996.

_____ [Alexander Olivier Exquemelin]. *Histoire des Aventuriers Flibustiers.* 1686. Reprint, edited by Réal Ouellet and Patrick Villiers. Paris: Presses de l'Université Paris-Sorbonne, 2005.

_____ [Alexander Olivier O'Exquemelin]. *Histoire des Avanturiers Flibustiers qui se sont Signalez dans les Indes.* 2 vols. Paris: Jacques Le Febvre, 1699.

_____ [J. Esquemeling]. *The History of the Bucaniers.* London: Tho. Malthus, 1684.

_____ [Joseph Esquemeling]. *The History of the Buccaneers of America.* 1699. Reprint, Boston: Sanborn, Carter and Bazin, 1856.

_____. *Piratas de la America, y Luz à la Defensa de las Costas de Indias Occidentales.* Translated from the Dutch by Alonso de Buena-Maison. Colonia Agrippina: Lorenza Struickman, 1681.

"Extract of a Letter from Capt. Andrew Kingston, Commander of the Lloyd Galley, carrying 12 Guns and 18 Men, who sail'd in February last from London for the Island of Jamaica, April 24, 1721." In *The Historical Register, Containing an Impartial Relation of All Transactions Foreign and Domestick*, vol. 6, edited by C. H. Green, 247–48. London: H. Meere, 1721.

Fairbanks, Douglas. "Prefatory." In *Douglas Fairbanks in "The Black Pirate."* New York: Longacre Press, 1926.

Fanthorpe, Lionel and Patricia. *Secrets of the World's Undiscovered Treasures.* Toronto: Dundern Press, 2009.

Farenhold, A. "Tattooing in the Navy, as Shown by the Records of the U.S.S. Independence." *United States Medical Bulletin*, vol. 2, no. 1 (January 1900): 37–39.

Fernández Duro, Cesáreo. *Armada Español des de la unión de los reinos de Castilla y de León.* 9 vols. Madrid: Sucesores de Rivadeneyra, 1895–1903.

Fictum, David. "The Firsts of Blackbeard: Exploring Edward Thatch's Early Days as a Pirate." Blog post, October 18, 2015, http://csphistorical.com.

Field, C. "The Marines in the Great Naval Mutinies of 1797–1802." In *Journal of the Royal United Service Institution, Whitehall, S. W.* Vol. 62 (February–November, 1917): 720–46.

Fillmore, John. *A Narration of the Captivity of John Fillmore and His Escape from the Pirates.* Portland, ME: B. Titcomb, 1792.

Flacourt, Etienne de. *Histoire de la Grande Isle Madagascar.* Paris: Alexandre Lesselin, 1658.

Florus. *Epitome of Roman History.* In *Sallust, Florus, and Velleius Paterculus,* edited by John Selby Watson. London: George Bell and Sons, 1889.

Forbin, Claude de. *Memoirs of the Count de Forbin.* 2 vols. London: J. Pemberton, 1731.

_____. *Mémoires du Comte de Forbin.* Reprint, Paris: Mercure de France, 1993.

Fox, E. T. *Jolly Rogers, the True History of Pirate Flags.* N.p.: Fox Historical, 2015.

Fox, George. *A Journal, or Historical Account of the Life, Travels, Sufferings, Christian Experiences and Labour of Love in the Work of the Ministry.* London: J. Sowle, 1709.

Franzén, Anders. "Kronan: Remants of a Warship's Past." *National Geographic,* vol. 175, no. 4 (April 1989): 438–65.

Fraser, George MacDonald. Introduction to *Captain Blood: His Odyssey* by Rafael Sabatini. Pleasantville, NY: Akadine Press, 1998.

Furbank, P. N., and W. R. Owens. *Defoe De-Attributions: A Critique of J. R. Moore's Checklist.* London: Hambledon Press, 1994.

Fury, Cheryl A. *Tides in the Affairs of Men: A Social History of Elizabethan Seamen, 1580–1603.* Westport, CT: Greenwood Press, 2002.

Gage, Thomas. *A New Survey of the West Indies.* London: A. Clark, 1677.

Gallay, Alan. *The Indian Slave Trade: The Rise of the English Empire in the America South 1670–1717.* New Haven, CT: Yale University Press, 2002.

García-Torralba Pérez, Enrique. *Las Fragatas de Vela de la Armada Española 1600–1850. (Su Evolución Técnica).* Madrid: self-published, 2011.

Garrote, Antonio. *Fábricar de Baseles.* 1691. Reprint, edited by Félix Moreno Sorli et al. Madrid: Centro Marítimo y Naval Castro Méndez Núñez, 2008.

Gasser, Jacques. "Les Mystérieuses Disparitions de Grammont." In *L'Aventure de la Flibuste*, edited by Michel Le Bris. Paris: Éditions Hoëbeke, 2002.

Gay, John. *Polly: An Opera*. 1729. Reprinted in *The Poetical Works of John Gay*. London: Oxford University, 1926.

Gaya, Louis de. *Traité des Armes*. Paris: Sebastien Cramoisy, 1678.

Gaztañeta e Iturribalzaga, José Antonio de. *Arte de Fabricar Reales, 1687–1691*. Reprint, edited by Francisco Fernández González, Cruz Apestegui Cardenal, and Fernando Miguélez García. Madrid: Lunwerg Editores, 1992.

Geena Davis Institute on Gender in Media. "'Eye Candy Is Not for Kids,' Says Davis." Press Release, October 5, 2010.

Gell, Robert. *An Essay toward the Amendment of the Last English-Translation of the Bible*. London: R. Norton for Andrew Crook, 1659.

Gemelli Careri, Giovanni Francesco [John Francis Gemelli Careri]. *A Voyage Round the World*. 1700. In Churchill, Awnsham, and John Churchill, eds. *A Collection of Voyages and Travels, Vol. 4*. London: John Walthoe et al, 1732.

Généalogie et Histoire de la Caraïbe, Bulletin 12 (January 1990), and Bulletin 78 (January 1996), accessible at www.ghcaraibe.org.

Gerhard, Peter. *Pirates of the Pacific, 1575–1742*. 1960. Reprint, Lincoln, NE: University of Nebraska, 1990.

Girard, P. J. F. *Traité des Armes*. Paris: Pierre de Hondt, 1740.

Goslinga, Cornelis Ch. *The Dutch in the Caribbean and in the Guianas 1680–1791*. Edited by Maria J. L. van Yperen. Assen/Masstricht: Van Gorcum, 1985.

Graves, Robert. *The Greek Myths*. 1955, 1960. Reprint, London: The Folio Society, 1996.

Grey, Charles. *Pirates of the Eastern Seas (1618–1723): A Lurid Page of History*. Edited by George MacMunn. London: Sampson Low, Marston, & Co., 1933.

Grose, Francis. *A Classical Dictionary of the Vulgar Tongue*. 2nd ed. London: S. Hooper, 1788.

Gueroult du Pas, P. Jacques. *Recuëil de Veües de Tous les Differens Bastimens de la Mer Mediterranée, et de l'Ocean; avec Leurs Noms et Usages.* 1710. Facsimile reprint, Nice: A.N.C.R.E., 2004.

Guilmartin, John F. Jr. *Galleons and Galleys.* London: Cassell, 2002.

Hackett, James. *Narrative of the Expedition Which Sailed from England in 1817, to Join the South American Patriots.* London: John Murray, 1818.

Hamilton, Archibald. *An Answer to an Anonymous Libel, Entitled Articles Exhibited Against Lord Archibald Hamilton, Late Governor of Jamaica; with Sundry Depositions and Proofs Relating to the Same.* London: 1718.

Haring, C. H. *The Buccaneers in the West Indies in the 17th Century.* 1910. Reprint, Hamden, CT: Archon Books, 1966.

Harris, Walter. *The History of the Life and Reign of William-Henry, Prince of Nassau and Orange.* Dublin: Edward Bate, 1749.

Hart, Stephen M. *A Companion to Spanish-American Literature.* London: Tamesis, 1999.

Hawkins, Richard. "Account of the Pirates in America, by Captain Hawkins." In *The Political State of Great Britain,* vol. 28 (July–December 1724), edited by Abel Boyer, 147–56. London: for the author, 1724.

[Head, Richard.] *The English Rogue: Continued, in the Life of Meriton Latroon.* London: Francis Kirkman, 1680.

_____. *The English Rogue: Described, in the Life of Meriton Latroon.* London: Henry Marsh, 1665.

Heredia, Ruth. *Romantic Prince: An Exploration of Rafael Sabatini in Two Parts. Part One: Seeking Sabatini.* Bangalore: Ruth Heredia, 2104.

_____. *Romantic Prince: An Exploration of Rafael Sabatini in Two Parts. Part Two: Reading Rafael.* Bangalore: Ruth Heredia, 2015.

Hexham, Henry, and Daniel Manly. *A Copious English and Netherdutch Dictionary.* Rotterdam: [Widdow of] Arnold Leers, 1675.

Hope, William. *The Compleat Fencing-Master.* London: Dorman Newman, 1691.

_____. *New, Short, and Easy Method of Fencing.* 3rd ed. London: G. Strahan, 1744.

Horne, Robert, et al. *An Account of What Passed at the Execution of the Late Duke of Monmouth*. London: Robert Horne et al, 1685.

Horner, Dave. *Shipwreck: A Saga of Sea Tragedy and Sunken Treasure*. Dobbs Ferry, NY: Sheridan House, 1999.

House of Commons. *Journals of the House of Commons*. Vol. 13. London: H.M. Stationery Office, 1803.

_____. *Observations on the Evidence Given before the Committees of the Privy Council and House of Commons in Support of the Bill for Abolishing the Slave Trade*. London: John Stockdale, 1791.

Hughson, Shirley Carter. *The Carolina Pirates and Colonial Commerce, 1670–1740*. 1894. Reprint, Spartanburg, South Carolina: The Reprint Company, 1992.

Hutchinson, William. *A Treatise on Naval Architecture*. 1794. Reprint, Annapolis: Naval Institute Press, 1969.

Hidrographía [Spain, Dept. of]. *Derrotero de las Islas Antillas y de las Costas Orientales de América*. 6th ed. Vol. 2. Madrid: T. Fortanet, 1865.

Irving, Washington [Geoffrey Crayon]. *Tales of a Traveller*. 2 vols. London: John Murray, 1824.

Jaeger, Gérard. *Les Femmes d'Abordage: Chroniques Historiques et Légendaires des Aventurières de la Mer*. Paris: Clancier-Guénaud, 1984.

Jameson, John F., ed. *Privateering and Piracy in the Colonial Period: Illustrative Documents*. New York: Macmillan Company, 1923.

Jefferys, Thomas. "The Virgin Islands from English and Danish Surveys By Thomas Jefferys Geographer to the King." London: Laurie & Whittle, 1794. BNE.

Johnson, Charles. *A General History of the Pyrates*. London: T. Warner, 1724.

_____. *A General History of the Robberies and Murders of the Most Notorious Pirates*. 1726. Reprint, New York: Dodd, Mead, 1926.

_____. *Histoire des Pirates Anglois*. Utrecht: Jacques Brodelet, 1725.

Johnston, Mary. *To Have and to Hold*. New York: Houghton and Mifflin, 1900.

Jones, Russ. "En Garde!" *Flashback*, vol. 1, no. 2 (June 1972): 21–29.

_____. "Rathbone." *Flashback*, vol. 1, no. 2 (June 1972): 30–31.

Joutel, Henri. *The Last Voyage Perform'd by La Salle.* 1714. Facsimile reprint, Ann Arbor, MI: University Microfilms, 1966.

Jouve, Jean. *Album Levant.* 1679. Reprinted in La France Maritime aut Temps de Louis XVII, edited by Michel Vergé-Franceschi and Eric Rieth. Paris: Editions du Layeur, 2001.

Jouvin, Albert (de Rochefort). *Le Voyageur d'Europe, Où Sont les Voyages de France, d'Italie et de Malthe, d'Espagne et de Portugal, des Pays Bas, d'Allemagne et de Pologne, d'Angleterre, de Danemark et de Suède.* 3 vols. [Paris]: D. Thierry, 1672.

Juarez Moreno, Juan. *Corsarios y Piratas en Veracruz y Campeche.* Seville: Escuela de Estudios Hispano-Americanos de Sevilla, 1972.

Khafi Khan. "Capture of a Royal Ship by the English. The English at Bombay." Reprinted in *The History of India, as Told by Its Own Historians: The Muhammadan Period*, vol. 8, by Sir Henry Miers Elliot and John Dowson. London: Trübner and Co., 1877.

Kingsley, Charles. *At Last: A Christmas in the West Indies.* 4th ed. London: Macmillan & Co., 1874.

Klausmann, Ulrike, Marion Meinzerin, and Gabriel Kuhn. *Women Pirates and the Politics of the Jolly Roger.* Translated by Tyler Austin and Nicholas Levis. Buffalo, NY: Black Rose Books, 1997.

Knight, Jesse F., and Stephen Darley. *The Last of the Great Swashbucklers: A Bio-Bibliography of Rafael Sabatini.* New Castle, DE: Oak Knoll Press, 2010.

Konstam, Angus. *Blackbeard: America's Most Notorious Pirate.* Hoboken, NJ: John Wiley & Sons, 2006.

L'Abbat [Labat]. *The Art of Fencing: Or the Use of the Smallsword.* 1696. Reprint, edited and translated by Andrew Mahon. Dublin: James Hoey, 1734.

Lacroix, Paul [Bibliophile Jacob]. *Military and Religious Life in the Middle Ages and at the Period of the Renaissance.* London: Chapman and Hall, 1874.

L'Estrange, Roger. *The Grand Pyrate; or the Life and Death of Capt. George Cusack, The great Sea-Robber.* London: Jonathan Edwin, 1676.

Labat, Jean-Baptiste. *Nouveau Voyage aux Isles de l'Amerique.* 2 vols. The Hague: P. Husson et al, 1724.

Lagarde, Pierre. Deposition in "Extrait des registres du greffe civil de l'île Martinique." ANF, C8 A rec. 4: fol. 414–16, originally transcribed online by Dominika Haraneder.

Lander, Richard. *Records of Captain Clapperton's Last Expedition to Africa.* Vol. 2. London: Henry Colburn and Richard Bentley, 1830.

Laprise, Raynald. "Les Débuts de la Carrier de Laurens De Graffe (1674–1681): Quelques Rectifications et Nouvelles Hypotheses." In *Figures de proue.* Québec: Le Diable Volant, 2011. http: www.ori-com.ca/yarl/D/degraffe1.pdf.

Lee, Nathaniel. *The Massacre of Paris: A Tragedy.* London: R. Bentley and M. Magnes, 1690.

Lee, Robert. E. *Blackbeard the Pirate: A Reappraisal of His Life and Times.* Winston-Salem, NC: John F. Blair, 1974.

Lefroy, J. H., ed. *Memorials of the Discovery and Early Settlement of the Bermudas or Somers Islands 1511–1687.* 2 vols. London: Longmans, Green, 1879.

Legrand, Paul, ed. *Annales de la Marine Nantaise (des Origines à 1830).* Nantes: V. J. Heron, 1908.

Leguat, François [François Maximilien Misson?]. *A New Voyage to the East-Indies by François Leguat and His Companions.* London: R. Bonwick et al, 1708.

Leip, Hans. *Bordbuch des Satans: Geschichte der Freibeuterei.* 1959. Reprint, Munich: List Verlag, 1966.

Lepers, Jean Baptiste. *La Tragique Histoire des Flibustiers: Histoire de Saint-Domingue et de l'Ile de la Tortue, Repaires des Flibustiers, Écrite vers 1715 par le Rév. P. Lepers.* Edited by Pierre-Bernard Berthelot. Paris: G. Crés, 1922.

Leslie, Charles. *A New and Exact Account of Jamaica.* 3rd ed. Edinburgh: R. Fleming, 1740.

Letainturier-Fradin, G. *La Maupin (1670–1707): Sa Vie, Ses Duels, Ses Aventures.* Paris: Ernest Flammarion, 1904.

Ligon, Richard. *A True and Exact History of the Island of Barbados.* 1673. Facsimile reprint, London: Frank Cass, 1998.

Linaje, José de Veita [Ioseph de Veitia Linage]. *Norte de la Contratacion de las Indias Occidentales.* Seville: Juan Francisco de Blas, 1672.

_____. *The Spanish Rule of Trade to the West-Indies.* 1702. Translated and edited by John Stevens. Facsimile reprint, New York: AMS Press, 1977.

Linon-Chipon, Sophie, and Sylvie Requemora. *Les Tyrans de la Mer: Pirates, Corsaires et Flibustiers.* Paris: Presses Paris Sorbonne, 2002.

Little, Benerson. *The Buccaneer's Realm: Pirate Life on the Spanish Main, 1674–1688.* Washington, DC: Potomac Books, 2007.

_____. "Eyewitness Images of Buccaneers and Their Vessels." *The Mariner's Mirror,* vol. 98, no. 3 (2012), 312–26.

_____. *How History's Greatest Pirates Pillaged, Plundered, and Got Away with It: The Stories, Techniques, and Tactics of the Most Feared Sea Rovers from 1500–1800.* Beverly, MA: Fair Winds Press, 2010.

_____. "El Mito Pirata." *Desperta Ferro* 17 (August 2015): 52–55.

_____. "The Origin of the Dread Pirate Banner, the Jolly Roger." *Pirates Magazine,* vol. 12 (April 2010): 9–14.

_____. *Pirate Hunting: The Fight Against Pirates, Privateers, and Sea Raiders from Antiquity to the Present.* Washington, DC: Potomac Books, 2010.

_____. *The Sea Rover's Practice: Pirate Tactics and Techniques, 1630–1730.* Washington, DC: Potomac Books, 2005.

_____. "Las Tácticas de los Piratas del Caribe." *Desperta Ferro* 17 (August 2015): 27–32.

_____. "To Arr! or Not to Arr! The Language of Pirates Real and Imagined." *Pirates Magazine,* no. 13 (2010): 9–14.

Lloyd, Christopher. "Bartholomew Sharp: Buccaneer," *Mariner's Mirror,* vol. 42, no. 4 (1956): 291–301.

Lloyd, Ludowick. *The Stratagems of Ierusalem: With the Martiall Lawes and Militarie Discipline, as Well of the Iewes, as of the Gentiles.* London: Thomas Creede, 1602.

Longfield-Jones, G. M. "The Case History of Sir H. M." *Medical History* 32 (1988), 449–60.

López Cogolludo, Diego. *Historia de Yucathan.* Madrid: Juan Garcia Infanzon, 1688.

Lubbock, Basil. *The Blackwall Frigates*. Glasgow: James Brown & Son, 1922.

Lucena Salmoral, Manuel. *Piratas, Bucaneros, Filibusteros y Corsarios en América*. Caracas: Grijalbo, 1994.

Lugo-Verná, A. et al. "Analysis of the Gulf of Mexico's Veracruz-Havana Route of La Flota de la Nueva España." *Journal of Maritime Archaeology* (May 2007): 24–47.

Macaulay, Thomas Babington. *The History of England from the Accession of James II*. 4 vols. New York: Harper & Brothers, Publishers, 1849–1856.

Maggs, F. B., ed. *Voyages and Travels in All Parts of the World: A Descriptive Catalog*. Vol. 5. London: Magg Bros. Ltd., 1962.

Mallet, Allain Manesson. *Description de l'Univers*. 4 vols. Paris: Denys Thierry, 1683.

Margry, Pierre. *Découvertes et Établissements de Français dans l'Ouest et dans le Sud de L'Amerique Septentrionale (1614–1754), Mémoires et Documents Originaux*. 4 vols. Paris: D. Jouaust, 1880.

———. *Relations et Mémoires Inédits Pour Servir à l'Histoire de la France dans les Pays d'Outre Mer*. Paris: Challamel, 1867.

Marley, David F. *Pirates of the Americas: Vol. 1: 1660–1685*. Santa Barbara, CA: ABC-CLIO, Inc., 2010.

———. *Pirates and Engineers*. Windsor, Ontario: Netherlandic Press, 1992.

———. *Pirates and Privateers of America*. Santa Barbara, CA: ABC-CLIO, Inc., 1995.

———. *Sack of Veracruz*. Windsor, Ontario: Netherlandic Press, 1993.

———. *Wars of the Americas: A Chronology of Armed Conflict in the Western Hemisphere*. 2nd. ed. Vol. 1. Santa Barbara, CA: ABC-CLIO, Inc., 2008.

Marryat, Frederick. *The Phantom Ship*. 1839. Reprint, London: George Routledge and Sons, 1874.

Marshall, John. *Royal Naval Biography*. London: Longman, et al, 1824.

Marvel, Andrew. "The last Instructions to a Painter about the Dutch Wars, 1667." In *Poems on Affairs of State: From the Time of Oliver Cromwell, to the Abdication of K. James the Second*, 54–77. 5th ed. N.p.: n.p., 1703.

Massertie, François. "*Journal de bord, du 19 mai 1686 au 8 juin 1690,*" and "*Journal de bord, du 8 juin 1690 au 4 septembre 1694.*" Manuscripts, held in the Bibliothèque nationale de France, ark:/12148/btv1b9060640j.

_____. "Journal de Bord d'un Flibustier (1686–1693)." Edited by Edward Ducéré. *Bulletin of the Société des Sciences et Arts de Bayonne.* Bayonne: Lamaignère, 1894, 477–520.

_____. "Journal de bord d'un Flibustier (1686–1693)." Edited by Edward Ducéré. *Bulletin of the Société des Sciences et Arts de Bayonne,* Premier Trimestre. Bayonne: Lamaignère, 1895, 17–27.

May, Charles. *An Account of the Wonderful Preservation of the Ship Terra Nova of London.* 1694. In *A Collection of Voyages and Travels*, vol. 6, edited by Awnsham Churchill and John Churchill. London: John Walthoe et al, 1732.

McBane, Donald. *The Expert Sword-Man's Companion or the True Art of Self-Defence.* Glasgow: James Duncan, 1728.

Meltons, Eduward, and Engelsch Edelmans. *Zeldzaame en Gedenkwaardige Zee- en Land-Reizen; Door Egypten, West-Indien, Perzien, Turkyen, Oost-Indien, en d'Aangrenzende Gewesten.* Amsterdam: Jan ten Hoorn, 1681.

Mercure Historique et Politique. The Hague: Henri van Bulderen, 1714.

Miège, Guy. *A New Dictionary, French and English.* London: Tho. Dawks, 1677.

Milla, José, and Agustín Gómez Carrillo. *Historia de la America Central, desde el Descubrimiento del País por los Españoles (1502) hasta su Independencia de la España (1821).* Vol. 2. Guatemala: Establecimiento Tipográfico De "el Progreso," 1882.

Milton, Giles. *White Gold: The Extraordinary Story of Thomas Pellow and Islam's One Million European Slaves.* New York: Farrar, Straus and Giroux, 2004.

Mitchell, Heidi. "Does Reading in Dim Light Hurt Your Eyes?" *Wall Street Journal* online, April 8, 2013, http://www.wsj.com.

Moreau de Saint-Méry, *A Topographical and Political Description of the Spanish Part of Saint-Domingo.* 2 vols. Translated by William Cobbett. Philadelphia: by the author, 1798.

[Mortier, Pieter]. *Le Neptune François, ou Atlas Nouveau des Cartes Marines*. Paris: H. Jaillot, 1693.

Murdoch, Steve. "John Brown: A Black Female Soldier in the Royal African Company." *World History Connected: The Online Journal of World History*, vol.2 (2004), http://worldhistoryconnected.press.illinois.edu/1.2/murdoch.html.

Murray, Dian A. "Cheng I Sao in Fact and Fiction." In *Bold in Her Breeches: Women Pirates Across the Ages*, edited by Jo Stanley. London: Pandora, 1995.

_____. *Pirates of the South China Coast, 1790–1810*. Stanford: Stanford University Press, 1987.

Mylne, Vivienne. *The Eighteenth-Century French Novel: Techniques of Illusion*. 2nd ed. Cambridge: Cambridge University, 1981.

Mythbusters. Episode 71: Pirate Special. First aired January 17, 2007.

Nalson, John. *The Complaint of Liberty & Property Against Arbitrary Government: Dedicated to all True English Men, and Lovers of Property, Laws, and Religion*. London: Robert Steele, 1681.

Nashe, Thomas. *Christs Tears Over Jerusalem*. 1593. In *The Works of Thomas Nashe*. 2 vols. Edited by Ronald B. McKerrow. London: A. H. Bullen, 1904.

Navarro, Juan José [Marques de la Victoria]. *Album del Marques de la Victoria [Architectura Naval Antigua y Moderna]*. Original manuscript. Facsimile reprint, edited by Jose Ignacio Gonzalez-Aller Hierro. Madrid: Lunwerg, 2007.

Nicollière-Teijeiro, sieur de la. "Un Pavillon de Pirate." In *La Bretagne Artistique, Pittoresque et Littéraire*, vol. 11 (1881): 281–84.

Nieuhoff, John. *Mr. John Nieuhoff's Remarkable Voyages and Travels to Brasil*. In *A Collection of Voyages and Travels*, edited by Awnsham Churchill, John Churchill, and John Locke. 3rd. ed. Vol. 2. London: Henry Lintot and John Osborn, 1744.

Le Nouveau Mercure. February, 1719. Paris: Guillaume Cavelier, 1719.

Oliver y Fullana, Nicolás de. *Recopilacion Historica de los Reynes, Guerras, Tumultos y Rebeliones de Ungria*. Cologne: Baltazar ab Egmont, 1687.

Olsen, Paul. "Sørøvere i Vestindien." *Siden Saxo* 3 (2003).

Orozco y Berra, Manuel, ed. *Apéndice al Diccionario Universal de Historia y de Geografía*. Vol. 1. Mexico: J. M. Andrade and F. Escalante, 1855.

Otway, Thomas. *The Soldiers Fortune*. 1681. In *The Works of Mr. Thomas Otway*. 2 vols. London: J. Tonson, 1712

Oudin, Cesar. *Le Tresor des Deux Langues Espagnolle et Françoise*. Paris: Sebastien Martin, 1660.

Ovington, John. *A Voyage to Suratt: In the Year, 1689*. London: Jacob Tonson, 1696.

Page, Thomas. *The Use of the Broad Sword*. Norwich, England: M. Chase, 1746.

Parish, James Robert. *Pirates and Seafaring Swashbucklers on the Hollywood Screen*. Jefferson, NC: McFarland & Company, 1995.

Park, Robert. *Defensive War by Sea in Five Parts*. London: Rich. Mount and Tho. Page, 1704.

Partenay. "Ainsy se fait voir le Petit Gouave au Sud-est et nord oist éloignée . . ." 1688. *Bibliothèque Nationale de France*, ark:/12148/btv1b5972789c.

Paterculus, Velleius. *Remains of His Compendium of the History of Rome*. In In *Sallust, Florus, and Velleius Paterculus*, edited by John Selby Watson. London: George Bell and Sons, 1889.

Pawson, Michael, and David Buisseret. "A Pirate at Port Royal in 1679," *Mariner's Mirror* 57, no. 3 (1971): 303–5.

_____. *Port Royal, Jamaica*. 1974. 2nd ed. Kingston: University of the West Indies Press, 2000.

Pepys, Samuel. *Samuel Pepys' Diary 1660–1669*. British Library.

Pérez Valenzuela, Pedro. *Historias de Piratas: Los Aventureros del Mar en la América Central*. Guatemala: C.A. Tipografía Nacional, 1936.

Perkins, Samuel. Deposition of Samuel Perkins. August 25, 1698. In *Privateering and Piracy in the Colonial Period: Illustrative Documents*, edited by John F. Jameson. New York: Macmillan Company, 1923.

Perrin, W. G. [William Gordon Perrin]. *British Flags: Their Early History, and Their Development at Sea; With an Account of the Origin of the Flag as a National Device*. Cambridge: Cambridge University, 1922.

Peru, Viceroyalty of. *Memorias de los Vireyes que Han Gobernado el Peru, Durante el Tiempo del Coloniaje Español.* Vol. 1. Lima: Librería Central de Felipe Bailly, 1859.

Phillips, Carla Rhan. *Los Tres Reyes 1628–1634: The Short Life of an Unlucky Spanish Galleon.* Minneapolis: University of Minnesota Press, 1990.

_____. *Six Galleons for the King of Spain.* Baltimore: Johns Hopkins University Press, 1986.

_____. *The Treasure of San José: Death at Sea in the War of the Spanish Succession.* Baltimore: Johns Hopkins, 2007.

Phillips, Edward, ed., [and J. K. Philobibl]. *The New World of English Words.* 7th ed. London: J. Philips, D. Rhodes, and J. Taylor, 1720.

Phillips, Thomas. *A Journal of a Voyage from England to Africa, and so forward to Barbados, in the Years 1693, and 1694.* In *A Collection of Voyages and Travels,* vol. 6, edited by Awnsham Churchill and John Churchill. London: John Walthoe et al, 1732.

Pitman, Henry. *A Relation of the Great Sufferings and Strange Adventures of Henry Pitman.* London: Andrew Sowle, 1689.

Playford, Henry. *Wit and Mirth: or, Pills to Purge Melancholy.* 2 vols. London: William Pearson, 1707.

Plutarch [Lucius Mestrius Plutarchus]. *The Lives of the Noble Grecians and Romans: The Dryden Translation.* Translated by John Dryden. Chicago: Encyclopedia Britannica, 1952.

Poe, Edgar Allan. "The Gold-Bug." In *Tales* by Edgar A. Poe. London: Wiley and Putnam, 1845.

Poildecoeur, François. Déclaration du Capitaine, June 17, 1718. Excerpted in *Voyages Français à Destination de la Mer du Sud Avant Bougainville (1695–1749)* by M. E. W. Dahlgren, 537–38 [115–16]. Paris: Imprimerie Nationale, 1907.

Polderman, Marie. *La Guyane Française, 1676–1763: Mise en Place et Évolution de la Société Coloniale, Tensions et Métissages.* Matoury Cedex, Guyane Française: Ibis Rouge Editions, 2004.

Polybius. *The Histories.* 6 vols. Translated by W. R. Paton. New York: G. P. Putnam's, 1922.

[Povey, Edward?]. "The Buccaneers on the Isthmus and in the South Sea. 1680–1682." In Jameson, *Privateering and Piracy*.

Povey, Francis. *The Sea-Gunners Companion, or Practical Rules, Explaining the Use of Ordnance and Other Stores in Sea Service*. London: Richard Mount, 1702.

Preble, George Henry. *Origin and History of the American Flag: And of the Naval and Yacht-Club Signals, Seals, and Arms, and Principal National Songs of the United States*. Vol. 1. Philadelphia: Nicholas L. Brown, 1917.

Pringle, Patrick. *Jolly Roger: The Story of the Great Age of Piracy*. New York: W. W. Norton, 1953.

Pyle, Howard. *An Attack on a Galleon*. Illustration for "The Fate of a Treasure-Town." *Harper's Monthly Magazine* (December 1905).

_____. *Buried Treasure*. Illustration in *Howard Pyle's Book of Pirates*. New York: Harper & Brothers, 1921.

_____. *The Buccaneer Was a Picturesque Fellow*. In "The Fate of a Treasure-Town" by Howard Pyle. *Harper's Monthly Magazine* (December 1905).

_____. *Extorting Tribute from the Citizens*. In "The Fate of a Treasure-Town" by Howard Pyle. *Harper's Monthly Magazine* (December 1905).

_____. *Howard Pyle's Book of Pirates*. New York: Harper & Brothers, 1921.

_____. *Kidd at Gardiner's Island*. Illustration for "Tom Chist and the Treasure Box." In *Howard Pyle's Book of Pirates*. New York: Harper & Brothers, 1921.

_____. *So the Treasure Was Divided*. In "The Fate of a Treasure-Town" by Howard Pyle. *Harper's Monthly Magazine* (December 1905).

_____. "Tom Chist and the Treasure Box." In *Howard Pyle's Book of Pirates*. New York: Harper & Brothers, 1921.

_____. *Walking the Plank*. Illustration for "Buccaneers and Marooners of the Spanish Main" by Howard Pyle. *Harper's New Monthly Magazine* (September 1887).

_____. *Which Shall Be Captain?* In "The Buccaneers" by Don C. Seitz. *Harper's Monthly Magazine* (January 1911).

_____. *Why Don't You End It?* In To *Have and to Hold* by Mary Johnston. New York: Houghton and Mifflin, 1900.

_____. "With the Buccaneers." In *Howard Pyle's Book of Pirates*. New York: Harper & Brothers, 1921.

Racault, "De l'Aventure Flibustière à la Piraterie Littéraire: Defoe, Leguat, le Deux Misson et la République Utopique de Libertalia." In *Les Tyrans de la Mer: Pirates, Corsaires et Flibustiers*, edited by Sophie Linon-Chipon and Sylvie Requemora, 243–64. Paris: Presses Paris Sorbonne, 2002.

Rediker, Marcus. "Liberty beneath the Jolly Roger: The Lives of Anne Bonny and Mary Read, Pirates." In *Bandits at Sea: A Pirates Reader*, edited by C. R. Pennell, 299–320. New York: New York University Press, 2001.

_____. *The Slave Ship: A Human History*. New York: Viking, 2007.

_____. *Villains of All Nations: Atlantic Pirates in the Golden Age*. Boston: Beacon Press, 2004.

Reynado, Feliz. *Collecion de los Tradados de Paz*. Vol. 2. Madrid: Antonio Marin et al, 1752.

Richard Wiseman. *Several Chirurgicall Treatises*. London: E. Flesher and J. Macock, 1676.

Richards, Jeffrey. *Swordsmen of the Silver Screen: From Douglas Fairbanks to Michael York*. London: Routledge & Keegan Paul, 1977.

Ringrose, Basil. "The Buccaneers of America: The Second Volume." In Exquemelin, *Buccaneers of America* (Crooke, 1684).

_____. *Buccaneer Atlas: Basil Ringrose's South Sea Waggoner*. Edited by Derek Howse and Norman J. W. Thrower. Berkeley: University of California Press, 1992.

_____. "Captains Sharp, Coxon, Sawkins, and Others . . ." In *The History of the Buccaneers of America* by Alexander Exquemelin [Joseph Esquemeling], 180–313. 1699. Reprint, Boston: Sanborn, Carter and Bazin, 1856.

Ritchie, Robert C. *Captain Kidd and the War Against the Pirates*. Cambridge: Harvard University Press, 1986.

Robbins, Rossell Hope. *The Encyclopedia of Witchcraft and Demonology*. New York: Crown Publishers, 1959.

Roberts, George. *The Four Years Voyages of Capt. George Roberts; Being a Series of Uncommon Events Which Befell Him.* 1726. Reprint, London: The Traveller's Library, 1930.

Robinson, Edmond. Deposition of Edmond Robinson. Excerpted in Hughson, Shirley Carter. *The Carolina Pirates and Colonial Commerce, 1670–1740.* 1894. Reprint, Spartanburg, South Carolina: The Reprint Company, 1992.

Robinson, J. H. *Journal of an Expedition 1400 Miles Up the Orinoco and 300 Up the Arauca.* London: Black, Young, and Young, 1822.

Roche, Jeremy. *The Journals of Jeremy Roche.* In *Three Sea Journals of Stuart Times*, edited by Bruce S. Ingram. London: Constable & Co., 1936.

Rogers, Woodes. *A Cruising Voyage 'Round the World.* 1712. Facsimile reprint, New York: Da Capo Press, 1969.

[Roggeveen, Jakob.] "Voyage of Commodore Roggewein." In *The World Displayed; or, a Curious Collection of Voyages and Travels*, edited by Samuel Johnson, Oliver Goldsmith, and Christopher Smart. Vol. 9. London: J. Newberry, 1760.

Rogoziński, Jan. *Honor Among Thieves: Captain Kidd, Henry Every, and the Pirate Democracy in the Indian Ocean.* Mechanicsburg, PA: Stackpole Books, 2000.

_____. *Pirates!* New York: Facts on File, Inc., 1995.

Rosenberg, Aubrey. *Tyssot de Patot and his work 1655–1738.* The Hague: Nijhoff, 1972.

Sabatini, Rafael. *The Black Swan.* Boston: Houghton Mifflin, 1931.

_____. *Captain Blood: His Odyssey.* Boston: Houghton Mifflin, 1922.

_____. *Captain Blood Returns.* New York: Grosset & Dunlap, 1930.

_____. *The Chronicles of Captain Blood.* London: Hutchinson, 1931.

_____. "The Duel on the Beach." In *Ladies' Home Journal* XLVIII, no. 9 (September 1931), 3–5, 47, 49–50, 52.

_____. *The Fortunes of Captain Blood.* New York: Grosset & Dunlap, 1936.

_____. *Torquemada and the Spanish Inquisition.* London: Stanley Paul & Co., [1913].

Sanders, Richard. *If a Pirate I Must Be . . . : The True Story of "Black Bart," King of the Caribbean Pirates.* New York: Aurium Press, 2007.

Scelle, Georges. *La Traite Négrière aux Indes de Castille, Contrats et Traités d'Assiento.* Paris, L. Larose & L. Tenin, 1906.

Scott, Walter. *The Fortunes of Nigel.* Boston: Samuel H. Parker, 1822.

———. *The Pirate.* 3 vols. Edinburgh: Archibald Constable and Co., 1822.

Seitz, Don C., ed. *The Tryal of Capt. William Kidd for Murther and Piracy.* 1936. Reprint, Mineola, NY: Dover Publications, 2001.

Serrano Mangas, Fernando. "El Proceso del Pirata Bartholomew Sharp, 1682." *Temas Amercanistas*, no. 4 (1984), 38–49.

Seutonius [Gaius Suetonius Tranquillus]. *Suetonius.* 2 vols. Edited by J. C. Rolfe. London: William Heinemann, 1914.

Sewall, Samuel. *The Diary of Samuel Sewell, 1674–1729.* Vol. 3. Boston: Massachusetts Historical Society, 1882.

Sharp, Bartholomew. *Captain Sharp's Journal of His Expedition.* In *A Collection of Original Voyages* by William Hacke. 1699. Facsimile reprint, edited by Glyndwr Williams. New York: Scholars' Facsimiles & Reprints, 1993.

Shelvocke, George, *A Voyage Around the World.* Facsimile reprint, 1726. New York: Da Capo Press, 1971.

Sierksma, Kl. *Flags of the World 1669–1670: A Seventeenth Century Manuscript.* Amsterdam: S. Emmering, 1966.

Simons, Nicholas. "A Memorandum of my Transactions since I sailed out of Newport in November 1723." In *Captured by Pirates: Two Diaries of 1724–1725*, edited by Robert Francis Seybolt. *The New England Quarterly*, vol. 2, no. 4 (October 1929): 663–69.

Simms, William Gilmore. *The Cassique of Kiawah: A Colonial Romance.* New York: Dodd, Mead & Co., 1859.

Sloane, Hans. *A Voyage to the Islands Madera, Barbados, Nieves, S. Christophers and Jamaica.* 2 vols. London: B. M. for the author, 1707.

Smith, Stacy L., and Marc Choueiti. "Gender Disparity On Screen and Behind the Camera in Family Films; The Executive Report." Los Angeles: University of Southern California, Annenberg School for Communication & Journalism, August 19, 2010. Available at www.thegeenadavisinstitute.org.

Smith, William. *A New Voyage to Guinea*. 2nd ed. London: John Nourse, 1745.

Smyth, William Henry. *The Sailor's Word-Book: An Alphabetical Digest of Nautical Terms*. Revised by E. Belcher. London: Blackie and Son, 1867.

Snelders, Stephen. *The Devil's Anarchy*. Brooklyn: Autonomedia, 2005.

Snelgrave, William. *A New Account of Some Parts of Guinea*. London: James, John, and Paul Knapton, 1734.

Spottiswood, Alexander. *The Official Letters of Alexander Spotswood, Lieutenant-Governor of the Colony of Virginia, 1710–1722*. Vol. 1. Richmond, VA: The Society, 1882.

Stanley, Jo, ed. *Bold in Her Breeches*. London: Pandora, 1995.

Stark, Suzanne J. *Female Tars: Women Aboard Ship in the Age of Sail*. Annapolis: Naval Institute Press, 1996.

State of Pennsylvania. *Minutes of the Provincial Council of Pennsylvania*. Vol. 3. Harrisburg, PA: Theophilus Fenn for the State of Pennsylvania, 1840.

Sterre, David van der. *Zeer Aanmerkelijke Reysen Gedaan door Jan Erasmus Reining*. Amsterdam: Jan ten Hoorn, 1691.

Stevenson, Robert Louis. "My First Book—'Treasure Island.'" In *Treasure Island* by Robert Louis Stevenson. New York: Longman's, Green and Co., 1910.

_____. *Treasure Island*. Illustrated by N. C. Wyeth. New York: Charles Scribner's Sons, 1911.

_____. *Treasure Island*. Illustrated by Don Irwin. Santa Rosa, CA: Classic Press, 1968.

Sturmy, Samuel. *The Mariner's Magazine*. London: E. Cotes et al, 1669.

Swanson, Gail. *Documentation of the Indians of the Florida Keys and Miami 1513–1765*. Haverford, PA: Infinity Publishing.com, 2003.

Tallemant des Réaux, Gédéon. *Les Historiettes de Tallemant des Reaux*. 3rd ed. Vol. 5. Paris: Techener Libraire, 1856.

Tarin, Pierre-Paul [le sieur de Cussy]. "Analyse d'une lettre de Cussy ([1687])." ANOM, FR ANOM COL C8A 4 F° 270.

_____. "Le sieur de Cussy à monseigneur le marquis de Seignelay." August 24, 1684. ANF: CAOM COL-C9A 1.

_____. "Le sieur de Cussy à Monseigneur le marquis de Seigneley." January 10, 1686. ANF, CAOM COL-C9A 1.

_____. "Mémoire du sieur de Cussy pour monseigneur le marquis de Seigneley." August 13, 1686. ANF, Colonies, CAOM COL-C9A 1.

_____. "Mémoire du sieur de Cussy pour Monseigneur le marquis de Seignelay," May 3, 1688. ANF, CAOM COL-C9A 1.

Taylor, John. *Jamaica in 1687: The Taylor Manuscript at the National Library of Jamaica.* Edited by David Buisseret. Kingston: University of West Indies Press, 2008.

Thucydides. *The History of the Peloponnesian War.* In *Great Books of the Western World: 6. Herodotus, Thucydides.* 1952. Translated by Richard Crawley. Reprint, revised by R. Feetham. Chicago: Encyclopedia Britannica, 1982.

Torres Ramirez, Bibiano. *La Armada de Barlovento.* Sevilla: Escuela de Estudios Hispano-Americanos de Sevilla, 1981.

Treich, Léon. *Les Gentilshommes de la Flibuste.* Illustrated by Van Rompaey. Paris: Editions de la Nouvelle France, 1944.

Twain, Mark. *The Adventures of Tom Sawyer.* Hartford, CT: American Publishing Company, 1876.

Tyssot de Patot, Simon. *Voyages et Avantures de Jaques Massé.* Bordeaux: Jaques l'Aveugle, 1710.

United Artists Corporation. Advertisement to Exhibitors, "Douglas Fairbanks in THE BLACK PIRATE." 1926.

Universidad y Casa de Contratación, Bilbao. *Ordenanzas de la ilustre Universidad, y Casa de contratacion de la m.n.y.m.1. villa de Bilbao, (insertos sus reales privilegios) aprobadas, y confirmadas por el rey nuestro señor don Phelipe Quinto (que Dios guarde) año de 1737.* Bilbao: Universidad y Casa de Contratación, 1775,

Updike, Wilkins. *Memoirs of the Rhode Island Bar.* Boston: Thomas H. Webb, 1842.

Vaissière, Pierre de. *Les Origines de la Colonisation et la Formation de la Société Française à Saint-Domingue.* Paris: Bureaux de la Revue, 1906.

Valentine, D. T., ed. *Manual of the Corporation of the City of New York for 1853.* Vol. 4. New York: Common Council of New York, 1853.

Vázquez, Germán. *Mujeres Piratas.* Madrid: Algaba Edicíones, 2004.

Vetancurt, Agustín de. *Chronica de la Provincia del Santo Evangelio de Mexico.* Mexico: Por doña Maria de Benavides viuda de Iuan de Ribera, 1697.

Vignols, Léon. *La Piraterie sur l'Atlantique au XVIIIe Siècle.* Rennes, France: Typographie Oberthur, 1890.

Villehuet, Jacques Bourdé de. *The Manœuverer, or Skilful Seaman: Being an Essay on the Theory and Practice of the Various Movements of a Ship at Sea.* Translated by the Chevalier de Sauseuil [Jean Nicolas]. London: S. Hooper, 1788.

_____. *Le Manœuvrier, ou Essai sur la Théorie et la Practique de Mouvements du Navire et des Évolutions Navales.* Paris: H. L. Guerin and L. F. Delatour, 1765.

Volney, C-F. [Constantin-François]. *Travels Through Syria and Egypt.* 2 vols. London: G. G. J. and J. Robinson, 1788.

Vrijman, L. C. *Dr. David Van der Sterre: Zeer Aenmerkelijke Reysen Gedaan Door Jan Erasmus Reyning.* Amsterdam: P. N. Van Kampen, 1937.

Wafer, Lionel. *A New Voyage & Description of the Isthmus of America.* 1699. Reprint, London: Oxford, for the Hakluyt Society, 1934.

[Walker, George?]. *The Voyages and Cruises of Commodore Walker.* 1760, Reprint, London: Cassell and Company, 1928.

Waller, John Augustine. *A Voyage in the West Indies: Containing Various Observations Made During a Residence in Barbados.* London: Sir Richard Phillips and Co., 1820.

Ward, Edward [Ned Ward]. "A Trip to New England." 1699. Reprinted in *Boston in 1682 and 1699.* Providence, RI: Club for Colonial Reprints, 1905.

_____. *The Wooden World.* 1751. Reprint, London: Society for Nautical Research, 1929.

Watson, John Selby, ed. *Sallust, Florus, and Velleius Paterculus.* London: George Bell and Sons, 1889.

Weddle, Robert S. In *The Handbook of Texas* online, s.v. "Armada de Barlovento," http://www.tshaonline.org/.

_____. *La Salle, the Mississippi, and the Gulf: Three Primary Documents.* College Station: Texas A&M University Press, 1987.

_____. *Wilderness Manhunt: The Spanish Search for La Salle.* College Station, TX: Texas A&M University Press, 2001.

Whiles, John. *Sedgemoor 1685.* 2nd ed. Chippenham, England: Picton Publishing, 1985.

Wilde-Ramsing, Mark. "Historical Background for the Queen Anne's Revenge Shipwreck Site." Research Report and Bulletin Series *QAR-R-09-02* (August 2009). Underwater Archaeology Branch, Office of State Archaeology, Department of Cultural Resources, State of North Carolina.

Willocks, William. "A Narrative About the *Mocha Frigatt.*" In Grey, *Pirates of the Eastern Seas.*

Wilson, Timothy. *Flags at Sea.* Annapolis: Naval Institute Press, 1999.

Witsen, Nicolaas, Cornelis van Eyk, and Carel Allard. *L'Art de Bâtir les Vaisseaux, Et d'en Perfectionner La Construction.* 2 vols. Amsterdam: David Morier, 1719.

Woodbridge, Benjamin M. "À Propos d'un Prisonnier à Pierre-Scize, Visité par Mme. De Sévigné." In *Publications of the Modern Language Association of America,* vol. 27, edited by William Guild Howard. Baltimore: J. H. Furst, 1912 (372–79).

Woodward, Colin. *The Republic of Pirates: Being the True and Surprising Story of the Caribbean Pirates and the Man Who Brought Them Down.* New York: Houghton Mifflin Harcourt, 2007.

Worth, John E. *The Struggle for the Georgia Coast.* Tuscaloosa, AL: University of Alabama Press, 2007.

Wright, J. Leitch, Jr., "Andrew Ranson: Seventeenth Century Pirate?", *Florida Historical Quarterly* 39 (1960–1961): 135–44.

Wycherley, William. *Miscellany Poems: As Satyrs, Epsitles, Love-Verses, Songs, Sonnets, &c.* London: C. Brome, F. Taylor, and B. Tooke, 1704.

_____. *The Plain-Dealer.* London: T. N. for James Magness and Rich. Bentley, 1677.

Ximénez, Francisco. *Historia de la Provincia de San Vicente de Chiapa y Guatemala de la Orden de Predicadores*. Vol. 2. Guatemala: Tipografía Nacional, 1930.

Yonge, Francis. *A Narrative of the Proceedings of the People of South-Carolina, in the Year 1719*. London: n.p., 1726.

Yun-lun, Yuan. *History of the Pirates Who Infested the China Sea, From 1807 to 1810*. 1830. Translated by Charles Friedrich Neumann. London: Oriental Translation Fund, 1831.

Acknowledgments

⊶⊷

It is always a pleasure to acknowledge in a public writing those who have done so much to help get a book into print. Every author, whether he or she admits it or not, is in debt to many people, whether simply from the support they gave or the ideas they inspired.

To begin, I cannot help but acknowledge the debt I owe to those whose acts or works have inspired me to write about pirates and privateers. Were it not for them, I might never have taken this path. I do not pass judgment here; I only note their great influence. They are buccaneer-surgeon and author Alexander Exquemelin and pirate chronicler Charles Johnson, whoever he really was. They are buccaneer-journalists William Dampier, Basil Ringrose, William Dick, Edward Povey, Bartholomew Sharp, John Cox, Lionel Wafer, and François Massertie.

They are privateers and journalists Woodes Rogers and George Shelvocke, *boucanier-* and filibuster-chronicling priests Jean-Baptiste Dutertre, Jean Baptiste-Labat, and Jean-Baptiste Lepers, and mariner-diarists Edward Barlow, Edward Coxere, Nathaniel Uring, and William Snelgrave. They are corsairs Jean Doublet, Jean Bart, René Duguay-Trouin, and Claude de Forbin; they are buccaneers Henry Morgan, Laurens de Graaf, Michel de Grammont, and the eighty-year-old buccaneer Swan; they are Spanish pirate hunter and gentleman Don Francisco de Peralta, Campechano turned Dutch pirate Diego the Mulatto, English naval officer Robert Maynard, and pirate-hunting Carolinian William Rhett. They are Anne Dieu-le-veult and all of her unnamed kindred spirits.

They include novelists Daniel Defoe, Sir Walter Scott, Jeffery Farnol, John Steinbeck, Leslie Charteris, Daphne du Maurier, William Goldman, George MacDonald Fraser, and especially Robert Louis Stevenson, Rafael Sabatini, Joseph Conrad, and Herman Melville, and all the films they inspired. I cannot leave out the compilers of the extraordinarily rich and useful *Calendars of State Papers, Colonial*, nor the paintings and stories of Howard Pyle, nor the paintings of his students N. C. Wyeth and Frank Schoonover, not to mention his descendants Andrew and Jamie, much less the poetry of John Masefield; the rousing film scores of Erich Wolfgang Korngold and his composer brethren; the swashbuckling films of Douglas Fairbanks, Errol Flynn, and Maureen O'Hara; the film swordplay choreography of Fred Cavens, William Hobbs, and Bob Anderson; and, of course, the childhood romance of Disney's Pirates of the Caribbean theme park ride.

Among those I have known in the flesh, once more I thank Ann Crispin, who has since sadly passed away, and Will Kiester, the former for pointing me to Fair Winds Press, the latter for *almost* publishing me a second time in an early iteration of this book: a corporate decision at the last minute ended the publisher's history line. To Cara Connors, an early editor who shares my excitement for fascinating truths brought forth from the dusty leaves of history and the depths of human nature, likewise go my many thanks.

My agent, Frank Weimann at Folio Literary Management, has my many thanks and great appreciation for finding a new publisher, Skyhorse Publications. At Skyhorse, my many thanks to my editor, Chris Evans, who has shepherded this manuscript through the publication process, and also to copy editor Deborah Goemans, proofreader Rita Samols, senior production editor Stacey Fischkelta, and editor Julia Abramoff, my first contact at Skyhorse.

To Shelley Barber, my favorite manuscript curator and designated librarian, my many thanks for her support, her New England pirate anecdotes, and her assistance with sources on the origin of pirate flag myths, including *le joli rouge*. My many thanks also to Chad Scales, friend, fellow fencer, and outstanding artist for the buccaneer and pirate flag illustrations in this book. For their enthusiasm at bringing pirate lore to a large audience, not to mention for hiring me as their historical consultant, my many thanks also to Jon Steinberg and Robert Levine co-creators of the STARZ network's *Black Sails* cable television series— and to all the *Black Sails* writers and crew I've worked with, all of them great people. My thanks to everyone at Firelock Games, for their enthusiasm for the subject of this book is boundless. My thanks in particular to Alex Aguila and Mike Tuñez for bringing me aboard, and to Christopher Tuñez, whose enthusiasm for finding an authentic female buccaneer led me to triple-check my research into the subject.

Of my many fencing friends, I give my thanks and high regard to Dr. Francis Zold, who has also passed away, and Dr. Eugene Hamori, both of whom fanned the flame of my love for swordplay, and to the members past and present of the New Orleans Fencing (now Fencers) Club, the USC and the Tulane Fencing Clubs, and the Huntsville Fencing Club, all swashbucklers and adventurers, rather than mere sportsmen and sportswomen, at heart.

Among my adventuresome friends, colleagues, and acquaintances, I cannot forget to note the fellow Navy SEALs I served with, nor their courage, deeds, and camaraderie.

To Ruth Heredia—friend, family, poet, literate raconteur, and Rafael Sabatini biographer extraordinaire—my great affection.

Especially, though, I thank my grandparents and great-grandparents, who told me tales of ghosts and buried treasures and let me roam in quest of them; my parents, who likewise encouraged me to do so on land and sea; my wife, Mary Crouch, who not only was indispensable in researching this book and helping with my Spanish translations, but also is my companion in adventure and life; my daughters, Courtney and Bree, who likewise aided my research, took adventures with me, and have long encouraged my separate adventures written and real, and now seek their own; and my infant son, Aidan, who will soon begin seeking his own adventures and discoveries.

Last, my many thanks to purveyors and repositories of old books, maps, papers, and films everywhere, and to everyone who has ever reminded me that life is an adventure best experienced firsthand.

About the Author

———◦⊸⊸◦———

Benerson Little is the author of *Fortune's Whelp*, a novel, and also of the following non-fiction titles: *The Sea Rover's Practice: Pirate Tactics and Techniques, 1630–1730; The Buccaneer's Realm: Pirate Life on the Spanish Main, 1674–1688; Pirate Hunting: The Fight against Pirates, Privateers, and Sea Raiders from Antiquity to the Present; How History's Greatest Pirates Pillaged, Plundered, and Got Away with It.* He is the author of numerous articles on pirates, has twice appeared in History Channel documentaries to discuss piracy, and serves as the historical consultant for Firelock Games and for the Starz pirate drama *Black Sails*. A former Navy SEAL, he has worked as a naval special warfare analyst, an intelligence analyst, and a consultant in maritime subjects, and he is a fencing instructor, both modern and historical, in his spare time.

Endnotes

The following endnotes use a short-form citation. For the complete reference to a full text, refer to the bibliography.

Abbreviations

AGI: Archivos General de Indias
ANF: Archives Nationales de France
ANOM: Archives Nationales d'Outre-Mer
BNF: Bibliothèque Nationale de France
CSPC: Calendar of State Papers Colonial, America and West Indies
CSPD: Calendar of State Papers, Domestic
PRCC: Public Records of the Colony of Connecticut

Preface

1   Stevenson, *Treasure Island* (1968).

Prologue

1   Regarding the proverb "Dead men tell no tales," used by Disney at the beginning of its Pirates of the Caribbean theme park attractions, it dates back at least two millennia—even Tom Sawyer uses

it when he plays pirate—and was used in one form or another by at least one pirate crew, that of Bartholomew Roberts. They told prisoners that in time of battle they must fight or "immediately be shot, that they should not tell tales." Its ultimate origin is probably "*mortui non mordent*," that is, "dead men don't bite," a Latin translation from Plutarch, in Greek originally.

2 The eyewitness images are part of the following charts: Cornuau, "Plan des Passes," 1685, BNF; Cornuau, "Plan du Cap et de Son Entrée," 1684, BNF; Cornuau, "Plan Ignographique du Fon et de l'Isle à Vache," 1686; Cornuau, "Plan Ignographique du Fon et de l'Isle à Vache," 1686 (different chart from previous); Cornuau, "Plan du Petit Goave, 1688, ANOM; Partenay, "Ainsy se Fait Voir le Petit Gouave," 1688, BNF; See also Little, "Eyewitness Images," 2012.

3 Dampier, *Voyages and Discoveries*, 138; Cornuau, "Plan du Cul de Sac de Léogane," 1685, among other Cornuau charts; Little, *Buccaneer's Realm*, 58. The French eyewitness illustrations cited above show hats with broad and moderate brims; most have feathers or plumes. Dampier describes and Cornuau, in several drawings, illustrates the cropped hat. The Monmouth Museum has a sixteenth-century Monmouth cap in its collection, and the Rijksmuseum has a collection of colorfully knitted whaler's caps, similar to Monmouth caps.

4 Hutchinson, *Treatise on Naval Architecture*, 297.

5 See for example: Cornuau, "Plan du Cap et de Son Entrée," "Plan Ignographique du Fon et de l'Isle à Vache" (both charts), "Plan du Petit Goave et de l'Acul," and Partenay, "Ainsy se Fait Voir le Petit Gouave."

6 Exquemelin, *Flibustiers du Nouveau Monde*, 33; Little, *Sea Rover's Practice*, 88.

7 Leslie, *New and Exact Account of Jamaica*, 35.

8 See for example, Partenay, "Ainsy se Fait Voir le Petit Gouave."

9 Anon., *Tryals of Captain John Rackam*, 18.

10 Diarist Samuel Pepys wore a black patch (perhaps a large beauty patch) to cover a large cold sore, and King William III once advised that a soldier remove the black patch covering the scar on his face, because "It's more honourable in a Soldier to wear a Scar than a Patch." See Pepys, *Diary*, 26 September 1664, and Coke, *Detection of the Court*, vol. 2:472.

11 Exquemelin, *Buccaneers of America* (1684), 60; Díaz del Castillo, *Historia verdadera*, vol. 1:213; Scott, *Fortunes of Nigel*, 255; Dickens, "Perils of Certain English Prisoners," 144; Little, "El Mito Pirata," 54.

12 Two of the principal inspirations for the myth appear to be *Mythbusters*, Episode 71, and articles similar to Mitchell, "Does Reading in Dim Light Hurt Your Eyes?"

13 See for example Johnson, *General History of the Robberies*, 307; Ward, "Trip to New England," 36; Ward, *Wooden World*, 92, and Taylor, *Jamaica in 1687*, 240.

14 Regarding pirates and liquor, see Dampier, *New Voyage*, 33–34, and Snelgrave, *New Account*, 234, 235.

15 Snelgrave, *New Account*, 217.

16 Cordingly, *Under the Black Flag*, 176; *Treasure Island*, Walt Disney Productions, 1950; *Blackbeard the Pirate*, RKO Radio Pictures, 1952; *Long John Silver*, 20th Century Fox, 1954.

17 See for example Ward, *Wooden World*, 98, and Duguay-Trouin, *Memoirs of M. du Gué-Trouin*, 182.

18 Johnson, *General History of the Robberies*, 237; Stevenson, *Treasure Island* (1911), 3; *Treasure Island*, RKO Radio Pictures, 1950; *The Tomahawk, or Censor General*, November 6, 1795, 37; Little, "To Arr or Not to Arr!," 9–14; Cordingly, *Under the Black Flag*, 176. "Shiver me timbers!" appears to be a nineteenth-century usage.

19 *Captain Blood*, Warner Brothers Pictures, 1935; Sturmy, *Mariner's Magazine*, 16, 19; Twain, *Adventures of Tom Sawyer*, chapter 8; Little, "To Arr or Not to Arr!," 9–14.

20 Wycherley, *Plain-Dealer*, 28; Brown, *Works of Mr. Thomas Brown*, vol. 3:250; *London Gazette*, 25 June 1688; Fox, *Journal*, 254. Regarding the play noting the jewel in the ear and the gunpowder spot, see prologue endnote 28.

21 Numerous paintings from the seventeenth and eighteenth centuries show African house slaves, as well as free Africans, both male and female, wearing long, dangling pearl earrings. A mid-seventeenth century painting of the Flemish school, *An African with a Sword*, shows an African male, possibly a slave trader, wearing earrings, which may be pearls, in each ear.

22 Exquemelin, *Flibustiers*, 176 (author's translation); Shomette, *Pirates on the Chesapeake*, 108; Johnson, *General History of the Robberies*, 211. See also Senior, *Pirates*, 37.

23 Fillmore, *Narration of the Captivity*, 16.

24 Examples of pirates and rings include Captain Richard Sawkins being given a gold ring by the governor of Panama; captured seaman Jonathan Barlow, who was threatened by Ned Low's crew if he did not part with his ring; and Captain John Philips, who wore two gold rings as described. See Ringrose, "The Buccaneers of America," 331; Barlow, "Memorandum of the Transactions," 659; and Fillmore, *Narration of the Captivity*, 16.

25 See Farenhold, "Tattooing in the Navy," 37–39, for the origin of the word "tattoo," as well as some examples of nineteenth-century tattoos among US Navy men. Much of our modern idea of sailor tattoos derives from nineteenth- and early twentieth-century naval traditions.

26 Volney, *Travels Through Syria*, vol. 2:311.

27 Dampier, *New Voyage*, 344; Farenhold, "Tattooing in the Navy," 39.

28 Wycherley, "Upon the Gun-powder Spot on a Lady's Hand," in *Miscellany Poems*, 78. Thomas Otway's Beau in *The Soldiers Fortune* (vol. 1:365, act 4) catalogs the "Age, Shape, Proportion, colour of Hair and Eyes, degrees of Complexion, Gun-powder Spots and Moles" of the "choicest Beauties about Town." A

seventeenth-century surgeon reported that he was often called on to remove gunpowder spots from persons who had them made in their youth and later wanted them removed. See Wiseman, *Several Chirurgicall Treatises*, 440. David Willson, a deserter from the British army in 1715, was described as having his initials "D. W." in gunpowder on his right hand. See *The London Gazette*, 10 September to 17 September 1715, no. 5363.

John Dickson Carr, novelist and historian, would seem to have agreed with my initial assessment of the gunpowder spot on the hand being a sign of the seaman: he writes, "as much the mark of the seaman as the gunpowder spot on his hand . . . ," almost certainly inspired by Wycherley in *The Plain-Dealer*, 28 (act 2, sc. 1). See Carr, *Devil in Velvet*, 107. The depth of Carr's research ability is attested to by his nonfiction *The Murder of Sir Edmund Godfrey*. However, we are both probably in error: Professor Ted Cotton, retired from Loyola University in New Orleans, in conversation with me some years ago, suggested the lines refer merely to the earring and gunpowder spot as being fashions of idle gentlemen. Add to this the evidence of Wycherley's poem in praise of a lady's gunpowder spot, along with similar evidence, and it is likely that the lines in *The Plain-Dealer* refer to a gentleman, not a seaman.

29 Wafer, *New Voyage and Description*, 83.

30 *The American Mercury*, 17 March 1720, no. 13.

31 Joutel, *Last Voyage*, 110, 117; Dièreville, *Relation of the Voyage*, 169–71, 296–97; Barroto, *Diary*, 180; Anon., *Voyage*, 238; Wafer, *New Voyage & Description*, 22; Farenhold, "Tattooing in the Navy," 37–39; Little, *Buccaneer's Realm*, 59; Little, "El Mito Pirata," 54.

32 See for example, May, *Account of the Wonderful Preservation*, 349–50; and Phillips, *Journal of a Voyage*, 233; and Brandes, "Dekzicht van een Oostindiëvaarder."

33 Dampier, *Voyages and Discoveries*, 212; Natière: The Saint-Malo Shipwrecks: Underwater Archaeology at Saint-Malo, http://www.epaves.corsaires.culture.fr/

34 Little, *Sea Rover's Practice*, 87–88, 207; Little, *Buccaneer's Realm*, 41, 58–59; Labat, *Nouveau Voyage aux Isles*, vol. 2:472; Avila, "Pillage de la ville de Veracruz," folio 3.

35 Labat, *Nouveau Voyage aux Isles*, vol. 2:472; Snelgrave, *New Account*, 255–56; Johnson, *General History of the Robberies*, 211.

36 Leslie, *New and Exact Account of Jamaica*, 35.

37 Regarding arms carried by pirates, see Exquemelin, *Flibustiers*, 89; Ringrose, "Buccaneers of America," 300; Avila, "Pillage de la ville de Veracruz," folio 3; Everard, *Relation*, 259; and Little, *Sea Rover's Practice*, 57–74. Regarding the way pirates wore and carried their arms, see the eyewitness illustrations noted above.

38 Exquemelin, *Flibustiers*, 89, 92.

39 The eyewitness illustrations noted above do not show any filibusters or *boucaniers* wearing baldrics.

40 Regarding English pirates wearing sashes, see for example Downing, *History of the Indian Wars*, 117.

41 Avila, "Pillage de la ville de Veracruz," folio 3.

42 Regarding pirates who carried more than two pistols, see Johnson, *General History of the Robberies*, 57, 92, 211; Snelgrave, *New Account*, 214; Barlow, "Memorandum of the Transactions," 663; and Simons, "Memorandum of my Transactions," 669. Blackbeard reportedly carried six "hanging in holsters, like bandoliers," Bartholomew Roberts reportedly carried four hanging from a silk sling, James Griffin wore four in his belt, and an unidentified pirate among Captain Shipton's crew wore three or four. The popular images of Blackbeard in the various editions of Johnson's work are conjectural, and therefore the manners in which he is shown wearing pistols are likewise conjectural.

43 The use of the silken sling among early eighteenth-century pirates is described by Johnson and has been confirmed archaeologically from the remains of the pirate ship *Whydah*; the end of the silk

was wrapped around the grip of a single pistol. In typical usage, a length of silk was attached at each end to each butt of a brace of pistols. See Johnson, *General History of the Robberies*, 211, photograph in Clifford and Turchi, *Pirate Prince*, and the artifact itself in the National Geographic *Whydah* exhibit.

44 Downing, *History of the Indian Wars*, 115.

45 Exquemelin, *Buccaneers of America* (1684), 60; Johnson, *General History of the Pyrates* (1724), 123; Johnson, *General History of the Robberies*, 92; [Povey?], "Buccaneers on the Isthmus," 88; Avila, "Pillage de la ville de Veracruz," folio 3. Regarding the identity of Charles Johnson, see Furbank and Owens, *Defoe De-Attributions*, and Bialuschewski, "Daniel Defoe, Nathaniel Mist." Defoe is no longer believed to have written the pirate history attributed to Johnson; Bialuschewski argues for Nathaniel Mist as the author.

46 Povey, *Sea-Gunners Companion*, 26.

47 [Head], *English Rogue: Continued*, 205.

48 Harris, *History of the Life*, 263.

49 Regarding socks resembling boots, see for example the illustrations in Collombon, *Traité de l'Exercice Militaire*. They are easily mistaken for boots—which some of the other figures are in fact wearing—if not examined closely. The form of such socks is admirably shown in color in many of Gestina ter Borch's watercolors in the Rijksmuseum. Regarding "cavalier" boots, a portrait of Prince Rupert as a 1660s naval commander shows him in these boots, but it is a nineteenth-century full-length copy of a 1666 three-quarter-length painting by Sir Peter Lely, part of the Flagmen of Lowestoff series. The later artist added the boots to the painting. See "Prince Rupert (1619–1682), 1st Duke of Cumberland and Count Palatine of the Rhine," Repro ID: BHC299, in the Royal Museums Greenwich.

50 Regarding seafaring boots, see for example Phillips, ed., *New World of English Words*, s.v. "Coker"; Brookes, *Art of Angling*, 98; Fury, *Tides in the Affairs of Men*, 162. There are several illustrations

in the collection of the Royal Museums, Greenwich, circa 1665, of Dutch fishermen and their boots.

51 [Dick?], "A Brief Account of Captain Sharp," 267; Davis, *Expedition of a Body*, 156; Johnson, *General History of the Robberies*, 176; Anon., *Tryals of Joseph Dawson*, 15.

Chapter 1

1 Anon., *Pacquet from Parnassus*, 16.

2 This narrative is derived from Massertie, *"Journal de bord, du 19 mai 1686 au 8 juin 1690,"* and *"Journal de bord, du 8 juin 1690 au 4 septembre 1694,"* throughout; Bradley, *Last Buccaneers*, throughout; and to a lesser degree, Gerhard, *Pirates of the Pacific*, 188–94. The attack on Acaponeta is described by Massertie, *"Journal de bord, du 19 mai 1686 au 8 juin 1690,"* but the pages are unnumbered, making reference difficult. Alternatively, see Massertie, *Journal de Bord*, ed. Ducére (1894), 512–20, and Bradley, *Last Buccaneers*, 60–62.

3 Regarding Banister (or Bannister), see Taylor, *Jamaica in 1687*, 48, 106–9; *CSPC 1681–1685*, nos. 1759, 1852, 1867, 2067; *CSPC 1685–1688*, nos. 193, 475, 661, 662, 754, 839, 1,127; *CSPD James II*, vol. 2, no. 961; Pawson and Buisseret, *Port Royal*, 69–74; and Moreau de Saint-Méry, *Topographical and Political Description of the Spanish Part*, vol. 1:176–77.

4 Lieutenant Governor Molesworth to William Blathwayt, *CSP 1685–1688*, no. 1127. Some sources, including the published transcriptions of Ducére and Bradley, have mistakenly transcribed Samana as Panama. However, not only do the English records of the attack on Banister at Samana correlate perfectly with the French description of events, and French records also record the incident as being at Samana, but an examination of the manuscript makes it clear that the word, written three times, is *Samana*, not Panama. See Massertie, *"Journal de bord, du 19 mai 1686 au 8 juin 1690"*; Massertie, *"Journal de bord, du 8 juin*

1690 au 4 septembre 1694"; and Tarin de Cussy, "Analyse d'une lettre de Cussy ([1687])."

5   Bradley, *Last Buccaneers*, 18; "Attachment to Monclova to Crown, 31 December, 1691," in Bradley, *Last Buccaneers*, 82, 83; "Attachment to Monclova to Marqués de los Velez," in Bradley, *Last Buccaneers*, 90.

6   Tarin de Cussy, "Le sieur de Cussy à Monseigneur le marquis de Seigneley"; Tarin de Cussy, "Analyse d'une lettre de Cussy ([1687])."

7   Massertie, "*Journal de bord, du 8 juin 1690 au 4 septembre 1694*," 15–17; Polderman, *La Guyane Française*, 68.

8   Tarin, "Mémoire du sieur de Cussy pour Monseigneur le marquis de Seignelay."

9   Buti and Hrodej, *Dictionnaire des Corsaires*, 12–13; Exquemelin, *Histoire des Aventuriers Flibustiers* (1686), eds. Ouellet and Villiers, 503; Little, *Buccaneer's Realm*, 45.

10 Exquemelin, *Les Flibustiers du Nouveau Monde* (1699), ed. Le Bris, 159–72; Buti and Hrodej, *Dictionnaire des Corsaires*, 12–13; Exquemelin, *Histoire des Aventuriers Flibustiers* (1686), eds. Ouellet and Villiers, 503.

11 See for example Rogers, *Cruising Voyage*, 166.

12 [Massertie], *Journal de Bord d'un Flibustier* (1894), 514. Author's translation.

13 This was common practice among pirates. See Ringrose, "Buccaneers of America," 312.

14 Danet, *Complete Dictionary of the Greek and Roman Antiquities*, s.v. "Castor."

15 [Massertie], *Journal de Bord d'un Flibustier* (1894), 516. Author's translation.

16 Ibid., 518. "*jeter un galette á son bord . . .*" Author's translation.

17 In general, see Little, *Sea Rover's Practice*, 134–61.

18 See for example de Lussan, *Journal du Voyage*, throughout.

19 Anon., "Jolly Roger."

20 Commission Départementale des Antiquités, *Mémoires de la Commission*, 528, no. 1027.

21 Castille, *Histoire de la Seconde République*, vol. 1:328.

22 The author has found no primary reference to "*joli rouge*" as the French name of the red banner of pirates or privateers in any period, and no secondary reference until 1921, although the reference does note that the hypothesis has been around for a while. See Anon., "Jolly Roger."

23 Field, "Marines in the Great Naval Mutinies," 743; Jacob, *Military and Religious Life*, 100; Lloyd, *Stratagems of Ierusalem*, 318; Marvel, "Last Instructions to a Painter," 68.

24 In general, see Little, *Sea Rover's Practice*, 111–19.

25 Ringrose, "Buccaneers of America," 300; Downing, *History of the Indian Wars*, 119.

26 Earle, *Pirate Wars*, 153–54.

27 Anon., *Pacquet from Parnassus*, 16.

28 *CSPC 1717–1718*, no. 298; Cordingly, *Under the Black Flag*, 119.

29 Hawkins, "Account of the Pirates in America," 153.

30 Anon., *Journal historique et littéraire*, 292.

31 Gell, *Essay Toward the Amendment*, 323.

32 "Nouvelles d'Espagne, de Portugal, et des Pais-Bas," 335; Nashe, *Christs Teares*, vol. 2:20 (re: Tamerlane); Baldæus, *True and Exact Description*, 766 (re: siege of Colombo, Ceylon, 1655-56); Oliver y Fullana, *Recopilacion Historica de los Reynes*, 248 (re: Turks at Pest, Hungary, 1686); Al-Shaṭi, *Wives of the Prophet*, 92 (re: origin of the Muslim black flag). My thanks to my wife, Mary Crouch, for pointing out this juxtaposition of opposites in black and white flags.

33 Coke, *Third Part of the Institutes*, chap. 49.

34 Preble, *Origin and History of the American Flag*, 52.

35 Franzén, "Kronan: Remants of a Warship's Past," 455.

36 In general regarding Roberts, see Johnson, *General History of the Robberies*, 167–254, and Anon., *Full and Exact Account*, throughout.

37 [Mortier], *Neptune François*, plate 5; Phillips, *Journal of a Voyage*, 212.

38 Hawkins, "Account of the Pirates in America," 152. See Fox, *Jolly Roger*, for the most complete list and description in print of Golden Age pirate flags.

39 Dulaien et al, "Liste charte partie ès règles," 370–71.

40 Poildecoeur, Déclaration du Capitaine, 537 [115]; *Le Nouveau Mercure*, 188.

41 Hawkins, "Account of the Pirates in America," 152.

42 Roggeveen, *Voyage of Commodore Roggewein*, 100–1.

43 *Boston Gazette*, August 15 to 20, 1720, no. 36; *Boston News-Letter*, August 22, 1720.

44 *CSPC 1720–1721*, no. 251i.

45 Ibid.; Anon., "Ring Mottos," 504.

46 Johnson, *General History of the Robberies*, 186–87, 191–92, 202–3.

47 Vignols, *Piraterie sur l'Atlantique*, 353–54 (author's translation); *CSPC 1717–1718*, no. 298; Poildecoeur, Déclaration du Capitaine, 537 [115] (author's translation); Robinson, Deposition of Edmond Robinson, 123.

48 Johnson, *General History of the Robberies*, 196, 202.

49 At least as early as 1812, the skull and crossbones was used on stage performers' clothing to identify a pirate. See for example Anon., "Principal Characters in the Sevens Wonders."

50 Barlow, *Journal*, vol. 2:484.

51 Testimony of John Eaton in Anon., *Tryals of Captain John Rackam*, 25; *Boston News-Letter*, June 9–16, 1718; *The Weekly-Journal or, Saturday's-Post*, April 11, 1718.

52 Beal, *Quelch's Gold*, 52-53.

53 Nicollière-Teijeiro, "Pavillon de Pirate," 281–84; Anon., "Statuts d'un Navire Forban," 223–24; Johnson, *General History of the Robberies*, 38, 42.

54 Nicollière-Teijeiro, "Pavillon de Pirate," 281–84; Anon., "Statuts d'un Navire Forban," 223–24; Vignols, *Piraterie sur l'Atlantique*, 369 (author's translation).

55 Lubbock, *Blackwall Frigates*, 92; Grey, *Pirates of the Eastern Seas*, 16 (facing).

56 Pringle, *Jolly Roger*, 112 (facing); Leip, *Bordbuch des Satans*, 291–92.

57 Cochran et al, *Pirates of the Spanish Main*, 109, 125; Botting, *Pirates*, 48-49.

58 Low's history as described here is based largely on Barlow, "Memorandum of the Transactions," 658–59; Ashton and Barnard, *Ashton's Memorial*; Johnson, *General History of the Robberies*, 284–305; Johnson, *Histoire des Pirates*, 294–311; Dow and Edmonds, *Pirates of the New England Coast*, 141–217; and Little, *How History's Greatest Pirates*, 176–95. Roberts's *Four Years Voyages of Capt. George Roberts* is commonly cited in regard to Low, but the fascinating dialogue comes across as heavily edited, if not entirely invented.

59 Johnson, *General History of the Robberies*, 317.

60 Vignols, *Piraterie sur l'Atlantique*, 353–54.

61 Hawkins, "Account of the Pirates in America," 152.

62 See for example a 1509 printer's mark described in Caille, *Histoire de l'Imprimerie*, vol. 2:77.

63 *Boston News-Letter*, July 25, 1723. This is the description misidentified in some works as that of John Quelch and his crew.

64 *Present State of Europe*, vol. 35, 355–56.

65 Anon., "Jolly Roger."

66 Anon., *Whole Tryal*, 1.

67 Regarding Low and Philips, see *Boston News-Letter*, June 4, 1724, and Johnson, *General History of the Robberies*, 317. Regarding Davis, see Fox, *Jolly Rogers*, 26–27.

68 Brown, *Works of Mr. Thomas Brown*, vol. 2:219.

69 Once each in Anon., *Whole Tryal*, 1, and Hawkins, "Account of the Pirates in America," 152; twice in Johnson, *General History*

of the Robberies, 196, 317. See Fox, *Jolly Rogers*, 26–27, for a possible fifth.

70 Anon., *New Canting Dictionary*, s.v. "Roger."

71 "Jolly Roger Twangdillo" in Playford, *Wit and Mirth*, vol. 2:113; [B. E. Gent.], *New Canting Dictionary*, s.v. "Roger"; Anon., *New Canting Dictionary*, s.v. "Roger."

72 This idea was originally discussed by historians E. T. Fox and David Fictum. See also Fox, *Jolly Rogers*, 26–27.

73 Anon., *New Canting Dictionary*, s.v. "Roger."

74 See Little, *Pirate Hunting*, 192.

75 Stevenson, *Treasure Island* (1911), in particular chapter 15, "I Strike the Jolly Roger"; Scott, *Pirate*, vol. 1:89, vol. 3:309; Simms, *Cassique of Kiawah*, 290. Scott uses both "Jolly Roger" and "Jolly Hodge." Hodge is a form of Roger.

76 Grose, *Classical Dictionary of the Vulgar Tongue*, s.v. "Roger, or Tib of the Buttery"; Smyth, *Sailor's Word-Book*, s.v. "Jolly Roger".

77 Milton, *White Gold*, 11; Witsen et al, *L'Art de Bâtir*, 24 (plate descriptions) and plate 89; Jouvin, *Voyageur d'Europe*, vol. 2:231–33; Dan, *Histoire de Barbarie*, 299; Nieuhoff, *Remarkable Voyages and Travels*, 2; *Boston Gazette*, August 15 to 20, 1720; *Boston News-Letter*, August 22, 1720. The "Pavillon des *Corsaires*" in Witsen et al is clearly a Barbary corsair flag of no quarter. It is printed on a plate of images of North African flags (squarely between *Salé* and *Maroc*, and among other Barbary states), and the description, which denotes a richly appointed flag, aligns with Père Pierre Dan's comment that he had seen Algerine corsair ensigns that were worth more than a thousand or twelve hundred livres. The term *corsaire* in French was reserved for privateers, including Barbary corsairs; *forban* and *pirate* were used for pirates, that is, for sea rovers who sailed without a lawful commission.

78 Crowne, *Ambitious Statesman*, 209. See also, from 1690, Lee, *Massacre of Paris*, 51: "To hang the Flag of a Damn'd Pyrat

forth . . ." Barbary corsairs often fought under foreign flags. See for example *The London Gazette*, April 25, 1670.

79 *The Daily Mail*, June 20, 2007, "Student restores rare Jolly Roger pirate flag to former glory," www.dailymail.co.uk, and December 16, 2011, "Red is for ruthless: Rare Jolly Roger pirate flag captured in north Africa battle 230 years ago goes on show for first time," www.dailymail.co.uk; Marshall, *Royal Naval Biography*, vol. 2:459–70. Curry entered the Royal Navy in 1780, but did not go to sea until 1786. He served in the Egyptian campaign, 1801–1802, and this appears to be the likely source of the flag. Of the three purported authentic "pirate" flags with skull and bones still in existence, the Curry flag had been held in a private collection, but was put on display in the National Museum of the Royal Navy as of 2011. The second is in the Åland Maritime Museum in Finland, and was purchased in North Africa and brought to Finland by a mariner. It may date to the late eighteenth or early nineteenth century. The third is in the St. Augustine Pirate & Treasure Museum in St. Augustine, Florida; the flag exhibit provides a date of 1850, but I was unable to obtain any information on provenance. See *This is Finland*, "Åland treasures maritime memories," June 2012, finland.fi/Public/default. aspx?contentid=250941, and the St. Augustine Pirate & Treasure Museum, www.thepiratemuseum.com.

80 See for example Nieuhoff, *Remarkable Voyages and Travels*, 2, and Jouvin, *Voyageur d'Europe*, vol. 2:231–33.

Chapter 2

1 Roche, *Journals of Jeremy Roche*, 95.
2 This narrative of Blackbeard's blockade of Charlestown is derived from Anon., *Tryals of Major Stede Bonnet*, iii–iv, 8; *CSPC 1717-1718*, nos. 551, 556, 660; *CSPC 1719-1720*, no. 541; and Johnson, *General History of the Robberies*, 46-48, 59-64. For Blackbeard in general, see Johnson, *General History of the*

Robberies; Lee, *Blackbeard the Pirate*; Konstam, *Blackbeard*; Brooks, "Born in Jamaica"; and Fictum, "The Firsts of Blackbeard."

3 For background, see Yonge, *Narrative of the Proceedings*; Hughson, *Carolina Pirates*; Crane, *Southern Frontier*; and Gallay, *Indian Slave Trade*.

4 Crisp et al, "Compleat Description of the Province of Carolina."

5 In general, see Wilde-Ramsing, "Historical Background," 6. See also *CSPC 1717-1718*, no. 298iii regarding possible Dutch origin.

6 Wilde-Ramsing, "Historical Background," 6.

7 Period estimates and reports of the mounted armament of Blackbeard's *Queen Anne's Revenge* varied greatly: 20, 22, 30, 36, 40, and 40 "od[d]" guns (cannon). One report suggested she could mount *as many as* 40. Anything more than thirty guns would require two full decks. However, the size of the ship and its single full deck limited the number of great guns she could carry to a range of 20 to 30, with 20 to 26 most likely. The full accounting may have included various swivel guns. Government officials may also have exaggerated the number of guns in order to solicit a greater naval presence. See *Boston News-Letter*, November 11, 1717; *Boston News-Letter*, June 9, 1718; *CSPC 1717-1718*, nos. 298, 298iii, 551, 556, 660; *Tryals of Major Stede Bonnet*, iii; Wilde-Ramsing, "Historical Background," 8-10; and Little, *Sea Rover's Practice*, 48.

8 *Boston News-Letter*, June 9-16, 1718; *The Weekly-Journal or, Saturday's-Post*, April 11, 1718.

9 Park, *Defensive War by Sea*, 126.

10 Deposition of Henry Bostock, excerpted in Cordingly, *Under the Black Flag*, 165–66; Letter from Mr. Maynard, in *The Weekly Journal or British Gazetteer*, April 25, 1719; Johnson, *General History of the Robberies*, 57.

11 Johnson, *General History of the Robberies*, 57.

12 Ibid.

13　Ibid.

14　Johnson, *General History of the Robberies*, 58.

15　Villehuet, *Manœuverer, or Skilful Seaman*, 214; Villehuet, *Manœuvrier, ou Essai sur la Théorie*, 256; Little, *Sea Rover's Practice*, 72-73; Arnoult, *Portrait de Jean Bart, en Pied*.

16　Johnson, *General History of the Robberies*, 60.

17　*CSPC 1717-1718*, no. 660.

18　In general see Anon., *Tryals of Major Stede Bonnet*.

19　In general see the narrative and quoted documents in Hughson, *Carolina Pirates*, 112-27.

20　Anon., *Tryals of Major Stede Bonnet*, 8; *CSPC 1717-1718*, no. 660.

21　Roche, *Journals of Jeremy Roche*, 95.

22　*Boston News-Letter*, June 16, 1718.

23　Spottiswood, October 22, 1718, in *Official Letters*.

24　This narrative is derived from *The Boston News-Letter*, February 16, 1719, and February 23, 1719; Cooke, *British Newspaper Accounts*; Johnson, *General History of the Robberies*, 50-55; and my extensive research into pirate and anti-pirate tactics, much of which was published in Little, *Sea Rover's Practice*.

25　Johnson, *General History of the Robberies*, 54. Johnson suggests that these bottle-explosives were "new-fashioned." In fact, they were one of several common sorts of improvised explosives used at the time at sea and ashore. See Little, *Sea Rover's Practice*, 72-73.

26　See for example Hope, *New, Short, and Easy Method*, 167.

27　Only a very few maritime cartridge boxes from this era have been recovered. Two are from the Phips expedition wreck of 1690; one is leather with a wooden box liner, the other leather and appears to be unlined, and is flat, with a single row of cartridges. The remnants of several cartridge boxes from the 1704 wreck of the privateer *La Dauphine* are drilled wood blocks to hold cartridges. The box from the 1717 wreck of the pirate ship *Whydah* is leather, with a wooden box liner, similar to that of the Phips box.

28 This narrative speculation on the nature of the swordplay between Maynard and Blackbeard is based on the account in *The Boston News-Letter*, February 23, 1719, and the author's long experience studying historical swordplay.

29 Hope, *New, Short, and Easy Method*, 177.

30 Johnson, *General History of the Robberies*, 54; Letter from Mr. Maynard, in *The Weekly Journal or British Gazetteer*, April 25, 1719.

31 In general see Little, *Buccaneer's Realm*.

32 Brooks, "Born in Jamaica," 279-83. See also Fictum, "The Firsts of Blackbeard."

33 *The Boston News-Letter*, June 19, 1718.

34 Regarding the difficulties of identifying flags at sea, see Little, *Sea Rover's Practice*, 111–19.

35 Johnson, *General History of the Robberies*, 56-58; L'Estrange, *Grand Pyrate*, 7-8.

36 Johnson, *General History of the Robberies*, 302; Johnson, *Histoire des Pirates*, 310–11; Barlow, "Memorandum of the Transactions," 659.

37 Bruckheimer, *MTV News* interview, March 19, 2010.

38 Lee, *Blackbeard*, 3.

39 Ibid., 168.

40 In general see the works of Marcus Rediker, and also Bialuschewski, "Daniel Defoe, Nathaniel Mist." Brooks, "Born in Jamaica," summarizes much of the "pirate as victim and rebel" argument throughout, and other viewpoints as well. The Marxist and similar "pirate as victim" argument ignores the very real nature and existence of the excessive violence that has always accompanied lawless, and often lawful, theft at sea throughout history. See for example Little, *Pirate Hunting*, throughout.

41 See Brooks, "Born in Jamaica," for a summary of scholarly arguments on the subject of Blackbeard and violence.

Chapter 3

1 Exquemelin, *Buccaneers of America* (Crooke, 1684), 111.

2 [Povey?], "Buccaneers on the Isthmus," 97.

3 The narrative of the crossing of the Isthmus of Darien, the attack on Santa Maria, the *armadilla* battle, and the capture of the *Trinity* is taken primarily from [Cox], *Voyages and Adventures*, 1-15; [Dick], "Brief Account of Captain Sharp," 262-66; Peru, Viceroyalty of, *Memorias de los Vireyes*, vol. 1:328; [Povey?], "Buccaneers on the Isthmus," 92-101; Ringrose, *Buccaneer's Atlas*, 124-127; Ringrose, "Buccaneers of America: The Second Volume," 301-28; and Sharp, *Captain Sharp's Journal*, 1-13. Details of buccaneer tactics can be found in Little, *Sea Rover's Practice*; Little, *Buccaneer's Realm*; and Little, *Pirate Hunting*.

4 [Cox], *Voyages and Adventures*, 9.

5 Ringrose, "Buccaneers of America," 307-308.

6 [Cox], *Voyages and Adventures*, 9.

7 Ringrose, "Buccaneers of America," 308.

8 Ibid., 319

9 Ibid., 321.

10 Ibid., 322.

11 [Cox], *Voyages and Adventures*, 13.

12 The author has test-fired a buccaneer gun several hundred times, under a variety of conditions, with a variety of loads in a variety of loading and firing positions, including from a canoe on the water.

13 Ringrose, "Buccaneers of America," 323.

14 Ibid.

15 The author's tests with cutlasses on haunches of meat, and of flintlock pistols fired at close range against targets covered by fabric, demonstrate the power of these hand-to-hand weapons.

16 Ringrose, "Buccaneers of America," 324.

17 Ibid.

18 Peru, Viceroyalty of, *Memorias de los Virreyes*, vol. 1:328. Author's translation.

19 Ringrose, "Buccaneers of America," 325.

20 [Povey?], "Buccaneers on the Isthmus," 100.

21 Exquemelin, *Buccaneers of America* (Crooke, 1684), 212-213.

22 Mallet, *Description de l'Univers*, vol. 1:252. See also Phillips, *Treasure of the San José*, 6-34.

23 Peru, *Memorias de los Vireyes*, 332.

24 Ibid.; [Dick], "Brief Account of Captain Sharp," 266; [Cox], *Voyages and Adventures*, 14; [Povey?], "Buccaneers on the Isthmus," 100; Ringrose, "Buccaneers of America," 328.

25 In general see Gaztañeta e Iturribalzaga, *Arte de Fabricar Reales*; Garrote, *Fábricar de Baseles*; Apestegui, "La Arquitectura Naval Entre 1660 y 1754;" García-Torralba Pérez, *Fragatas de Vela de la Armada Española*; Torres Ramirez, *Armada de Barlovento*; Phillips, *Treasure of the San José*; and Guilmartin, *Galleons and Galleys*.

26 See for example Peru, *Memorias de los Vireyes*, 342.

27 Rogers, *Cruising Voyage*, 150.

28 Exquemelin, *Buccaneers of America* (1684), 144.

29 In general see Little, *Sea Rover's Practice*, 41-56, for a discussion of canoes and other small sea-roving vessels.

30 *CSPC, 1677-1680*, no. 53.

31 Exquemelin, *Buccaneers of America* (Crooke, 1684), 111.

32 See for example Jouve, *Album Levant*, illustrations 4 and 5; du Pas, *Recüeil de Veües*, illustration 19 in the Mediterranean section; and Navarro, *Architectura Naval Antigua y Moderna*, 68.

33 In general see Little, *Sea Rover's Practice*, 54-55; Little, *Buccaneer's Realm*, 14; Baker, *Sloops & Shallops*; and Evans, "Defining Jamaica Sloops."

34 The narrative of the Nathanial & Charles is derived from Council Minutes, July 22, 1718, in State of Pennsylvania, *Minutes of the Provincial Council*, 41-46.

35 Ibid., 42.

36 Ibid.
37 Ibid., 43.
38 Ibid., 44.
39 Ibid.
40 Ibid.
41 See for example Dampier, *New Voyage*, 63, and Snelgrave, *New Account*, in general.
42 The Le Grand narrative is derived from the various early Dutch, Spanish, English, and French editions of Exquemelin's *Buccaneers of America*.
43 Charlevoix, *Histoire de l'Isle Espagnole*, vol. 2:57.
44 Exquemelin, *Buccaneers of America* (Crooke, 1684), 57.
45 Ibid.
46 Little, *Buccaneer's Realm*, 52.
47 Lepers, *Tragique Histoire*, 70; Charlevoix, *Histoire de l'Isle Espagnole*, vol. 2:57.
48 Duro, *Armada Español*, vol. 5:164; Haring, *Buccaneers in the West Indies*, 135, note 1.
49 Rogoziński, *Pirates!*, 194-95.
50 Lepers, *Tragique Histoire*, 70; Charlevoix, *Histoire de l'Isle Espagnole*, vol. 2:57; Marley, *Pirates of the Americas*, 16; Cauna, "Flibustiers Basques et Gascons," 151-52.
51 In general see Pyle, *Howard Pyle's Book of Pirates*.

Chapter 4

1 Anon., *Sad and Dreadful News*, 1.
2 This narrative, its dialogue imagined, is derived largely from Plutarch, *Lives*, 577, and Florus, *Epitome of Roman History*, 361-62.
3 In general see Little, *Pirate Hunting*, 47-69, on the subject of Mediterranean piracy in this era.
4 Plutarch, *Lives*, 577; Paterculus, *Remains of His Compendium*, 479–80; Suetonius, *Suetonius*, vol. 1:5, 7, 95.

5   Plutarch, *Lives*, 510–12.

6   Chaucer, *Canterbury Tales*, 13 (Prologue, "The Sailor"). See also Little, *Pirate Hunting*, 87-109, on Middle Ages piracy.

7   The l'Ollonois narrative is derived primarily from the early Dutch, Spanish, English, and French editions of Exquemelin's *Buccaneers of America*. Except where otherwise noted, the tortures described are taken from Exquemelin.

8   Exquemelin, *Buccaneers of America* (1678), 86.

9   Exquemelin, *Flibustiers*, 128. Author's translation.

10 Exquemelin, *Buccaneers of America* (1678), 84.

11 Ibid., 87.

12 *CSPC 1669-1674*, no. 138.

13 Ibid., 167; Exquemelin, *Buccaneers of America* (Crooke, 1684), 215; Anon., *Sad and Dreadful News*, 1; Robbins, *Encyclopedia of Witchcraft*, s.v. "torture"; Sabatini, *Captain Blood*, 159; Sabatini, *Torquemada*, in general.

14 Exquemelin, *Buccaneers of America* (1678), 87.

15 Ibid., 167.

16 *CSPC 1681-1685*, no. 1,313.

17 Meltons and Edelmans, *Zeldzaame en Gedenkwaardige*, plate following page 206,

18 Personal experience, and Disney Enterprises, *Pirates of the Caribbean* attraction soundtrack, track 3.

19 Exquemelin, *Buccaneers of America* (1678), 123-25.

20 Ibid., 88.

21 *London Gazette*, December 26, 1670.

22 [Povey?], "Buccaneers in the South Sea," 113-14; Ringrose, "Buccaneers of America," 402–5.

23 Labat, *Nouveau Voyages aux Isles*, vol. 6:477-78; Ligon, *True and Exact History*, 5.

24 Anon., *Full and Exact Account*, 39.

25 In general see de Lussan, *Journal du Voyage Fait a la Mer de Sud*, or any of the other editions listed in the bibliography.

26 Exquemelin, *Buccaneers of America* (Crooke, 1684), 139; [Cox], *Voyages and Adventures*, 58.

27 Exquemelin, *Buccaneers of America* (1678), 67.

28 In general see Barlow, "Memorandum of the Transactions," 658-59; Ashton and Barnard, *Ashton's Memorial*; Johnson, *General History of the Robberies*, 284-305; Johnson, *Histoire des Pirates*, 294-311.

29 *CSPC 1669-1674*, no. 138.

30 Avila, "Pillage de la Ville de Veracruz," folio 5.

31 "Abstract, E. I. Co. Letters from Bombay, October 12, 1695," in Jameson, *Privateering and Piracy*, 159.

32 Khafi Khan, "Capture of a Royal Ship by the English," 350-51.

33 "Extract of Suratt General Letter," 17, "Extract of Bombay General Letter," 18, in House of Commons, *Journals of the House of Commons*, vol. 13.

34 South, "Narrative of Captain Thomas South," 17; *American Weekly Mercury*, September 8, 1720.

35 Snelgrave, *New Account*, 256-57.

36 Ibid.

37 Little, *Buccaneer's Realm*, 87-89.

38 Sabatini, *Captain Blood*, 108.

39 Scott, *Pirate*, vol. 3:281.

40 Robinson, *Journal of an Expedition*, 312.

41 This narrative is taken from Hackett, *Narrative of the Expedition*, 119-21, and in general.

42 Ibid., 119-21.

43 Grose, *Classical Dictionary*, s.v. "walking the plank."

44 This narrative is taken from House of Commons, *Observations on the Evidence*, 96-106.

45 Pyle, *Walking the Plank*, illustration.

46 Anon., "Sailor's Definition," 356-57.

47 Barrie, *Peter Pan and Wendy*, 178.

Chapter 5

1 Smith, *New Voyage to Guinea*, 242.

2 Johnson, *General History of the Robberies*, 187.

3 This narrative is derived largely from *American Weekly Mercury*, September 22, 1720; *Boston Gazette*, September 5, 1720; *Weekly Journal*, November 26, 1720; *CSPC 1720-1721*, no. 513; and to a lesser extent Johnson, *General History of the Robberies*, 187-89. Descriptions of blackstrap may be found in Diéreville, *Relation of the Voyage*, 91, 256, and Johnson, *General History of the Robberies*, 312.

4 Johnson, *General History of the Robberies*, 211.

5 *Boston Gazette*, September 5, 1720.

6 *CSPC 1720-1721*, no. 513; *American Weekly Mercury*, September 22, 1720; *Boston Gazette*, September 5, 1720.

7 *CSPC 1720-1721*, no. 463iii.

8 Breverton, *Black Bart Roberts*: the subtitle is *The Greatest Pirate of Them All*.

9 See for example, Little, *Pirate Hunting*, on the great pirate fleets and empires of antiquity and the Middle Ages.

10 See for example Little, *How History's Greatest Pirates*, chapters 11 and 12.

11 *American Weekly Mercury*, September 22, 1720; *Boston Gazette*, September 5, 1720.

12 *Weekly Journal*, November 26, 1720, excerpted in Breverton, *Black Bart Roberts*, 93.

13 See note 8 in this chapter.

14 Johnson, *General History of the Robberies*, 244.

15 Anon., *A Full and Exact Account*, 42-44, 48-49.

16 Ibid., 63.

17 Ibid., 84-86.

18 See for example *Boston Gazette*, September 5, 1720.

19 *American Weekly Mercury*, September 8, 1720; Breverton, *Black Bart Roberts*, 156.

20 Ibid., 21, 56.

21 Dampier, *New Voyage*, 30.

22 *CSPC 1720-1721*, no. 463iii.

23 "Extract of a Letter from Capt. Andrew Kingston," 247-48.

24 Anon., *A Full and Exact Account*, throughout.

25 Rediker, *Slave Ship*, 22.

26 See for example "Extract of a Letter from Capt. Andrew Kingston," 247, and, Anon., *Full and Exact Account*, v, 8.

27 Johnson, *General History of the Robberies*, 203–4.

28 Anon., *Full and Exact Account*, iv, 27, 39, 40. See also Johnson, *General History of the Robberies*, 203-4.

29 Ibid.

30 Johnson, *General History of the Robberies*, 195-96.

31 Ibid.

32 Sanders, *If a Pirate I Must Be*, 18.

33 Anon., *Tryals of Captain John Rackam*, 20; Johnson, *General History of the Robberies*, 211. The term "black man" could also mean a man of African descent. Full context is everything, but is often lacking.

34 *CSPC 1720-1721*, no. 501; Anon., *Full and Exact Account*, 46.

35 Johnson, *General History of the Robberies*, 212.

36 Anon., *Full and Exact Account*, 5.

37 This narrative is derived from Anon., *Full and Exact Account*, iv–vi, 3-8, with additional details throughout; Atkins, *Voyage to Guinea*, 191-94, 262-63; and Johnson, *General History of the Robberies*, 205-11, 236-38.

38 Regarding the distance of pistol shot as "yardarm to yardarm," see Duguay-Trouin, *Memoirs of M. du Gué-Trouin*, 91.

39 Anon., *Full and Exact Account*, 69, 70, 73.

40 *Weekly Journal: Or, Saturday's Post*, June 20, 1724; Johnson, *General History of the Robberies*, 283; *American Weekly Mercury*, June 20, 1723; Fillmore, *Narration of the Captivity*, 16.

41 Fillmore, *Narration of the Captivity*, 16. John Fillmore was the great-grandfather of President Millard Fillmore.

Chapter 6

1 Everard, *Relation of Three Years Sufferings*, 259.

2 The Bennett narrative is derived from the somewhat sparse details in *CSPC 1674-1675*, no. 1,129; *CSPC 1677-1681* nos. 203, 203i, 2203ii; Maggs, *Voyages and Travels*, vol. 5:323, summarized from the Letter-book of Henry Coventry, 1674-1679; Marley, *Pirates of the Americas*, 43; Ximénez, *Historia de la Provincia*, 381 (book 5, chapter 30); and the author's research, detailed in *Sea Rover's Practice* and *Buccaneer's Realm*, on how attacks at sea were conducted.

3 *CSPC 1677–1681*, no. 203ii; "A List of Ships Under the Command of Admiral Morgan," PRO CO 138/1, f. 105, reprinted in *Life of Sir Henry Morgan*, appendix 1.

4 Marley, in *Pirates of the Americas*, 47, describes Bennett's crew as twenty men.

5 Little, *Buccaneer's Realm*, 226-27, 251.

6 See Little, *Sea Rover's Practice*, 120-28, for details on chasing at sea.

7 Blunt, *American Coast Pilot*, 430-31.

8 See Little, *Sea Rover's Practice*, 79-83, for details on buccaneer intelligence gathering.

9 "A List of Ships Under the Command of Admiral Morgan," PRO CO 138/1, f. 105, reprinted in *Life of Sir Henry Morgan*, appendix 1.

10 Exquemelin, *Buccaneers of America* (1678), 117.

11 Taylor, *Jamaica in 1687*, 106–7; *CSPD James II*, vol. 2, no. 961.

12 *CSPC 1685-1688*, no. 678v.

13 Anon., "Letters Concerning the English Expedition," 142.

14 Anon., Diseño ó plano del Fuerte y Plataforma de San Vicente, en Santa Marta.

15 Sabatini, *Captain Blood*, 89-90; *Captain Blood*, Warner Brothers, 1935; Desjeans, *Relation de l'Expédition de Carthagène*, in general; Downing, *Compendious History*, in general.

16 Laprise, "Débuts de la Carrier de Laurens De Graffe," 6, suggests circumstantially that it may have been Jean de Grammont commanding the smaller vessel. His account, along with that in *CSPC 1677-1680*, no. 53, notes only two attacking vessels. The Spanish account, however, notes three. See Guardiola and Padilla, eds., *Revista del Archivo*, 91.

17 Ximénez, *Historia de la Provincia*, 381 (libro 5, capitulo 30).); "Registro del navío: 'San Pablo, 'AGI, Contratacion,1227,N.1. Some of the vessel's *registros* and lists of goods, as well as Ximénez, give the ship's name as *el gran San Pablo*, although other *registros* note only *San Pablo*. See for example, "Registro del navío: 'San Pablo,' AGI, Contratacion,1230,N.3, and "Bienes de difuntos: Domingo Caravallo," AGI, Contratacion,460,N.2,R.1. Spanish tonnage was often calculated as either merchantman or man-of-war. In *toneladas de guerra*, the *San Pablo* would be roughly 544 tons.

18 *CSPC 1675-1676*, no. 1129.

19 This account is derived from *CSPC 1677-1680*, no. 53; Ximénez, *Historia de la Provincia*, 381 (libro 5, capitulo 30); Laprise, "Débuts de la Carrier de Laurens De Graffe," 5-6; Marley, *Pirates of the Americas*, 43; Exquemelin, *Buccaneers of America* (1699), 84-85; Exquemelin, *Flibustiers*, 139; Exquemelin, *Histoire des Avanturiers,* vol. 1:275-76; Milla and Carrillo, *Historia de la America Central*, vol. 2:359; Camus, *L'Île de la Tortue*, 77; *Dictionnaire de l'Académie Française*, 1st ed., 1694, s.v. "saucisson"; Pérez Valenzuela, *Historias de Piratas*, 85; Little, *Buccaneer's Realm*, 73-75, 79-81; and the author's research, detailed in *Sea Rover's Practice* and *Buccaneer's Realm*, on how attacks at sea were conducted.

20 Cooper, *Red Rover*, vol. 2:295.

21 Ximénez, *Historia de la Provincia*, 381 (libro 5, capitulo 30). See also Milla and Carrillo, *Historia de la America Central*, vol. 2:359.

22 Ximénez, *Historia de la Provincia*, 381 (libro 5, capitulo 30). Author's translation, with the significant assistance of Mary Crouch.

23 Ibid. Santa Rosa de Lima was canonized in 1671.

24 *CSPC 1677–1680*, no. 53.

25 Regarding the honorific "sieur de Graff," see for example Vaissière, *Origines de la Colonisation*, 70.

26 Exquemelin, *Flibustiers*, 165-66; Avila, "Pillage de la ville de Veracruz," folio 2; *CSPC 1681-1685*, nos. 1,461, 1,649m 1,718; *CSPC 1689-1692*, no. 980; Vetancurt, *Chronica de la Provincia*, 77; Laprise, "Débuts de la Carrier de Laurens De Graffe," 1-10; Lepers, *Tragique Histoire*, 219. Occasionally one hears that the foregoing description of de Graff was written by Charlevoix in the eighteenth century, but it is in fact from Exquemelin, cited above, who probably met de Graff in 1697 in Saint-Domingue when the buccaneer-surgeon is believed to have served with de Pointis's expedition against Cartagena.

27 See for example Avila, "Pillage de la ville de Veracruz," folio 2, and Vetancurt, *Chronica de la Provincia*, 77. Avila notes that he was a gunner or a pilot.

28 Linaje, *Rule of Trade*, 349-52.

29 Marley, *Pirates of the Americas*, vol. 1:362-363.

30 Laprise, "Débuts de la Carrier de Laurens De Graffe," 5.

31 Ibid.

32 In general see Laprise, "Débuts de la Carrier de Laurens De Graffe," 1-10, and Marley, *Pirates of the Americas*, vol. 1:98-107, 362-63.

33 *CSPC 1681–1685*, no. 158.

34 Ibid., no. 709.

35 Exquemelin, *Buccaneers of America* (Malthus, 1684), 10.

36 *CSPC 1681-1685*, no. 709.

37 This narrative is derived from *CSPC 1681-1685*, no. 1563; de Lussan, *Journal du Voyage*, 11; Registro: Asiento de Negros, AGI, Indiferente, 2768, L.4, 140-141, 171; Juarez Moreno, *Cosarios y*

Piratas, 290-91; Gasser, "Les Mystérieuses Disparitions," 222-24; Marley, *Pirates of the Americas*, vol. 1:102-103; Reynado, *Collecion de los Tradados*, 497-98; Scelle, *La Traite Négrière*, 647, 654-55; and Tarin de Cussy, "Le sieur de Cussy à Monseigneur le Marquis de Seignelay". AGI 171 above, Scelle, and *Collecion de los Tradados* list the ships as the *San Francisco Javier* and the *San Joseph*; Lynch's letter names them *St. Francisco* and *Lapaz*; de Cussy's letter includes no names. De Cussy, and Gasser via de Cussy's letter, note the *San Francisco* as armed with 48 guns, the *La Paz* with 40; de Lussan notes that the ships later were armed with 50 and 44 guns, respectively; Juarez Moreno notes 40 and 35, respectively; Marley, 40 and 34; Lynch does not mention armament; Scelle, quoting Spanish documents, notes original armaments in Spain as 34 and 38 guns; Reynado notes their original Spanish armaments as 34 and 30 (either Scelle or Reynado have misread the original document). Juarez Moreno, citing Spanish documents, describes the galliot as armed with 28 guns, most of which must surely have been swivels. Regarding the number of guns carried aboard ship, usually the number was even, but odd numbers are seen in various records.

38 *CSPC 1681-1685*, no. 1563

39 This narrative is derived from Exquemelin, *Flibustiers*, 166-68; "Analyse d'une lettre de Cussy ([1687])"; Moreno, *Corsarios y Piratas*, 375-89; Gasser, "Les Mystérieuses Disparitions," 240-42; Torres Ramirez, *Armada de Barlovento*, 133-35; Marley, *Pirates of the Americas*, 107–8; de Lussan, *Journal du Voyage*, 11. Juarez Moreno's account, relying heavily on and quoting original sources, is the most detailed secondary account.

40 The *Nuestra Señora de Jonjon* is referred to in period Spanish documents as both an *urca* and a *fragata*, and more generally as a *navio* (ship) and a *bajel de velas* (sailing vessel). The reference to *urca* in this case may be to the distinct hull of the ship or possibly to its being originally used as a cargo vessel, although the common term was *navio mercante*. *Urcas* and *fragatas* were distinct

ship types. Small to medium *urcas* (fluyts) were suitable as *guar-das costas*, given their flat bottoms and often shallow drafts, but so were small frigates. Regarding the ship's name, Spanish documents of 1682 tend to use the spelling *Jonjon*; documents of 1686 noting her sale and decommissioning from the Armada de Barlovento, as well as most modern historians, use *Honhon*. I have used *Jonjon* both for its place in early documents as well for as its modern association with both Yucatan and the Virgin of Jonjon. See Cartas del Virrey Marques de la Laguna, AGI, Mexico, 52, no.10, 28 February 1681, 1–8; Cartas del Virrey Marques de la Laguna, AGI, Mexico, 53, R. 2, no. 24, 30 December 1682, 1-9; Registro: Armada de Barlovento, AGI, Indiferente, 2516, L.4, 570-75 (26 June 1686), 596-97 (3 April 1686); and endnote 60 below.

41 López Cogolludo, *Historia de Yucathan*, libro IV, cap. XIX, 233; Hidrografía [Spain, Dept. of], *Derrotero de las Islas Antillas*, 402–03, s.v. "Nuestra Señora de Jonjon"; Orozco y Berra, *Apéndice al Diccionario Universal*, 706; Benevides C., *Ecab, Poblado y Provincia*, 17, 61-62.

42 Torres Ramirez, *Armada de Barlovento*, 115-16, 314. The French give the number of guns as 60 and 56, respectively. See "Analyse d'une lettre de Cussy ([1687])."

43 Agarat, "Plan de Porto Bello." Both ships were in Portobello in 1682 in disrepair. See Torres Ramirez, *Armada de Barlovento*, 122-23; Marley, *Pirates of the Americas*, vol. 1:32. The Agarat chart describes the Burgos as the "Gallion pour la deffence du Port," and the *Conceptión* as the "Vaisseau pour la deffence du Port," which were their duties at the time.

44 See for example Garrote, *Fábricar de Baseles*. The usual Dutch stern construction would need to have been modified in order to support these galleries.

45 Regarding great guns of the Armada de Barlovento, see García-Torralba Pérez, *Las Fragatas de Vela*, 53-54, 64.

46 Ibid.

47 de Lussan, *Journal du Voyage*, 11.

48 Exquemelin, *Flibustiers*, 166. Author's translation.

49 See for example Rogers, *Cruising Voyage*, 299.

50 Ibid., 166-68; Sabatini, *Captain Blood*, 219-23.

51 *The Handbook of Texas Online*, Texas State Historical Association, http://www.tshaonline.org, s.v. "Armada de Barlovento." Robert S. Weddle is cited as the entry's author.

Chapter 7

1 Pitman, *Relation of the Great Sufferings*, 19.

2 This narrative is derived primarily from *CSPC 1685-1688*, nos. 210, 505, 602, 617x, 1,356, and 1,522; associated documentation in Lefroy, *Memorials of the Discovery*, 543-52; and Ringrose, *Buccaneer's Atlas*, 32.

3 *CSPC 1685-1688*, no. 210.

4 Ibid., no. 552.i.

5 The author has not located this exact title, even in reference. However, it almost certainly is a misquote for *English Liberties: or, the Freeborn Subject's Inheritance*, published in 1680 and an object of confiscation by the government of James II. See [Cary], *English Liberties*, and *CSPD James II*, vol. 1, no. 1,885. There are also texts that argue in opposition, most notably Nalson's *The Complaint of Liberty*, published in 1681.

6 *CSPC 1685-1688*, no. 210.

7 "Analyse d'une lettre de Cussy ([1687])"; [Povey], "Buccaneers on the Isthmus," 98, and throughout; Little, *How History's Greatest Pirates*, 120-37.

8 *CSPC 1681-1685*, no. 1522.

9 See for example Serrano Mangas, "Proceso del Pirata Bartholomew Sharp."

10 *CSPC 1685-1688*, no. 210.

11 Ibid., no. 505.

12 Ibid., no. 602.

13 Ibid., no. 617x.

14 Ibid., no. 617iv; William Peniston, paraphrased in Ringrose, *Buccaneer's Atlas*, 32.

15 *CSPC 1685-1688*, no. 1,356.

16 Olsen, "Sørøvere i Vestindien," 8.

17 Snelgrave, *New Account*, 225.

18 Ibid., 216.

19 Anon., *Full and Exact Account*, 45.

20 Thucydides, *Peloponnesian War*, 350.

21 Anon., *Importance of Jamaica*, 23.

22 See for example *CSPC 1681-1685*, no. 1,163. The examples are numerous during the last quarter of the seventeenth century and well into the eighteenth.

23 *CSPC 1716-1717*, no. 158vii.

24 See for example *CSPC 1716-1717*, nos. 158iii, 308.

25 See for example Saleban Aadan Barqad, quoted by the Associated Press, "US Navy attacks Somali 'pirates,'" *TimesOnline*, March 20, 2006, http://www.timesonline.co.uk/.

26 Ibid., 253.

27 Anon., *Trials of Eight Persons*, 11.

28 In general see Little, *Pirate Hunting*, 162-67.

29 Little, *Sea Rover's Practice*, 34-38; Little, *Buccaneer's Realm*, 223-29.

30 Anon., *Full and Exact Account*, 68.

31 *CSPC 1681-1685*, no. 740; G.H.C. Bulletin 78, January 1996, 1527, *Généalogie et Histoire de la Caraïbe*, accessible at www.ghcaraibe.org.

32 de Lussan, *Journal du Voyage*, 18.

33 Agreement to Commit Piracy, June 30, 1683 in Jameson, *Privateering and Piracy*, 142; Little, *Buccaneer's Realm*, 223-24.

34 Little, *Buccaneer's Realm*, 10.

35 *CSP 1681-1685*, no. 1863iv.

36 This narrative is drawn largely from Pitman, *Relation of the Great Sufferings*.

37 Ibid., 3.

38 Ibid.

39 Ibid., 5.

40 Macaulay, *History of England*, vol. 1:596.

41 Pitman, *Relation of the Great Sufferings*, 10-12.

42 Ibid., 14.

43 In general see Worth, *Struggle for the Georgia Coast*, for background.

44 Pitman, *Relation of the Great Sufferings*, 20.

45 Ibid., 19.

46 Ibid., 27.

Chapter 8

1 al-Mûsili, *An Arab's Journey*, 84.

2 This narrative is derived from Sterre, *Zeer Aanmerkelijke Reysen*, 22-23, 52; Vrijman, *Dr. David Van der Sterre*, 55-72; the early Dutch, Spanish, English, and French editions of Exquemelin's *The Buccaneers of America*; Marley, *Pirates of the Americas*, vol. 1:147-51; Snelders, *Devil's Anarchy*, 116-20; with additional analysis and commentary based on the author's study and practice of historical swordplay.

3 *CSPC 1661-1668*, no. 1,894.

4 Dampier, *New Voyage*, 30.

5 Exquemelin, *Buccaneers of America* (Crooke, 1684), 73.

6 Sloane, *Voyage to the Islands*, vol. 1:lxxiii.

7 In general, see Little, *Sea Rover's Practice*, for buccaneer tactics at sea.

8 Exquemelin, *Buccaneers of America* (1678), 66.

9 Sterre, *Zeer Aanmerkelijke Reysen*, 23; Vrijman, *Dr. David Van der Sterre*, 64; Hexham and Manly, *Copious English and Netherdutch Dictionary*, s.v. "sabel," "sabelen"; Miège, *New Dictionary, French and English*, s.v. "sable."

10 Hope, *New, Short, and Easy Method*, 132-133; Page, *Use of the Broad Sword*, 17-19.

11 *Merriam-Webster's 11th Collegiate Dictionary*, s.v. "snickersnee."

12 Sterre, *Zeer Aanmerkelijke Reysen*, 23.

13 Ibid., 52.

14 Dampier, *Voyages and Discoveries*, 162.

15 Wiseman, *Several Chirurgicall Treatises*, 399-400.

16 Exquemelin, *Bucaniers of America* (Malthus, 1684), 44-45.

17 Cornuau, "Plan de la Petite-Rivière de Léogane."

18 Park, *Defensive War by Sea*, 71.

19 Exquemelin, *Flibustiers*, 150.

20 Smith, *New Voyage to Guinea*, 66-67.

21 Gaya, *Treatise of the Arms*, 11-12.

22 Khan, "Capture of a Royal Ship by the English," 350.

23 See for example Duguay-Trouin, *Memoirs of M. du Gué-Trouin*, 22; [Walker?], *Commodore Walker*, 158-159.

24 Exquemelin, *Buccaneers of America* (1678), 59-60, 109-110; Exquemelin, *Flibustiers*, 74.

25 Johnson, *General History of the Robberies*, 232.

26 Goslinga, *Dutch in the Caribbean*, 245.

27 See Anon., *Remarks on the Life and Death*.

28 Sabatini, *Captain Blood*, 166.

29 Ibid., 167.

30 Sabatini, *Black Swan*, 249; McBane, *Expert Sword-Man's Companion*, 21; Hope, *New, Short, and Easy Method*, 110-112; Hope, *Compleat Fencing-Master*, 100-102. For more detail on swordplay in Sabatini novels, see Heredia, *Romantic Prince: Reading Rafael*.

31 Email, Ruth Heredia to the author, January 8, 2016. See also Behlmer, ed., *The Sea Hawk*, 12, quoting Grant Overton quoting Sabatini. For a thorough understanding of the literary and historical influences on Rafael Sabatin, see Heredia, *Romantic Prince: Seeking Sabatini*.

32 Johnson, *General History of the Robberies*, 195.

33 In general, see Little, *Sea Rover's Practice*, and Little, *Buccaneer's Realm*.

34 See for example Anon., *Full and Exact Account*, 62, 74.

35 Vrijman, *Dr. David Van der Sterre*, 56-57; Duguay-Trouin, *Memoirs of M. du Gué-Trouin*, 15.

36 This account is drawn largely from Avila, "Pillage de la ville de Veracruz," folio 10; Exquemelin, *Flibustiers*, 173-76; Anon. [Philip Ayers?], *Captain Van Horn's Taking*, 119-20; *CSPC 1681-1685*, nos. 963, 1,163; al-Mûsili, *An Arab's Journey*, 84; and Marley, *Sack of Veracruz*, 57-58.

37 Exquemelin, *Flibustiers*, 173.

38 *CSPC 1681-1685*, no. 1,163.

39 Exquemelin, *Flibustiers*, 173.

40 Avila, "Pillage de la ville de Veracruz," folio 10. Author's translation, with many thanks for the assistance of Mary Crouch.

41 "Demande de pardon du capitaine Laurens De Graff," 25 January 1685.

Chapter 9

1 Taylor, *Jamaica in 1687*, 240.

2 Moon, planet, and star positions were checked via several means, including Stellarium software, version 0.11.1. An estimated position off Point Negril, Jamaica, was determined, from which latitude and longitude were taken; the position did not need to be exact. The Julian date was converted to Gregorian.

3 Hamilton, "Answer," 73.

4 This narrative is derived primarily from Anon., *Tryals of Captain John Rackam*, and Johnson, *General History of the Robberies*, 118-41. The accounts have been interpreted through my study of sea roving and pirate hunting tactics.

5 Hamilton, "Answer," 70-73.

6 Ibid., 52; *CSPC 1716-1717*, no. 308.

7 Johnson, *General History of the Robberies*, 127.

8 Hawkins, "Account of the Pirates in America," 149.

9 The range is noted in Povey, *Sea-Gunners Companion*, 42, and matches the author's experience with test firings of a swivel gun loading with musketballs.

10 The dialogue is based on eyewitness testimony in Anon., *Tryals of Captain John Rackam*, 14.

11 Willocks, "Narrative," 144.

12 Anon., *Tryals of Captain John Rackam*, 19; Johnson, *General History of the Robberies*, 122.

13 Johnson, *General History of the Robberies*, 131.

14 Johnson, *General History of the Robberies*, 141.

15 Anon., *Tryals of Captain John Rackam*, 14.

16 Ibid., 18.

17 [Head], *English Rogue: Described*, 272.

18 Johnson, *General History of the Robberies*, 108.

19 In general regarding women pirates, seafarers, and warriors during this period, see Appleby, *Women and English* Piracy; Creighton, *Iron Men, Wooden Women*; Druett, *She Captains*; Dugaw, *Warrior Women and Popular Balladry*; Eastman, *Pirate Trial*; Stanley, *Bold in Her Breeches*; Stark, *Female Tars*; and Vázquez, *Mujeres Piratas*. Klausmann, *Women Pirates*, is occasionally cited by historians but is highly speculative and unreliable.

20 Exquemelin, *Flibustiers*, 116; Vázquez, *Mujeres Piratas*, 201-205; Jaeger, *Femmes d'Abordage*, 56-62. See also Treich, *Gentilshommes de la Flibuste*.

21 Regarding these "pseudo-memoirs," see Mylne, *Eighteenth-Century French Novel*, 39.

22 In general see Courtilz de Sandras, *Memoires de Madame la Marquise de Fresne*; Mylne, *Eighteenth-Century French Novel*, 39; Woodbridge, "À Propos d'un Prisonnier," 373-77; Tallemant des Réaux, *Historiettes*, 407.

23 Records associated with the privateering activities of Lars and Ingela Gathenhielm are identified and summarized in Bes et al, *Baltic Connections*, vol. 1:2023-24.

24 This narrative is derived from Lepers, *Tragique Histoire*, 90-91, 201-202; 219; Charlevoix, *Histoire de l'Isle* Espagnole, vol. 2:270-71, 291-92; Vaissière, *Origines de la Colonisation*, 70; Chapin, *Buccaneers*, 246 note 2; *Relations et Mémoires Inédits*, 282; Laprise, "Débuts de la Carrier de Laurens De Graffe," throughout; G.H.C. Bulletin 12, January 1990, 96-97; *Généalogie et Histoire de la Caraïbe*, accessible at www.ghcaraibe. org; G.H.C. Bulletin 78, January 1996, 1527, *Généalogie et Histoire de la Caraïbe*, accessible at www.ghcaraibe.org; "Brevet de naturalité pour Laurent de Graff et sa femme"; "Au Marquis d'Harcourt au Sujet de Rapatriement de Madame *de Graff*"; "Au Marquis d'Harcourt au Sujet du Retour des Prisonniers"; del Monte y Tejada, *Historia de Santo Domingo*, vol. 3:53.

25 Joutel, *Last Voyage*, 9-10.

26 Lepers, *Tragique Histoire*, 90-91.

27 d'Auger, "Analyse d'une lettre d'*Auger* (Charles)," in which de Graff's death is noted. Note also, "*Baldran de Graff (Laurent Corneille)*, dit Laurencillo, gentilhomme de port établi en *Hollande*, à la Martinique, lettres de naturalité (5 août 1685), brevet de grâce ayant tué son associé (13 août 1685), major à la *Tortue* (30 septembre 1686), lieutenant de roi (1er juin 1691), ordre de venir à la cour (23 mars 1696), capitaine de frégate (26 septembre 1697), décédé à Saint-Domingue en 1704."

28 G.H.C. Bulletin 78, January 1996, 1527, *Généalogie et Histoire de la Caraïbe*, accessible at www.ghcaraibe.org.

29 "Examination of John Dann, August 3, 1696," in Jameson, *Piracy and Privateering*, 171.

30 *CSPC 1685-1688*, no. 1,382.

31 This narrative is derived primarily from *CSPC 1685-1688*, nos. 678x, 768, 913, 1,111, 1,111i, 1,111ii, 1,356, 1,382, 1,405,

1,449, 1,624, 1,733, 1,733i, and Little, *Buccaneer's Realm*, 35, 62, 67, 69-70, 167, 213, 219, 236.

32 *CSPC 1685-1688*, no. 1,382.

33 See Eruaso, *Lieutenant Nun*.

34 See Arzáns de Orsúa y Vela, *Tales of Potosí*, 58-70.

35 See Letainturier-Fradin, *La Maupin*.

36 Casanova, *History of My Life*, vol. 2, chapter 2.

37 In general see Burg, *Sodomy and the Pirate Tradition*.

38 The argument that pirates of this era were functioning homosexual communities is overwhelmed by the evidence against it, including eyewitness accounts of the large number female prostitutes in pirate ports, there to practice their trade with pirates. It also faces the non sequitur of a purportedly homosexual pirate crew throwing one of its own in irons for sodomy. See Little, *Buccaneer's Realm*, 169, 297 note 25.

39 Snelgrave, *New Account*, 256-57; Anon., *Full and Exact Account*, 34.

40 Phillips, *Journal of a Voyage*, 179. Murdoch, in "John Brown: A Black Female Soldier in the Royal African Company," states that she was a black (of African descent) woman, based on Phillips description: "a likely black girl." Captain Phillips used the terms "black" and "blacks" to describe Africans, but the term "black girl" could also mean a white woman with black hair and dark (i.e. olive) complexion. Phillips also uses the terms "negro" and "negroes," but not "African" or "Africans."

41 Geena Davis, "Eye Candy," 1.

42 Polybius, *Histories*, vol. 1:249-59.

43 See Chambers, *Ireland's Pirate Queen*; Chambers, "'The Pirate Queen of Ireland': Grace O'Malley"; Murray, "Cheng I Sao in Fact and Fiction"; Murray, *Pirates of the South China Coast*; Yunlun, *History of the Pirates*.

44 Graves, *Greek Myths*, 525–526;

45 Arzáns, *Tales of Potosí*, 58.

Chapter 10

1   Gage, *New Survey*, 428-29.

2   [Povey], "Buccaneers on the Isthmus," 115.

3   This account is derived from Cooke, *Voyage to the South Sea*, vol. 1:290-92; [Cox], *Voyages and Adventures*, 54-60; Dagnino, *Correjimiento de Arica*, 136-38; Dampier, *New Voyage*, 175-76; [Dick], "Brief Account of Captain Sharp," 274-75; Little, *Buccaneer's Realm*, 181-82; Little, *Sea Rover's Practice*, 1-9, 214-18; Peru, Viceroyalty of, *Memorias de los Virreyes*, vol. 1:237-38, 251, 334-35; [Povey?], "Buccaneers on the Isthmus," 114-15; Ringrose, *Buccaneer's Atlas*, 18-19, 215-16; Ringrose, "Buccaneers of America: The Second Volume," 404-409; Sharp, *Captain Sharp's Journal*, 47-48; and Wafer, *New Voyage & Description*, 121. Details of buccaneer tactics ashore can be found in Little, *Buccaneer's Realm*, 171-87.

4   Arzáns, *Tales of Potosí*, 116.

5   [Cox], *Voyages and Adventures*, 55.

6   Ibid., 57.

7   Ibid., 70-71.

8   Johnson, *General History of the Robberies*, 150.

9   Anon., *Full and Exact Account*, 8.

10 *CSPC 1720-1721*, 463iii.

11 [Cox], *Voyages and Adventures*, 79.

12 Anon., *Full and Exact Account*, 74. See also 55, 76.

13 Gage, *New Survey*, 428-29; Little, *How History's Greatest Pirates*, 66-83.

14 *CSPC 1675-1676*, no. 1178.

15 *CSPC 1716-1717*, nos. 158v, 158vii, 308, 604i.

16 Massertie, "Journal de Bord" (1894), 482.

17 See for example Exquemelin, *Flibustiers*, 165-66.

18 Avila, "Pillage de la ville de Veracruz," folio 2; Vetancurt, *Chronica de la Provincia*, 77.

19 Laprise, "Débuts de la Carrier de Laurens De Graffe," 1-10; Exquemelin, *Flibustiers*, 165-66.

20 Shelvocke, *Voyage Around the World*, 219-224.

21 Gardiner, "Copy of the Narrative," 30.

22 *CSPC 1700*, no. 354xvii; *CSPD William III*, vol. 11, 348.

23 See for example Phillips, *Journal of a Voyage*, throughout.

24 *CSPC 1700*, no. 354xvii.

25 Weddle, *Wilderness Manhunt*, 72; Juarez Moreno, *Corsarios y Piratas*, 287, 303; Wright, "Andrew Ranson," 140, 144.

26 Ringrose, "Buccaneers of America," 323-24.

27 *CSPC 1681-1685*, no. 1163.

28 Dampier, *Voyages and Discoveries*, 148-149.

29 Ringrose, "Buccaneers of America," 435-36; *CSPC 1681-1685*, no. 872; *CSPC 1685-1688*, no. 1,313.

30 This account is derived from Anon., *Tryals of Major Stede Bonnet*, iii–vi, 28-31.

31 Ibid., v.

32 Ibid.

33 Ibid., 30.

34 Ibid.

35 Ibid., 31.

Chapter 11

1 "Earl of Bellomont to the Lords of Trade, July 22, 1699," in Brodhead and Bailey, *Documents Relative to the Colonial History*, vol. 4:532.

2 St. Augustine, *City of God*, 4.4.

3 Johnson, *General History of the Robberies*, 482.

4 This narrative is taken from Johnson, *General History of the Robberies*, 340-72.

5 Johnson, *General History of the Robberies*, 348.

6 Ibid., 398.

7 Ibid.

8 In general see Racault, "De l'Aventure Flibustière," 243-264.

9 In general see Rogoziński, *Honor Among Thieves*.

10 Baldridge, "Deposition of Adam Baldridge," 184; Johnson, *General History of the Robberies*, 416.

11 Deposition of Jeremiah Tay, July 6, 1694" and "Deposition of Samuel Perkins, August 25, 1698," in Jameson, *Privateering and Piracy*, 150, 177; *CSPC 1697-1698*, nos. 473, 473ii, 473xvii, 904.

12 Anon., *Mery Tales*, 134-136.

13 Alaux and t'Serstevens, *Memoirs of a Buccaneer*, v–vi; Johnson, *General History of the Robberies*, 430.

14 Downing, *Compendious History*, 92.

15 See Leguat, *New Voyage to the East-Indies*.

16 See Tyssot de Patot, *Voyages et Avantures*, throughout, and Rosenberg, *Tyssot de Patot*, 84-85.

17 This narrative is drawn primarily from "Examination of John Dann, August 3, 1696," 165-71; "Deposition of Samual Perkins, August 25, 1698," 175-78; "Deposition of Adam Baldridge, May 5, 1699," 180-87; "Examination of Edward Buckmaster, June 6, 1699," in Jameson, *Privateering and Piracy*, 198-99; "Lords of Trade to the Earl of Bellomont, October 25, 1698," in Brodhead and Bailey, *Documents Relative to the Colonial History*, vol. 4:412-14; Cruger, "John Cruger's Report of his Voyage," 466-68, in Valentine, *Manual of the Corporation of the City*.

18 Dellon, *Voyage*, 19.

19 Ibid.

20 "Deposition of Adam Baldridge, May 5, 1699," 181.

21 Ovington, *Voyage to Suratt*, 103.

22 "Examination of Edward Buckmaster, June 6, 1699," in Jameson, *Privateering and Piracy*, 198-99; *CSPC 1699*, no. 512.

23 *CSPC 1699*, no. 530i; "Examination of John Dann, August 3, 1696," 168, in Jameson, *Privateering and Piracy*.

24 "Deposition of Adam Baldridge, May 5, 1699," 180 note 2, in Jameson, *Privateering and Piracy*.

25 *CSPC 1699*, no. 384.

26 "Lords of Trade to the Earl of Bellomont, October 25, 1698," in Brodhead and Bailey, *Documents Relative to the Colonial History*, vol. 4:413.

27 Cruger, "John Cruger's Report of his Voyage," 467, in Valentine, *Manual of the Corporation*.

28 This account is drawn primarily from John Plantain's narrative, and of various descriptions of, in Downing, *Compendious History*, throughout.

29 Downing, *Compendious History*, 114.

30 Ibid., 129.

31 Ibid., 133.

Chapter 12

1 May, *Account of the Wonderful Preservation*, vol. 6:345.

2 *Boston News-Letter*, August 22, 1720.

3 This account of the sack of Veracruz and Grammont's journey afterward is drawn from Avila, "Pillage de la Ville de Veracruz," throughout; Anon., *Captain Van Horn's Taking*, 115-20; CSPC *1681-1685*, no. 1163; Dampier, *Discoveries*, 209-210; "Declaration of Juan Clar," in Worth, *Struggle for the Georgia Coast*, 149-51; Exquemelin, *Flibustiers*, 159-164; Gasser, "Les Mystérieuses Disparitions," 218-20; Gemelli Careri, *Voyage*, 526-27, 539; Joutel, *Last Voyage*, 189-91; Juarez Moreno, *Cosarios y Piratas*, 165-254; Marley, *Sack of Veracruz*, throughout; Anon., "Relation du voyage des Flibustiers"; and Uring, *Voyages*, 148-49.

4 Exquemelin, *Flibustiers*, 331.

5 See for example Lugo-Fernández et al, "Analysis of the Gulf of Mexico's Veracruz-Havana Route."

6 *PRCC 1678-1689*, 119, 416.

7 Gemelli-Carreri, *Voyage Round the World*, 537; Alonso et al, "Monedas de la Fragata," 2-4; Horner, *Shipwreck*, 262-263.

8 Anon., *Captain Kidd Burying His Bible.*

9 Anon., *Trials of Eight Persons*, 24.

10 Exquemelin, *Flibustiers*, 332.

11 Ibid., 178-79.

12 Grose, *Classical Dictionary*, s.v. "burning shame."

13 Forbin, *Mémoirs*, 48; Exquemelin, *Flibustiers*, 178-179.

14 This narrative is taken primarily from documents relating to the alledged piracies of Captain William Kidd in Jameson, *Privateering and Piracy*, 190-257, and in House of Commons, *Journals of the House of Commons*, vol. 13:11-39; and Anon., *Arraignment, Tryal, and Condemnation*, throughout.

15 Cooper, *Sea Lions*, 12, 14, 28, et al.

16 Gardiner, "Narrative of John Gardiner," in Jameson, *Privateering and Piracy*, 221.

17 Ibid., 222.

18 "Lord Bellomont to Lords of Trade," in Jameson, *Privateering and Piracy*, 227.

19 Ibid., 228.

20 Gardiner, "Narrative of John Gardiner," in Jameson, *Privateering and Piracy*, 222.

21 Jameson, *Privateering and Piracy*, 253-257.

22 Downing, *Compendious History*, 121, 124, 128.

23 Taylor, *Jamaica in 1687*, 129-130.

24 Downing, *Compendious History*, 212.

25 Pitman, *Relation of the Great Sufferings*, 34-35.

26 This account is taken from Vignols, *Piraterie sur l'Atlantique*, 367-380.

27 Downing, *Compendious History*, 124.

28 Ibid., 124-125.

29 Barton, *Disappointment*, 49, and throughout. For details regarding the writing and intended performance, see the editor's introduction. There are references to Freemasons in the play; in them treasure-hunting conspiracy theorists will doubtless find further

reason to continue in vain their searches for Templar-pirate associations, not to mention for associated conspiracy and treasure.

30 Irving, *Tales of a Traveller*, vol. 2:246.

31 Ibid., vol. 2:251.

32 Ibid., vol. 2:326-327.

33 Wafer, *New Voyage & Description*, 123.

34 Marryat, *Phantom Ship*, 279.

35 Dumas, *The Count of Monte Cristo*, chapter 18.

36 Anon., "The Last Pirate Treasure Delusion"; Enfield [Connecticut] Historical Society, "A Ghost Story."

37 Stevenson, *Treasure Island* (1911), 3.

38 See Stevenson, "My First Book—'Treasure Island.'"

39 Kingsley, *At Last*, 13.

40 Cleve, *On the Geology*, 12-13.

41 Waller, *Voyage in the West Indies*, 31.

42 Dampier, *New Voyage*, 107.

43 Anon., *Captain Kidd Burying His Bible*.

44 See for example Fanthorpe, *Secrets of the World's*, 206-208. The Oak Island treasure hunters should consider that the pit was not intended to hide treasure, but was made for some other purpose of engineering. Any treasure found there may have been placed there as an afterthought—hiding valuables in wells and similar places was common.

45 Cooper, *History of the Navy*, 58-59.

46 Author's experience. The author is not at liberty to discuss the details of the suspected treasure sites of those who have consulted him.

47 Cooper, *Sea Lions*, vol. 1:88.

48 Labat, *Nouveau Voyage*, vol. 5:338; Jefferys, "Virgin Islands from English and Danish Surveys." Treasure Point is probably Nutmeg Point today.

49 This account is derived from Beeston, "Journal Kept by Col. William Beeston," 298; *CSPC 1681-1685*, nos. 552, 600, 668, 769, 1,590i; "L'intendant Patoulet au ministre Colbert [extrait],

2 November 1679," Archives nationales, Colonies, C8 A rec. 1, fol. 222-229, reprinted in *Les Archives de la Flibuste*, <http://us.geocities.com/trebutor/archives/D1670/D7808lemoign. html; Horner, *Shipwreck*, throughout; Little, *Buccaneer's Realm*, 121-127; Marley, *Pirates of the Americas*, 59-60; Swanson, *Documentation of the Indians*, 26, 80.

50 Pitman, *Relation of the Great Sufferings*, 28.

51 Barton, *Disappointment*, 39.

Index